S0-ABB-390

BEST RECIPES

. . .

From the Backs of Boxes, Bottles, Cans & Jars

. . .

CEIL DYER

BEST RECIPES

. . .

From the Backs of Boxes, Bottles, Cans & Jars

. . .

CEIL DYER

CHARTWELL BOOKS

Quarto is the authority on a wide range of topics.

Quarto educates, entertains and enriches the lives of our readers—enthusiasts and lovers of hands-on living.

www.quartoknows.com

This edition published in 2017 by
Chartwell Books
an imprint of Book Sales
a division of Quarto Publishing Group USA Inc.
142 West 36th Street, 4th Floor
New York, New York 10018
www.quartoknows.com

This edition published by arrangement with McGraw-Hill Education.

10 9 8 7 6 5 4 3 2 1

ISBN: 978-0-7858-3523-3

Editor: Milton Creek Editorial Services
Cover Design: Jen Cogliantry

Printed in China

Previously published in three volumes as:
Best Recipes from the Backs of Boxes, Bottles, Cans and Jars
More Recipes from the Backs of Boxes, Bottles, Cans and Jars
Even More Recipes from the Backs of Boxes, Bottles, Cans and Jars

Contents

Introduction

This is in essence *your* book—or, to put it more accurately, the cookbook you would have undoubtedly compiled if only you had time for the project. For here are the recipes you meant to save from that jar, can or box top, recipes you and your friends have asked for, a good number your mother's generation requested, and even a few of your grandmother's choices. Recipes you meant to save but didn't, those from magazine ads you may have torn out intending to file away someday, but that someday never came. In short, here is the cookbook you have always wanted: a treasury of the very best efforts of America's food producers.

In compiling this book I have come to appreciate how really lucky we are in this country; not only do we have an abundance of food, we are rich in the variety and quality of food produced and distributed to us by our food companies. It is apparently not enough for a company to sell a can of beets; they must be the best beets obtainable. Grown especially for the packer, they are superior to begin with. They must then be expertly canned for maximum flavor and best texture. Nor does the effort to get a good product to your table end there; a team of good cooks goes to work to create new and delicious ways for you to serve those beets; testing and retesting until they are satisfied the results are letter-perfect and that you, the customer, will be pleased. Flour millers, sugar refiners, convenience food producers, meat packers, canners and purveyors of spices, sauces and dressings, all give time and effort in abundance to produce not just good food, but to give you the best possible way to cook and serve their products. No other industry tries harder to please you; after all, do automobile makers offer to teach you to drive? Does the maker of carpets give expert professional decorating service? But the food people! Virtual armies of talented home economists, chefs and just plain good cooks labor long and hard to create recipes that are not only good, but perfect, time after time after time.

As anyone knows, the measure of a good cookbook is the absolute reliability of the recipes; almost anyone with a little knowledge of food can *write* a good recipe, but one that can be depended upon for uniformly good results is the only one that counts in the kitchen.

Good recipes, plain-jane or fancy, are the result of testing; making the casserole, stew or cake from scratch under average home kitchen conditions, then doing it over and over again until every detail is crystal-clear and the results are uniformly perfect.

Good recipes are also those that offer a new food idea, new combinations that perhaps you haven't thought of before; but that too requires testing and experimenting. Not every food "love affair" ends in a happy "marriage." A good idea is only as good as it looks and tastes, and that means trying out idea after idea until indeed the recipe is as good as it sounds. For the truth is that all good cookbooks are written at the kitchen counter, not at the typewriter; and, while the poet may find inspiration in a sunset, cookbook writers must find theirs at the stove. I have sifted through over fifteen hundred recipes from different sources to select the best, you may be sure that every one will be a success, a can't-fail predictable success, every time you make it. America's best cooks have made certain of that.

Happy cooking!

1.
Appetizers, Snacks, Noshes and Such

That "something before" or the hospitable hors d'oeuvre, be it for a casual "stop by for a drink" or a full-blown cocktail party, is ever a challenge. Too much or too heavy is too bad, too little a disappointment, but have no qualms, for easy delicious "starters" are at hand from the good cooks who contributed their best to this book.

These talented people also passed along a few tips for a successful cocktail party that can be useful to any host or hostess. I include them here for your pleasure. . . .

An electric wok, usually available in handsome colors, is a very useful substitute for a chafing dish. In my opinion, it is a bit more dependable and requires less watching.

Serve a variety of breads, toasts and crackers; remember, cheese and highly flavored spreads and pâtés are at their best when the breads or crackers are not too highly flavored. Choose thin slices of cocktail rye, rounds of French® or Italian loaves, homemade melba toast made from thin white bread, unsalted water biscuits and the like. Too much seasoning in the crackers ruins the cook's efforts.

Do serve raw vegetables for dipping. Try celery stalks, carrot sticks, thin slices of turnip, apple, cauliflowerets, endive stalks and the like—great for flavor, and the calorie-conscious will love you.

Do, please do, have plenty of ice, loads of it; nothing cools off a party like warm drinks.

Serve enough! People like to munch at a party, and even a small gathering can consume an amazing amount of food. Endless variety isn't necessary, but whatever you serve it should be plentiful.

If you are a "helpless" host or hostess it pays to set up a buffet where people can help themselves. A bar tray with a generous ice bucket will probably occupy one end of the table, with a chafing dish or wok holding the stage at the other. Cold dips, cheeses and spreads make up the balance of the array.

Avoid cocktail foods that require individual serving plates; fork foods too are out unless you have help at hand to gather up the remains. The best advice for all but very formal occasions is: stick to finger foods.

Do have plenty of cocktail napkins. Paper ones are definitely okay; there are very attractive ones available, but have lots of them. Nothing is worse than needing a napkin at a party and finding none available.

The important thing is to have a good time. The recipes included here should certainly assure you of that. Great-tasting, easy, imaginative, they are from some of the best cooks in the business. I am certain you will enjoy every one.

Party Cheese Ball

We couldn't put together a cookbook of favorite recipes without Philadelphia Cream Cheese, the all-time star of the appetizer tray.

- 2 8-ounce packages Philadelphia Brand Cream Cheese
- 2 8-ounce cups shredded Cracker Barrel sharp Cheddar cheese
- 1 Tbs. chopped pimiento
- 1 Tbs. chopped green pepper
- 1 Tbs. finely chopped onion
- 2 tsp. Worcestershire sauce
- 1 tsp. lemon juice
- Dash of cayenne
- Dash of salt
- Finely chopped pecans

Combine softened cream cheese and Cheddar cheese, mixing until well blended. Add pimiento, green pepper, onion, Worcestershire sauce, lemon juice and seasonings; mix well. Chill. Shape into ball; roll in nuts. Serve with crackers.

During the party season, leftover cheese ball can be reshaped and refrigerated until the next event. Will keep up to one week.

Roast Beef Party Snacks

This great idea is from the Underwood Red Devil Roast Beef Spread label.

- 12–15 melba rounds
- 1 (4¾ ounces) can Underwood Roast Beef Spread
- ½ cup grated Cheddar cheese
- 1 Tbs. minced onion

Spread melba round with roast beef spread. Top with grated cheese and minced onion. Broil for 3 to 5 minutes or until cheese bubbles. Makes 12–15 snacks.

PICKLE IDEAS FOR YOUR PARTY

From Heinz®

Pick Pockets

Mix well 2 cups finely grated American cheese, ½ cup softened butter or margarine. Using pastry blender, cut in 1 cup all-purpose flour, dash cayenne. Divide into 2 balls; chill. Cut 36 strips (2 × ½-inch) from Heinz® Dill or Sweet Pickles. Roll each ball to ⅛-inch thickness on floured board; cut in rectangles (2½ × 2-inch). Wrap a pickle strip in dough; seal ends well. Place on ungreased baking sheets. Bake in 425°F. oven, 12 to 15 minutes. Makes 3 dozen.

Dill Fondue Balls

Combine 2 slightly beaten egg whites, 1 cup grated Swiss cheese, ⅓ cup chopped Heinz® Dills, dash garlic salt. Drop by teaspoonsful into ½ cup dry bread crumbs; roll and coat well, forming small balls. Chill until ready to serve. Fry in deep fat (375°F.) until golden brown, 2 to 3 minutes. Drain on absorbent paper. Makes 2 dozen appetizers.

Peppy Bean Dip

An easy great and money-saving appetizer from the Old El Paso Refried Beans can.

- 1 (16-ounces) can Old El Paso Refried Beans
- 1 cup dairy sour cream
- 3 to 5 Old El Paso Pickled jalapeño peppers seeded and rinsed
- Shredded Cheddar cheese
- Sliced green onion
- Old El Paso Tostada Shells, broken

Blend together refried beans and sour cream. Finely chop the jalapeño peppers; mix well with bean mixture. Spoon into serving bowl; garnish with shredded Cheddar cheese and sliced green onion, if desired. Serve with broken tostada shells for dippers. Makes 2¾ cups.

Chippy Cheese Ball

This is an especially good cheese ball to make for your next party. Frito-Lay's test kitchen director tells us it improves with chilling, so it's easy to make ahead and store in your refrigerator or freezer. (Note: if you place it in the freezer be sure to defrost completely before serving.)

- 1 lb. sharp Cheddar cheese, grated
- ¼ lb. Roquefort cheese, crumbled
- ½ lb. cream cheese
- 2 tsps. Worcestershire sauce
- 2 Tbs. grated onion
- ¼ tsp. cayenne pepper
- 1¼ cups crushed Lay's Brand Sour Cream & Onion Flavored Potato Chips

Have cheeses at room temperature. Blend well with mixer or pastry blender. Add Worcestershire sauce, onion, pepper, and ¼ cup of the crushed Lay's Brand Sour Cream & Onion

Flavored Potato Chips. Shape into ball and roll in remaining chips until completely covered. Chill well.

Deviled Ham Stuffed Cucumbers

A perfect appetizer from Underwood; easy, great-tasting, low in calories and light on the budget. Could you ask for more?

- 2 medium cucumbers
- 1 4½-ounce can Underwood Deviled Ham
- 1 hard-cooked egg, coarsely chopped
- 1 Tbs. finely chopped onion
- 1 Tbs. finely chopped sour pickle
- 1 tsp. prepared mustard

Cut cucumbers in half lengthwise and scoop out seeds. In a bowl, mix together deviled ham, chopped egg, onion, pickle and mustard. Spoon mixture into cucumber shells. Chill. When ready to serve, cut cucumber diagonally into 1-inch pieces. Makes about 2 dozen hors d'oeuvres.

Guacamole With Green Chili Peppers

More people write to the Avocado Advisory Board for this classic recipe than almost any they have printed during the past decade. Serve with toasted tortillas as a cocktail dip or with tomatoes and Boston lettuce as an appetizer.

- 4 avocados, mashed or puréed
- ½ cup finely chopped canned green chili peppers
- ¼ cup minced onion
- 1 tsp. salt
- ½ cup lemon juice

Combine ingredients. Cover and chill. Makes 3 cups.

Mushroom Liver Pâté

Underwood created this luxurious-tasting pâté for your next party. Make it ahead and chill well; it tastes even better the day after it's made.

2 Tbs. butter or margarine
⅔ cup chopped fresh mushrooms
⅓ cup chopped onion
2 cans (4¾-ounce) Underwood Liverwurst Spread
2 Tbs. brandy
2 tsps. dried chives
½ tsp. Ac'cent flavor enhancer

Melt butter in a skillet over medium low heat. Add mushrooms and onions; sauté 10 minutes, until all moisture has evaporated. Stir in liverwurst spread, brandy, chives and flavor enhancer. Spoon into a serving bowl. Chill. Serve cold with crackers. Makes 1½ cups spread.

Eggplant Spread

Here's a sophisticated vegetable appetizer from Ac'cent. Serve it on crisp melba toast.

1 large eggplant (2 lbs.)
1 cup chopped onion
⅓ cup chopped celery
⅓ cup chopped green pepper
2 cloves garlic, finely chopped
¼ cup vegetable oil
2 medium tomatoes, peeled and chopped
1 tsp. Ac'cent flavor enhancer
1 tsp. salt
¼ tsp. ground black pepper
2 Tbs. lemon juice
1 loaf (8-ounces) party rye bread

Preheat oven to 425°F. Bake eggplant on rack in the center of oven 1 hour, until soft. In a large saucepan over low heat, sauté onions, celery, green pepper and garlic in oil for 10 minutes. Remove skin from cooled baked eggplant and finely chop the pulp. Add chopper pulp to the onion mixture and stir in tomatoes, Ac'cent, salt and pepper. Bring mixture to a boil, stirring constantly, reduce heat, cover and simmer 1 hour. Remove cover and cook 30 minutes longer, stirring occasionally. Stir in lemon juice. Refrigerate 3 hours. Serve chilled with party rye bread. Makes 3 cups.

Lipton California Dip

Here's the recipe that started all those great cocktail dips; perfect for parties. Make as much or as little as you need in minutes. It's been going strong since 1954.

In small bowl blend 1 envelope Lipton Onion Soup Mix with 2 cups (16 ounces) sour cream; chill. Makes about 2 cups dip. *Variations:*

California Vegetable Dip: Add 1 green pepper, chopped; 1 tomato, chopped; and 2 tsp. chili powder.

California Blue Cheese Dip: Add ¼ lb. blue cheese, crumbled, and ¼ cup finely chopped walnuts.

California Shrimp Dip: Add 1 cup finely chopped cooked shrimp and ¼ cup ketchup.

California Clam Dip: Add 1 can (7½ ounces) minced clams, drained, and 2 Tbs. chili sauce.

Who knows how to give a better party than the lighthearted people at Bacardi® Rum down in Miami? Here are four great hors d'oeuvres from their national advertising. Mix up a bunch of Daiquiris and the party is on!

Chicken Liver Dip

Cut ½ lb. chicken livers into small pieces. Melt 2 Tbs. butter or margarine with 1 clove pressed or minced garlic. Sauté livers till cooked through. Remove from heat. Stir in 3 Tbs. Bacardi® Dark Rum.* Cool. Combine mixture in a blender with 1 package (8 ounces) softened cream cheese, ¼ cup plain yogurt, ½ tsp. salt, ¼ tsp. crumbled basil. Blend smooth. Salt and pepper to taste. Chill several hours. Serve with crackers and/or raw vegetable pieces. Makes about 1⅓ cups.

Liverwurst Spread

Mash 1 package (8 ounces) liverwurst with fork. Mix in 4 slices cooked crumbled bacon, 1 Tbs. snipped chives, 1 Tbs. Bacardi® Dark Rum,* 3 Tbs. softened butter or margarine. Serve with melba toast or crisp crackers. Makes 1 cup.

Sautéed Shrimp

Marinate 1½ lbs. medium shrimp, shelled and deveined, in ½ cup Bacardi® Light Rum* several hours. Melt ¼ cup butter or margarine in large frying pan. Add shrimp and rum mixture with ½ tsp. garlic salt. Sauté 8 to 10 minutes or until shrimp cook through. Sprinkle ⅓ cup grated Parmesan cheese and ground pepper over shrimp. Broil 2 to 3 minutes or until cheese browns. Serve hot. Makes about 36 servings.

Mini Meat Balls

Combine 1½ Tbs. Bacardi® Light Rum,* 2 Tbs. soy sauce, 1 pressed garlic clove and 1 tsp. ground ginger; blend.

* Unless otherwise specified all recipes suggesting use of Bacardi® Light or Dark Rum refer only to 80-proof rum.

Add 1 lb. ground beef chuck. Blend well. Shape into balls about 1 inch in diameter. Bake at 300°F., 12 to 15 minutes, turning once. Serve with wooden picks.

Hot Crabmeat Appetizer

Kraft® terms this scrumptious concoction one of their classics. I call it a short cut to becoming the hostess with the mostest. Nobody, but nobody, can resist it!

- 1 8-ounce package Philadelphia Brand Cream Cheese
- 1½ cups (7½-ounce can) flaked drained crabmeat
- 2 Tbs. finely chopped onion
- 2 Tbs. milk
- ½ tsp. cream-style horseradish
- ¼ tsp. salt
- Dash of pepper
- ⅓ cup sliced almonds, toasted

Combine softened cream cheese, crabmeat, onion, milk, horseradish and seasonings, mixing until well blended. Spoon into 9-inch pie plate or oven-proof dish; sprinkle with nuts. Bake at 375°F. 15 minutes. Serve as a dip or a spread with crackers, chips or raw vegetables. Makes about 2 cups.

Sausage and Hot Mustard Sauce

In 1965 Swift & Co. printed this recipe, Brown 'N Serve Sausages with Hot Mustard Sauce, on their sausage package. For well over ten years people have consistently asked for the recipe.

- 1 8-ounce package Swift Premium Brown 'N Serve Sausage, any flavor

Cut sausage links in halves. Brown according to package directions. Keep hot on hot tray or in chafing dish. Spear sausage pieces with smooth toothpicks. Serve with Hot Mustard Sauce for dipping. Makes 20 appetizers.

Hot Mustard Sauce

2 Tbs. butter or margarine
1 Tbs. flour
½ tsp. salt
1 cup water
1 beef bouillon cube
⅓ cup Dijon-style mustard
2 tsps. horseradish
2 Tbs. sugar

Melt butter in a saucepan. Stir in flour and salt. Gradually add water. Add bouillon cube, mustard, horseradish and sugar. Stir and cook until sauce thickens. Makes 1½ cups.

QUICK AND EASY APPETIZERS

These are some great ideas for "made-in-a-minute" appetizers from Kraft®.

- Marinate cooked shrimp in Kraft® Italian Dressing for several hours in the refrigerator. Drain and arrange on picks with pitted ripe olives.
- Spread thin ham slices with Philadelphia Brand Whipped Cream Cheese. Roll up and chill. Cut into 1¼-inch pieces.
- Marinate fresh mushroom caps and frozen cooked artichoke hearts in Kraft® Caesar Dressing for several hours in the refrigerator. Drain and serve on picks.
- Spread thin slices of French® bread with soft margarine. Top with Kraft® Shredded Mozzarella Cheese. Heat at 350° until cheese melts.

- Combine flaked crabmeat with enough Kraft® Real Mayonnaise to moisten. Season lightly with curry powder. Serve as a spread with melba toast or sesame crackers.
- Serve melon balls, pineapple chunks and apple wedges as dippers with Kraft® Blue Cheese Sour Cream Dip.
- Spread one 8-ounce package Philadelphia Brand Cream Cheese with chutney and serve with crackers.
- Stuff large mushroom caps with Philadelphia Brand Whipped Cream Cheese blended with bacon and horseradish, chives or onions.
- Simmer cocktail sausages, ham or luncheon meat cubes in Kraft® barbecue sauce. Keep warm in chafing dish or over a warmer.
- Sauté shrimp or scallops in Parkay® margarine. Season with dill weed. Serve in chafing dish or over a warmer.

Antipasto for Eight

Progresso Foods suggests this Roman-style appetizer for a buffet supper or cocktail party.

¼ lb. each prosciutto, salami, ham
2 2-ounce cans Anchovy Fillets
1 large can Progresso Tuna Fish
1 15-ounce can Progresso Artichoke Hearts in Brine, drained
1 7½-ounce can Caponata
1 jar Olive Condite or Olive Appetizer
¼ jar Roasted Peppers
1 can Giant Ripe Olives
1 jar Pepper Salad
1 Sliced tomatoes
celery hearts, cut in halves lengthwise
2 or 3 hard-cooked eggs, cut in quarters
Pure Olive Oil
Pure Wine Vinegar

Use a large round platter or lazy susan. Arrange tuna fish in center and surround with all other ingredients, forming a pretty pattern. Serve with cruets of olive oil and vinegar for individual seasoning.

Party Mix

Ralson Purina tells me that this is their long-time, all-time favorite. First record of it in the Checkerboard Kitchens files goes back to 1952.

- 6 Tbs. butter or margarine
- 1 tsp. seasoned salt
- 4 tsps. Worcestershire sauce
- 2 cups Corn Chex cereal
- 2 cups Rice Chex cereal
- 2 cups Wheat Chex cereal
- ¾ cup salted mixed nuts

Preheat oven to 250°F. Heat butter in 13 × 9 × 2-inch baking pan in oven until melted. Remove. Stir in seasoned salt and Worcestershire sauce. Add Chex and nuts. Mix until all pieces are coated. Heat in oven 45 minutes. Stir every 15 minutes. Spread on absorbent paper to cool. Makes 6¾ cups.

Note: Party Mix may be frozen, so make a double batch. Thaw at room temperature in container in which it was stored.

Oriental Ham Tidbits

Armour cooks dreamed this one up a dozen years ago and they are still getting requests for the recipe. It's "nothing-to-it" easy and it is downright irresistible.

1 cup plum or red currant jelly
½ cup lemon juice
2 Tbs. cornstarch
1 lb. Golden Star Ham by Armour, cut into ¾-inch cubes
1 8-oz. can water chestnuts, drained, cut in half
1 green pepper, cut into 1-inch chunks

In large skillet, combine jelly, lemon juice and cornstarch. Heat, stirring constantly, until thickened. Add ham, water chestnuts and green pepper, stirring to coat pieces; heat through. Serve with wooden picks. Makes 5 cups.

Barbecued Cocktail Franks

This was said to have originated in Texas. It could have been, but Hunt's® was first to print the recipe. Perhaps you should double the recipe.

1 6-oz. can Hunt's® Tomato Paste
2 cups water
2 Tbs. *each*: minced onion, Worcestershire sauce and light brown sugar, firmly packed
1 Tbs. *each*: white vinegar and molasses
1 tsp. *each*: lemon juice and dry mustard
½ tsp. salt
1 lb. cocktail frankfurters.

In a large saucepan, combine all ingredients except frankfurters. Bring to boil, stirring frequently; reduce heat. Add franks; simmer 10 minutes. Serve with toothpicks. Makes 32 appetizers.

Horseradish Dip

From a can of Bumble Bee® Pink Salmon an especially flavorful and different dip.

1 15½-oz. can Bumble Bee® Pink Salmon
1 8-oz. package cream cheese, softened
¼ cup dairy sour cream
¼ cup horseradish
½ tsp. salt
⅛ tsp. garlic powder
Crisp romaine lettuce
Paprika
Crackers
Celery sticks

Drain salmon. Remove skin, if desired. Mash bones. Beat cream cheese, sour cream, horseradish, salt and garlic powder until smooth. Beat in salmon and bones until blended. Arrange romaine lettuce in a bowl. Spoon in salmon mixture. Sprinkle with paprika. Serve with crackers and celery sticks. Makes 6–8 servings.

Hot Chili-Cheese Dip

A South-of-the-Border original from Armour, zesty with flavor, this dip is a firmly established favorite that pleases just about everybody.

1 15-oz. can Armour Star Chili (no beans)
1 4-oz. can chopped green chilies
1 lb. processed American cheese, shredded
1 Tbs. Worcestershire sauce
Corn chips

Combine all ingredients, except chips; heat, stirring occasionally, over low heat until cheese melts. Serve heated as a dip with chips. Makes 4 cups.

Liptauer Spread

Kraft® tells me this simple but simply fabulous spread has won rave notices ever since it appeared in their advertising fifteen years ago.

1 8-oz. package Philadelphia Brand Cream Cheese
½ cup soft Parkay® Margarine
2 Tbs. finely chopped onion
1½ tsps. anchovy paste
1 tsp. Kraft® Pure Prepared Mustard
1 tsp. capers, chopped
1 tsp. caraway seed
1 tsp. paprika

Combine softened cream cheese and margarine, mixing until well blended. Add remaining ingredients; mix well. Chill. Serve as a spread with French® or pumpernickel bread. Makes 1½ cups.

These festive cheese balls are as tempting and delicious today as they were when Lea & Perrins® created them years ago.

Coventry Cheese Ball

1 8-oz. package cream cheese, softened
1 cup (4 oz.) shredded sharp Cheddar cheese
¼ cup minced onion
2 Tbs. minced parsley
1 tsp. Lea & Perrins® Worcestershire Sauce
¼ tsp. salt

In a bowl blend cream and Cheddar cheeses. Add onion, parsley, Lea & Perrins®, and salt; blend well. Shape into a ball. Chill and serve with assorted crackers, if desired. Makes 1 cheese ball.

Harlequin Cheese Ball: Add 2 Tbs. finely diced pimiento, 1 tsp. prepared brown mustard, and 1 clove garlic, crushed, to basic cheese mixture. Shape into a ball. Chill. Garnish with pimiento stars, if desired.

Holiday Cheese Ball: Add 1 Tbs. caraway to basic cheese mixture. Shape into a ball. Chill. Sprinkle ribbons of paprika and chopped parsley around ball.

Fruit and Nut Cheese Ball: Add 1 8¼-oz. can crushed pineapple, well drained, and ⅓ cup finely chopped nuts to basic cheese mixture. Shape into a ball; roll in ⅓ cup finely chopped nuts. Chill.

Chicken Liver Paté

Planters Peanut Oil Company thought up this paté to make your entertaining life easy—and successful. I stir in about 2 Tbs. of good brandy, but I leave that up to you; it's great either way.

½ cup Planters Peanut Oil
½ cup diced onion
1 lb. cooked chicken livers
1 hard-cooked egg
1 tsp. salt
⅛ tsp. pepper

Heat Planters Peanut Oil in a heavy skillet; add diced onion and sauté until transparent, about 5 minutes. Allow to cool in skillet. Grind or chop together chicken livers, egg and entire contents of skillet. Stir in salt and pepper. Chill until ready to serve. Makes about 1½ cups spread.

Bacon-Onion Pinwheels

Remember these? The recipe appeared in a Kraft® advertisement fifteen years ago. It's high on the list of Kraft's® "most wanted" recipes.

½ cup finely chopped onion
⅓ cup soft Parkay® Margarine
6 crisply cooked bacon slices, crumbled
2 Tbs. chopped parsley
2 8-oz. cans Pillsbury's® Refrigerated Quick-Crescent Dinner Rolls

Combine onion, margarine, bacon and parsley; mix well. Separate dough into eight rectangles; firmly press perforations to seal. Spread margarine mixture over dough. Roll up each rectangle, starting at short end; cut into four slices. Place on ungreased cookie sheet, cut-side down; flatten slightly. Bake at 375°F; 15–20 minutes or until golden brown. Makes approximately 2½ dozen.

From the Bisquick "No Time to Cook" summer recipe book here are two appetizers that get raves whenever they are served:

Zucchini Appetizers

3 cups thinly sliced unpared zucchini (about 4 small)
1 cup Bisquick baking mix
½ cup finely chopped onion
½ cup grated Parmesan cheese
2 Tbs. snipped parsley
½ tsp. salt
½ tsp. seasoned salt
½ tsp. dried marjoram or oregano leaves
Dash of pepper
1 clove garlic, finely chopped
½ cup vegetable oil
4 eggs, slightly beaten

Heat oven to 350°F. Grease oblong pan, 13 × 9 × 2 inches. Mix all ingredients; spread in pan. Bake until golden brown, about 25 minutes. Cut into about 2- × 1-inch pieces. Makes 4 dozen appetizers.

Mushroom-Cheese Appetizers

2 cups Bisquick baking mix
½ cup cold water
¼ lb. bulk pork sausage
¼ cup finely chopped green onions (with tops)
¾ cup mayonnaise or salad dressing
35 medium mushrooms (about 1 lb.)
2 cups shredded Cheddar cheese (about 8 oz.)
Paprika

Heat oven to 350°F. Grease oblong pan, 13 × 9 × 2 inches. Mix baking mix and water until soft dough forms; beat vigorously 20 strokes. Press dough in bottom of pan with floured hands. Cook and stir sausage in skillet until brown; drain. Mix sausage, onions and mayonnaise. Remove stems from mushrooms. Finely chop stems; stir into sausage mixture. Fill mushroom caps with sausage mixture. Place mushrooms in rows on dough in pan; sprinkle with cheese and paprika. Cover pan loosely with aluminum foil. Bake 20 minutes; remove foil. Bake until cheese is bubbly, 5–10 minutes. Let stand 15 minutes; cut into pieces. Makes 35 appetizers.

Barbecued Korean-Style Short Ribs

Adapted by Kikkoman, this authentic Korean recipe is a West Coast favorite.

4 lbs. pre-cut beef short ribs, 2½ inches long
½ cup Kikkoman Soy Sauce

¼ cup water
1 Tbs. sugar
1 Tbs. sesame seed, toasted
1 tsp. Tabasco Pepper Sauce
½ tsp. garlic powder

Score meaty side of ribs, ½ inch apart, ½ inch deep, lengthwise and crosswise. Combine remaining ingredients. Marinate ribs in sauce in plastic bag 2 hours. Broil 2 inches from heat 15 minutes, or until ribs are brown and crisp on all sides.

Sweet-and-Sour Franks

You just wouldn't believe a humble frankfurter could taste so elegant. No wonder this quickie has been a Lea & Perrins® "asked-for" recipe for years.

½ cup red currant jelly
½ cup prepared brown mustard
2 Tbs. minced onion
1 Tbs. Lea & Perrins® Worcestershire Sauce
1 lb. frankfurters, cut into 1-inch chunks

In a medium saucepan mix jelly, mustard, onion and Lea & Perrins®; bring to boiling point. Add frankfurters; return to boiling point. Reduce heat and simmer, covered, for 15 minutes, stirring occasionally. If desired, serve hot from a chafing dish with cocktail picks. Makes about 32 hors d'oeuvres.

Seasoned Pop Corn

Trust American know-how, especially when it comes to casual entertaining. For casual entertaining at its best (and easiest) here are a few ideas from Jolly Time Pop Corn.

Blue Cheese Pop Corn: Melt 1 cup butter or margarine. Stir in 1 package blue cheese salad dressing mix. Toss with 6 quarts freshly popped Jolly Time Pop Corn.

Parmesan Pop Corn: Melt ¼ cup butter. Pour over 2 quarts popped Jolly Time Pop Corn. Add ½ cup grated Parmesan cheese and ½ tsp. salt. Mix well.

Herb Seasoned Pop Corn: Melt 3 Tbs. butter or margarine. Stir in ½ tsp. salt. Combine 1 tsp. thyme, ½ tsp. basil, ½ tsp. oregano and ½ tsp. rosemary. Add to butter. Pour over 2 quarts freshly popped Jolly Time Pop Corn. Toss well.

Curry Seasoned Pop Corn: Melt 3 Tbs. butter or margarine. Stir in ½ tsp. salt, 1 tsp. curry powder, ¼ tsp. ground cinnamon, and ¼ tsp. ground ginger. Toss with 2 quarts popped Jolly Time Pop Corn.

Flavored Pop Corn: Sprinkle one or more of the following over hot buttered Jolly Time Pop Corn:

Garlic salt
Celery salt
Seasoned salt
Hickory flavored salt
Chili powder
Grated American cheese
Dry soup mix
Dill weed
Butter flavored salt
Bacon-flavored bits

Party Mix

2 quarts popped Jolly Time Pop Corn
2 cups slim pretzel sticks
2 cups cheese curls
½ tsp. seasoned salt
¼ cup butter or margarine
1 Tbs. Worcestershire sauce
½ tsp. garlic salt

In a shallow baking pan, mix popped corn, pretzel sticks and cheese curls. Melt butter or margarine in small saucepan and stir in seasonings. Pour over dry ingredients and mix well. Bake at 250°F. for about 45 minutes, stirring several times. Makes about 2½ quarts. NOTE: 1 cup dry roasted peanuts may be added.

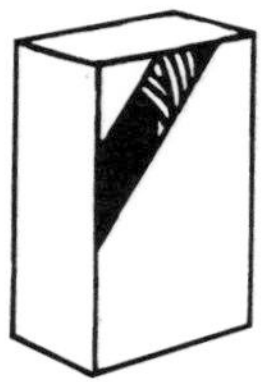

Crispy Snack

- 3 quarts unsalted, popped Jolly Time Pop Corn
- ¼ cup butter or margarine, melted
- ½ 3¼-oz. can French® fried onions
- ¼ cup bacon bits or bacon-flavored bits
- Salt to taste

Toss popped corn with melted butter. Stir in French® fried onions and bacon bits. Sprinkle with salt. Place mixture on a jelly roll pan or baking sheet. Heat in 250°F. oven 5 minutes, serve hot.

Bacon-Cheese Pop Corn

- 4 quarts popped Jolly Time Pop Corn
- ⅓ cup butter or margarine, melted
- ½ tsp. seasoned salt
- ½ tsp. hickory-smoked salt
- ⅓ cup grated Parmesan or American cheese
- ⅓ cup bacon-flavored bits

Pour freshly popped pop corn in a large bowl. Combine butter with seasoned hickory-smoked salt. Pour over pop corn; toss well to coat. Sprinkle with cheese and bacon bits. Toss again and serve while warm.

Curry Party Mix

A new twist to that old favorite Chex® Party Mix. It's great for party snacking, but did you know it makes a perfect accompaniment to any curry dish? Inexpensive too!

½ cup butter or margarine
1¼ tsps. seasoned salt
1¼ – 2 tsps. curry powder
4½ tsps. Worcestershire sauce
2 cups Corn Chex® cereal
2 cups Rice Chex® cereal
2 cups Wheat Chex® cereal
2 cups Bran Chex® cereal
1 cup chow mein noodles
1 cup golden raisins

Preheat oven to 250°F. Heat butter in large shallow roasting pan (about 15 × 10 × 2 inches) in oven until melted. Remove. Stir in seasonings. Add Chex, noodles, and raisins. Mix until all pieces are coated. Heat in oven 1 hour. Stir every 15 minutes. Spread on absorbent paper to cool. Makes about 10 cups.

Chex® No-Cook Party Mix

Perfect for parties; this party mix is also great for children's after-school snacks. Tastes so good they won't know how good for them it really is.

1 cup Corn Chex® cereal
1 cup Rice Chex® cereal
1 cup Wheat Chex® cereal
1 cup Bran Chex® cereal
2 cups cheese-flavored corn puff balls
¾ cup broken pretzel sticks
1 cup peanut butter-flavored chips

Mix all ingredients together. Store tightly covered. Makes about 7 cups.

QUICK-AND-EASY APPETIZERS

These quickies from Hillshire Farms®—all for sausage fans in a hurry for something really good.

Piggy Wraps

1 package Hillshire Farm® Sausage
1 package refrigerated crescent dough

Cut Sausage into desired shapes. Wrap in dough. Bake at 400°F. for 5 minutes or until golden brown. May be frozen.

Sweet and Saucy

Equal parts currant jelly and ketchup
1 package Hillshire Farm® Sausage, cut up

Heat jelly and ketchup in saucepan. Add bite-size pieces of Sausage and heat until Sausage is hot. Serve with toothpicks.

Italian Nachos

1 package Hillshire Farm® Italian Smoked Sausage
1 bag tortilla chips
Monterey Jack or taco-flavored cheese
Sour cream for garnish (optional)

Place thinly sliced Sausage on tortilla chips. Top with cheese and broil until cheese melts. If desired, garnish with sour cream.

Pickled Shrimp

Charleston, South Carolina, takes credit for "inventing" Pickled Shrimp but you can thank the French® Company for this easy version.

1 to 1½ pounds cooked, shelled and deveined medium or large shrimp
2 medium-size onions, thinly sliced and rings separated
16 to 20 bay leaves
1 to 1½ cups Piquant French® Dressing (opposite)
Crackers

In medium-size bowl arrange alternate layers of shrimp, onion rings and bay leaves. Pour dressing over the top, pressing down so top layer is covered. Let stand in refrigerator at least

24 hours to blend flavors. Serve as an hors d'oeuvre on crackers, as a cocktail or in a salad.

Piquant French® Dressing

- 1 tsp. Colman's® (dry) Mustard
- 1 tsp. water
- 1½ cups oil
- ⅔ cup vinegar
- 1 Tbs. French's® Worcestershire Sauce
- 1½ tsps. salt
- 1 tsp. sugar
- 1 tsp. paprika
- ¼ tsp. cayenne pepper

Mix mustard with water and let stand 10 minutes to develop flavor. Combine all ingredients in a jar. Cover tightly and shake.

Crab Ball Hors d'Oeuvre

This outstanding recipe appeared in national magazine advertising a couple of years ago from Wakefield® Snow Crabmeat and it's become a great favorite. Walnuts can be used instead of pecans.

- 1 6-oz. package Snow Crabmeat
- 1 8-oz. package cream cheese, softened
- 2 tsps. chopped chives
- ¼ tsp. garlic powder
- ¼ tsp. salt
- ½ cup chopped pecans

Thaw and drain crabmeat. Blend softened cream cheese, chives, garlic powder and salt. Fold in crabmeat. Shape into log or ball. Roll in pecans. Serve with crackers or fresh vegetables.

Spinach Beef Dip

Armour's® test kitchen director tells me that this label recipe was the first dip to use thawed but uncooked spinach as an ingredient. It's terrific; so easy to make ahead and store in your refrigerator until party time, and it tastes even better for waiting.

1 10-oz. package frozen chopped spinach, thawed and drained
1 8-oz. package cream cheese, softened
1 cup mayonnaise
½ cup chopped green onions
1 Tbs. dillweed
1 2½-oz. jar Armour® Star Sliced Dried Beef, rinsed and chopped
Assorted crackers

Combine spinach, cream cheese, mayonnaise, green onions and dillweed in container of electric blender; process on high speed 1 to 2 minutes or until smooth and creamy. Fold in Dried Beef. Chill. Serve with crackers. Makes 3 cups.

Make-Ahead Ham & Mushroom Paté

This recipe from the label of Underwood® Deviled Ham was one of their most popular. It's well worth keeping in your permanent file. Easy to make and very special in flavor.

1 Tbs. butter or margarine
¼ lb. coarsely chopped fresh mushrooms
2 4½-oz. cans Underwood® Deviled Ham
1 3-oz. package cream cheese, softened
¼ tsp. ground thyme
Party bread slices

Day before:
Melt butter in a skillet and sauté mushrooms over medium heat until tender. Combine Deviled Ham, cream cheese and thyme; blend well. Stir in sautéed mushrooms. Cover and chill overnight. Serve on party bread slices. Makes 1¾ cups paté.

Cheesy Corn Spread

Whole kernel corn is the surprise ingredient in this recipe. It's a favorite with the home-economists at the Green Giant® test kitchens and with me, too—as well as with literally hundreds of other good cooks.

- 12 oz. (3 cups) shredded sharp Cheddar cheese
- ½ cup dairy sour cream
- ½ cup salad dressing or mayonnaise
- ¼ cup finely chopped onion
- ½ tsp. salt
- 1 12-oz. can Green Giant® Mexicorn Golden Whole Kernel Corn with Sweet Peppers, drained

Bring cheese to room temperature. In large bowl, crumble cheese with fork or blend with mixer to form small bits. Mix in remaining ingredients, except corn, until well blended. Stir in corn. Cover; chill several hours or overnight. Can be stored in the refrigerator up to 1 week. Serve with raw vegetables or crackers. Makes 3½ cups.

Tropical Fruit Nibbles

The Almond Growers test kitchens say serve this lovely fruit with wooden picks . . . and a tropical drink I hope?

- ¼ cup light rum
- ¼ cup orange juice
- 1 tsp. French's® Almond Extract or Coconut Flavor
- Melon balls, pineapple chunks, grapes, or other fresh fruit.

Combine rum, orange juice and extract; pour over fruit and refrigerate 30 minutes. Serve with wooden picks.

Alaska Shrimp Quiche

Wakefield® test-kitchen cooks suggest this deluxe quiche for a buffet supper or cocktail party.

- 1 6-oz. package Shrimp
- 1 9-inch pie shell
- 4 eggs
- 1 cup half-and-half
- ½ tsp. salt
- 1 4-oz can sliced mushrooms, drained
- 1 tsp. chopped chives
- Dash pepper
- Dash nutmeg
- ½ cup grated Swiss cheese

Thaw and drain Shrimp well. Beat together the eggs, half-and-half and seasonings. Place mushrooms and shrimp in bottom of pie shell. Sprinkle with cheese. Add egg mixture and bake at 375°F. for 35 to 40 minutes or until center is firm. To prepare quiche ahead, bake 10 minutes less than directed; cool, then wrap and freeze. When ready to use, unwrap and bake at 325°F. for 25 minutes.

Alternate suggestions: For a delicious Alaska Crab Quiche, substitute one 6-oz. package Wakefield® Alaska Crabmeat for the shrimp. Or, in place of 1 cup half-and-half, use ¾ cup half-and-half and ¼ cup dry sherry.

Swiss and Bacon Squares

Bisquick® suggested this "no time to cook" recipe for a luncheon or supper dish. I put it under Appetizers because it's great cut into bite-size squares and served warm as a "go with" for wine, beer or just about anything else you care to serve.

- 2 cups Bisquick® Baking Mix
- ½ cup cold water
- 1 8-oz. package natural Swiss cheese slices
- 1 lb. bacon, crisply fried and crumbled
- 4 eggs
- ½ cup milk
- ½ tsp. onion salt

Heat oven to 425°F. Grease baking dish, 13 × 9 × 2 inches. Mix baking mix and water until soft dough forms; beat vigorously 20 strokes. Gently smooth into ball on floured cloth-covered board. Knead 10 times. Pat in dish with floured hands, pressing ½ inch up sides. Top with cheese slices, overlapping edges; sprinkle with bacon; mix remaining ingredients; pour over bacon. Bake until edges are golden brown and knife inserted near center comes out clean, about 20 minutes. Makes 6 to 8 servings as a main course or 12 to 16 servings as an appetizer.

Rumaki Canapés

Americans discovered Rumaki appetizers about 10 years ago, but while great tasting they were troublesome to make. Not so these Ramaki Canapés. The recipe is from those clever Underwood® cooks—easy to prepare and devilishly good.

- 2 4¾-oz. cans of Underwood® Liverwurst Spread
- 2 tsps. soy sauce
- ½ tsp. brown sugar
- ¼ cup chopped water chestnuts
- ½ lb. raw bacon
- Buttered toast rounds

In a small bowl, combine Liverwurst Spread, soy sauce and brown sugar and mix well. Add water chestnuts and mix. Chill. While mixture is chilling, prepare bacon crumbs. Fry bacon in a frying pan until crisp and let drain on paper toweling. When bacon has cooled, break into small crumbles and set aside. Spoon chilled liverwurst mixture onto prepared toast rounds and top with crumbled bacon. Chill covered until ready to use. Makes 30 hors d'oeuvres.

Deviled Ham Stuffed Cucumbers

The Underwood® Deviled Ham people dreamed up this elegant vegetable appetizer almost 10 years ago, but it's just right for today to serve with drinks.

2 medium cucumbers
1 4½-oz. can Underwood® Deviled Ham
1 hard-cooked egg, coarsely chopped
1 Tbs. finely chopped onion
1 Tbs. finely chopped sour pickle
1 tsp. prepared mustard

Cut cucumbers in half lengthwise and scoop out seeds. In a bowl, mix together deviled ham, chopped egg, onion, pickle and mustard. Spoon mixture into cucumber shells. Chill. When ready to serve, cut cucumber diagonally into 1-inch pieces. Makes about 2 dozen hors d'oeuvres.

Slimster's Guacamole

A long-time favorite from the French® Company. It was especially popular back in the 1940's, and is even more so today when everyone is thinking thin.

1 cup low-fat cottage cheese
1 medium-size avocado, peeled and cut in chunks
1 tomato, peeled and cut in chunks

2 Tbs. lemon juice
1 Tbs. French's® Worcestershire Sauce
1 tsp. French's® Garlic Salt
⅛ tsp. French's® Cayenne Pepper
Cauliflowerets, carrot sticks, celery sticks, green or red pepper squares, green onions, cucumber sticks.

Combine cottage cheese, avocado, tomato, lemon juice, Worcestershire Sauce, Garlic Salt, and Cayenne Pepper in blender; blend until smooth. Serve as dip with vegetables. Makes about 2 cups dip (about 300 calories per cup).

Almond Cheese Pinecone

The full-page color ad in national magazines showing this absolutely beautiful appetizer sent literally thousands of cooks to the market for Blue Diamond® Almonds. It's terrific—a show-stopper and crowd-pleaser for sure.

2 8-oz. packages cream cheese, softened
2 5-oz. jars pasteurized process cheese spread with pimiento
½ lb. blue cheese, crumbled
¼ cup minced green onion
½ tsp. Worcestershire sauce
2 cups Blue Diamond® Blanched Whole Almonds, toasted
Pine sprigs for garnish
Crackers

In large bowl with mixer at medium speed, beat cream cheese, cheese spread with pimiento and blue cheese until smooth. With spoon, stir in green onions and Worcestershire sauce. Cover and refrigerate about one hour. On work surface, with hands, shape cheese mixture into shape of large pinecone. Arrange on wooden board. Beginning at narrow end of cone, carefully press almonds about ¼ inch deep into cheese mixture in rows, making sure that pointed end of each almond extends at a slight angle. Continue pressing almonds into cheese mixture in rows, with rows slightly overlapping, until all cheese is covered. Garnish pinecone with pine sprigs. Serve with crackers. Makes about 25 servings.

Toasty Bread Slices

This isn't so much a recipe as simply an idea—but what an idea! For anything from a full-scale Italian meal to a TV snack, to go with your favorite beverage: a glass of red wine, an icy cold beer or a chilly mug of milk, from Parkay®.

½ cup soft Parkay® Margarine
⅓ cup crushed French® fried onions
1 Vienna bread loaf, sliced

Combine margarine and onions; spread on one side of each bread slice. Place bread slices spread-side up on ungreased cookie sheet. Bake at 400°F. 12 to 15 minutes or until lightly browned.

Variation: Substitute ⅓ cup Kraft® Grated Parmesan Cheese for onions.

Mushroom Bread

A unique bread from the Kraft® kitchens that resembles a pizza without sauce. Serve as an hors d'oeuvre or cut into small wedges as a snack.

1 8-oz. can refrigerated crescent rolls
2 cups mushroom slices
¼ cup margarine, melted
Kraft® Grated Parmesan Cheese
¼ tsp. marjoram

Separate dough into triangles. Place on ungreased 12-inch pizza pan; press out dough to fit pan. Toss mushrooms with margarine; arrange on dough. Sprinkle with cheese and marjoram. Bake at 375°F. 20 to 25 minutes.

Variations: Shredded Mozzarella, Monterey Jack or Swiss cheese are excellent alternates for Parmesan.

Cocktail Meatballs

So simple and so good. These meatballs from *Campbell's® 100 Best Recipes* cookbook can be shaped, browned and refrigerated hours before the party. Then it's a breeze to heat them in sauce shortly before serving.

1 lb. ground beef
1 egg, slightly beaten
2 Tbs. fine dry bread crumbs
½ tsp. salt
½ cup finely chopped onion
⅓ cup finely chopped green pepper
2 Tbs. butter or margarine
1 10¾-oz. can Campbell's® Condensed Tomato Soup
2 Tbs. brown sugar
1 Tbs. vinegar
1 Tbs. Worcestershire sauce
1 tsp. prepared mustard
Dash hot pepper sauce

Mix thoroughly beef, egg, bread crumbs and salt; shape into 50 small ½-inch meatballs. Arrange in shallow baking pan (12 × 8 × 2 inches). Broil 4 inches from heat until browned; turn once. Pour off fat. Meanwhile, in saucepan, cook onion and green pepper in butter until tender. Add meatballs and remaining ingredients. Cover; cook over low heat 10 minutes. Stir occasionally. Makes about 3½ cups.

Pepperoni Pizzas

A fast-food favorite from Hellmann's® and Best Foods® Real Mayonnaise to make at home.

- 1 cup shredded Mozzarella cheese (about 4 ozs.)
- 1 cup sliced pitted ripe olives
- 4 ounces pepperoni, chopped
- ½ cup Hellmann's® Best Foods® Real Mayonnaise
- ¼ tsp. Italian seasoning
- 4 English muffins, split, toasted

In medium bowl stir together first 5 ingredients. Spoon onto muffin halves. Broil 6 inches from source of heat about 5 minutes or until browned. Makes 8.

Texas Style Pizza

The French® Company combined two favorites of mine—chili and pizza—to come up with this new classic.

- ½ lb. ground beef
- 1 envelope French's® Chili-O Seasoning Mix
- 1 16-oz. can tomatoes
- 1 package active dry yeast
- ¾ cup warm water
- 2¼ cups biscuit mix
- ½ cup corn meal

1 15-oz. can kidney beans, drained and rinsed

Shredded Cheddar or American cheese

Brown ground beef in large skillet, stirring to crumble; pour off excess fat. Stir in seasoning mix, tomatoes and beans; simmer, uncovered, 10 minutes. Sprinkle yeast over warm water in large mixing bowl; stir to dissolve. Add biscuit mix and corn meal; stir until smooth. Knead 25 strokes on floured surface. Divide in half, roll or pat each to a 14-inch circle on greased pizza pan or baking sheet. Spoon filling on top of crust; sprinkle with cheese. Bake at 425°F. for 15 to 20 minutes, until crust is golden brown. Makes 6 to 8 servings.

Easy Deep-Dish Pizza

Takes no longer to make than a trip to the local pizzeria and is twice as good. This recipe showed up everywhere—on the box, in national ads and in the *Creative Recipes with Bisquick®* book—and was a smash hit then as it is now.

3 cup Bisquick® Baking Mix
¾ cup cold water
1 lb. ground beef
½ cup chopped onion
½ tsp. salt
2 cloves garlic, crushed
1 15-oz. can tomato sauce
1 tsp. Italian seasoning
1 4½-oz. jar sliced mushrooms, drained
½ cup chopped green pepper
2 cups shredded Mozzarella cheese (about 8 ozs.)

Heat oven to 425°F. Lightly grease jelly roll pan, 15½ × 10½ × 1 inch, or cookie sheet. Mix baking mix and water until soft dough forms; beat vigorously 20 strokes. Gently smooth dough into ball on floured cloth-covered board. Knead 20 times. Pat dough in bottom and up sides of pan with floured hands. Or roll into rectangle, 13 × 10 inches, and place on cookie sheet; pinch edges of rectangle, forming ¾-inch rim.

Cook and stir ground beef, onion, salt and garlic until beef is brown. Mix tomato sauce and Italian seasoning; spread over dough. Spoon beef mixture over sauce. Top with remaining ingredients. Bake until crust is golden brown, about 20 minutes. Makes 8 servings.

Sour Cream Pizza Strips

A 1979 third-prize winner of Borden's® Contest for recipes using sour cream. These strips taste super good and there's this bonus: they can be made ahead and reheated.

- 2 cups biscuit baking mix
- ⅔ cup Borden® Milk
- 1 tsp. Italian seasoning
- 1 8-oz. container Borden® Sour Cream
- ⅓ cup mayonnaise or salad dressing
- ¼ cup Borden® Grated Parmesan and Romano Cheese
- ¼ cup chopped onion
- 3 Tbs. chopped pimiento
- 1 Tbs. chopped parsley
- ½ tsp. garlic powder

Preheat oven to 400°F. In medium bowl, combine baking mix, Milk and Italian seasoning; stir to make soft dough. Turn onto well-floured surface; knead lightly 10 to 12 strokes. Pat dough onto bottom and up sides of greased 13 × 9-inch baking dish, making a small rim. In medium bowl, mix remaining ingredients; spread evenly over dough. Bake 20 to 25 minutes or until golden. Cut into rectangles. Serve warm. Refrigerate leftovers.

Chili Quesadilla

Quesadilla is Mexico's answer to Italian Pizza and French® Quiche. This is Hormel's® adaptation. Best served hot, good any way.

2 10 to 12-inch prepared flour tortillas
1 15-oz. can Hormel® Chili (with beans or no beans)
1 Tbs. chopped onion
½ tsp. garlic powder
2 tsp. green chilies, chopped
½ cup Monterey Jack cheese, grated
½ cup Cheddar cheese, grated
Red onion rings

Bake tortillas in 350°F. oven 2 minutes per side. Heat Hormel® Chili, adding onion, garlic powder, chilies. Sprinkle Monterey Jack cheese over tortillas, then spread thinly on chili mixture. Sprinkle Cheddar cheese on top, heat 8 minutes in 350°F. oven. Garnish with red onion rings.

A PAIR OF PLANTERS® TEX-MEX FAST-FOOD SPECIALS

For the past five years requests have been pouring in to the Planters® test kitchens for easy to prepare "Tex-Mex" recipes. Here are two of their most popular. They are super delicious as well as fast and easy to make.

Beef Tacos

2 Tbs. Planters® Peanut Oil
1 lb. ground beef
½ cup chopped onion
1 medium clove garlic, minced
1 8-oz. can tomato sauce
1 tsp. salt
Generous dash ground black pepper
12 prepared taco shells
Grated cheese
Shredded lettuce

Heat Planters® Peanut Oil in skillet over medium-high heat. Add ground beef and brown, stirring to break up beef. Add onion and garlic; continue cooking until onion is tender. Mix in tomato sauce, salt and pepper. Heat, stirring occasionally. Spoon beef mixture into prepared taco shells. Top with cheese and lettuce. Serve hot. Makes 12 servings.

Chicken Enchiladas

- ⅓ cup Planters® Peanut Oil
- ½ cup finely chopped onion
- 2 cloves garlic, crushed
- ½ cup flour
- 1 13¼-oz. can chicken broth
- 1⅔ cups water
- ½ cup enchilada sauce
- 1 Tbs. chili powder
- ½ tsp. salt
- 1¼ cups coarsely shredded Cheddar cheese (about 5 ozs.)
- 1½ cups diced cooked chicken or turkey
- ¼ cup sliced pitted ripe olives
- 8 7-inch Piñata® Corn Tortillas

Heat Planters® Peanut Oil in a saucepan over medium heat; add onion and garlic and cook until tender. Stir in flour, mixing until smooth. Gradually add chicken broth, water and enchilada sauce, mixing until smooth. Stir in chili powder and salt. Cook over medium heat, stirring constantly, until thick. Reserving ½ cup cheese, mix remaining cheese with chicken and olives. Dip Piñata® Corn Tortillas in prepared sauce for about 5 seconds. Spoon 3 Tbs. chicken filling across center of each; roll up and place seam side down, in a shallow 2½-quart baking dish. Pour remaining sauce over tortillas. Bake at 350°F. for 15 minutes. Sprinkle with reserved cheese and continue baking 10 minutes. Garnish with sliced ripe olives if desired and serve immediately. Makes 4 servings.

A.1.® INTERNATIONAL STEAKBURGERS

From the A.1.® Steak Sauce people comes this original Californian idea for "super plus" hamburgers. I've also included three variations—all equally good.

Basic A.1.® Hamburgers

1½ lbs. ground beef
1½ tsps. salt (optional)
¼ cup A.1.® Steak Sauce

In medium bowl, lightly combine all ingredients. Form 6 patties to fit bread shape of your choice. Broil, barbecue or pan fry until cooked as desired. Makes 6.

English Cheddar Burgers

1 cup shredded sharp yellow Cheddar cheese (4 ozs.)
2 Tbs. minced fresh onion
1 medium clove garlic, crushed
2 Tbs. A.1.® Steak Sauce
6 Basic A.1.® Hamburgers, cooked
6 English muffins, fork split, toasted and buttered

Combine cheese, onion, garlic and A.1. Spread 2 Tbs. over each cooked hamburger patty. Broil to melt cheese. Serve on muffins. Makes 6.

Greek Burgers

- 1 cup (4 ozs.) Feta cheese, rinsed and crumbled
- ¼ cup sliced ripe olives
- 1 Tbs. A.1.® Steak Sauce
- 1 tsp. lemon juice
- 2 Tbs. mayonnaise
- 6 Basic A.1.® Hamburgers, cooked
- 3 Pita (or pocket) bread, cut in half
- 6 tomato slices
- Shredded lettuce

Combine cheese, olives, A.1.®, lemon juice and mayonnaise. Place hamburgers in Pita bread. Spoon topping over hamburgers. Heat in preheated 425°F. oven 5 minutes. Garnish with tomato and lettuce. Makes 6.

Lipton® Onion Burgers

A famous Lipton® Onion Soup mix combination that has become an American classic.

- 1 envelope Lipton® Onion Soup mix
- ½ cup water
- 2 lbs. ground beef

In large bowl, combine Onion Soup mix, water and ground beef. Shape into 8 patties. Grill or broil until done. Makes 8 servings.

San Francisco Burgers

- 2 large, ripe avocados, peeled and mashed
- 2 Tbs. A.1.® Steak Sauce
- ½ tsp. salt
- ¼ cup minced fresh onion
- 4 slices bacon, cooked, drained, and crumbled
- 6 Basic A.1.® Hamburgers, cooked
- 6 tomato slices
- 12 slices San Francisco sour-dough bread, toasted

Combine avocado, A.1.®, salt, onion, and bacon. Serve hamburgers, topped with sauce and tomato, on toast. Makes 6.

Corned Beef Funburger

What's a funburger? It's a hamburger with a super great-tasting filling. It's an Underwood® theory that makes sense and great eating.

3 hamburger rolls, sliced, heated
1 4½-oz. can Underwood® Corned Beef Spread
¾ tsp. horseradish
3 Tbs. chopped walnuts
3 green pepper rings
3 Tbs. drained crushed pineapple

Partially hollow top half of each roll. Combine corned beef spread and horseradish, spread on bottom half. Sprinkle corned beef mixture with nuts, top with a pepper ring, fill ring with pineapple and cover with top half of roll. Makes 3 sandwiches.

Hamburgers Angostura

Dione Lucas made her original recipe for Hamburger Angostura® famous on TV in the late 1950's.

2 lbs. ground beef
2 tsps. salt
½ tsp. pepper
2 tsps. Angostura®
½ cup ice water

Combine meat with salt and pepper. Mix Angostura® with ice water and pour over meat. Blend thoroughly and shape into 8 patties. Broil or pan-fry hamburgers quickly to desired degree of doneness. Serve hot with sauce (below):

Sauce

1 8-oz. can tomato sauce
¼ cup water
1 tsp. Angostura®
1 Tbs. minced onion
2 Tbs. minced green pepper
2 Tbs. minced celery

Combine all ingredients and simmer 10 minutes. Makes 8 patties.

Super Burger Topper

Every time I've ever served this burger topping someone wants the recipe, and that someone usually gives it to someone else. The good cook at Heinz® who dreamed it up should be given a medal by hamburger fans.

½ cup chopped green pepper
¼ cup chopped onion
1 Tbs. salad oil
½ cup Heinz® Tomato Ketchup
⅓ cup water
½ tsp. chili powder
¼ tsp. salt

Sauté green pepper and onion in salad oil until tender. Stir in ketchup, water, chili powder and salt; simmer 10 to 15 minutes, stirring occasionally. Serve on hot dogs, hamburgers or other meat sandwiches. Makes about 1 cup.

Bavarian Wranglers® Franks

Here's a new one to me, but it may not be to you. It was printed on the Wranglers® package a few years ago.

4 Wranglers® Smoked Franks
1⅓ cups prepared German potato salad
2 Tbs. chopped parsley
4 slices crusty French® bread
Hormel bacon bits

Split meaty, smoky-tasting Wranglers® Franks almost to one end. Slash sides lightly and form into circle, fastening with toothpicks. Place on baking sheet. Stir parsley into potato salad; spoon ⅓ cup into each frank. Bake 10 minutes at 350°F. Top each bread slice with stuffed frank; garnish with bacon bits. Makes 4.

Spicy Muffins

A nosh, a snack, a sandwich—you name it. It's a new classic from a new company, Frieda's of California, and you most certainly will want the recipe in your permanent file of great quick and easy recipes.

1½ cups cottage cheese
½ cup wheat germ
2 Tbs. chopped chilies
¼ tsp. basil, dried and crushed
¼ tsp. oregano
¼ tsp. salt
4 to 6 whole wheat English muffin halves, toasted
tomato slices
Cheddar cheese slices
Minced parsley

Combine first 6 ingredients and mound on English muffin halves. On each muffin, place a slice of tomato and criss-cross with 2 strips of sliced Cheddar cheese. Broil 3 to 4 inches from source of heat for 5 minutes, or until cheese melts. Sprinkle with minced parsley. Makes 4 to 6 open-faced sandwiches.

Vegetable Rarebit

A 1940's classic, from the second edition of the *Pet® Evaporated Milk Cookbook*. Quick, easy and so good—a hearty snack supper dish to please just about everyone.

	For 2	For 4	For 6
Grated American cheese or sliced, packaged variety	1 cup (3 ozs.)	1¾ cups (5 ozs.)	2½ cups (½ lb.)
Pet® Milk	¼ cup	½ cup	¾ cup
Salt	¼ tsp.	½ tsp.	¾ tsp.
Dry mustard	¼ tsp.	½ tsp.	¾ tsp.
Kidney beans, drained and canned*	¾ cup	1½ cups	2¼ cups
Bread, white or whole wheat	2 slices	4 slices	6 slices
Fresh tomatoes, cut in ½-inch slices**	1 large	2 large	3 large
Salt	⅛ tsp.	¼ tsp.	½ tsp.
Pepper	few grains	few grains	⅛ tsp.

For cheese sauce, mix together grated cheese, Pet® Milk, salt and dry mustard. Cook over boiling water until cheese melts and mixture is smooth, stirring frequently. Add kidney beans and keep warm until needed. Turn on oven and set at 375°F. Toast bread on one side only, then put bread, toasted side up, in shallow baking pan. Arrange sliced tomatoes on

* Cooked, dried red, pink or kidney beans may also be used. You will need to soak about 6 hours or overnight ⅓ cup beans in 1¾ cups water for 2, ⅔ cup beans in 3 cups water for 4 and 1 cup beans in 4 cups water for 6. In the morning, add ¼ tsp. salt for 2, ½ tsp. salt for 4, and ¾ tsp. salt for 6, then cover and boil 1 hour or until tender.

** Drained canned tomatoes may be used in place of fresh tomatoes. You will need ⅔ cup for 2, 1⅓ cups for 4 and 2 cups for 6.

top of toast and sprinkle with salt and pepper. Bake until tomatoes are thoroughly heated, about 5 minutes. Put on serving plates and serve at once with cheese sauce.

French's® Tomato Rarebit

My mother always served rarebits after a night of dancing to a big-name band at the local country club. Great these days while watching the late show on TV.

- 2 large tomatoes, halved
- Sugar
- Salt and freshly ground pepper
- 2 Tbs. (¼ stick) butter
- 1 Tbs. prepared mustard
- ½ tsp. dry mustard
- 2 tsps. French's® Worcestershire Sauce
- ½ tsp. paprika
- ¼ tsp. salt
- 1 lb. sharp Cheddar cheese, cut into ½-inch cubes
- ½ cup beer or ale
- 2 egg yolks
- ¼ cup whipping cream or milk
- Toast

Preheat broiler. Sprinkle tomatoes generously with sugar, salt and pepper. Place on baking sheet and broil just until tender, turning once to cook both sides. Turn oven to low and keep tomatoes warm. Melt butter in top of double boiler or chafing dish over simmering water. Add mustards, Worcestershire, paprika and salt and stir well to blend. Add cheese, making sure water does not boil or cheese will become tough. (Some stringiness may occur, but mixture will incorporate as cheese warms.) Allow most of cheese to melt, stirring frequently. Add beer and continue stirring until cheese is completely melted. Beat yolks with cream and add slowly to cheese mixture, stirring until blended and thickened. Spoon immediately over warm tomatoes. Arrange toast around edge of dish. Makes 4 servings.

Chicken and Asparagus Rarebit

Very elegant and great-tasting too. A party dish that can come from your emergency shelf whenever there are unexpected guests. The idea is from Swanson® and it's such a good one it's proven to be one of their most popular recipes.

1 10¾-oz. can Campbell's® Condensed Cream of Chicken Soup
¼ cup water
1 cup shredded Cheddar cheese
1 5-oz can Swanson® Chunk Chicken
Cooked asparagus spears
Toast

In saucepan, combine soup, water and cheese. Heat until cheese melts; stir occasionally. Add chicken; heat. Arrange asparagus on toast; pour chicken mixture over asparagus. Makes about 2½ cups, or 3 servings.

Cheese Fondue

The nice thing about this lovely fondue is that it won't get stringy, separate or become gummy as ordinary fondues are apt to do. From *Campbell's® 100 Best Recipes* cookbook.

1 cup Sauterne or other dry white wine
1 large clove garlic, minced
1 lb. natural Swiss cheese, cubed or shredded
¼ cup flour
1 11-oz. can Campbell's® Condensed Cheddar Cheese Soup
French® or Italian bread cubes*

In saucepan or fondue pot, simmer wine and garlic. Combine cheese and flour; gradually blend into wine. Heat until cheese melts; stir often. Blend in soup. Heat, stirring until smooth. Spear bread with fork or toothpick and dip into fondue. Makes about 4 cups.

Unsalted Nut Butter

People write Planters® Peanut test kitchens every day for the "how-to" of nut butters. This one is elegant, tastes divine and is good for you, too—no salt is added.

2 cups Planters® Dry Roasted Unsalted Cashews or Unsalted Peanuts
3 Tbs. Planters® Oil
1 tsp. honey

* Also use bite-size pieces of cooked artichoke hearts, franks, lobster or shrimp.

Place Planters® Dry Roasted Unsalted Cashews or Unsalted Peanuts in blender or food processor. Blend on high speed until coarsely chopped. Continue blending, adding Planters® Oil in a steady stream. Add honey and blend until smooth and creamy. Makes ¼ cup.

2.
The Main Dish: Meats, Poultry, Fish and Seafood, Pasta, Sauces and Meatless Main Courses

There are still a few people in this country who persist in putting food, especially main course dishes, into separate categories such as "gourmet" food, "health" food, "convenience" food and such. They even go as far as to separate family food from party food; but this is ridiculous. Except for personal preference and/or prejudice there are only two kinds of food: truly flavorful and satisfying food and food that is disappointingly dull. Truly flavorful food *is* gourmet food and only healthful food is really satisfying. Whether it is convenient and thrifty besides depends very much on the recipe used, but with know-how it can be not one but all of these things.

Each recipe in this chapter was developed by an expert and very knowledgeable cook who "knew how" to make it a multi-category dish: flavorful, healthful, easy to prepare, relatively economical even in these inflated times and, especially, convenient for you, the cook. In fact these are no ordinary recipes; from a simple, but simply superb, Irish Stew developed by James Beard, no less, to a very continental Steak with Fresh Tomato Sauce from the Pompeian® Olive Oil Company, they are very special indeed. Each one is a more-for-your-money dish, satisfying, kind to your pocketbook and easily prepared.

In addition to beef, pork and chicken recipes, there are fish specialties ranging from crispy fish 'n' chips to a delicate Flounder au Gratin, special enough for a dinner party.

As for pasta, no self-respecting cookbook would go to press without a portfolio of recipes for America's favorite ethnic food. And what pasta recipes! Easier than ever, kinder than a rich uncle to the budget, and as popular as peanuts at the circus. They include some totally new ways to prepare your favorites and I know you'll love them. Last, but not least, a few delicate quiches and main-course pies, lovely stars for a luncheon party and a sophisticated choice for festive supper.

West Coast Broiled Flank Steak

Out in California, the Sunkist Lemon Growers tell me, this is the only way to broil a steak.

- 1 flank steak, about 1½ pounds
- 1 onion, thinly sliced
- 1 tsp. fresh grated lemon peel
- ½ cup fresh squeezed lemon juice
- 2 Tbs. sugar
- ½ tsp. salt
- ½ tsp. oregano, crushed
- ⅛ tsp. coarse black pepper
- 2 Tbs. soy sauce
- 1 Tbs. butter

Trim any fat or membrane from steak. With knife, score steak ⅛ inch deep on both sides in diamond design. Layer half of onions in plastic bag or glass dish. Place steak on top of onions, cover with remaining onion. Thoroughly combine remaining ingredients except butter; pour over steak and onions. Marinate 2 to 3 hours or overnight in refrigerator, turning several times. Remove steak from marinade; wipe partially dry with paper towel. Drain onions and reserve. Place steak on cold broiler pan, 3 to 5 inches from source of heat in preheated broiler. Broil 3 to 5 minutes on each side. Meanwhile, sauté onions in butter until soft. To serve, cut steak across grain in very thin slices; top with onions. Makes 4 servings.

Marinated Steak

A truly inspired way to transform a tough chuck steak into as tender and flavorful a steak as any you've ever eaten. The recipe is on the label of Regina® Cooking Sherry—has been for years.

1 1½-lb. flank, London broil or chuck steak
½ cup *each* Regina® Cooking Sherry and Japanese Soy Sauce
2 Tbs. cooking oil
1 large clove garlic, minced
¼ tsp. ground ginger

Score steak in criss-cross pattern on both sides. Combine remaining ingredients in shallow dish. Marinate steak, covered, for several hours or overnight. Turn occasionally. Grill or broil until cooked as desired. Serves 6.

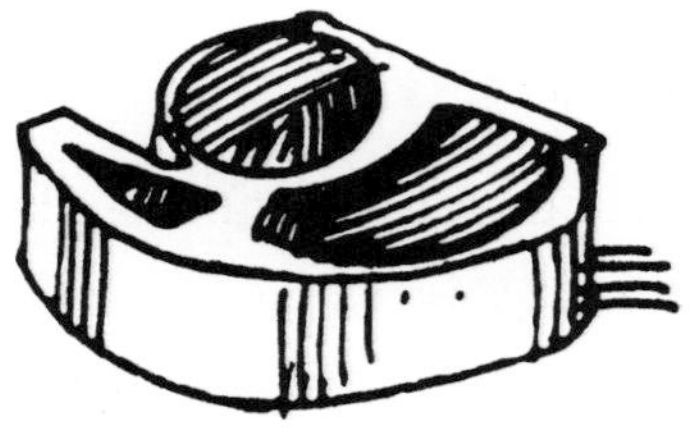

Beefsteak with Fresh Tomato Sauce

Here's a Continental way with steak from Pompeian® Olive Oil, and a tip for cutting the cost of a steak dinner; substitute inexpensive, thin-sliced bottom round steak for more expensive cuts and serve both steak and sauce over rice. Elegant and delicious.

2 lbs. ripe tomatoes, peeled and chopped coarsely
2 Tbs. Pompeian® Olive Oil
4 garlic cloves, sliced
Salt
Pepper
Oregano
Fresh basil or parsley to taste
6 small rump or sirloin steaks

Cook tomatoes, Pompeian® Olive Oil, garlic, salt and pepper until tomatoes are soft and begin to give off their juice. Add oregano, fresh basil or parsley to taste, if desired. Pound small rump or sirloin steaks until they are about ¼-inch thick, season with salt and pepper, and pan broil quickly in small amount of Pompeian® Olive Oil to the desired stage of doneness. Spread the tomato sauce over steaks, cover the pan and cook the steaks for about 5 minutes, or longer if a tougher cut of beef is used. Serve very hot with the sauce. Serves 6.

Flank Steak Creole

A great way to make inexpensive flank steak into a superb tasting and positively elegant entrée. Pepperidge Farm® put it on their Herb Seasoned Stuffing Mix over a dozen years ago.

1½ to 2½ lbs. flank steak
⅓ cup butter or margarine
2 Tbs. chopped onion
2 Tbs. chopped green pepper
1 Tbs. tomato paste
½ tsp. horseradish
½ tsp. salt
¼ tsp. sugar
½ cup water
2 cups Pepperidge Farm® Herb Seasoned Stuffing Mix
1 10½-oz. can condensed beef broth
1 Tbs. tomato paste
1½ Tbs. corn starch

Preheat oven to 500°F. Score one side of steak in a diamond pattern and rub with salt and pepper. Melt butter in a saucepan and sauté onion and green pepper until tender. Stir in 1 Tbs. tomato paste, horseradish, salt, sugar, water and stuffing. Place mixture down center on unscored side of steak, but not quite to the ends. Fold ends over stuffing, then bring together and overlap long sides. Skewer together. Place in a shallow baking pan and roast for 15 minutes. Reduce heat to 350°F. and continue baking 40 to 50 minutes. Meanwhile, combine beef broth, remaining tomato paste and corn starch in a saucepan. Bring to a boil, stirring, and boil 1 minute until shiny and thickened. Pass with the sliced steak. Makes 4 to 6 servings.

Easy-Does-it Swiss Steak

An all-time Hunt-Wesson® favorite and not just because it's simple to prepare, but because it tastes simply superb.

3 Tbs. pure vegetable oil
2 lbs. round steak, 1-inch thick
¼ cup flour
1 envelope dry onion soup mix
1 8-oz. can Hunt's® Tomato Sauce
½ cup water

Pour oil in 7½ × 12 × 1½-inch baking dish. Place in oven at 400°F. While dish and oil heat, trim steak and pound 2 Tbs. flour into each side. Place in heated baking dish; turn to coat both sides. Sprinkle on soup mix. Pour Hunt's® Tomato Sauce mixed with water over all. Cover tightly. Reduce oven temperature to 325°F. Bake 2½ to 3 hours until fork tender. Skim excess fat from gravy. Makes 6 servings.

Beef en Brochette

One of the most popular recipes to ever appear on the Heinz® 57 Sauce bottle. Serve over rice, add a glass of red wine to the menu, and your guests and family will be impressed by the simple elegance of this delicious meal.

- 1 13¼-oz. can pineapple chunks
- ½ cup Heinz® 57 Sauce
- 2 Tbs. dry white wine
- 1 Tbs. salad oil
- ½ tsp. salt
- Dash pepper
- 2 lbs. beef sirloin tip or top round, cut into 1-inch cubes
- Salt and pepper

Drain pineapple, reserving ½ cup liquid. Cover and refrigerate pineapple chunks. Combine the ½ cup pineapple liquid with Heinz® 57 Sauce and next 4 ingredients; pour over meat. Marinate 2 to 3 hours in refrigerator, turning occasionally. Thread meat and pineapple chunks alternately on six (12-inch) skewers, allowing 4 to 5 pieces of meat and 5 to 6 pieces of pineapple for each skewer. Brush with marinade; season lightly with salt and pepper. Grill or broil 3 inches from heat source 5 minutes on each side for medium rare. Makes 6 servings.

Grits and Grillades

This is South Louisiana cooking at its very best. The recipe was developed by people who truly know fine food—The McIlhenny's, who make Tabasco® pepper sauce in Louisiana's Cajun country.

- 2 lbs. beef round, thinly sliced
- 6 Tbs. bacon drippings or salad oil
- 4 Tbs. all-purpose flour
- 1 medium onion, chopped
- 1 green pepper, chopped
- 1 clove garlic, chopped
- 1 bay leaf
- 1 Tbs. chopped parsley
- 2 tsps. salt

- 1 cup peeled and cubed tomatoes
- 1½ cups water
- 1 tsp. Tabasco® pepper sauce
- ½ tsp. thyme
- 3 cups hot cooked grits

Brown meat in oil in deep skillet. Remove meat. Add flour and brown, stirring constantly. Add onion and tomatoes. Simmer a few minutes. Add meat, water, pepper, garlic, bay leaf, parsley, salt, Tabasco® pepper sauce and thyme. Cover and simmer for 1½ hours or until meat is very tender, adding water if necessary to make sauce the consistency of thick gravy. Serve grillades with portion of hot grits on the side. Serves 4 to 6.

Note: If you live in a part of the country where grits are not available, you may serve grillades with hot cooked rice.

Hungarian Goulash

This easy to prepare goulash has been a favorite for years in the Pet® Milk Company Consumer Services Kitchen. It's hard to believe, but the original version appeared in their *Pet® Gold Cookbook* back in 1932.

- 1½ lbs. round steak, cut in ½-inch cubes
- 3 Tbs. oil
- ⅓ cup all-purpose flour
- 1 Tbs. paprika
- 1 tsp. salt
- ¼ tsp. pepper
- ¼ tsp. garlic powder
- 1 medium onion, thinly sliced
- 1 1-lb. can whole tomatoes
- ⅓ cup water
- ⅔ cup Pet® Evaporated Milk

Brown meat in hot oil in large saucepan. Mix together flour, paprika, salt, pepper and garlic powder. Stir into meat mixture. Add onion, tomatoes and water. Cover. Simmer

1 hour, stirring occasionally. Gradually stir Pet® Evaporated Milk into hot mixture. Simmer 15 minutes, stirring frequently. Serve over hot buttered noodles. Makes 6½-cup servings.

Hungarian Pot Roast

This super-flavored pot roast recipe has been on the top twenty "most wanted" lists at the Hunt-Wesson® test kitchens for over 15 years.

- 1 3- to 4-lb. lean chuck or rump roast
- 1½ tsp. paprika
- 2 tsps. salt
- ¼ tsp. pepper
- 2 Tbs. pure vegetable oil
- ½ cup water
- 1 bay leaf
- 8 to 10 small whole white onions
- 8 small carrots, pared
- 2 8-oz cans Hunt's® Tomato Sauce with Mushrooms
- 1 clove garlic, minced
- ½ tsp. onion salt
- 2 Tbs. minced parsley
- 1 cup sour cream (optional)

Trim excess fat from meat. Sprinkle with paprika, salt and pepper. Brown in oil in Dutch oven over medium heat. Add water and bay leaf; simmer, covered, 2 hours or until meat is almost tender. Skim off fat. Place onions and carrots around meat. Add Hunt's® Sauce, garlic and onion salt. Cover; simmer 50 to 60 minutes longer until meat and vegetables are tender.

Add parsley. Just before serving, remove from heat and gradually stir in sour cream, if desired. Makes 6 to 8 servings.

Roast Chuck Neapolitan

One of the easiest recipes ever to appear on a Campbell's® Soup label and one of the best tasting ways you'll ever find to cook this inexpensive cut of meat.

- 1 3½-lb. boned chuck roast (about 2 inches thick)
- 2 Tbs. shortening
- 1 10¾-oz. can Campbell's® Condensed Tomato Soup
- ½ cup water
- 1 cup sliced onion
- 1 large clove garlic, minced
- 2 tsps. oregano, crushed
- Generous dash pepper

In large heavy pan, brown meat in shortening. Pour off fat. Stir in remaining ingredients. Cover; cook over low heat 2½ hours or until tender. Spoon off fat. Thicken sauce if desired. Makes 6 servings.

Oven-Baked Short Ribs with Garden Vegetables

I always thought this was my mother's "own" original recipe—until it was sent to me by an old friend who had long ago clipped it from the Argo-Kingsford® Corn Starch box.

- 3 lbs. beef short ribs
- 1 tsp. salt
- ¼ tsp. pepper
- 1 lb. carrots, cleaned and halved
- 1 lb. potatoes, pared and halved
- ½ lb. fresh green beans
- 4 small white onions
- 1 13¾-oz. can beef broth
- 2 tsps. prepared mustard
- 2 Tbs. horseradish
- 2 Tbs. Argo-Kingsford's® Corn Starch
- ¼ cup water

Trim excess fat from meat. Place in 13 × 9 × 2-inch baking pan; sprinkle with salt and pepper. Bake uncovered in 350°F. oven 2 hours; drain fat. Add next 4 ingredients. Mix broth, horseradish and mustard; pour over meat and vegetables. Cover with foil; bake 1 to 1½ hours longer or until tender. Arrange meat and vegetables on serving platter; keep warm. Strain broth; remove excess fat. Add water, if necessary, to make 2 cups and return to baking pan. Mix Corn Starch and ¼ cup cool water; stir into pan. Bring to boil 1 minute. Serve gravy with meat and vegetables. Makes 4 servings.

Po-Man's Ribs and Rice

A very popular "stick to the ribs" kind of recipe. Up-dated by home-economists at the Tabasco® Test Kitchens.

- 2 to 3 lbs. short ribs
- 1 10½-oz. can condensed onion soup
- 1 4-oz. can mushrooms
- 1 cup beef bouillon
- ½ tsp. salt
- ½ to 1 tsp. Tabasco® pepper sauce
- Hot cooked rice

Brown short ribs in Dutch oven. Combine remaining ingredients except rice, plus ½ cup water. Pour over ribs. Cover and simmer about 2½ hours. Serve with hot cooked rice. Makes 4 servings.

Salisbury Steak, Onion Gravy

Remember Salisbury steak? This label recipe comes from *Campbell's® 100 Best Recipes* cookbook.

- 1 10½-oz. can Campbell's® Condensed Onion Soup
- 1½ lbs. ground beef
- ½ cup fine dry bread crumbs
- 1 egg, slightly beaten
- ¼ tsp. salt
- Dash pepper
- 1 Tbs. flour
- ¼ cup ketchup
- ¼ cup water
- 1 tsp. Worcestershire sauce
- ½ tsp. prepared mustard

In bowl, combine ⅓ cup Soup with beef, crumbs, egg, salt and pepper. Shape into 6 oval patties. In skillet, brown patties; pour off fat. Gradually blend remaining soup into flour until smooth. Add to skillet with remaining ingredients; stir to loosen browned bits. Cover; cook over low heat 20 minutes or until done. Stir occasionally. Makes 6 servings.

Skillet Stuffed Peppers

From one of the most popular booklets ever printed by the A.1.® Sauce people. It's recipes like this that make for easy preparation and grand eating.

- ½ cup converted rice, cooked
- ¾ lb. ground beef
- ¼ cup minced, fresh onion
- 3 Tbs. A.1.® Steak Sauce
- 1 tsp. salt
- ¼ tsp. pepper
- 1 8-oz. can tomato sauce
- 1 12-oz. can whole kernel corn, drained
- 6 large green peppers
- 6 medium carrots, peeled and cut into 1-inch pieces
- 3 Tbs. butter (or margarine)
- ½ cup water

While rice is cooking, in medium skillet brown beef until crumbly. Drain. Add onion. Cook until onion is soft. Remove from heat. Mix in A.1.®, salt, pepper, tomato sauce, corn and rice. Cut tops, seeds and membranes from peppers. Discard. Fill peppers with meat and rice mixture. In 10-inch skillet, place peppers and carrots. Add butter and water. Simmer, covered, 30 to 40 minutes, or until carrots are tender. Serves 6.

Quick Chinese Pepper Steak

The Ehlers people tell us their favorite package recipe is this easy Chinese pepper steak. You can cook it in minutes in your wok or electric skillet.

- 1 lb. round steak, cut ½ inch thick
- 2 Tbs. salad oil
- 1 medium onion, sliced
- 1 medium green pepper, sliced
- 1 envelope Au Jus Gravy Mix
- ¾ cup water
- 4 tsps. soy sauce
- ½ tsp. ground ginger
- 3 cups hot cooked rice

Cut meat in half lengthwise with a sharp knife, then crosswise into thin slices. Cook meat, onion and pepper in skillet in hot oil until meat is browned. Stir in remaining ingredients except rice. Cook 5 minutes, stirring constantly. Serve over rice. Makes 4 servings.

Korean-Style Flank Steak

The secret of this spicy steak recipe is the Karo Dark Corn Syrup. It's different and delicious.

- 1½–2lbs. flank steak
- ¼ cup sesame seeds
- ¼ cup corn oil
- ¼ cup soy sauce
- ¼ cup Karo Dark Corn Syrup
- 1 small onion, sliced
- 1 clove garlic, crushed
- ¼ tsp. black pepper
- ¼ tsp. ground ginger

Remove tendons and trim steak. Score meat. In shallow baking dish stir together sesame seeds, corn oil, soy sauce, corn syrup, onion, garlic, pepper and ginger. Add steak, turning to coat. Refrigerate, turning once, several hours or overnight. Broil steak about 6 inches from source of heat, turning once, about 8 minutes, or until cooked to desired doneness. Slice steak diagonally and serve immediately. Makes about 6 servings.

Ranchero Supper Stew

Lipton adapted this authentic Texas recipe for their Onion Soup Mix packaging. It's a great spicy meal in one. Serve with hot cornbread for a true ranch-house supper.

- 2 Tbs. oil
- 1½ lbs. beef cubes
- 1 envelope Lipton Onion Soup Mix
- 2 cans (16 ounces) whole tomatoes, undrained
- 1 cup water
- 2 tsps. chili powder
- 2 carrots, thinly sliced
- 1 green pepper, chopped
- ½ cup celery, thinly sliced
- 2 potatoes, diced

In large skillet, heat oil and brown beef; add onion soup mix blended with tomatoes, water, and chili powder. Simmer, stirring occasionally, 30 minutes. Add carrots, green pepper, celery, and potatoes; cook covered 45 minutes or until vegetables are tender and gravy is slightly thickened. Makes about 6 servings.

Horseradish Dressing for Cold Meats

This zippy dressing is a great accompaniment to cold meat. I also recommend it spooned over hot broiled hamburgers.

- 1 cup Hellmann's Real Mayonnaise (or Best Foods)
- ½ cup buttermilk
- 2 Tbs. finely chopped green onion
- 1½ Tbs. horseradish
- ½ tsp. salt
- ⅛ tsp. pepper

Combine all ingredients. Cover; chill 1 hour. Serve over slices of beef, tomato and onions. Makes 1⅔ cups.

Red-Hot Stir-Fry

From Dole® comes one of the best stir-fry dishes I've ever tried. Serve it with hot with just-cooked thin noodles for a change.

- 2 large stalks broccoli
- 1 lb. beef top round
- ¼ cup oil
- 1 can (20-ounce) Dole® Pineapple Chunks, in syrup
- ¼ cup soy sauce
- 2 Tbs. vinegar
- ½ tsp. crushed red pepper
- 2 Tbs. cornstarch
- 1 cup fresh bean sprouts
- 2 Tbs. sesame seeds, toasted

Trim and slice broccoli diagonally. Slice beef in strips across the grain. Heat oil in wok or skillet till very hot. Add broccoli and stir fry 2 to 3 minutes until barely tender. Add beef strips and cook just until brown. Drain pineapple reserving syrup. Mix syrup with soy sauce, vinegar, red pepper and cornstarch. Add pineapple, bean sprouts and sauce mixture to beef. Heat and stir until thickened. Sprinkle with sesame seeds. Serve over rice or noodles if desired. Makes 4 servings.

Mock Sauerbraten

Good German housewives used to spend days making sauerbraten. Ehler Pot Roast Gravy Mix makes it simple and simply delicious with this easy recipe from the back of their Pot Roast Gravy envelope.

- 1 package (½-ounce) Pot Roast Cooking and Gravy Mix
- ¾ cup water
- ½ cup dry red wine
- ¼ cup red wine vinegar
- ⅛ tsp. ground cloves
- 1 3- to 4-lb. pot roast
- 4 carrots, quartered
- 2 onions, quartered
- ¼ to ½ cup sour cream
- ¼ cup gingersnap cookie crumbs

Combine gravy mix, water, wine, vinegar and cloves in a 4-quart Dutch oven and stir to blend well. Add pot roast, cover and cook in a preheated 350° oven for 2 hours. Add carrots and onions, cover and cook 1 hour longer. Remove pot from oven and set meat aside on warm platter. Stir sour cream and gingersnap crumbs into sauce. Serve sauce separately. Makes 6 servings.

Note: Leftover meat may be sliced and served cold with Horseradish Dressing.

Spanish Pot Roast

One of the first recipes demonstrated on Kraft's® famous "complete meal" television commercials. A great-tasting flavorful one-pot meal. Save leftovers to serve cold with Kraft® horseradish.

- 3- to 4-lb. pot roast
- 1 8-ounce bottle Kraft® Catalina French® Dressing
- ¾ cup water
- 8 small onions
- 8 small potatoes
- 1 cup stuffed green olive slices
- 2 Tbs. flour

Brown meat in ¼ cup dressing. Add remaining dressing and ½ cup water. Cover; simmer 2 hours and 15 minutes. Add onions, potatoes and olives; continue simmering 45 minutes, until meat and vegetables are tender. Remove meat and vegetables to warm serving platter. Gradually add remaining ¼ cup water to flour, stirring until well blended. Gradually add flour mixture to hot liquid in pan; cook, stirring constantly, until mixture boils and thickens. Simmer 3 minutes, stirring constantly. Serve with meat and vegetables. Makes 6 to 8 servings.

In 1976 the Uncle Ben's Rice Company held a contest for the best recipe using their Converted Rice, Quick Rice, Long Grain and Wild Rice mixture or Stuff 'n Such Stuffing mix. Here are three of their prize-winning recipes for your collection. Collector's items they surely are. Each one is super-delicious. If you lost the one you clipped and thought you saved, rejoice! Here it is!

Stuffed Beef Ranchero

Family flank steak in a glamorous new dress.

2 1½-lb. flank steaks
3 tsp. instant meat tenderizer
1 6-ounce package Uncle Ben's Stuff 'n Such Traditional Sage Flavor
1 egg, beaten slightly
½ lb. ground pork sausage
1 medium green pepper, chopped
½ cup finely chopped onion
1 6-ounce jar stuffed green olives, sliced
1 10½-ounce can condensed beef broth
1 medium ripe tomato, chopped
1 Tbs. flour
2 Tbs. cold water

Pound steaks thin enough to stuff and roll easily. Sprinkle both sides of steaks with tenderizer and treat as manufacturer suggests on package label. Prepare Stuff 'n Such according to package directions, using ¾ cup water. Add egg to stuffing; mix well. Cook sausage meat, pepper and onion in skillet until sausage is lightly browned and onion is tender, about 5 minutes. Drain off excess fat. Add olives and sausage mixture to stuffing and mix well. Spread 1½ cups stuffing on each steak. Roll each steak and tie securely with string. Place steaks in a 13½ × 8½-inch baking dish. Pour broth mixed with tomato over steaks. Bake at 350°F. oven for 1 hour or less until meat is tender yet rare, basting occasionally. Place remaining stuffing in aluminum-foil packet and bake for 30 minutes. Cool meat rolls 5 minutes before slicing. Combine flour and cold water; mix until free of lumps. Stir into pan drippings; continue stirring over medium heat until thickened. Serve with additional stuffing and gravy. Makes 8 to 10 servings.

Reuben Croquettes

A completely new flavor for ever-welcome crisp croquettes.

- ½ cup Uncle Ben's Converted Brand Rice
- 1 1-lb can sauerkraut
- 1 12-ounce can corned beef
- ¼ cup chopped onion
- 3 eggs
- 1 cup shredded Swiss cheese
- 1 tsp. salt
- ¼ tsp. pepper
- 2 Tbs. water
- 1½ cups fine dry breadcrumbs
- 1 cup mayonnaise
- ⅓ cup milk
- ¼ cup prepared mustard
- 4 tsps. lemon juice
- Oil for frying

Cook rice according to package directions for half the basic recipe. Drain sauerkraut very well, pressing out as much liquid as possible. Chop sauerkraut and corned beef very fine. Add onion, 2 eggs, cooked rice, cheese, salt and pepper; mix well. Shape into 18 croquettes or balls, using ¼ cup of mixture for each. Combine remaining egg and water; beat slightly. Roll each croquette in crumbs, then egg mixture, and again in crumbs. Let dry 10 minutes. Fry croquettes in hot shallow oil, 5 to 7 minutes, turning once, or bake in 450°F.

oven for 10 minutes, turn and bake 10 minutes longer. Serve with sauce. Makes 18 croquettes or 6 servings.

Sauce: Combine and mix mayonnaise, milk, mustard and lemon juice.

Cheesy Rice Roll-Ups

Delicate crêpes with an elegant wild rice filling.

Crêpes:

- ¾ cup milk
- 3 eggs
- ¼ tsp. salt
- ¾ cup all-purpose flour
- Melted butter or margarine

Filling:

- 1 (6-ounce) package Uncle Ben's Long Grain and Wild Rice
- 1 lb. ground lean beef
- 1 (4-ounce) can sliced mushrooms, drained

Sauce:

- ¼ cup butter or margarine
- 2 Tbs. all-purpose flour
- 1 10¾-ounce can condensed cream of mushroom soup
- 1½ cups milk
- 1 cup shredded process American cheese

Prepare crêpes. Combine milk, eggs and salt in small mixing bowl; beat slightly. Add flour; beat until smooth. Cover and refrigerate 1 hour. Lightly butter a 6-inch frypan. Pour 2 Tbs. of crêpe batter into pan; rotate pan quickly to spread evenly. Cook until lightly browned. Turn; brown lightly on second side and turn out. Keep warm.

Prepare filling. Cook contents of rice and seasoning packets according to package directions. Cook ground beef until crumbly; drain. Add cooked rice and mushrooms; mix well. Fill each crêpe with ⅓ cup rice mixture; roll up. Place on large heatproof platter or 13½ × 8½-inch baking dish.

Prepare sauce. Melt butter or margarine; stir in flour, then soup and milk. Cook until thickened, stirring constantly.

Stir in remaining rice mixture. Pour over filled crêpes. Sprinkle with cheese. Bake at 350°F. oven until cheese is melted, 15 to 20 minutes. Makes 6 servings, 2 crêpes per serving.

Best Beef Bourguignon

True beef bourguignon from Holland House Wines.

- ½ lb. mushrooms, sliced
- ¼ cup butter
- 3 slices bacon, cut up
- 2 lbs. boneless beef, cut in 2-inch cubes
- 2 Tbs. flour
- 2 cloves garlic, crushed
- 1 Tbs. tomato paste
- 1¼ cups Holland House Red Cooking Wine
- 2 beef bouillon cubes
- 2 Tbs. sugar
- ¼ tsp. salt
- ¼ tsp. thyme
- 1 small bay leaf
- 1 peppercorn
- ½ lb. small white onions

In large pot, sauté mushrooms in butter; remove mushrooms and set aside. Fry bacon until crisp; remove and set aside. Add meat to drippings and brown well. Blend in flour. Add garlic, tomato paste, wine and seasonings. Cover and simmer for 2 hours, stirring occasionally. Add onions, mushrooms and bacon; simmer 1 hour longer. Add additional wine if liquid has evaporated. Garnish with cherry tomatoes and serve over rice if desired.

Best Ever Meat Loaf

In 1916 Campbell's published "Help for the Hostess," the first cookbook to use canned soup as an ingredient. This succulent meat loaf made its debut in the first edition and it's been going strong ever since. Here is the up-to-date version with four popular variations.

- 1 10¾-ounce can Campbell's Condensed Cream of Mushroom or Golden Mushroom Soup
- 2 lbs. ground beef
- ½ cup fine dry breadcrumbs
- 1 egg, slightly beaten
- ⅓ cup finely chopped onion
- 1 tsp. salt
- ⅓ cup water

Mix thoroughly ½ cup soup, beef, breadcrumbs, egg, onion, and salt. Shape *firmly* into loaf (8 × 4-inch); place in shallow baking pan. Bake at 375°F. for 1 hour, 15 minutes. In saucepan, blend remaining soup, water, and 2 to 3 Tbs. drippings. Heat; stir occasionally. Serve with loaf. Makes 6 to 8 servings.

Frosted Meat Loaf: Prepare loaf as above; bake for 1 hour. Frost loaf with 4 cups mashed potatoes; sprinkle with shredded Cheddar cheese. Bake 15 minutes more.

Swedish Meat Loaf: Add ½ tsp. nutmeg to loaf. Blend remaining soup with ⅓ cup sour cream; omit drippings and water. Serve over loaf; sprinkle with additional nutmeg. Garnish with thinly sliced cucumber.

Meat Loaf Wellington: Crescent Rolls (Refrigerated): Prepare loaf as above. Bake at 375°F. for 1 hour. Spoon off fat. Separate 1 package (8 ounces) refrigerated crescent dinner rolls; place crosswise over top and down sides of meat loaf, overlapping slightly. Bake 15 minutes more.

Patty Shells: Thaw 1 package (10 ounces) frozen patty shells. Prepare loaf as above. Bake at 375°F. for 30 minutes. Spoon off fat. Increase oven temperature to 400°F. On floured board, roll 5 patty shells into rectangle (12 × 8-inch); prick several times with fork. Cover top and sides of loaf with pastry. Decorate top with remaining patty shell, rolled and cut into fancy shapes. Bake 45 minutes more or until golden brown. Serve with sauce.

Souperburgers

Back in 1959 Campbell's test kitchens developed this "souper" easy hearty main dish. Good cooks around the country still write in for the recipe. The results never disappoint them.

- 1 lb. ground beef
- ½ cup chopped onion
- 1 can Campbell's Chicken Gumbo Soup
- 2 Tbs. ketchup
- 1 Tbs. prepared mustard
- 6 buns, split and toasted

Brown beef and cook onion in skillet until tender (use shortening, if necessary); stir to separate meat. Add soup and seasonings. Heat; stir often. Serve on buns. Makes about 3 cups.

Saucy Meatballs

Adapt this recipe to your next party by serving it from a chafing dish with cocktail picks and omitting the noodles. It's from Heinz® 57 Sauce and has been a 4-star favorite for over ten years.

- 1 lb. lean ground beef
- ⅔ cup grated Parmesan cheese
- ½ cup seasoned dry bread crumbs
- ½ cup milk
- 1 egg, slightly beaten
- 2 Tbs. shortening
- 1 Tbs. flour
- 1 28-ozs. can tomatoes, cut into bite-size pieces
- ⅓ to ½ cup Heinz® 57 Sauce
- 1 Tbs. sugar
- ½ tsp. salt
- Hot buttered noodles

Combine first 5 ingredients. Shape into 20 meatballs using a rounded Tbs. for each. Brown well in shortening. Drain excess fat. Sprinkle flour over meatballs; stir gently to coat meatballs. Combine tomatoes, Heinz® 57 Sauce, sugar and salt; pour over meatballs. Simmer uncovered, 25 minutes or until sauce is desired consistency, stirring occasionally. Serve meatballs and sauce over noodles. Makes 5 servings (about 3 cups sauce).

Sweet-Sour Meatballs

Another easy, delicious and different way with meatballs from Heinz®.

- 1 lb. lean ground beef
- 1 egg, slightly beaten
- 1 tsp. salt
- Dash pepper
- 2 Tbs. shortening
- 1 medium green pepper, cut into strips
- 1 medium onion, sliced
- 1½ cups pineapple juice
- ¼ cup Heinz® 57 Sauce
- Hot buttered rice

Lightly combine first 4 ingredients; form into 16 meatballs. Partially brown meatballs in shortening. Add green pepper and onion; sauté until vegetables are tender. Stir in pineapple juice and Heinz® 57 Sauce. Cover; simmer 15 to 20 minutes or until meatballs are cooked. Thicken sauce with corn starch/water mixture, if desired. Serve over rice. Makes 4 servings.

Cheeseburger Pie

Remember this? It was a teen-age favorite way back before pizza became popular—and it still is. A feature recipe found on the Bisquick® Baking Mix box back in the 1960's.

- 1 cup Bisquick® Baking Mix
- ¼ cup cold water
- 1 lb. ground beef
- ½ cup chopped onion
- ½ tsp. salt
- ¼ tsp. pepper
- 2 Tbs. Bisquick® Baking Mix
- 1 Tbs. Worcestershire sauce
- 2 eggs
- 1 cup small curd creamed cottage cheese
- 2 medium tomatoes, sliced
- 1 cup shredded Cheddar cheese (about 4 ozs.)

Heat oven to 375°F. Mix 1 cup Bisquick® Baking Mix and the water until soft dough forms; beat vigorously 20 strokes. Gently smooth dough into ball on floured cloth-covered board. Knead 5 times. Roll dough 2 inches larger than inverted pie plate, 9 × 1¼ inches. Ease into plate; flute edge if desired. Cook and stir ground beef and onion until beef is brown; drain. Stir in salt, pepper, 2 Tbs. Bisquick® Baking Mix and the Worcestershire sauce. Spoon into pie crust. Mix eggs and cottage cheese; pour over beef mixture. Arrange tomato slices in circle on top; sprinkle with Cheddar cheese. Bake until set, about 30 minutes. Makes 6 to 8 servings.

Tangy Meat Loaf

A "best of the best" recipes from the Wheat Chex® cereal permanent file of all-time favorites.

½ cup ketchup
2 Tbs. brown sugar
½ tsp. powdered mustard
4 tsps. Worcestershire sauce
2 tsps. seasoned salt
1½ tsps. onion powder
¼ tsp. garlic powder
¼ tsp. ground black pepper
1 egg
2 Tbs. finely chopped green pepper
1½ cups Wheat Chex® cereal
1½ lbs. ground beef

In large bowl combine ketchup, brown sugar and mustard. Reserve 4 Tbs. mixture for topping. To remaining mixture add Worcestershire sauce, salt, onion, garlic powder, pepper and egg. Blend well. Stir in green pepper and Wheat Chex.® Let stand 5 minutes. Break up Wheat Chex.® Add ground beef. Mix well. Shape into loaf in shallow baking pan. Bake in 350°F. oven for 65 minutes. Spread top with reserved ketchup mixture. Bake additional 15 minutes. Makes about 6 servings.

Skillet Barbecued Pork Chops

Simply terrific! One of the first recipes to appear on the Kikkoman® Teriyaki Sauce label. Still one of the best.

6 pork chops, ½-inch thick
1 Tbs. salad oil
¾ cup water
¼ cup Kikkoman® Teriyaki Sauce
¼ cup tomato ketchup
4 tsps. brown sugar, packed
4 tsps. corn starch

Brown chops slowly in hot oil on both sides; drain. Combine ½ cup water with next 3 ingredients; pour over chops. Cover and simmer 30 minutes; turn chops over and cook 30 minutes longer. Remove from pan. Dissolve corn starch in remaining water; stir into pan. Cook and stir until sauce boils and thickens. Return chops and coat both sides with sauce. Makes 6 servings.

7-Layer Casserole

A recipe for liberated cooks, so quick and easy, developed long before cooks were liberated. So delicious it is one of the most popular ever from the Hunt-Wesson® kitchens.

- 1 cup uncooked rice
- 1 1-lb. can whole kernel corn, undrained
- 1 tsp. seasoned salt
- ¼ tsp. seasoned pepper
- 1 beef bouillon cube
- ¾ cup boiling water
- 1 15-oz. can Hunt's® Tomato Sauce with Tomato Bits
- 1 tsp. Worcestershire sauce
- 1 tsp. Italian herb seasoning
- 1 cup chopped onion
- ½ cup *each*: chopped green pepper and celery
- 1 lb. lean ground beef
- 1 cup shredded mild Cheddar cheese
- 2 Tbs. imitation bacon bits

In 2-quart casserole, arrange ingredients in layers in the following order:

Rice mixed well with corn, half the salt and pepper, bouillon cube and boiling water.

Half of Hunt's® Tomato Sauce that has been mixed with Worcestershire sauce and Italian seasoning.

Chopped onion, green pepper and celery.

Uncooked ground beef, remaining salt and pepper.

Remaining Hunt's® Tomato Sauce mixture. Cover tightly; bake at 375°F. 45 minutes.

Sprinkle with cheese; bake, uncovered, 15 minutes longer.

Top with bacon bits before serving.

Makes 4 to 6 servings.

Silverado Taco Casserole

Would a Texas woman like me pass up this recipe? I found it on a package of Ortega® Taco Shells but, as they told me at the Ortega® test kitchens, so did a couple of 100,000 other aficionados of Tex-Mex food. If you like that South-of-the-Border flavor, you'll love this casserole.

- 10 Ortega® Taco Shells, coarsely broken
- 1½ lbs. ground beef
- 1 1¼-oz. package Ortega® Taco Seasoning Mix
- ½ cup water
- 2 Tbs. dried minced onion
- 1 8-oz. can tomato sauce
- 2 cups (½ lb.) grated Monterey Jack cheese
- 1 large tomato, cut in wedges
- 6 stuffed green olives, sliced
- Ortega® Taco Sauce

In lightly greased 1½-quart casserole, place one half taco chips. Set aside. In 10-inch skillet, brown beef until crumbled. Drain. Add taco seasoning mix and water. Simmer, uncovered, 10 minutes. Stir in onion and tomato sauce. Spoon meat mixture over taco shells. Sprinkle with 1½ cups cheese. Place remaining taco chips over cheese. Sprinkle with remaining cheese. Arrange tomato wedges and olives attractively on top. Bake in preheated 350°F. oven 15 to 20 minutes or until hot and bubbly. Serve with Ortega® Taco Sauce. Makes 6 servings.

Stuffed Cabbage with Creamy Horseradish Sauce

It's positively amazing and really rather wonderful what a good cook can create with no-nonsense supermarket ingredients. This recipe from the A.1.® Sauce test kitchen is a classic example. It's extraordinarily good and positively elegant to look at and serve.

- 1 firm medium head cabbage
- 1 egg, beaten
- 1 lb. lean ground beef
- 3 Tbs. A.1.® Steak Sauce
- 2 Tbs. horseradish
- 2 Tbs. minced fresh onion
- 1 tsp. salt
- ½ tsp. pepper
- 2 Tbs. dry bread crumbs
- Creamy Horseradish Sauce (page 80)

Remove damaged outer leaves of cabbage. Slice off 1 inch of cabbage top. Remove inner leaves. Reserve top. Scoop out center of cabbage leaving ¾-inch cabbage shell. Finely chop 1 cup of removed cabbage leaves. Combine remaining ingredients and chopped cabbage. Pack into cabbage cavity. Replace top. Tie stuffed cabbage in cheesecloth. Place on rack, or nest of crinkled foil, in 4-quart saucepan. Pour 2 cups water in bottom of pan. Steam for 1 hour. Remove cheesecloth carefully from cabbage. Cut in wedges and serve with Creamy Horseradish Sauce. Serves 6.

Creamy Horseradish Sauce

¼ cup butter (or margarine)
¼ cup flour
1 tsp. salt
¼ tsp. pepper
2¼ cups milk
2 Tbs. horseradish
1 Tbs. A.1.® Steak Sauce

In 2-quart saucepan, melt butter. Stir in flour. Cook, stirring constantly, for 2 minutes. Add salt, pepper, milk, horseradish and A.1.® Cook, stirring occasionally, until thickened. Spoon over stuffed cabbage.

Mustard-Glazed Ham

This version of a classic Southern method of treating ham made its bow in a Grey Poupon® Dijon Mustard advertisement about a dozen years ago. Great looking on a buffet table, great tasting too.

1 precooked ham, about 8 lbs. (or 5-lb. canned ham)
Whole cloves
1½ cups firmly-packed dark brown sugar
½ cup maple-flavored syrup
2 Tbs. Grey Poupon® Dijon Mustard
1 Tbs. corn starch
1 1 lb., 4-oz. can unsweetened crushed pineapple

Cut rind off ham, if present. Score top surface of ham, stud with cloves, and place, fat side up, on a rack in a shallow baking pan. Bake in a preheated oven (350°F.) approximately 15 minutes per pound, or follow wrapper directions. Combine sugar, syrup and mustard. Use ¾ cup of glaze to baste ham every 10 minutes during last 30 to 45 minutes of baking. Stir corn starch into remaining glaze in saucepan. Add pineapple with juice. Simmer, stirring constantly, until sauce thickens. Serve sauce with ham.

Golden Praline Ham

Beautiful is what you'll call this prize-winning ham recipe from Hormel.®

1 Hormel® Cure/81 Ham
1 16-oz. jar apricot-pineapple preserves
½ cup brown sugar
Pecan halves and Maraschino cherries for garnish

Combine apricot-pineapple preserves with brown sugar and heat in saucepan, stirring well. Spread mixture over Hormel® Cure/81 Ham for last half hour of baking. When ham is finished, garnish with alternating diagonal rows of pecan halves and cherry halves.

Swiss Hamlets

The Oscar Mayer® people tell me their favorite package recipe is this easy but elegant dish. It can be put together in minutes, so you can relax and watch the evening news on TV while it bakes.

1 6 to 8 oz. package Oscar Mayer® brand smoked cooked ham, chopped ham, honey loaf or luxury loaf
4 slices Swiss cheese, 4-inches square
1 10-oz. package frozen broccoli spears, thawed
Dill Mustard Sauce (page 82)

Top two slices of meat with slice of cheese and one-fourth of broccoli; roll and secure with wooden toothpicks. Place in small shallow baking dish. Repeat. Top with sauce. Bake in 350°F. oven for about 30 minutes. Remove toothpicks; serve with Dill Mustard Sauce. Makes 2 servings.

Dill Mustard Sauce

- 1 1-oz. package white sauce mix
- ¼ cup sour cream
- 1 Tbs. prepared mustard
- ¼ tsp. dill weed

Prepare white sauce according to package directions. Stir in rest of ingredients.

Spaghettini Bolognese

From the Hunt's® Tomato Paste Collection, a 1960 recipe that's still as economical to prepare (well almost) as it has been delicious to eat.

- ¼ lb. mushrooms, sliced
- 1 carrot, sliced
- 1 clove garlic, crushed
- ½ cup *each:* chopped onion, celery and green pepper
- 2 Tbs. Wesson Oil
- ¾ lb. Italian sausage, casings removed
- 2 6-oz. or 1 12-oz. can Hunt's® Tomato Paste
- 3 cups water
- ¼ cup dry red wine (optional)
- 1 tsp. sugar
- ¼ tsp. Italian herb seasoning
- 1 lb. spaghettini, cooked and drained

Sauté mushrooms, carrot, garlic, onion, celery and green pepper in hot oil in Dutch oven. Add sausage; cook until sausage loses redness; drain fat. Add remaining ingredients except spaghettini. Simmer, uncovered, 30 to 40 minutes, stirring occasionally. Serve over hot spaghettini. Makes 6 to 8 servings.

Bucks County Lamb Stew

A 1930 classic from the Argo-Kingsford® Corn Starch package. Its down-home flavor has never gone out of style.

- 3 Tbs. corn oil
- 2 lbs. lamb stew meat, cut into 2-inch cubes
- 1 beef bouillon cube
- 2 tsps. salt
- 1 bay leaf
- ¼ tsp. crushed dried thyme leaves
- 4½ cups water
- 6 carrots
- 12 small white onions
- ¼ cup Argo-Kingsford's® Corn Starch

In skillet heat corn oil over medium heat. Add beef; brown on all sides. Add next 4 ingredients and 4 cups of the water. Cover; bring to boil. Reduce heat; simmer 1½ hours. Add carrots and onions. Simmer ½ hour or until tender. Mix Corn Starch and ½ cup water. Stir into beef mixture. Bring to boil, stirring constantly; boil 1 minute. Makes 6 servings.

Irish Stew

This recipe, from a booklet put out by the Tabasco® pepper sauce people, was developed by James Beard. It's great tasting, but so simple to prepare any novice can do it.

- 3 lbs. lamb; shoulder chops, breast
- 2 large potatoes for each person
- 2 medium onions per person
- 1 or 2 carrots per person
- 1 tsp. thyme
- 1 tsp. Tabasco® pepper sauce
- 1 bay leaf
- Salt to taste
- Water to cover

Arrange lamb, which should have a minimum of fat, in alternating layers with potatoes, onions (thickly sliced) and carrots. Add the seasonings and just cover with water or broth. Cover and either simmer on top of the stove or cook in a 325°F. oven for 1½ to 2 hours or until meat is tender. Test for seasoning and serve with crisp bread and a good salad. Serves 4 to 6.

Hiram Walker's Supreme Brandy Burgers

These are supreme all right, just the best burgers I have ever devoured.

- 2 shallots (or scallions) finely chopped
- 4 Tbs. butter
- 1 lb. ground lean chuck
- ¼ lb. boiled ham, ground
- 4 Tbs. ice water
- 1 egg slightly beaten
- Pinch of thyme
- Freshly ground pepper
- Flour
- 1 Tbs. oil
- ¼ cup beef consommé
- ¼ cup Hiram Walker Apricot Flavored Brandy
- 2 Tbs. butter
- Parsley

Sauté the shallots, add the next 7 ingredients. Wet hands and shape into patties. Refrigerate for 1 hour. Dust patties with flour; sauté in oil and keep in warm oven. Add consommé, Apricot Brandy, and cook five minutes. Add butter and pour over patties. Sprinkle with parsley.

Old El Paso Guacamole

- 2 California avocados, peeled and barely mashed
- ⅓ cup onion, chopped
- ⅓ cup Old El Paso Chopped Green Chilies
- ⅔ cup tomato, chopped
- 2 Tbs. Old El Paso Taco Sauce
- 1 Tbs. lemon or lime juice
- 1¼ tsp. sugar
- ½ tsp. garlic powder

Prepare all ingredients. In a medium bowl, carefully mix all ingredients. Makes 2⅔ cups.

Double the recipe so you'll have plenty of this zesty dip for tortilla chips and chilled fresh vegetables. Will keep 2 to 3 days refrigerated.

Avocado Tostadas

"Next time you feel like having a little excitement, stay at home and enjoy it. Crunchy 'Old El Paso' Tostada Shells heaped with refried beans and ground beef; smothered with zesty California avocado guacamole and layers of shredded lettuce, olives and Cheddar. Top with even more cool, golden-green guacamole, and a dab of tangy sour cream. It's a feast for eight that you can make in minutes." The Avocado Advisory Board and Old El Paso Foods sent us these words about their Avocado Tostadas. All we can add is, bravo!

- 8 Old El Paso Tostada Shells
- 1 can (16-ounces) Old El Paso Refried Beans
- 4 cups browned ground beef
- 2¾ cups guacamole
- ½ cup sliced black olives
- 4 cups shredded lettuce
- 1 cup grated Cheddar cheese
- ½ cup sour cream
- Old El Paso Taco Sauce
- Season to taste

Prepare all ingredients. Heat tostada shells according to package directions. In separate skillets heat beans and browned meat. Assemble tostadas by spreading equal portions of beans on each shell. Next layer equal portions of meat and guacamole (reserving about ¾ cup guacamole to garnish tops of tostadas); add olives, lettuce and cheese. Top each with a large spoonful of guacamole and a dollop of sour cream. If desired, Old El Paso hot or mild Taco Sauce may be sprinkled over tostada. Makes 8 servings.

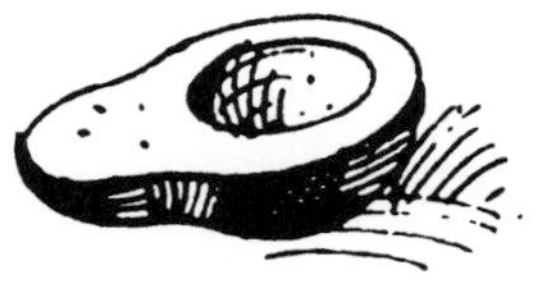

Tamale Pie

This is an "old love." Way back in depression days tamale pie made a great inexpensive supper. It still does. This version from Elam's Yellow Corn Meal box is extra good.

- 1½ cups cold water
- 1½ cups Stone Ground 100% Whole Yellow Corn Meal
- 1½ tsps. salt
- 2 cups boiling water
- 1 lb. ground beef chuck or round
- ½ cup chopped onion
- 2 Tbs. flour
- 1 tsp. chili powder
- 1 can (1 lb.) tomatoes
- 1 can (8 ounces) tomato sauce
- 1 can (8¾ ounces) whole kernel corn, drained (1 cup)

Combine and mix cold water and corn meal. Add ½ tsp. salt to boiling water. Add corn-meal mixture, stirring constantly, bring to a boil. Partially cover pan; cook slowly 7 minutes, stirring often. Line bottom and sides of greased 2-quart casserole with cooked mush. Cook beef and onion in frypan until beef is brown and crumbly. Stir in flour, remaining 1 tsp. salt and chili powder. Add tomatoes, breaking them up into chunks with spoon. Stir in tomato sauce and corn. Spoon into mush-lined casserole. Bake in 350°F. oven until hot and bubbly, 40 to 45 minutes. Makes 6 servings.

Frito Chili Pie Casserole

Did you know the very first Fritos were made with an old converted potato ricer? Mrs. Daisy Dean Doolin (mother of Elmer Doolin, the founder of the Frito Company) was the cook and Elmer was the route salesman for the corn chips. Nobody seems to know just when some talented cook combined Fritos and chili in this casserole dish, but it's Fritos' most-asked-for recipe.

3 cups Fritos Brand Corn Chips
1 large onion, chopped
1 can (19 ounces) chili
1 cup grated American cheese

Place 2 cups of Fritos Brand Corn Chips in a baking dish. Arrange chopped onion and half of grated cheese on the corn chips. Pour chili over onion and cheese. Top with the remaining corn chips and grated cheese. Bake at 350° F. for 15 to 20 minutes. Makes 4 to 6 servings.

Enchiladas

Would a Texas girl like me put together a cookbook of famous recipes without one for enchiladas? Certainly not this one, so here is Kraft's® classic version of this great dish.

1 lb. ground beef
1 16-ounce can tomatoes
1 6-ounce can tomato paste
½ cup water
½ cup chopped onion
1 Tbs. chili powder
1¼ tsps. salt
¼ tsp. pepper
1 8-ounce package tortillas
Oil
2 cups (8 ounces) shredded Kraft® sharp Cheddar cheese

Brown meat; drain. Add tomatoes, tomato paste, water, onion and seasonings; simmer 10 minutes. Fry tortillas in hot oil until softened; drain. Place rounded tablespoonful of meat sauce and cheese on each tortilla; roll up tightly. Place seam side down in 11¾ × 7½-inch baking dish; top with remaining sauce and cheese. Cover with aluminum foil; bake at 375°F. for 25 minutes. Makes 6 to 8 servings.

To make ahead: Prepare recipe as directed. Cover; refrigerate overnight. Bake at 375°F. for 50 minutes.

Hot Mexican Beef Salad

I'm sorry, I couldn't resist just one more South of the Border recipe. It's simply spectacular! Hot salad made with meat sauce, shredded lettuce and sharp Cheddar—festive and different for entertaining or family suppers.

1 lb. ground beef
¼ cup chopped onion
1 16-ounce can kidney beans, drained
½ cup Catalina French® dressing
½ cup water
1 Tbs. chili powder
1 qt. shredded lettuce
½ cup sliced green onion
2 cups (8 ounces) shredded Kraft® sharp Cheddar cheese

Brown meat; drain. Add onion; cook until tender. Stir in beans, dressing, water and chili powder; simmer 15 minutes. Combine lettuce and green onion. Add meat mixture and 1½ cups cheese; mix lightly. Top with remaining cheese. Makes 4 to 6 servings.

For variety, serve with toppings such as sour cream, sliced avocado, tortilla chips and sliced ripe olives.

Veal Parmigiana

Progresso Foods printed this Italian classic recipe on their Redi-Flavored Bread Crumbs package.

1 lb. veal cutlets
1 or 2 eggs, beaten
Progresso Redi-Flavored Bread Crumbs
¼ cup Progresso Pure Olive Oil
1 8-ounce can Progresso Tomato Sauce
Progresso Grated Parmesan Cheese
Slices of Mozzarella cheese

Dip cutlets in beaten egg, then in bread crumbs, and fry in hot olive oil until golden-brown on both sides. Place cutlets in a baking pan, pour tomato sauce over each, sprinkle with Parmesan cheese, and top each cutlet with slices of Mozzarella. Bake in a 375°F. oven for about 15 to 20 minutes, until Mozzarella has melted.

San Giorgio Marzetti

A Neapolitan-style recipe for a great casserole. Enjoy half tonight, freeze half for a work-free dinner whenever you're in the mood to dine *italiano*.

- 8 ounces San Giorgio Medium Egg Noodles
- 1 lb. lean ground beef
- ¾ cup finely chopped onion
- ½ tsp. salt
- 1 16-ounce jar San Giorgio Spaghetti Sauce with Mushrooms
- ½ cup green pepper slivers
- ½ cup thinly sliced celery
- 1 cup frozen peas
- 1 cup tomato juice
- 1 Tbs. Worcestershire sauce
- ½ tsp. crushed oregano
- ⅛ tsp. pepper
- 1 cup shredded Cheddar cheese
- San Giorgio Grated Parmesan cheese

Prepare medium egg noodles as directed on package. Brown beef and onion in a heavy skillet until the pink disappears, breaking up the pieces as it cooks; pour off fat. Sprinkle the meat with salt. Add the remaining ingredients, except for cheeses. Simmer, covered for 10 minutes. Add the hot drained noodles and blend. Stir until hot; remove from heat. Blend in Cheddar cheese. Serve in a hot casserole, garnished with Parmesan cheese. Makes 8 (1 cup) servings.

Variation: If you desire, place half of the mixture in a freezer container, cover and freeze. Allow to defrost, sprinkle with buttered San Giorgio Seasoned Bread Crumbs and bake.

Lasagne Italiano

Authentic Italian lasagne—a Kraft® "classic" from the mid-1950s.

- 1 lb. ground beef
- ½ cup chopped onion
- 1 6-ounce can tomato paste
- 1½ cups water
- 1 garlic clove, minced
- 2 tsps. salt
- ¾ tsp. oregano leaves
- ¼ tsp. pepper
- 8 ounces lasagne noodles, cooked, drained
- 1 lb. ricotta or cottage cheese
- 2 6-ounce packages Kraft® Mozzarella cheese slices
- ½ cup grated Parmesan cheese

Brown meat; drain. Add onion; cook until tender. Stir in tomato paste, water and seasonings. Cover; simmer 30 minutes. In 11¾ × 7½-inch baking dish, layer half of noodles, meat sauce, ricotta cheese and Mozzarella cheese; repeat layers. Sprinkle with Parmesan cheese. Bake at 375°F. 30 minutes. Let stand 10 minutes before serving. Makes 6 to 8 servings.

Grand-Mott's Roast Pork

Was there anything ever as good as a roast of pork, crispy brown outside, done to a creamy turn inside? Yes, one that has been glazed with apple sauce, molasses and spices as in this recipe from the Mott's Apple Sauce jar.

- 4 to 6 lbs. pork loin roast
- ⅓ cup Mott's Apple Sauce
- ⅓ cup Grandma's Molasses
- ¼ tsp. ground ginger
- 1 clove garlic, crushed

Have meat retailer loosen chine (back) bone. Place roast fat side up on rack in open roasting pan. Insert meat thermometer with bulb in thickest part not touching bone. Roast in 325°F. oven 2 to 2½ hours or until meat thermometer registers 170°F. In saucepan, combine apple sauce, molasses, ginger and garlic over medium heat. Brush pork with glaze every 10 minutes during last ½ hour of cooking. Serve pork with remaining apple sauce. Makes 8 to 10 servings.

Avocado With Chili Con Carne

If you have never tried chili with avocados you have never had one of the "specialties" of Southern California. The Avocado Advisory Board first published this super combination just a few years ago but its fame spread across the country in short order.

- 3 medium onions, coarsely chopped
- 4 cloves garlic
- 3 Tbs. bacon fat or butter
- 2 lbs. round of beef, diced
- 1 lb. lean pork, diced
- ⅓ cup chili powder
- 1 Tbs. flour
- 1 can (1 lb., 12 ounces) pear-shaped tomatoes
- 3 bay leaves
- 1 Tbs. *each:* salt, oregano, brown sugar, wine vinegar
- 2 cups pimiento-stuffed olives
- 4 avocados, halved and peeled

In large saucepan, cook onions and garlic in bacon fat until golden brown. Remove and reserve onions; discard garlic. Brown the meat in same pan over high heat. Stir in onions, chili powder and flour. Add tomatoes, bay leaves, salt, oregano, sugar and vinegar; bring to boil. Cover and simmer 2 hours, stirring occasionally. Discard bay leaves. Stir in olives; cook 30 minutes longer. Serve over avocado halves. Makes 8 servings.

Special Indoor Barbecued Spare Ribs With Sauce

From the Tabasco Sauce people in Creole Louisiana comes this classic red-hot barbecued ribs recipe. The sauce is equally good for barbecued chicken, and just try it over grilled hamburgers.

- 1 large onion, chopped
- ¼ cup Wesson Oil
- 1 (6-ounce) can tomato paste
- ½ cup water
- 1 beef bouillon cube
- ¼ cup Worcestershire sauce
- ¼ cup soy sauce
- ¼ cup white vinegar
- 2 Tbs. honey
- 2 tsps. Tabasco sauce
- 2 tsps. salt
- 1½ tsps. Liquid Smoke
- 1 large clove garlic, minced
- 1 tsp. dry mustard
- 4 to 5 lb. pork spare ribs

In small saucepan, sauté onion in Wesson Oil until transparent. Add remaining ingredients except spare ribs. Mix well. Simmer 15 minutes. Pour over spare ribs in large glass baking dish; let stand 1 hour, turning occasionally. Arrange on shallow rack or broiler pan. Bake at 350° F. about 1½ to 2 hours. Turn ribs and baste with remaining barbecue sauce two or three times during baking. Cut in portions to serve. Makes 4 servings.

Cantonese Apricot Pork

The Apricot Advisory Board featured the recipe for this unusual Oriental dish in their advertising a decade ago; it's still an asked-for favorite. Perhaps it started today's popular trend toward using fruit in main-course recipes.

- 1½ lb. lean, boneless pork*
- 2 Tbs. salad oil
- 2 cups sliced celery
- ½ cup sliced scallions
- 2 large cloves garlic, minced
- ⅓ cup soy sauce
- ½ tsp. powdered ginger
- 1 8-ounce can water chestnuts, drained and sliced
- 1 30-ounce can apricot halves, drained
- Salt, pepper
- Rice

Slice pork into thin strips. Heat oil in wok; gradually add celery, scallions and garlic. Stir-fry over high heat (about 5 minutes) until tender but crisp; remove vegetables and set aside. Add pork to seasoned oil and stir-fry over high heat until lightly browned (about 10 minutes); mix in soy sauce and ginger. Reduce heat to medium; return vegetables to wok with water chestnuts; heat until hot, stirring constantly. Gently mix in apricots. Remove wok from heat immediately after mixing in apricots to prevent them from getting too soft. Season to taste with salt and pepper. Serve with rice. Makes 6 servings.

Lemony Ham Slice

A new idea from Oscar Mayer, so good they put it on their Oscar Mayer Jubilee Ham Slice package.

- 1 lemon
- ½ cup brown sugar
- 1 Tbs. prepared mustard
- 1 Oscar Mayer Ham Slice

Lemon Sauce: Grate peel of one lemon; cut lemon in half. Thinly slice one half; squeeze juice from other half. Combine peel, juice, brown sugar, mustard. Add lemon slices. Broil

* For a good money-saving dish use leftover pork.

ham slice 4 inches from heat for 5 minutes; turn and top with sauce. Broil 3 minutes until sauce bubbles. Makes 2 servings.

Quick Sweet and Sour Pork

Like Oriental food? You'll love this easy recipe from the label of Karo Corn Syrup.

- 2 Tbs. corn oil
- 1 lb. boneless pork, cut in 1-inch cubes
- 1 can (20 ounces) pineapple chunks in juice
- ½ cup Karo Light or Dark Corn Syrup
- ¼ cup cider vinegar
- 2 Tbs. ketchup
- 2 Tbs. soy sauce
- 1 clove garlic, crushed
- 1 small pepper, cut in 1-inch squares
- 2 Tbs. corn starch
- 2 Tbs. water
- Hot cooked rice or Chinese noodles

In large skillet heat corn oil over medium-high heat; add pork and brown on all sides. Add pineapple, corn syrup, vinegar, ketchup, soy sauce and garlic. Bring to boil. Reduce heat; simmer uncovered, stirring occasionally, 10 minutes or until pork is tender. Add green pepper. Mix corn starch and water; stir into pork mixture. Stirring constantly, bring to boil over medium heat and boil 1 minute. Serve over rice or noodles. Serves 4.

Jambalaya

This 1898 Creole recipe came from the McIlhenny family who have been making Tabasco Sauce down on Avery Island in Louisiana for three-quarters of a century. The recipe first appeared in print back in the Thirties. Since then good cooks have made endless adaptations. Shrimp and chicken are favorite additions and the sausage is often omitted to suit today's taste for lighter meals.

- ½ lb. fresh pork
- 1 onion
- 1 clove garlic
- ½ lb. cured ham
- 6 small smoked pork sausages
- 2 Tbs. lard or butter
- 1 bay leaf
- 1 sprig parsley
- 1 sprig thyme or ¼ tsp. dried leaf thyme
- 1 whole clove
- 1½ quarts beef or chicken broth
- ½ tsp. Tabasco
- ¾ tsp. salt
- 1 cup uncooked rice

Cut pork (lean and fat) into cubes about ½-inch square. Chop onion and garlic very fine. Dice ham and cut sausage into pieces. Melt lard in a heavy iron pot or Dutch oven. Add onion, garlic, pork and ham; brown slowly, stirring frequently. Add sausage, bay leaf, parsley, thyme and clove; cook about 5 minutes. Add broth, Tabasco and salt; bring mixture to a boil. Add washed rice. Cover and simmer gently a half hour or longer until rice is tender. Stir often to mix well. Season to taste. Makes 4 to 6 servings.

Beans and Franks

Remember this? It's an old-time favorite combination. The recipe first appeared on Van Camp's Pork and Beans cans way back before World War II.

- 3 Tbs. chopped onion
- 2 Tbs. butter or margarine
- 1 can (1 lb., 15 ounces) Van Camp's Pork and Beans
- 6 wieners, sliced penny-style
- ⅓ cup brown sugar
- 1 tsp. prepared mustard
- 1 tsp. celery salt

Sauté onion in butter until tender. Combine onion with remaining ingredients in a 2-quart casserole. Bake, uncovered, at 350°F. for 40 minutes, stirring occasionally. Makes 6 servings.

Western Pot Roast

This pot roast is standard fare when there are hungry men around. Lea & Perrins® perfected the recipe and it's been a favorite for over a decade.

- 3 lbs. beef brisket or boneless round or chuck roast
- 1 cup chopped onion
- 1 cup ketchup
- ¼ cup Lea & Perrins® Worcestershire Sauce
- 2 Tbs. brown sugar
- 2 Tbs. cider vinegar
- 2 tsps. salt

In heavy pot brown on all sides beef brisket or boneless round or chuck roast in oil. Add chopped onion; cook until golden. Combine ketchup, Lea & Perrins® Worcestershire Sauce, brown sugar, cider vinegar and salt; pour over meat. Simmer, covered, until meat is tender, about 3 hours. Serve sliced with sauce along with onions, carrots and potato chunks if desired. Serves 8.

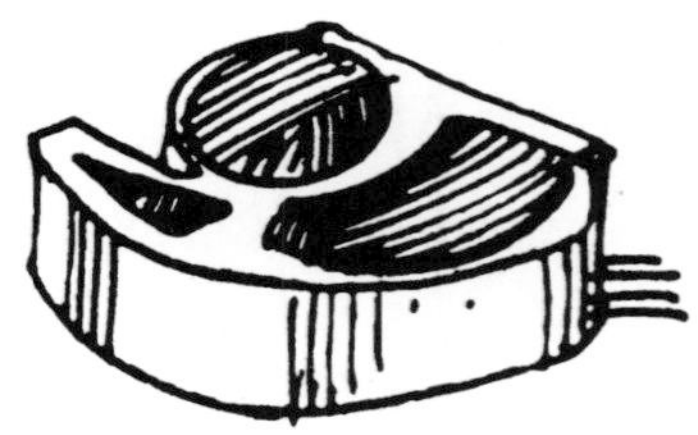

Marinated Steak Italiano

You know this recipe but had just forgotten? Well remember and enjoy. It's Wish-Bone's contribution to the pleasures of charcoal cookery.

- 2½- to 3-lb. London broil or chuck steak
- ½ cup Wish-Bone Italian Dressing

In large baking dish, place meat and cover with Wish-Bone Italian Dressing. Marinate, turning occasionally, about 3 hours. Broil steak, preferably over charcoal, turning once. Makes about 6 servings.

Variation: Add ¼ cup soy sauce and ¼ cup brown sugar to Wish-Bone® Italian Dressing before marinating.

Onion Chuck Steak

From Lipton comes one of the best tasting, easy, "bake-in-foil" dishes I've ever tasted. Serve it with baked potatoes and broiled tomato slices for a cooked all-in-the oven meal.

1½ lb. boneless chuck steak
2 envelopes Lipton Onion Cup-a-Soup
1 2½-oz. jar sliced mushrooms, drained

Preheat oven to 375°F. Place meat on foil in shallow baking pan. Sprinkle both sides with Lipton Onion Cup-a-Soup; top with mushrooms. Wrap loosely, sealing airtight with double fold; bake 1 hour. Makes about 4 servings.

Swiss Steak

Another Campbell soup label recipe that remains consistently in favor. Not just because it's easy, they told me at the Campbell Test Kitchens, but because this particular combination of steak and sauce happens to be especially good.

1½ lb. round steak
1 Tbs. vegetable shortening
½ cup chopped canned tomatoes
¼ cup chopped onion
¼ cup water
Dash pepper

Pound steak; cut into serving-size pieces. In heavy skillet, brown steak in shortening; pour off fat. Add remaining ingredients. Cover; simmer 1½ hours or until done. Stir often. Makes 4–6 servings.

Kikkoman Chuck Steak Teriyaki

An original American-Oriental recipe from Kikkoman. Inexpensive chuck steak is basted with a thick tomato-teri sauce and grilled to juicy, tender perfection.

2½ lb. chuck steak (about 1½ inches thick)
Meat tenderizer
⅔ cup Kikkoman Teriyaki Sauce
1 6-oz. can tomato paste
¼ cup salad oil

Prepare meat with a meat tenderizer according to label directions. Combine remaining 3 ingredients; brush over meat. Place on grill 3–4 inches from hot coals. Cook about 15 minutes. Turn steak over and brush with additional sauce. Cook to desired degree of doneness. Heat remaining sauce and serve with steak. Makes 4 servings.

New England Boiled Dinner

New Englanders know what to put on the table on a frosty night: it's this classic boiled dinner; and you know something, they are so right. Campbell's makes it easy for you to make it perfect. Warm gingerbread with whipped cream for dessert, anyone?

3 lb. boneless beef round rump roast
1 lb. rutabagas, peeled & sliced ¼-inch thick

- 2 tsps. shortening
- 2 10¾-oz. cans Campbell's Onion Soup
- 1 tsp. prepared horseradish
- 1 medium bay leaf
- 1 medium clove garlic, minced
- 6 medium carrots (about 1 lb.) peeled & cut in 2-inch pieces
- 8 whole potatoes (about 1 lb.), peeled
- 1 medium head cabbage (about 2 lbs.) cut in 6 wedges
- ½ cup water
- ¼ cup flour

In large heavy pan, brown meat in shortening; pour off fat. Add soup, horseradish, bay leaf, and garlic. Cover; cook over low heat 2 hours. Add carrots and rutabagas. Cook 30 minutes. Stir occasionally. Add potatoes; place cabbage on top. Cook 30 minutes more or until done. Remove meat and vegetables to serving platter; keep warm. Meanwhile, blend water into flour until smooth; stir into sauce. Cook, stirring until thickened. Makes 6 servings.

Salisbury Steak

The 1930's: President-elect Roosevelt was soon to be in the White House, "prosperity was just around the corner" and "things were sure to get better," but hourly wages were still only 44¢. In Depression days ingenious cooks believed "there just had to be another way to cook hamburger." There was: Salisbury steak. You may not believe it, but some people, including me, like it better than porterhouse. You may too when you try this version from the French® Company.

- 1 egg
- ½ cup dry bread crumbs
- ½ cup tomato juice
- 1 Tbs. French's® Minced Onions

1 lb. ground beef
1 envelope French's® Mushroom Gravy Mix
1 cup water

Combine egg, bread crumbs, tomato juice and onions; add ground beef. Shape into oblong patties, brown in skillet. Add gravy mix and water, stirring until smooth. Cover and simmer 10 minutes. Makes 4 servings.

Beef Burgundy with Rice

An American adaptation of a French® classic from the Uncle Ben's® rice box that's just as great tasting as it is easy to prepare.

5 medium onions, thinly sliced
2 Tbs. bacon drippings or shortening
2 lbs. boneless beef chuck, cut into 1½-inch cubes
2 Tbs. flour
Salt, pepper, thyme, marjoram to taste
½ cup beef bouillon
1 cup dry red wine
½ pound fresh mushrooms, sliced
4 cups hot cooked Uncle Ben's ® Converted Brand Rice

In heavy skillet, cook onions in bacon drippings until brown. Remove onions and set aside. Add more bacon drippings to skillet if necessary. Add beef cubes to drippings and brown well on all sides. Sprinkle beef with flour and seasonings. Stir in bouillon and wine. Cover and simmer very slowly for 2½–3 hours, or until meat is tender. If necessary, add more bouillon and red wine (1 part bouillon to 2 parts wine) to keep the meat barely covered with the liquid. Return onions to pan and add mushrooms. Cook 30 minutes longer, adding more liquid if necessary. Adjust seasonings to taste. Serve over hot cooked rice.

Dutch Meat Loaf

One of the most requested label recipes from Hunt's® Tomato Sauce. The brown sugar tomato sauce topping makes it especially good.

1½ lbs. lean ground beef
1 cup fresh bread crumbs
1 medium onion, chopped
1 8-oz. can Hunt's® Tomato Sauce
1 egg
1½ tsps. salt
¼ tsp. pepper
¾ cup water
2 Tbs. brown sugar, packed
2 Tbs. prepared mustard
1 Tbs. vinegar

In medium bowl, lightly mix beef, bread crumbs, onion, ½ can Hunt's® Tomato Sauce, egg, salt and pepper. Shape into loaf in shallow baking pan. Combine remaining Hunt's® Sauce with rest of ingredients; pour over loaf. Bake at 350°F. 1¼ hours. Baste loaf several times. Makes 5–6 servings.

Rodeo Hash

This quick cooking, one-skillet supper dish has gained in popularity over the years. It's one of the best from Campbell's back-of-the-label recipes.

1 lb. ground beef
3 cups diced raw potatoes
1 cup sliced celery
2 T. shortening
1 can Campbell's Golden Mushroom Soup
½ cup water
¼ cup chili sauce
½ tsp. salt
Generous dash pepper

In skillet, brown beef in shortening with potatoes and celery; stir to separate meat. Pour off fat. Add remaining ingredients. Cover; simmer 10 minutes. Stir often. Makes 4½ cups.

Chili Beef and Beans

A chili con carne dish that's ready in 15 minutes on top of the stove. It's one of the ever popular "adaptable" recipes developed by the home economists at Campbell's test kitchen. I garnish this dish with avocado slices, minced green onion and grated Monterey Jack cheese. No doubt, you'll have your own ideas.

1 lb. ground beef
1 cup chopped onion
1 large clove garlic, minced
2 tsps. chili powder
2 16-oz. cans Campbell's Pork and Beans in Tomato Sauce
1 10-oz. can tomatoes and green chilies

In large saucepan, brown beef and cook onion, combined with garlic and chili powder, until tender (use shortening if necessary); stir to separate meat. Add remaining ingredients. Bring to boil; reduce heat. Simmer 10 minutes; stir occasionally. Makes about 6½ cups, 6 servings.

Veal Goulash

Originally a Hungarian dish, this goulash is so good it has become an international favorite. Easy and economical, it's a great choice for a buffet supper. The recipe is from the Planters Peanut Oil cookbook.

- 2 lbs. veal cubes
- 1 Tbs. paprika
- ¼ cup Planters Peanut Oil
- 1¼ cups chopped onions
- 2 medium tomatoes, peeled and wedged
- 1 8-oz. can tomato sauce
- 2 tsps. salt
- Hot cooked noodles

Dredge veal with paprika, set aside. Heat Planters Peanut Oil in Dutch oven. Add chopped onions and sauté until lightly browned; remove onions using slotted spoon and set aside. Brown dredged veal on all sides. Return onions to Dutch oven. Stir in tomatoes, tomato sauce and salt. Simmer gently, uncovered, about 1 hour, or until veal is tender. Serve over noodles. Makes about 6 servings.

Meatballs with Spaghetti

No collection of American favorites would be complete without this Italian-style dish. Hunt's® has perfected the recipe for the label of their Tomato Paste can.

- 2 eggs, beaten
- 2 6-oz. or 1 12-oz. can Hunt's® Tomato Paste
- ¼ cup minced onion
- ¼ cup grated Parmesan cheese
- 2 Tbs. minced parsley
- 1 clove garlic, minced
- 2 tsp. salt
- 1 lb. ground beef
- ¾ cup soft bread crumbs
- 3 Tbs. Wesson Oil
- 2½ cups hot water
- 1½ tsps. sugar
- 1 tsp. basil
- 1 tsp. oregano
- 1 tsp. pepper
- 1 lb. spaghetti, cooked and drained

In a bowl, mix together eggs, 1 Tbs. Hunt's® Tomato Paste, onion, cheese, parsley, garlic and 1 tsp. salt. Add beef and bread crumbs; mix thoroughly. Form into 20 balls, about 1 inch in diameter. Lightly brown in a Dutch oven on all sides in hot oil; drain. Blend remaining Hunt's® Tomato Paste with hot water, sugar, basil, oregano, 1 tsp. salt and the pepper in a bowl. Pour over meatballs. Cover; simmer 10 minutes. Uncover; simmer 10 minutes longer. Serve over spaghetti. Makes 6 servings.

Golden Glaze Ham

Armour tells me this is a Midwest farm recipe and I can believe it. Only a good farm cook would dream up using a jar of apple jelly to glaze a ham and is it delicious!

1 5-lb. Armour Golden Star Ham
1 10-oz. jar apple jelly
1 tsp. lemon juice
½ tsp. cinnamon
Dash of nutmeg

Heat oven to 325°F. Score surface of ham. Heat ham according to label instructions. Combine remaining ingredients in small saucepan. Heat, stirring occasionally, until jelly melts. Spoon glaze over ham during last 30 minutes of heating time.

Pork Chops Parisienne

An old-world recipe to prepare in new-world record time. I found it, of all places, on a package of Del Monte dried pitted prunes. I think you'll be glad I did.

- 4 1-inch center cut pork chops
- 1 cup dry white wine
- 12 Del Monte Pitted Prunes
- 1 cup heavy whipping cream
- 1 Tbs. red currant jelly

In skillet, brown pork chops. Add ¼ cup wine and simmer, covered, 25 minutes. Place Del Monte prunes and ¾ cup wine in oven-proof dish; heat in 300°F. oven for 20 minutes. Remove pork chops to heated platter. To skillet add whipping cream and currant jelly; cook quickly over high heat, stirring constantly, until sauce is thick and shiny. Pour over pork chops. Garnish with baked prunes in wine.

Pork Chops 'n' Vegetables

This is an old favorite from Lea & Perrins® advertising. It's a soul-satisfying dish that needs only some good crusty bread and a crisp salad to round out the meal. Reheatable too for make-ahead cooks.

- 2 Tbs. oil
- 6 pork loin chops, ½-inch thick
- 1 green pepper, cut into strips
- 2 Tbs. flour
- 1 10½-oz. can condensed onion soup
- 2 Tbs. Lea & Perrins® Worcestershire Sauce
- 1 tsp. garlic powder
- 1 tsp. salt
- 2 medium tomatoes, cut in wedges

In large skillet heat oil. Add chops, 3 at a time; brown well on both sides; remove and set aside. Add green pepper; saute for 3 minutes; remove and set aside. Stir in flour; cook and stir for 1 minute. Blend in next 4 ingredients. Bring to boiling point. Return chops to skillet; spoon sauce over chops. Cover and simmer until chops are tender, about 1 hour. Stir in tomatoes and sautéed green pepper. Cover and simmer 5 minutes longer. Serves 6.

Sweet and Sour Pork Skillet

If you like pork, you'll love this recipe. It's been an all-time favorite since 1957 when it first appeared on the back of the Uncle Ben's® Converted Brand Rice package.

- 1 lb. boneless pork, cut in ¾-inch cubes
- 1 13½-oz. can pineapple tidbits
- ¼ cup vinegar
- 1½ tsps. salt
- ½ tsp. garlic salt
- 2 Tbs. sugar
- 1 cup Uncle Ben's® Converted Brand Rice
- 1 green pepper, cut into small squares
- 1 tomato, cut into thin wedges

Brown pork in cooking oil in 10-inch skillet; drain. Drain pineapple tidbits, reserving liquid. Add water to liquid to make 2½ cups. Add liquid, vinegar, salt, garlic salt and sugar to pork; stir. Bring to boil. Reduce heat, cover and cook over low heat 20 minutes. Remove cover, stir in rice. Cover and continue cooking about 25 minutes or until liquid is absorbed and pork is tender. Stir in pineapple tidbits, green pepper and tomato wedges. Heat through. Makes 4–6 servings.

Variations: Nice to add sliced water chestnuts or bamboo shoots at end of cooking, or substitute cubed ham or cubed uncooked chicken for pork.

Braised Ginger Pork

Nobody seems to have a better knack for Chinese dishes than the Planters Peanut Oil cooks. After all Peanut Oil *is* the traditional cooking oil of China.

2 lbs. lean 1-inch pork cubes
Flour
3 Tbs. Planters Peanut Oil
⅓ cup chicken broth
⅓ cup soy sauce
2 Tbs. sherry
¼ cup chopped green or yellow onion
1 small clove garlic, crushed or minced
1 Tbs. sugar
1 tsp. ground ginger
Dash pepper
Hot cooked rice

Dredge meat in flour. Heat Planters Peanut Oil in Dutch oven or large skillet. Add half of meat and brown quickly; remove meat and set aside. Brown remaining meat; remove and set aside. Pour off excess oil from pan. Combine chicken broth, soy sauce and sherry. Add onion, garlic, sugar, ginger and pepper. Place in cooking pan along with meat. Simmer, covered, for 15 minutes, or until meat is tender. Serve over rice. Makes about 6 servings.

Speedy Baked Beans with Wieners

The Oscar Mayer Company tells me that this quick-cooking baked beans recipe has been a consumer favorite ever since it first appeared on their bacon package a decade ago.

1 8-oz. package Oscar Mayer Bacon
3 1-lb. cans baked beans
½ cup chopped onion
¼ cup firmly packed brown sugar
1 Tbs. molasses

2 tsps. Worcestershire sauce
½ tsp. dry mustard
1 1-lb. package Oscar Mayer Wieners cut up

Cut bacon into 1-inch pieces; cook in skillet until crisp; add remaining ingredients. Simmer, covered, for 15 minutes. Makes 6 servings.

Country Fried Chicken

As American as the Fourth of July—and just right for a picnic. This country fried chicken has been a "most requested favorite" ever since it was first developed especially for the back label of the Crisco shortening can.

1 2½- to 3-lb. frying chicken, cut-up or use chicken pieces
Crisco Shortening
½ cup milk
1 egg
1 cup flour
2 tsps. garlic salt
2 tsps. MSG
1 tsp. paprika
¼ tsp. poultry seasoning
1 tsp. black pepper

Blend milk and egg. Combine flour and seasonings in plastic or paper bag. Shake chicken in seasoned flour. Dip chicken pieces in milk/egg mixture. Shake chicken a *second* time in seasoning mixture to coat thoroughly and evenly.

To Pan Fry: Melt Crisco in skillet to about ½- to 1-inch deep and heat to 365°F. Brown chicken on all sides. Reduce heat (275°F.) and continue cooking until chicken is tender, about 30–40 minutes. Do not cover. Turn chicken several times during cooking. Drain on paper towels.

To Deep Fry: Prepare as above and cook in deep Crisco heated to 365°F. for 15–18 minutes. Drain on paper towels. Makes about 4 servings.

Variation: For extra-spicy chicken: Increase poultry seasoning to ½ tsp. and black pepper to 2 tsps.

Oven-Fried Chicken

From the Betty Crocker Kitchens a sure-fire way to crispy, flavorful oven-fried chicken plus four interesting variations. An asked-for recipe for years and it's not surprising!

1 Tbs. margarine or butter
⅔ cup Bisquick® Baking Mix
1½ tsps. paprika
1¼ tsps. salt
¼ tsp. pepper
2½- to 3½-lb. broiler-fryer chicken, cut up

Heat oven to 425°F. Heat margarine in rectangular pan, 13 × 9 × 2 inches, until melted. Mix baking mix, paprika, salt and pepper; coat chicken. Place chicken, skin side down, in pan. Bake uncovered 35 minutes. Turn; bake until done, about 15 minutes longer. Makes 6 servings.

Variations:

Italian Coating: Add 1 Tbs. Italian seasoning and ½ tsp. garlic powder.

Mexican Coating: Decrease baking mix to ½ cup. Add 2 Tbs. cornmeal and 1 to 2 Tbs. chili powder.

Parmesan Coating: Decrease baking mix to ⅓ cup and salt to 1 tsp. Add ½ cup grated Parmesan cheese.

Sesame-Herb Coating: Decrease salt to 1 tsp. Add 2 Tbs. sesame seed and 2 tsps. each dried thyme leaves, ground sage and parsley flakes.

Zesty Orange Barbecued Chicken

Now when was it someone started using orange juice concentrate as a marinade? I don't remember, but those clever Kikkoman cooks give us an up-to-date version that combines it with Kikkoman Teriyaki Sauce for sensational results.

1 6-oz. can frozen orange juice concentrate, thawed
¼ cup Kikkoman Teriyaki Sauce
1 Tbs. instant minced onion
1 tsp. parsley flakes
½ tsp. garlic powder
¼ tsp. black pepper
8–10 pieces frying chicken

Combine all ingredients, except chicken; let stand 10 minutes. Place chicken and sauce in large plastic bag; press air out and close securely. Refrigerate 8 hours or overnight, turning over occasionally. Remove chicken; reserve marinade. Place on grill 6–8 inches from hot coals. Cook about 20 minutes on each side; baste with reserved marinade during last 15 minutes of cooking time. Makes 6–8 servings.

Chicken Continental

This richly European-flavored entrée appeared recently in national magazines and has won hundreds of fans—including one woman who found herself in a dilemma when the recipe she clipped was lost forever behind her gigantic stove. But the story ended happily. When her letter reached the ever-obliging folks at Kikkoman, a specially typed replica was quickly sent to her.

3 lbs. frying chicken pieces
¼ cup flour (about)
2 Tbs. salad oil
1 4-oz. can sliced mushrooms
1 16-oz. can tomatoes, chopped
⅓ cup Kikkoman Soy Sauce
1 clove garlic, minced
1 medium onion, sliced
¼ cup sliced pitted black olives (optional)
3 cups hot cooked rice (cooked according to package directions)

Coat chicken pieces thoroughly with flour; brown slowly in hot oil. Meanwhile, drain mushrooms, reserving liquid. Combine mushroom liquid with tomatoes, soy sauce and garlic. Add to chicken with onion and stir to combine. Cover and simmer 45 minutes, or until chicken is tender. Stir in mushrooms and olives; bring to boil. Serve over fluffy rice. Pass additional soy sauce, if desired. Makes 4–6 servings.

Sunshine Chicken

A truly unusual and delicious recipe for a party cookout from the R. T. French® Company.

¼ cup French's® Prepared Mustard
¼ cup pineapple juice
1 Tbs. brown sugar
8 slices lean bacon
2 whole chicken breasts, split, boned, skinned and sliced in half crosswise, making 8 pieces in all.

In small mixing bowl, combine mustard, pineapple juice, and brown sugar, mixing until sugar is dissolved. Wrap each chicken piece with bacon, fastening with wooden picks. Brush mustard sauce over chicken and bacon. Grill over hot coals about 10 minutes, turning frequently and brushing with additional mustard sauce. Remove wooden picks. To serve, spoon remaining sauce over chicken. Makes 4 servings.

Pizza Chicken Italiano

Here's a rich Italian treatment for chicken devised by Del Monte for their "no taste like home" series of recipes.

- 2 whole chicken breasts (split, boned, skinned)
- 1 15-oz. can Del Monte Tomato Sauce
- 1½ tsp. oregano
- 1 tsp. chopped parsley
- ½ tsp. each garlic salt, onion powder and sugar
- 1 2¼-oz. can sliced ripe olives, drained
- 4 slices Mozzarella cheese

Place chicken in 2-quart baking dish. Combine tomato sauce, oregano, chopped parsley, garlic salt, onion powder and sugar. Pour over chicken, cover, and bake at 425°F. for 15 minutes. Top with olives and Mozzarella cheese and continue to bake, uncovered, for 10 minutes. Designed for oven-to-table service. Serves 4.

Wild Rice—Chicken Supreme

This is the recipe that convinced literally a million Americans that Uncle Ben's® Long Grain and Wild Rice was indeed worth the price.

- 1 6-oz. package Uncle Ben's® Long Grain and Wild Rice
- ¼ cup butter or margarine
- ⅓ cup chopped onion
- ⅓ cup flour
- 1 tsp. salt
- Dash black pepper
- 1 cup half & half
- 1 cup chicken broth
- 2 cups cubed cooked chicken
- ⅓ cup chopped pimiento
- ⅓ cup chopped parsley
- ¼ cup chopped almonds

Prepare contents of rice and seasoning packets according to package directions. Meanwhile, melt butter in large saucepan. Add onion and cook over low heat until tender. Stir in flour, salt and pepper. Gradually stir in half & half and chicken broth. Cook, stirring constantly, until thickened. Stir in chicken, pimiento, parsley, almonds and cooked rice. Place in 2-quart casserole. Bake, uncovered, in 425°F. oven for 30 minutes. Makes 6–8 servings.

Savory Crescent Chicken Squares

A $25,000 Grand Prize Winner at the 25th Pillsbury Bake-Off® Contest in 1974, and it is good! Just about everybody wants *this* recipe, so here it is. I like to serve it with a cream sauce and tiny green peas.

- 1 3-oz. package cream cheese, softened
- 3 Tbs. margarine or butter, melted
- 2 cups cubed cooked chicken or two 5-oz. cans boned chicken
- ¼ tsp. salt
- ⅛ tsp. pepper

2 Tbs. milk
1 Tbs. chopped chives or onion
1 Tbs. chopped pimiento, if desired
1 8-oz. can Pillsbury Refrigerated Quick Crescent Dinner Rolls
¾ cup seasoned croutons, crushed

Heat oven to 350°F. In medium bowl, blend cream cheese and 2 Tbs. of the margarine until smooth. Add next 6 ingredients; mix well. Separate dough into 4 rectangles; firmly press perforations around edges together to seal. Spoon ½ cup meat mixture onto center of each rectangle. Pull 4 corners of dough to top center of chicken mixture, twist slightly and seal edges. Place on ungreased cookie sheet. Brush tops with reserved 1 Tbs. margarine; sprinkle with crouton crumbs. Bake at 350°F. for 20–25 minutes or until golden brown. Serves 4.

Pineapple Chicken in Patty Shells

When we wanted to impress anybody back in Shreveport, Louisiana, we served creamed chicken in patty shells. Now Pepperidge Farm gives this elegant new version of an old favorite.

1 package Pepperidge Farm Patty Shells
½ cup chopped onion
2 Tbs. butter or margarine
1 cup orange juice
¼ cup brown sugar
1 8-oz. can undrained crushed pineapple
¼ tsp. ground cinnamon
1½ Tbs. cornstarch
2 cups cubed cooked chicken
1 package frozen pea pods
¼ cup toasted slivered almonds

Prepare patty shells according to package directions. Meanwhile, in a saucepan, cook onion in butter until tender. Add orange juice, brown sugar, pineapple, cinnamon and cornstarch. Cook, stirring, over medium heat until thickened and smooth. Add chicken and pea pods and heat. Spoon into patty shells. Garnish with almonds. Makes 6 servings.

Country Cornish Hens

Sausage stuffing—as traditional as pumpkin pie in the heartland of America—now goes elegant with sherry-basted Rock Cornish hens. A special favorite from Parkay's® test kitchens.

- ½ lb. bulk pork sausage
- 2 cups bread cubes, toasted
- 1 cup chopped, peeled apples
- ½ cup celery slices
- ⅓ cup raisins
- ⅓ cup chopped onion
- ¾ cup Parkay® Margarine, melted
- ⅓ cup sherry
- ¼ tsp. sage
- ¼ tsp. salt
- Dash of pepper
- 6 1- to 1½-lb. Rock Cornish hens

Brown meat; drain. Add bread, apples, celery, raisins, onion, ¼ cup margarine, 2 Tbs. sherry and seasonings; mix well. Lightly stuff hens with dressing mixture; close openings with skewers. Bake at 400°F. 1 hour or until tender, basting occasionally with combined remaining margarine and sherry. Garnish with celery leaves, if desired. Makes 6 servings.

Stuffed Turkey

No self-respecting Southerner would dream of using anything but corn bread stuffing for the holiday bird but now Campbell's has perfected a new variation on the traditional version that even a Yankee would love.

- 6 slices bacon
- 1 cup celery, sliced
- ½ cup chopped onion
- 1 8½-oz. package herb-seasoned stuffing mix
- 2 cups coarse cornbread crumbs
- 1 10½-oz. can Campbell's Condensed Chicken Broth
- 1 egg, slightly beaten
- 10-pound turkey
- 1 10¾-oz. can Campbell's Condensed Cream of Mushroom Soup
- ½ cup whole berry cranberry sauce
- ¼ cup orange juice

In skillet, cook bacon until crisp; remove and crumble. Pour off all but 2 Tbs. drippings. Cook celery and onion in drippings until tender. Toss lightly with stuffing mix, cornbread, broth, and egg. Fill cavity of turkey loosely with stuffing. Truss; place in roasting pan. Cover with foil. Roast at 325°F. for about 4 hours (25 minutes per pound or until tender). Uncover last hour to brown. Remove turkey to serving platter. Skim fat from drippings; add remaining ingredients. Heat; stir to loosen browned bits. Makes 12 servings.

Beer Batter Fish or Shrimp

A fast and fabulous batter from Bisquick® Baking Mix kitchens for fresh-caught or fresh-bought fish or shrimp.

- Vegetable oil
- 1 lb. fish fillets or cooked large shrimp (or ½ lb. of each)
- 3 to 4 Tbs. Bisquick® Baking Mix
- 1 cup Bisquick® Baking Mix
- ½ tsp. salt
- 1 egg
- ½ cup beer

Heat vegetable oil (1½ inches) in heavy saucepan or deep fat fryer to 350°F. Cut fish in serving-size pieces. Lightly coat fish or shrimp with 3 to 4 Tbs. baking mix. Mix 1 cup baking mix, the salt, egg and beer until smooth. Dip fish or shrimp into batter, letting excess drip into bowl. Fry until golden brown, about 2 minutes on each side; drain. Makes 4 servings.

Quiche Lorraine With Bacon

A lovely appetizer or a great luncheon or supper main dish. For cocktail party fare use this recipe from the Armour Bacon package for individual quiches, substituting 8 frozen tart shells for the pie shell.

- 1½ cups milk
- 4 eggs, slightly beaten
- ½ tsp. salt
- Dash of cayenne
- 2 cups (8 ounces) shredded Swiss cheese
- 2 Tbs. flour
- ½ lb. Armour Star Bacon, crisply cooked, crumbled
- 1 9-inch unbaked pastry shell

Heat oven to 350°F. Combine milk, eggs and seasonings; mix well. Toss cheese with flour; add cheese mixture and bacon to egg mixture. Pour into pastry shell. Bake at 350°F. 40 to 45 minutes. Makes 6 servings.

Kellogg's Crunchy Baked Chicken Variations

An easy delicious change from fried chicken.

Wash 3 lbs. frying chicken pieces. Pat dry. For any of the following variations, dip chicken in liquid mixture. Coat evenly with crumb mixture. Place in single layer, skin side up, in well-greased or foil-lined shallow baking pan. Drizzle with 3 Tbs. melted margarine, or butter if desired. Bake in oven at 350°F. about 1 hour or until chicken is tender. Do not cover pan or turn chicken while baking. Makes 6 servings.

Corn-Crisped Chicken: Dip in ½ cup evaporated milk. Coat with mixture of 1 cup Corn Flake Crumbs, 1 tsp. salt and ⅛ tsp. pepper.

California Crusty Chicken: Dip in mixture of ¼ cup melted margarine or butter, 3 Tbs. lemon juice and 1 tsp. grated lemon peel. Coat with mixture of 1¼ cups Corn Flake Crumbs, 1½ tsp. salt and ¼ tsp. pepper.

Baked Chicken Italiano: Dip in ½ cup Italian-style salad dressing. If desired, marinate chicken in dressing for at least 1 hour. Coat with 1¼ cups Corn Flake Crumbs.

Oven-Fried Chicken: Dip in mixture of 1 slightly beaten egg and 2 Tbs. milk. Coat with mixture of 1¼ cups Corn Flake Crumbs, 1½ tsps. salt and ¼ tsp. pepper.

Parmesan Crisped Chicken: Dip in mixture of 1 slightly beaten egg and 2 Tbs. milk. Coat with mixture of ¾ cup Corn Flake Crumbs, 1½ tsps. salt, ¼ tsp. pepper and ½ cup grated Parmesan cheese.

Zesty Crisped Chicken: Dip in mixture of 1 slightly beaten egg and ¼ cup soy sauce. Coat with 1¼ cups Corn Flake Crumbs.

Kellogg's Croutettes Roast Poultry Guide

Here's how to stuff and roast "le bird," be it chicken or turkey.

Wash poultry, drain and dry. Turn wing tips back. Spoon prepared Croutettes stuffing (see Stuffing Guide) into neck and body cavities. Fasten cavities by securing skin with skewers.

Place bird, breast side up, in roasting pan. Insert meat thermometer in inner thigh muscle. Brush skin with melted margarine or butter. Roast in oven at 325°F. until meat thermometer reaches 180°F. to 185°F.

To check stuffing temperature, remove thermometer from thigh and insert in body cavity. Thermometer should register 165°F. If meat thermometer is not used, allow about 25 minutes per pound, depending on size of bird. When drumstick moves up and down easily and leg joint gives readily, bird is done.

To bake extra stuffing, spoon into buttered baking dish, cover and bake at 350°F. about 30 minutes.

For Basic Stuffing, pour Croutettes croutons into large mixing bowl. Add melted margarine or butter while tossing gently. Stir lightly while adding hot water or stock. (Amount of water may be varied, depending on preference for a fluffy or moist stuffing.)

For Celery-Onion Stuffing, cook celery and onions in the melted margarine until tender before mixing with Croutettes croutons.

Croutettes Stuffing Guide

Poultry weight	*3 – 5 lbs.*	*6 – 8 lbs.*	*9 – 11 lbs.*	*12 – 15 lbs.*	*16 – 19 lbs.*	*20 lbs. and over*
Croutettes croutons (7-oz. pkg., 7 cups)	½ pkg.	1 pkg.	1½ pkgs.	2 pkgs.	2½ pkgs.	3 pkgs.
Melted margarine or butter	¼ – ⅓ cup	½ – ⅔ cup	¾ – 1 cup	1 – 1¼ cups	1¼ – 1½ cups	1½ – 2 cups
Hot water or stock	¾ cup	1½ cups	2¼ cups	3 cups	3¾ cups	4½ cups
Finely chopped celery	¼ cup	½ cup	1 cup	1 cup	1¼ cups	1½ cups
Chopped onions	2 Tbs.	¼ cup	½ cup	½ cup	⅔ cup	¾ cup

Chicken Oriental

The greatest recipes come from the most surprising people! This recipe from the jar of Mott's Apple Sauce is fabulously good. Try it and see.

2 to 3 lbs. chicken pieces

Marinade Ingredients:

1 cup Mott's Apple Sauce
½ cup soy sauce
1 clove garlic, minced
½ tsp. ground ginger
3 drops Tabasco

Combine marinade ingredients. Pour over meat. Refrigerate 8 to 12 hours. Drain meat and place on rack in baking pan. Bake covered for 1 hour at 350°F. Then uncover and baste with marinade; bake 15 minutes. Turn pieces, baste again, and bake for 15 more minutes. (Final "baking-and-basting" may be done on charcoal grill.) Makes 4 to 6 servings.

Chicken À L'Orange

Created by a famous French® chef almost twenty years ago, this recipe appeared for years in Cointreau advertising; it's an especially pretty dish for a dinner party.

2 broiler-size (2- to 2½-lb.) chickens, quartered
2 Tbs. butter
½ tsp. salt
¼ tsp. pepper
¼ tsp. paprika
¼ tsp. dried tarragon
½ cup minced green onion
1 clove garlic, peeled and minced
½ cup finely chopped celery
4 more Tbs. butter
¼ cup Cointreau
2 Tbs. lemon juice
2 cups chicken stock or broth
¼ cup tomato paste
Minced parsley for garnish

Preheat oven to 375°F. Arrange quartered chicken pieces in a long shallow baking dish. Bake in preheated oven for 30 minutes, turning pieces twice during cooking. In a small skillet melt butter, stir in salt, pepper, paprika and tarragon; pour evenly over chicken pieces. Continue to bake for about 15 minutes, until chicken is tender and browned. While chicken bakes prepare sauce; sauté onion, garlic and celery in butter until soft. Add remaining ingredients; stir until blended; bring to boil; lower heat and let simmer very gently about 30 minutes or until thick and smooth. Arrange chicken pieces on serving platter. Pour sauce over and sprinkle with parsley. Makes 8 servings.

Broiled Chicken Italiano

This is so easy and so good you'll wonder why no one thought of it before. The Wish-Bone Salad Dressing people did, back in 1972 when it appeared on their Italian Dressing label.

2½- to 3-lb. chicken, cut into serving pieces
Salt
½ cup Wish-Bone Italian Dressing

Place chicken on broiler rack, sprinkle with salt and brush with Wish-Bone Italian Dressing. Broil about 45 minutes, basting with remaining dressing and turning chicken frequently. Makes about 4 servings.

Tangy Chicken

The Heinz® Company has been printing this extra-easy chicken recipe on their 57 Sauce bottles for years. It's such a favorite customers probably wouldn't let them take it off.

- 2 to 2½ lbs. broiler-fryer pieces
- 2 Tbs. butter or margarine
- ½ cup Heinz® 57 Sauce
- ½ cup water

Brown chicken in skillet in butter. Combine 57 Sauce and water; pour over chicken. Cover; simmer, basting occasionally, 30 to 40 minutes or until chicken is tender. Remove cover last 10 minutes of cooking. Skim excess fat from sauce before serving. Spoon sauce over chicken. Makes 4 servings (about ¾ cup sauce).

Baked Chicken That Makes Its Own Gravy

In 1964 the Carnation Evaporated Milk label featured this savory recipe for chicken, and it's been an asked-for special ever since. Chicken and gravy fans love it. Add hot cooked rice and a tomato salad for a true Deep-South supper.

- 3 to 3½ lbs. frying chicken pieces
- ¼ cup flour
- ¼ cup melted butter
- ⅔ cup undiluted Carnation Evaporated Milk
- 1 can (10¾ ounces) condensed cream of mushroom soup
- 1 cup (4 ounces) grated process American cheese
- ½ tsp. salt
- ⅛ tsp. pepper
- 2 cups (1-lb. can) drained whole onions
- ¼ lb. sliced mushrooms
- Dash paprika

Coat chicken with flour. Arrange chicken in single layer with skin down in melted butter in 13 × 9 × 2-inch baking dish. Bake uncovered in 425°F. oven for 30 minutes. Turn chicken, bake until brown, 15 to 20 minutes longer, until tender. Remove from oven and reduce temperature to 325°F. Pour off excess fat. Combine evaporated milk, soup, cheese, salt, and pepper. Add onions and mushrooms to chicken. Pour soup mixture over chicken. Sprinkle with paprika. Cover dish with foil. Return to oven for 15 to 20 minutes. Serves 6.

Chicken With Lime

Every year the Delmarva Chicken Association (*Delaware/Maryland/Virginia,*) sponsors a chicken cooking contest. For one of the "best of the best" try this 1977 winning recipe created by Mrs. Sally B. Lilley of Chevy Chase, Maryland.

- 1 broiler-fryer chicken, cut in parts
- 1 tsp. salt
- ¼ tsp. black pepper
- ¼ cup corn oil
- 1 Tbs. minced onion
- 1 clove garlic, minced
- ½ tsp. ground cumin
- ½ tsp. ground coriander seed
- ¼ tsp. crushed red pepper
- ¼ tsp. turmeric
- 2 Tbs. soy sauce
- 2 limes, quartered

Sprinkle chicken with salt and black pepper. Heat corn oil in large fry pan over medium heat. Add chicken and brown on all sides. Push chicken to side of pan. Add onion and garlic; sauté until golden. Add cumin, coriander, red pepper and turmeric. Stir around to distribute. Add soy sauce. Reduce heat and cook slowly, covered, stirring frequently about 20 minutes or until fork can be inserted in chicken with ease. Serve over rice. Squeeze 1 lime on chicken before serving, section remaining lime to squeeze on chicken while eating. Makes 4 servings.

Progresso's Chicken Cacciatore

A virtual Italian opera of flavors. Serve it with piping-hot just-cooked spaghetti and freshly grated Parmesan cheese.

- 2½ to 3-lb. spring chicken, cut into pieces
- ¼ cup Progresso Pure Olive Oil
- 1 medium onion, chopped
- 1 clove garlic, minced
- 1 tsp. Progresso Basil
- 1 Tbs. parsley
- ¼ cup Sherry, Marsala or white wine
- Salt and pepper
- 1 can (17-ounce) Progresso Peeled Tomatoes, cut up (or ½ 35-ounce can)

Brown chicken pieces in hot olive oil until lightly colored; add onion, garlic, basil and parsley and brown along with chicken until chicken is golden-brown and vegetables are soft and slightly colored. Wet with wine and allow to evaporate. Season with salt and pepper to taste. Add tomatoes and their juices. Cover and simmer for about 20 to 30 minutes or until chicken is tender and sauce has thickened a little.

Easy Chicken Tetrazzini

Ehlers Gravy Mix for Chicken makes short work of a very special supper dish from this recipe printed on the Ehlers envelope for the past five years. Madame Tetrazzini, who inspired the original dish, would have approved.

- 1 8-ounce package spaghetti
- 1 envelope Ehlers Gravy Mix for Chicken
- 1¼ cups milk
- ¼ cup cooking sherry
- 2 cups cooked, cubed chicken
- 1 4-ounce can sliced mushrooms, drained
- 2 Tbs. grated Parmesan cheese

Preheat oven to 350°F. Prepare spaghetti as label directs; drain. Place spaghetti in a greased 8-inch-square baking dish. Mix together remaining ingredients, except cheese. Pour mixture over spaghetti. Sprinkle with cheese. Bake 45 minutes, until bubbly. Let stand 5 minutes before serving. Makes 4 servings.

Chicken Macaroni Triumph

An elegant party dish, flavored with white wine. Easy and quick, it's from Mueller's Sea Shell Macaroni package.

- 3 whole chicken breasts, boned, skin removed
- 3 slices boiled ham, cut in half
- 3 slices American cheese, cut in half
- 2 Tbs. butter or margarine
- 1 (10¾ ounce) can condensed cream of mushroom soup
- ½ cup dry white wine
- ¼ cup milk or light cream
- Salt and pepper
- 8 ounces (3½ to 4 cups) Mueller's Sea Shell Macaroni
- 1 9-ounce package frozen cut green beans, cooked

Cut chicken breasts in half; pound with flat side of knife. On each piece of chicken place a piece of ham and cheese. Roll, tucking cheese in; fasten with toothpicks. Brown rolls in butter in skillet; remove toothpicks; place in 11 × 8 × 2-inch baking dish. Blend soup, wine and milk into drippings; season to taste with salt and pepper; pour over chicken. Bake at 350°F. about 45 minutes or until tender. Meanwhile, cook macaroni as directed on package; drain. In large serving dish, combine green beans and macaroni; stir in sauce from chicken; arrange chicken rolls on top. Makes 4 to 6 servings.

Avocado With Curried Chicken

This heavenly idea was introduced by the Avocado Advisory Board a dozen years ago. It's a gourmet dish, perfect for a festive lunch or supper party, and it probably started today's popular trend for serving hot avocado main dishes.

- ¼ cup butter (½ stick)
- ½ cup chopped pared apple
- ¼ cup chopped onion
- 1 clove garlic, crushed
- 1 Tbs. curry powder
- ¼ cup flour
- 1 cup light cream
- 1 cup chicken bouillon
- 1 tsp. salt
- ⅛ tsp. pepper
- 2 cups cut-up, cooked chicken
- 3 or 4 avocados, halved and peeled
- 3 to 4 cups cooked rice
- Condiments, given below

In saucepan, sauté apple, onion, garlic and curry powder in butter until onion is crisp-tender. Stir in flour. Gradually add cream and bouillon; cook and stir until sauce boils 1 minute. Add salt, pepper and chicken. Cook over low heat 10 minutes. Arrange avocado halves on rice in heat-proof serving dish. Heat in 350°F. (moderate) oven about 5 minutes. Spoon curried chicken over avocado halves. Serve with Indian or Euphrates bread and a choice of these condiments: chopped egg, crumbled bacon, sweet mixed pickles, coconut, raisins, chutney, Bombay duck, preserved ginger, chopped peanuts. Makes 6 servings.

Baked Chicken Salad

Here's a really different chicken recipe people have asked for time and time again.

- 2 Tbs. corn oil margarine
- 1 cup thinly sliced celery
- ½ cup chopped onion
- ½ cup Hellmann's Real Mayonnaise or Best Foods Real Mayonnaise
- ½ cup dairy sour cream
- 1 Tbs. lemon juice
- ½ tsp. salt
- ⅛ tsp. pepper
- 2 cups cubed cooked chicken
- ½ cup slivered almonds, toasted
- 1 can (6 ounces) sliced mushrooms, drained
- ¼ cup crushed potato chips

In large skillet melt margarine over medium heat. Add celery and onion; cook about 4 minutes or until tender. Remove from heat. Stir in next 5 ingredients until well blended. Add chicken, almonds and mushrooms; toss to coat well. Spoon into 1½-quart casserole. Sprinkle with potato chips. Bake in 325°F. oven 25 to 30 minutes or until hot. Makes 4 to 6 servings.

Microwave Directions: In 1½-quart microproof casserole microwave margarine with full power until melted. Stir in celery and onion; microwave 3 minutes. Stir in next 5 ingredients. Add chicken, almonds and mushrooms; toss to coat well. Microwave 5 minutes or until hot, stirring once and sprinkling with potato chips after 3 minutes.

Tyson's Food's Kintail Cornish Game Hens

The original recipe bowed in 1970 in a Tyson ad; it's a festive way to serve these versatile birds and an especially pretty dinner-party mainstay. Count on one whole bird per guest. There won't be any leftovers!

2 Tyson brand Cornish Hens, thawed
1 cup cooked wild rice (or mixture wild and long grain) with some chopped apple pieces and chopped pecans added
3 Tbs. butter or margarine
8 Tbs. orange marmalade
2 Tbs. lemon juice
¼ cup brandy

Salt cavity and stuff game hens with rice, apple, pecan mixture. Place hens on foil in pan. Over medium heat, melt butter. Add orange marmalade, lemon juice and brandy. Stir until heated. Brush some of marmalade mixture over hens, coating them well. Cover hens with foil. Bake in a preheated 350°F. oven for 30 minutes. Uncover and baste frequently with pan drippings and more marmalade mixture, adding more brandy if desired, for one hour more. Makes 2 servings.

Tyson's Cornish Hens Steamed in Foil

Tyson Foods advertised their Cornish hens with this easy recipe just a few years ago, but it became so popular it's termed a classic.

4 Tyson brand Cornish Hens, thawed

For each Cornish Hen:

1 square of foil, 16 inches at least
½ tsp. salt
Few grindings pepper
¼ tsp. sage or thyme
1 sprig parsley
1 to 2 tsp. butter

Preheat oven to 350°F. Season each hen with salt, pepper, sage or thyme. Place on foil, lay a sprig of parsley on top of hen and wrap securely in foil. Place hens on baking sheet or in baking pan. Place in oven for 1 hour. Remove hens and raise heat to 425°F. Carefully open foil (watch out for escaping steam) to expose hens. Brush with butter and return to oven to brown for 5 to 10 minutes. Serve hens with juices accumulated in foil. Makes 4 servings.

Crispy Fried Fish

"Even people who aren't enthusiastic about fish love this recipe. We've made it on lots of seaside "cookouts" over fires built in the sand with fish caught minutes before," says the director of the R. T. French® Company's test kitchen. This unusual recipe appeared in French's® advertising in 1972.

- 2 eggs
- ¼ cup French's® Prepared Mustard
- 1 tsp. French's® Parsley Flakes
- ½ tsp. French's® Seafood Seasoning
- 1½ lbs. fish fillets
- French's® Big Tate Mashed Potato Flakes
- Oil or melted shortening

Beat together eggs, mustard, parsley, and seafood seasoning. Dip fish in the mustard mixture; roll in potato flakes. Fry in hot oil or shortening 3 to 4 minutes on each side or until fish flakes easily and is golden brown. Makes 4 servings.

Veal Scaloppine al Marsala

If ever there was a dish tailor-made for quick cooking and pure enjoyment, it is this classic Italian recipe from the label of Holland House® Marsala Cooking Wine. Plain buttered noodles make a fine accompaniment.

- 4 veal scallops (about 1 lb., cut from leg, each about ⅛ inch thick)
- Salt
- Pepper
- 3 Tbs. butter or margarine
- 1 clove garlic, crushed
- 1 Tbs. butter or margarine
- ½ lb. mushrooms, sliced
- ½ cup Holland House® Marsala Cooking Wine

Dredge veal in flour and add salt and pepper to taste. Melt 3 Tbs. butter or margarine in skillet; brown garlic. Then add veal, browning quickly. Remove veal to shallow baking pan. Add 1 Tbs. butter to skillet and brown mushrooms. Add Holland House® Marsala Cooking Wine and bring to boil. Simmer approximately 2 minutes to blend flavors. Pour wine-mushroom sauce over veal. Cover pan and bake approximately 20 minutes at 350°F. Serves 2 to 3.

Broiled Chicken Deluxe

When Delmarva® staged their first National Chicken Cooking Contest in 1949, this recipe was the winner. It is a well thought-out method for broiling chicken, obviously by a very knowledgeable cook. You can learn quite a bit about broiling food in general just by reading the recipe. The final results cannot be improved.

- 1 broiler-fryer chicken, halved
- ½ lemon
- 2 tsps. salt
- ¼ tsp. pepper
- ½ tsp. paprika
- ½ cup butter, melted, divided
- 2 tsps. granulated sugar

In broiler pan place chicken skin side up. Rub surface of chicken with lemon, squeezing some juice onto meat. In bowl mix together salt, pepper and paprika. Sprinkle mixture over chicken. Brush with ½ of the butter; sprinkle with sugar. Place broiler pan as far from heat as possible and cook at 450°F. for 10 minutes allowing seasonings to penetrate. Move broiler pan up so that chicken is 3 to 6 inches from the heat in gas range or 6 to 9 inches from heat in electric range. Broil, basting frequently with remaining butter and turning to insure even browning, about 35 minutes or until fork can be inserted in chicken with ease. Makes 2 large servings.

Chicken Marseillaise

An American adaptation of a French® classic and a much requested recipe from the Kraft® Kitchens.

- 1 2½- to 3-lb. broiler-fryer, cut up
- Kraft® Catalina French® Dressing
- 1 16-oz. can tomatoes
- 8 onion slices, ¼-inch thick
- 1 tsp. salt
- ½ tsp. celery seed
- ¼ tsp. pepper
- ¼ cup wine or water
- 2 Tbs. flour

Brown chicken in ⅓ cup dressing over low heat. Add ¼ cup dressing, tomatoes, onion and seasonings. Cover; simmer 45 minutes. Remove chicken and vegetables to serving platter. Gradually add wine to flour, stirring until well blended. Gradually add flour mixture to hot liquid in pan; cook stirring constantly. Serve with chicken and vegetables. Makes 4 servings.

Chicken Jardiniere au Vermouth

There are many variations of this elegant French® recipe, but this version from Holland House® is so easy that it's hard to believe it tastes as good as it does.

1 3-lb. broiler chicken, cut into pieces
1 clove garlic, crushed
2 Tbs. oil
1 carrot
1 small zucchini
1 stalk celery
¼ tsp. thyme
¼ tsp. pepper
1 cup Holland House® Vermouth Cooking Wine
1 cup frozen peas
1 small can whole mushrooms
2 tsps. corn starch

Rub chicken with garlic. Heat oil in saucepan, add chicken and brown on both sides. Add fresh vegetables (all cut into 2-inch-by-¼-inch sticks), thyme, pepper and Holland House® Cooking Wine. Stir to deglaze pan. Cover and simmer 30 minutes. Add peas and mushrooms. Stir in corn starch/water mixture. Bring to a boil, simmer 5 more minutes and serve. Makes 6 servings.

Orange Glazed Chicken

The Pompeian® Olive Oil Company considers this their best label recipe. It's the one most often used by food editors of top newspapers across the country.

½ cup Pompeian® Olive Oil
½ cup orange juice
1 Tbs. wine vinegar
1 tsp. salt
1 tsp. instant choppped onion
¼ tsp. ginger or cumin
1 chicken, about 3 lbs.

Combine olive oil, juice, vinegar and salt; crush the instant onion with mortar and pestle or back of wooden spoon, blend with the ginger or cumin. Add to the juice mixture. Marinate either whole or cut-up chicken in the sauce for 1 hour or longer; baste with the marinade as it cooks over charcoal or in the broiler or rotisserie oven. Makes 1 cup sauce.

Oven-Fried Chicken and Bananas

It's hard to choose favorites, but if you twisted my arm I'd have to admit that this South Seas—style dish from the inside of the label from a can of Coco Casa® Cream of Coconut is tops on my list.

- 2 chickens, about 3 lbs. each, cut up
- Salt and pepper
- 1 cup Coco Casa® Cream of Coconut
- 2 Tbs. lemon juice
- 6 medium-size bananas
- 2½ cups cornflake crumbs
- ¾ cup melted butter or margarine

Sprinkle chicken pieces on all sides with salt and pepper. In a bowl, mix Coco Casa® Cream of Coconut and lemon juice. Peel bananas and cut each banana into halves crosswise. Brush chicken and bananas thickly with coconut mixture and roll in crumbs, pressing firmly to make them adhere. Brush a baking pan with some of the butter. Place chicken pieces in a single layer into pan and drizzle with half of the butter. Bake in preheated 350°F. oven for 45 minutes. Add bananas and drizzle with remaining butter. Bake for another 15 minutes. Serves 6.

Oven-Fried Chicken

One of the first and still one of the best oven-fried chicken recipes to appear on a package. It is from Pepperidge Farm® test kitchens.

¼ cup butter or margarine
2 cups Pepperidge Farm® Herb Seasoned Stuffing, crushed
1 tsp. salt
2- to 3-lb. chicken, cut up
1 egg
1 tablespoon water
Gravy (below)

Preheat oven to 425°F. Put butter in shallow baking pan and place in oven until melted. Meanwhile combine crushed suffing and salt in a plastic bag. Dip chicken parts in egg that has been beaten with water. Then shake, a few pieces at a time, in bag until well coated. Place chicken, skin side down, in melted butter. Do not layer in pan. Bake, uncovered, 30 minutes, turn and continue baking for 15 minutes. Serves 4.

Gravy

1 10¾-oz. can chicken gravy
½ cup sour cream

Combine canned gravy with sour cream and heat to just below boiling.

Baked Yogurt Chicken

Love this chicken! Everyone does; it's a "most-requested" recipe at the Dannon® Yogurt kitchens.

1 cut-up frying chicken, 2½ to 3 lbs.
Salt and pepper
6 Tbs. butter or margarine
2 Tbs. flour
1 Tbs. paprika
2 cups Dannon® Plain Yogurt
¼ lb. fresh mushrooms, cleaned and sliced
2 Tbs. fresh lemon juice
2 Tbs. chopped fresh dill or parsley

Wash chicken pieces and wipe dry. Add salt and pepper. In a large pan, melt 4 Tbs. of butter; fry chicken until golden brown. Remove to buttered shallow baking dish. Sprinkle flour and paprika into pan juices and cook, stirring for 1 minute. Stir in yogurt and mix well. Spoon over chicken. Sauté mushrooms in remaining 2 Tbs. of butter and lemon juice for 1 minute and spoon over pan. Sprinkle with the dill. Bake, covered, in preheated moderate oven (325°F.) for about 1¼ hours, or until chicken is tender. Serves about 4.

Sweet 'N' Smoky Oven-Barbecued Chicken

This chicken recipe is still as great as it was in 1966 when it won top place at the Delmarva® National Chicken Cooking Contest. The delicious flavor comes from a master-blend glaze of ketchup, mustard, oil, vinegar and maple syrup—delicious!!

- 1 broiler-fryer chicken, cut in serving pieces
- ½ cup of water
- 1 large onion, sliced
- 1 tsp. hickory-smoked salt
- ¼ tsp. pepper
- Barbecue Sauce (opposite)

Place chicken, skin side up, in baking pan. Pour water around chicken. Tuck onion slices in and around the chicken. Sprinkle with hickory smoked salt and pepper. Bake chicken, uncovered, for 30 minutes in 375°F. oven. Mix ketchup and mustard, add oil, vinegar and maple syrup. Pour Barbecue Sauce over chicken and bake 30 minutes longer, or until fork can be inserted in chicken with ease. Makes 4 servings.

Barbecue Sauce

½ cup ketchup
2 Tbs. prepared mustard
½ cup cooking oil
¼ cup vinegar
½ cup maple syrup

Combine above ingredients.

Chicken Argentina

The California Olive Industry used this recipe in a national advertising campaign. The resulting fan letters were enthusiastic to say the least. "Delicate and unique," "light and elegant," "just great," "superb," they wrote. After testing, I agree—it's all that and more.

1 frying chicken (3 lbs.), cut in pieces
1 lime
1 tsp. salt
½ tsp. pepper
¾ tsp. paprika
1½ cups pitted California ripe olives
¼ cup oil
1 large onion, chopped
1 medium green pepper, sliced
1 medium red pepper, sliced
1½ cups orange juice

Marinate chicken pieces in juice from the lime (approximately ⅓ cup) for at least 30 minutes. Combine salt, pepper and paprika; sprinkle over chicken. Brown on all sides in oil. Place chicken in baking pan, add olives, onion, green pepper, red pepper and orange juice. Cover and bake at 350°F. for 45 minutes or until chicken is tender. Remove chicken to platter. Serve with pan juices. Serves 4.

Pettengill Schoolhouse Chicken Pie

Here is a recipe usually sent to consumers who write the Argo-Kingsford® Corn Starch kitchens requesting "something real good to take to a covered dish supper," and it is *real good*!

- 2 Tbs. margarine
- 1 cup sliced mushrooms
- 1 clove garlic, minced
- 2 Tbs. Argo-Kingsford's® Corn Starch
- 1½ cups milk
- 2½ cups cooked chicken, cut into bite-size pieces
- 2 cups fresh peas, cooked
- 1 whole pimiento, chopped
- ½ tsp. dried thyme leaves
- 1 tsp. salt
- ¼ tsp. pepper
- 1 recipe double-crust pastry

In skillet melt margarine. Add mushrooms and garlic. Sauté over medium heat until lightly browned. In saucepan stir together Corn Starch and milk until smooth. Mix in mushrooms, garlic and pan drippings. Bring to a boil over medium heat, stirring constantly, and boil 1 minute. Stir in next 6 ingredients. Pour into pastry-lined 9-inch pie plate. Cover pie with pastry; seal and flute edge. Cut slits in top. Bake in 375°F. oven 35 minutes or until crust is golden brown. Serves 6 to 8.

Country-Style Chicken Kiev

Land O Lakes® printed this easy, elegant chicken recipe on their unsalted butter package. It has been voted one of their best by the executive staff.

- ½ cup fine dry bread crumbs
- 2 Tbs. grated Parmesan cheese
- 1 tsp. *each* basil leaves and oregano leaves
- 2 chicken breasts, split (about 1½ lbs.)
- ¼ cup white wine *or* apple juice

½ tsp. garlic salt
¼ tsp. salt
⅔ cup Land O Lakes® Sweet Cream Butter, melted
¼ cup chopped green onion
¼ cup chopped fresh parsley

Heat oven to 375°F. Combine bread crumbs, Parmesan cheese, basil, oregano, garlic salt and salt. Dip chicken breasts in melted Butter, then coat with crumb mixture; *reserve* remaining butter. Place chicken skin side up in ungreased 9-inch square baking dish. Bake for 50 to 60 minutes or until chicken is fork tender. Meanwhile, add wine, green onion and parsley to reserved melted butter (about ½ cup). When chicken is golden brown, pour butter sauce over chicken. Continue baking for 3 to 5 minutes or until sauce is heated through. Serve with sauce spooned over. Makes 4 servings.

Indian Chicken Curry

This recipe from a Coco Casa® Cream of Coconut label is as authentic a curry dish as any you are apt to find this side of New Delhi.

⅓ cup butter or margarine
1 large onion, chopped
1 cup chopped celery
2 tart apples, peeled and chopped
1 Tbs. curry powder
6 Tbs. flour
1 cup chicken broth
½ cup Coco Casa® Cream of Coconut
2 cups (1 pint) half-and-half
3 cups diced cooked chicken, turkey or lamb
Salt and pepper

In a large saucepan, melt butter and sauté onion, celery and apples for 5 minutes. Stir in curry and flour. Gradually stir in chicken broth, cream of coconut and half-and-half. Stir over moderate heat until sauce bubbles and thickens. Stir in chicken and season to taste with salt and pepper. Serve spooned over rice. Makes 6 to 8 servings.

Glazed Turkey Roast

A new recipe using thrifty frozen turkey loaf—a gift from Pepperidge Farm.® So good, it's destined to becme a classic.

- Turkey roast*
- Apricot jam or preserves
- 1 cup dried apricots
- 1 cup water
- 1 Tbs. brown sugar
- 1 Tbs. lemon juice
- ½ cup butter or margarine
- 1 8-oz. package Pepperidge Farm® Herb Seasoned Cube Stuffing
- ½ cup slivered almonds
- ¼ tsp. salt

Roast turkey according to package directions. For glaze, brush top of the roast with apricot jam frequently during the last 30 minutes. Meanwhile place the apricots, water, brown sugar and lemon juice in a small saucepan and simmer for 5 minutes. Drain, reserving the liquid. Add water to liquid to make 1 cup. Place in a large saucepan with butter and heat until butter is melted. Stir in stuffing, almonds and salt. Cut apricots in strips and add to mixture. Place in a 1-quart baking dish and bake alongside of turkey for the last 25 minutes. To serve: make a bed of dressing on a hot platter and place roast on top.

* Turkey roasts vary from 2 to 4½ lbs. in size. They can be all white meat or a combination of white and dark. Some come with prepared gravy. For best results use a meat thermometer and roast to 185°F. Let stand 10 minutes before slicing. Allow ⅓-lb. meat for each serving.

Mexican Turkey Bake

Were you looking for another way to use that leftover turkey? This one was found in a neat little give-away folder of recipes in a box of Uncle Ben's Converted® Brand Rice. It proved to be the most popular dish in that folder and no wonder. I tried it and it was a real success.

- 1 cup Uncle Ben's Converted® Brand Rice
- 1 can (about 3 ozs.) mild green chilies, drained and chopped
- 3 cups cubed cooked turkey
- 1 12-oz. can Mexican-style corn with sweet peppers, drained
- 1 10-oz. can enchilada sauce
- ¾ tsp. salt
- 1 cup dairy sour cream

Prepare rice according to package directions. Reserve 1 Tbs. chilies for garnish. Combine remaining chilies, turkey, corn, enchilada sauce, salt and cooked rice in large bowl. Spoon into greased baking dish 12 × 7½ × 2 inches. Cover and bake at 350°F. until hot, about 25 minutes. Spoon sour cream down center; garnish with reserved chilies. Makes 6 servings.

Polynesian Turkey and Noodles

Mueller's® developed this really great and different-tasting recipe to make good use of leftover turkey.

- 2 cups cubed cooked turkey
- 1 egg, slightly beaten
- ¼ cup corn starch
- 2 Tbs. cooking oil
- 1 13½-oz. can pineapple chunks, drained (reserve juice)
- ½ cup sugar
- ½ cup cider vinegar
- 1 medium green pepper, cut in strips
- 2 Tbs. corn starch
- ¼ cup water
- 1 tsp. soy sauce
- 4 large carrots, cooked and cut in 1-inch pieces
- 8 oz. (5 cups) Mueller's® Klops® Egg Noodles

Dip turkey pieces in egg; roll in ¼ cup corn starch until coated. In skillet, brown turkey pieces in oil; remove and set aside. Add enough water to reserved pineapple juice to make 1 cup; add to skillet along with sugar, vinegar and green pepper. Heat to boiling, stirring constantly. Reduce heat; cover and simmer 2 minutes. Blend 2 Tbs. corn starch and ¼ cup water; stir into skillet. Heat, stirring constantly, until mixture thickens and boils; cook 1 minute. Stir in pineapple chunks, soy sauce, carrots and turkey pieces; heat. Meanwhile, cook Egg Noodles as directed on package; drain. Serve turkey over noodles. Makes 4 to 6 servings.

Old-Fashioned Turkey Stuffing and Variations

It's on the package, it's *always* been on the package and I guess it will always *be* on the package. Good cooks have relied on this recipe from Pepperidge Farm® for twenty years. I highly recommend the Giblet variation—it's the one my mother used every Thanksgiving Day for as far back as I can remember.

¾ cup chopped onion
1 cup chopped celery
1 cup butter or margarine
2 cups water
1 1-lb. package Pepperidge Farm® Herb-Seasoned Stuffing

In a large saucepan, sauté the onion and celery in butter until tender but not browned. Stir in water and then stuffing. Makes enough to fill a 12- to 16-lb turkey.

Variations: Try the following with a 1-lb. bag of herb-seasoned stuffing, prepared according to package directions:

Parsley
1 cup chopped parsley, ¾ cup chopped onion and 1 cup chopped celery sautéed in 1 cup butter.

Oriental
¼ cup chopped onion, ½ cup chopped celery, 1 cup sliced mushrooms and ½ cup sliced water chestnuts sautéed in 1 cup butter.

Nut
1 cup chopped celery, ½ cup onion and 1 cup nuts sautéed in 1 cup butter. Almonds, Brazil nuts, chestnuts, filberts, pecans or walnuts may be used.

Giblet
Simmer turkey giblets with seasonings 2 to 3 hours. Remove liver after 10 to 20 minutes. Drain, reserving broth; chop coarsely. Sauté ¾ cup chopped onion and 1 cup chopped celery in 1 cup butter. Use reserved broth in place of water in recipe. Stir chopped giblets and liver into stuffing.

Fish Fillets Sauterne

This may well have been the first recipe your mother (or grandmother) ever prepared with wine. It first appeared in 1935 on the back label of a bottle of Regina® Cooking Sauterne. I still use it, often adding my own touch—a sprinkling of slivered almonds sautéed in butter until golden.

¼ cup butter
½ cup Regina® Cooking Sauterne
⅛ tsp. pepper
1 Tbs. dried parsley flakes
2 lb. white fish fillets (sole, flounder, haddock)

Melt butter in large skillet. Stir in Sauterne, pepper and parsley. Place fish in pan. Spoon sauce over fish. Simmer, covered, 5 to 10 minutes or until fish flakes easily with a fork. Remove fish to warm platter. Boil sauce until slightly thickened. Spoon sauce over fish. Serves 6.

Sole in Almond Shrimp Sauce

This entrée, in a velvety sauce garnished with tiny coral shrimp and golden almonds, makes a truly memorable meal. It's one of the most popular from the permanent files at the Blue Diamond® Almonds test kitchens.

- 1 to 1½ lbs. sole fillets
- 1 cup dry white wine
- 3 ozs. cooked baby shrimp
- 4 Tbs. butter
- 2 Tbs. all-purpose flour
- ½ cup half-and-half
- ¼ tsp. salt
- Dash pepper
- ⅓ cup Blue Diamond® Blanched Slivered Almonds, toasted

Poach fillets in wine in 350°F. oven until fish flakes easily with fork, but is still moist, 15 to 20 minutes. *Do not overcook.* Reserve ¼ cup shrimp; mash remaining with 2 Tbs. butter; set aside. In small saucepan, heat 2 remaining Tbs. butter. Add flour; cook 2 to 3 minutes. Gradually stir in half-and-half. Cook and stir over medium heat until sauce begins to thicken. Stir in ½ cup of fish cooking liquid; continue cooking and stirring until sauce boils. Reduce heat, add shrimp butter, salt and pepper; stir until butter melts. Stir in ¼ cup of the almonds. Arrange fillets on serving platter. Pour sauce over; garnish with remaining shrimp and almonds. Makes 4 servings.

Creole Snapper

A Creole dish from the Kikkoman® test kitchens that proves you don't have to be Creole to develop a terrific Louisiana-style baked fish recipe.

- 2 lbs. fresh or frozen red snapper fillets (thawed, if frozen)
- 6 Tbs. Kikkoman® Teriyaki Sauce, divided
- 4 Tbs. lemon juice, divided
- 1 Tbs. vegetable oil
- ½ cup diced celery
- ½ cup diced green pepper
- ½ cup diced onion
- ¼ tsp. Tabasco® pepper sauce
- 1 cup diced tomatoes

Cut fish fillets into serving portions; drain thoroughly on paper towels. Combine 4 Tbs. Kikkoman® Teriyaki Sauce and 1 Tbs. lemon juice in large shallow pan. Arrange fish, in single layer, in sauce; marinate 15 minutes, turning over once. Bake fish in sauce in preheated 350°F. oven 12 to 15 minutes, or until fish flakes easily with fork. Meanwhile, heat oil in large frying pan. Add celery, green pepper and onion and sauté over medium heat until tender, yet crisp. Stir in remaining 2 Tbs. Teriyaki Sauce, 3 Tbs. lemon juice and pepper sauce; bring to boil. Add tomatoes and cook only until heated through, stirring constantly. To serve, remove fish from sauce; top with tomato mixture and serve immediately. Makes 6 servings.

Fillets Baked in Sour Cream

This is the sophisticated kind of dish you'd expect to find in an expensive French® restaurant, but it's surprisingly easy to prepare. A 4-star favorite ever since it was printed about 10 years ago in a booklet on "The Art Of Seasoning" prepared by the Tabasco® pepper sauce test kitchens.

- 4 tsps. butter or margarine, divided
- 2 lbs. fish fillets (sole, haddock or flounder)
- 1 tsp. salt
- ½ tsp. Tabasco® pepper sauce
- 1 Tbs. paprika
- ¼ cup grated Parmesan cheese
- 1 cup (8 ozs.) sour cream
- ¼ cup fine dry bread crumbs

Grease 2-quart baking dish with 1 tsp. of the butter. Arrange fish in baking dish. Blend salt, Tabasco® pepper sauce, paprika and Parmesan cheese into sour cream. Spread over fish. Top with bread crumbs and dot with remaining 3 tsps. butter. Bake, uncovered, in 350°F. oven 30 minutes until fish is easily flaked with a fork. Serve with lemon slices, if desired. Makes 4 to 6 servings.

Baked Fish Fillets José

Baked fish takes on a Mexican flavor when you follow the directions on the label of the Ortega® Taco Dinner package.

- 1 7-oz. package Ortega® Taco Dinner (Shells, Seasoning and Sauce)
- 2 lbs. fish fillets
- ½ cup butter (or margarine), melted

Heat Taco Shells according to package directions. In food processor or blender, finely crush shells. Blend in Taco

Seasoning. Dip fish in butter. Coat with crumbs. Arrange in shallow baking dish. Bake in preheated 425°F. oven 15 to 20 minutes or until fish flakes easily with a fork. Serve with Ortega® Taco Sauce. Makes 6 servings.

Tuna Shortcake

This is one of America's "stand by" Campbell's® Soup recipes. Try it as a 4 A.M. breakfast after a night of serious partying or as a 1 P.M. brunch the next day. It's a hot lunch for the young set or a light supper dish for an "I hate to cook" night. It's one of those "add a" recipes—add a dash of white wine, a can of sliced mushrooms, a handful of slivered almonds—and serve on cornbread squares, English muffins or what have you.

1 can Campbell's® Cream of Chicken Soup
¼ cup milk
1 7-oz. can tuna, drained and flaked
1 cup cooked peas
1 Tbs. chopped pimiento

In saucepan, combine ingredients. Heat; stir often. Serve over biscuits. Makes about 2½ cups.

Tuna Pie

One of the first recipes used to introduce Pepperidge Farm® Frozen Patty Shells. A step up from tuna salad sandwiches, wouldn't you say?

2 Tbs. butter or margarine
½ cup slivered almonds
2 6½-oz. cans tuna, drained
2 10½-oz. cans condensed cream of mushroom soup, undiluted
⅓ cup sherry

- 1 16-oz. can cut green beans, drained
- 1 6-oz. can sliced mushrooms, drained
- 1 10-oz. package Pepperidge Farm® frozen Patty Shells
- 1 egg, well beaten

Thaw package of Patty Shells in refrigerator overnight or on a kitchen counter until workable, always keeping them cold to the touch. In a skillet, heat butter and sauté almonds until golden. Stir in tuna, green beans, mushrooms, soup and sherry. Pour mixture into a shallow 1½-quart casserole. Stack 3 Patty Shells one atop the other. On a lightly floured surface roll out to about 4 × 9 inches. With a cookie cutter cut pastry into 2-inch rounds. Repeat with remaining Patty Shells. Place rounds on a cookie sheet and brush tops with beaten egg. Bake casserole and pastry rounds in 400°F. oven for 15 to 20 minutes or until rounds are puffed and brown. Place puff pastry rounds over the top of the tuna casserole. Serve at once. Serves 6.

Salmon Sour Cream Puffs

Borden® Sour Cream sponsored a national recipe contest back in the 1970's and out of 10,000 recipes entered, 14 were selected and appeared in a booklet called "Award Winning Recipes made with Borden® Sour Cream." This one won second prize.

- 1 15½-oz. can salmon, drained
- 1½ cups soft bread crumbs (about 4 slices)
- 1 8-oz. container Borden® Sour Cream
- 2 eggs, separated
- 2 Tbs. chopped chives
- ¼ tsp. salt
- Dash pepper
- 1 to 1¼ cups finely chopped almonds
- Vegetable oil
- Lemon wedges

Remove skin and bones from salmon. In large bowl, combine salmon, crumbs, Borden® Sour Cream, egg yolks, chives, salt and pepper; mix well. Beat egg whites until stiff; fold into salmon mixture. On large sheet of wax paper, sprinkle half the almonds. Drop heaping tablespoonfuls of salmon mixture onto almonds; sprinkle remaining almonds over top. In large skillet, heat oil; lift puffs with spatula into skillet. Brown on each side. Serve hot with lemon wedges. Refrigerate leftovers. Makes 6 servings.

Szechuan Shrimp

Based on a dish served in a famous New York Chinese restaurant, this recipe appeared in a Planters® Peanut Oil ad in the late 1970's. It is pleasantly hot with a touch of sweetness—an authentic Szechuan-style dish.

½ cup minced bamboo shoots
½ cup minced scallions
¼ tsp. minced fresh ginger root
3 large cloves garlic, minced
¼ tsp. liquid hot pepper sauce
2 Tbs. sugar
½ cup ketchup
3 Tbs. Dry Sack® Sherry
1 Tbs. soy sauce
1½ tsps. sesame oil *or* 1 Tbs. toasted sesame seeds
1 Tbs. corn starch
3 Tbs. water
1½ cups Planters® Peanut Oil
1 lb. shelled and deveined raw shrimp

Combine bamboo shoots, scallions, ginger, garlic and red pepper sauce in a small bowl. In second bowl combine sugar, ketchup, Dry Sack Sherry, soy sauce and sesame oil or seeds. In third bowl mix corn starch and water. Heat Planters® Peanut Oil in wok or large skillet to 400°F. Have ready a large strainer with a bowl underneath. Add shrimp to hot oil, stirring until done, about 2 minutes. Pour oil and shrimp into strainer to drain. Heat 2 Tbs. of the strained oil in same wok or skillet over high heat. Add scallion mixture and stir-fry 1 minute. Add drained shrimp and continue to stir-fry 30 seconds. Pour in ketchup mixture. Cook stirring, 30 seconds. Blend corn starch and water and add to wok. Cook and stir until slightly thickened. Serves 4.

TWO OUTSTANDING SAUCES FOR FISH FROM SUNKIST LEMONS

Shakespeare wrote:
"... the sauce
to meat is ceremony:
Meeting were bare without it."

Which is very true, and if you would transform simple broiled fish, whip up one of these sauces from the Sunkist Lemon people's advertising—they are indeed "repeat specials."

Lemon Mustard Sauce

- 2 Tbs. butter or margarine
- 2 Tbs. flour
- ½ tsp. salt
- ⅛ tsp. pepper
- 1 cup hot water
- 1 tsp. prepared mustard
- Grated peel and juice of ½ fresh Sunkist Lemon
- ½ cup mayonnaise or salad dressing

In saucepan, melt butter. Remove from heat; stir in flour, salt and pepper. Gradually blend in water and mustard. Cook over medium heat, stirring until thickened. Add lemon peel and juice. Remove from heat; blend in mayonnaise. Makes about 1⅓ cups.

Lemon Tartar Sauce

- ½ cup mayonnaise or salad dressing
- 2 Tbs. finely chopped dill pickle
- 2 Tbs. finely chopped green onion
- 1 Tbs. chopped canned pimiento, optional
- 1 tsp. fresh grated Sunkist Lemon peel
- 2 tsps. fresh squeezed lemon juice

In small bowl, combine all ingredients. Makes about ¾ cup.

Clam Crunch

I am fascinated by this recipe and the story behind it. Ralston Purina tells me it was "one of the winners in our Chex Create-A-Recipe Contest several years ago. It was sent in by a ninety-one-year-old Connecticut woman."

- ¼ cup all-purpose flour
- ½ tsp. baking powder
- ¼ tsp. salt
- ⅛ tsp. black pepper
- 1 Tbs. snipped parsley
- 1 (6½-ounce) can minced clams, drained (reserve liquid)
- 1 egg, beaten
- 2 cups Rice Chex cereal
- Cooking oil
- Sour cream, optional

In medium bowl combine flour, baking powder, salt, pepper and parsley. Slowly stir in clam liquid until smooth. Add egg and clams. Mix well. Stir in Rice Chex to coat. Let stand 10 minutes. Stir to combine. Heat oil (⅛-inch deep) in skillet. Drop 1 heaping tablespoon clam mixture into hot oil. Pat with spoon to form 3-inch patty. Repeat to form 8 patties. Brown over medium heat. Turn. Brown. Drain on absorbent paper. Serve immediately. Top with sour cream if desired. Makes 4 servings.

Scrumptious Shrimp Suprême

This title from Wish Bone Salad Dressing may sound a bit fancy but wait until you taste it! Serve with a medley of rice, peas and parsley for a perfect shore-side dinner.

- 1 (8-ounce) bottle Wish-Bone Italian Dressing
- 1 cup chili sauce
- 2 Tbs. corn syrup
- 2 lbs. large shrimp, shelled and cleaned
- 4 lemons, cut into wedges

In large bowl, blend Wish-Bone Italian Dressing with chili sauce and corn syrup; add shrimp. Cover and marinate in refrigerator 2 hours, turning occasionally. On skewers, alternately thread shrimp and lemons. Grill or broil, turning and basting frequently with remaining marinade, 15 minutes or until shrimp is done. Makes about 6 servings.

Crabby Rice Enchiladas

A truly unusual and delicious idea for a party, lunch or supper from Uncle Ben's Rice.

- 1 cup Uncle Ben's Converted Brand Rice
- 1 or 2 6-ounce packages frozen crabmeat, thawed and diced
- ¼ cup chopped green onion
- ½ lb. Monterey Jack cheese, shredded
- 1 10-ounce can enchilada sauce
- ⅓ cup cooking oil
- 16 corn tortillas
- 1 cup dairy sour cream (more if desired)
- Pitted ripe olives, quartered, for garnish—optional

Cook rice according to package directions. Stir crabmeat, onion, 1 cup cheese and 3 Tbs. enchilada sauce into cooked rice. Heat oil in small skillet. Heat tortillas, one at a time, until soft. Drain on paper toweling. Spread each tortilla down center with about ¼ cup rice mixture. Roll up. Arrange in 13½ × 8½-inch baking dish. Pour remaining enchilada sauce over tortillas. Cover with aluminum foil, crimping it tightly to edges of dish. Bake at 350°F. for 25 minutes. Uncover. Sprinkle with remaining cheese. Return to oven until thoroughly heated and cheese melts, 5 to 10 minutes. Top with sour cream; garnish with olives if desired. Makes 8 servings.

Southern Shrimp and Dumplings

A great way to make a small amount of shrimp into a delicious dinner for four, from the Mueller's Dumpling Macaroni package.

- 2 Tbs. butter or margarine
- ½ cup thinly sliced onion
- ½ cup thinly sliced green pepper
- ⅛ tsp. pepper
- Dash cayenne
- 2 bay leaves

1 clove garlic, mashed
1 can (1 pound) tomatoes
2 tsps. salt
8 ounces cooked shrimp
6 ounces (3 cups) Mueller's Dumpling Macaroni

Melt butter in skillet; add onion, green pepper and garlic; cook until crisp-tender but not brown. Stir in tomatoes and seasonings; cover and simmer about 10 minutes. Add shrimp; heat a few minutes; remove bay leaves. Meanwhile, cook macaroni as directed on package; drain. Serve shrimp mixture over macaroni. Makes 4 servings.

Seven Seas Casserole

Apparently this speedy, delicious casserole is a winning combination, a flavorful mix of rice, tuna, peas and cheese, for the recipe first appeared on the Minute Rice box in 1957.

1⅓ cups water
1 (10¾-ounce) can condensed cream of mushroom or celery soup
¼ cup finely chopped onion, optional
1 tsp. lemon juice, optional
¼ tsp. salt
Dash of pepper
1⅓ cups Minute Rice
1 (10-ounce) package Birds Eye® 5 Minute Sweet Green Peas, partially thawed
1 (7-ounce) can tuna, drained and flaked
½ cup grated Cheddar cheese
Paprika

Combine water, soup, onion, lemon juice, salt and pepper in a saucepan. Bring to a boil, stirring occasionally, over medium heat. Pour about half of soup mixture into a greased 1½-quart casserole. Then, in separate layers, add rice, peas and tuna. Add remaining soup mixture. Sprinkle with cheese and paprika. Cover and bake at 375°F. for 10 minutes. Stir; then cover and continue baking for 10 to 15 minutes longer. Makes about 5½ cups or 4 servings.

Perfect Tuna Casserole

How many ovens in the United States and around the world have baked this famous casserole?

- 1 10¾-ounce can Campbell's Condensed Cream of Celery or Mushroom Soup
- 1 can tuna (about 7 ounces), drained and flaked
- ¼ cup milk
- 2 hard-cooked eggs, sliced
- 1 cup cooked peas
- ½ cup slightly crumbled potato chips

In 1-quart casserole, blend soup and milk; stir in tuna, eggs and peas. Bake at 350°F. for 25 minutes or until hot; stir. Top with chips; bake 5 minutes more. Makes about 4 cups.

Pacific Salmon Loaf

The cooks at Kraft® tell us this salmon, cucumber and dill combination is a favorite with their television viewers.

- 1 16-ounce can salmon, drained, flaked
- ½ cup dry bread crumbs
- ½ cup Kraft® Real Mayonnaise
- ½ cup chopped onion
- ¼ cup chopped celery
- ¼ cup chopped green pepper
- 1 egg, beaten
- 1 tsp. salt
- Cucumber Sauce

Combine ingredients except Cucumber Sauce; mix lightly. Shape into loaf in shallow baking dish. Bake at 350°F. for 40 minutes. Serve with:

Cucumber Sauce

½ cup Kraft® Real Mayonnaise
½ cup dairy sour cream
½ cup finely chopped cucumber
2 Tbs. chopped onion
½ tsp. dill weed

Combine ingredients; mix well. Makes 6 to 8 servings.

Boatman's Stew

Quick, easy and very "down east," this hearty fish soup was featured on the Hunt's® Tomato Paste can back in the 1960's and is still a top favorite today.

2 lbs. firm-fleshed white fish (cod, haddock or halibut), cut in large chunks
Salt
2 onions, sliced
2 Tbs. Wesson Oil
1 6-oz. can Hunt's® Tomato Paste
3 cups water
½ tsp. *each*: red pepper and black pepper
1 cup finely chopped parsley
⅓ cup dry white wine
6 slices of Italian bread (toasted, if desired)

Sprinkle fish with ½ tsp. salt; let stand 1 hour. Meanwhile, lightly brown onion in hot oil; drain. Stir in water, Hunt's® Tomato Paste, red pepper, black pepper, 1½ tsps. salt, parsley and wine. Simmer 20 minutes. Add fish, simmer about 10 minutes longer or just until fish flakes easily with a fork.

To serve, place a slice of bread in each soup bowl; ladle soup over. Makes 6 servings.

Shrimp de Jonghe

Shrimp de Jonghe was created many years ago by Papa de Jonghe for the patrons of his popular Chicago restaurant. Although the restaurant is no longer in existence a never-fail version of this classic recipe has been developed by the Planters Peanut Oil expert cooks.

⅓ cup Planters Peanut Oil
½ cup flaked coconut
¼ cup fine dry bread crumbs
3 Tbs. chopped parsley
1 Tbs. minced garlic
¾ tsp. salt
¼ tsp. paprika
Dash cayenne
2 pounds uncooked shrimp, shelled and deveined
½ cup sherry

Combine Planters Peanut Oil, coconut, bread crumbs, chopped parsley, minced garlic, salt, paprika and cayenne. Reserve about ¼ cup of mixture for topping. Toss shrimp lightly in remaining mixture until shrimp are well coated. Turn into lightly oiled 1½-quart casserole. Pour sherry over shrimp and sprinkle with reserved mixture. Bake, uncovered, in moderate oven (375°F.) until shrimp are tender. Makes 4–6 servings.

Avocados with Curried Chicken

This unusual dish was first featured in the Avocado Grower's advertising a decade ago. Everyone seemed to love it and it may have started the trend of serving avocado as a hot dish.

- ¼ cup butter (½ stick)
- ½ cup chopped, pared apple
- ¼ cup chopped onion
- 1 clove garlic, crushed
- 1 Tbs. curry powder
- ¼ cup flour
- 1 cup light cream
- 1 cup chicken bouillon
- 1 tsp. salt
- ⅛ tsp. pepper
- 2 cups cooked chicken, cut up or 1½ lbs. shrimp, cooked, shelled and cleaned.
- 3 or 4 avocados, halved and peeled
- 3–4 cups cooked rice
- Condiments, given below

In saucepan: sauté apple, onion, garlic and curry powder in the butter until onion is crisp-tender. Stir in flour. Gradually add cream and bouillon; cook and stir until sauce boils 1 minute. Add salt, pepper and chicken or shrimp. Cook over low heat 10 minutes. Arrange avocado halves on rice in heatproof serving dish. Heat in 350°F. (moderate) oven for about 5 minutes. Spoon curried chicken or shrimp over avocado halves. Serve with Indian or Euphrates bread and a choice of these condiments: chopped egg, crumbled bacon, sweet mixed pickles, coconut, raisins, chutney, Bombay duck, preserved ginger, chopped peanuts. Makes 6–8 servings.

Stuffed Flounder Supreme

Fish is America's latest "favorite food" but Wish-Bone® printed this recipe on the label of their Deluxe French® dressing more than ten years ago. Maybe it started the trend to the ever-increasing popularity of fish.

½ cup Wish-Bone® Deluxe French® Dressing
1 lb. flounder fillets
¾ cup seasoned croutons, crushed
¼ cup finely chopped celery

Preheat oven to 350°F. Brush 2 Tbs. Wish-Bone® Deluxe French® Dressing on top side of fillets. In small bowl, combine ¼ cup dressing, croutons, and celery; equally divide mixture on fillets and roll up. Brush fillets with remaining dressing and bake 35 minutes or until fish flakes. Makes about 4 servings.

Flounder Au Gratin

Back in my mother's family there was my cousin, John Jay, who served this elegant baked flounder, but wouldn't, for the longest time, tell me how he did it. John was a fine cook who enjoyed his reputation as a gourmet and he didn't want me to know it was so easy to prepare. It's a Hellmann's® Best Foods original.

¼ cup fine dry bread crumbs
¼ cup grated Parmesan cheese
1 pound flounder or sole fillets
¼ cup Hellmann's® Best Foods Real Mayonnaise

In shallow dish or on sheet of waxed paper combine crumbs and cheese. Brush all sides of fillets with Real Mayonnaise; coat with crumb mixture. Arrange in single layer in shallow baking pan. Bake in 375°F. oven 20–25 minutes or until golden and fish flakes easily. Makes 4 servings.

Barbecued Red Snapper

A "cook out" or "cook in" favorite and definitely a Hunt-Wesson® classic. This recipe first appeared on the Hunt Tomato Paste label in the 1950's.

2 lbs. red snapper steaks or fillets
1 6-oz. can Hunt's® Tomato Paste
⅓ cup water
2 Tbs. lime juice
2 Tbs. Worcestershire sauce
1 Tbs. sugar
1 Tbs. Wesson Oil
1 tsp. salt
⅛ tsp. garlic salt

Thaw fish if frozen; cut into serving-size portions. Combine remaining ingredients in a small bowl. Arrange fish on grill or broiler pan about 4 inches from heat source. Brush generously with sauce. Cook 6–10 minutes. Turn, brush with more sauce and cook 7–10 minutes longer or just until fish flakes when tested with a fork (length of cooking time depends on thickness of fish). Do not overcook. Makes 6 servings.

Imperial Fish Baltimore

A lovely, easy, inexpensive casserole from Lea & Perrins®. Good enough for company, easy enough for every day.

3 Tbs. butter or margarine, divided
½ cup diced green pepper
¼ cup mayonnaise
2 tsps. Lea & Perrins® Worcestershire Sauce
¼ tsp. salt
¼ tsp. powdered mustard
2 cups flaked cooked white fish

¾ cup soft bread crumbs
¼ cup chopped pimiento
½ tsp. paprika

In a medium saucepan melt 1 Tbs. of the butter. Add green pepper; sauté for 2 minutes. Remove from heat; stir in mayonnaise, Lea & Perrins®, salt and mustard. Gently blend in fish. Turn into a buttered 1-quart casserole. In a small saucepan melt remaining 2 Tbs. butter. Stir in bread crumbs, pimiento, and paprika. Sprinkle over fish mixture. Bake in a preheated moderate oven (350°F.) until crumbs are golden, about 30 minutes. Makes 4 servings.

Stuffin'-Topped Halibut

Parkay® published this easy way to transform frozen halibut steaks into a festive dish in their cookbook several years ago. It's a special favorite for Friday night supper.

2 cups soft bread crumbs
½ cup Squeeze Parkay® Margarine
½ cup chopped celery
¼ cup chopped onion
¼ tsp. sage
¼ tsp. salt
4 frozen halibut steaks, ¾-inch thick (thawed)

Combine crumbs, margarine, celery, onion and seasonings; mix well. Place fish in 11¾ × 7½-inch baking dish; top with crumbs mixture. Bake at 350°F., 30–35 minutes or until crumbs mixture is golden brown and fish flakes easily with fork. Makes 4 servings.

Variations: Substitute salmon steaks for halibut. Substitute dill weed for sage.

Crisco's® French-Fried Butterfly Shrimp

Simply spectacular and not in the least difficult to prepare. For a great, almost no-work menu, serve hot shrimp with made-ahead coleslaw and canned shoestring potatoes.

- 2 lbs. shelled, deveined shrimp
- 1 cup sifted all-purpose enriched flour
- ½ tsp. sugar
- ½ tsp. salt
- 1 cup ice water
- 2 Tbs. Crisco® Oil
- 1 egg
- Crisco® Oil for deep frying
- Hot sauce

With a sharp knife slit shrimp deeply down back without cutting all the way through. Wash shrimp and dry between paper towels. In a bowl, combine flour, sugar and salt. Add ice water, 2 Tbs. Crisco® Oil and the egg; beat until smooth. Dip shrimp, a few at a time, into the mixture. Fry in deep Crisco® Oil heated to 375°F. Cook for 3 to 5 minutes, until golden brown. Drain on paper towels. Serve hot with your favorite hot sauce. Makes 6 servings.

The Luxury Liner

It's no shrimp boat! Built by Holland House® Wine and California avocados, it is indeed a luxury liner.

- 2 Tbs. butter
- ½ cup onion, finely chopped
- 1 cup zucchini, finely diced
- ½ cup Holland House® Sherry Cooking Wine
- ½ lb. medium-size fresh or frozen shrimp,* shelled and deveined
- 1 Tbs. corn starch, dissolved in 2 Tbs. cold water
- 1 Tbs. bread crumbs

*Chicken breast cut into ¼-inch cubes may be substituted.

- ½ cup water
- 2 Tbs. tomato sauce or 1 ripe tomato, chopped
- 1 chicken-flavor bouillon cube
- 3 California avocados, halved, pitted and peeled

Melt butter in saucepan. Add onion and zucchini and cook 5 minutes over medium heat. Stir in sherry, water, bouillon cube and tomato. Cook 3 minutes over high heat. Add shrimp and cook, stirring, about 1 minute until shrimp turn pink. Add corn starch mixture and cook, stirring, until mixture comes to boil. Remove from heat. Place avocado halves on baking dish. Fill each half with shrimp mixture, spooning remainder of sauce around them. Sprinkle with crumbs and broil 1 to 2 minutes until crumbs brown. Serve immediately, as an appetizer for 6 or luncheon entrée for 3.

Classic Crab Newburg

Here is the recipe most Americans use when preparing this adaptation of a lobster dish created at New York's famed Delmonico Restaurant during the Gay Nineties. It's on the Wakefield® Snow Crabmeat package and has been as long as I can remember.

- 1 6-oz. package Snow Crabmeat
- ¼ cup butter
- 2 Tbs. flour
- ½ tsp. salt
- ⅛ tsp. nutmeg
- ⅛ tsp. cayenne
- 2 cups half-and-half or light cream
- 3 egg yolks, slightly beaten
- 1½ Tbs. dry sherry
- Hot, cooked rice

Thaw and drain Crabmeat. Melt butter in medium saucepan. Add flour, salt, nutmeg and cayenne. Stir until smooth. Gradually add half-and-half. Cook over medium heat 8 to

10 minutes or until slightly thickened, stirring constantly. Gradually add ½ cup hot sauce mixture to egg yolks, beating to blend. Add egg yolk mixture to remaining sauce mixture; mix well. Add crab and crab liquid. Cook 1 to 2 minutes or until thickened, stirring constantly. Remove from heat. Stir in sherry. Serve over hot, cooked rice. Serves 4 to 5.

Crab Louis

After much reviewing and reminiscing, the Campbell® Soup test kitchens selected this recipe as one of the all-time best from their extensive files.

- 1 10¾ oz. can Campbell's® Condensed Cream of Celery Soup
- ½ cup chili sauce
- ¼ cup mayonnaise
- 2 Tbs. finely chopped onion
- Generous dash pepper
- ¼ cup heavy cream, whipped
- 4 cups cooked flaked crab meat (about 1½ lbs.)
- Hard-cooked egg, cut in wedges
- Tomatoes, cut in wedges

Blend Soup, chili sauce, mayonnaise, onion and pepper; fold in whipped cream. Add crab; chill. Place crab on bed of lettuce. Garnish with egg and tomato. Makes about 4 cups.

Deviled Seafood

One of the simplest and nicest party dishes is this one from the Pepperidge Farm® test kitchens. If you don't already have it (it was first printed 8 years ago), you most certainly should.

- ¼ cup finely chopped green pepper
- ¼ cup finely chopped onion
- 1 cup finely chopped celery
- 1 tsp. Worcestershire sauce
- ½ tsp. salt
- 1 6- to 7-oz. can shrimp, drained
- 1 6- to 7-oz. can crab meat, flaked
- 2 cups Pepperidge Farm® Herb-Seasoned Stuffing, crushed
- 1 cup mayonnaise

Stir together all ingredients until blended. Spoon into a 1-quart shallow casserole or 8 oven-proof shells. Bake at 350°F. for 30 minutes or until lightly browned. Serves 6 to 8.

Creamy Mustard Sauce

This classic, positively superb, old English sauce recipe has been on the sides of Colman's Dry Mustard cans for almost 30 years. A positive "must" for every good cook's file.

- 2 to 3 tsps. Colman's® Mustard (dry)
- 2 to 3 tsps. water
- ¼ cup vinegar
- 1 cup heavy cream
- ½ cup beef bouillon
- 1 Tbs. corn starch
- ¼ tsp. salt
- 1 Tbs. butter

Combine Colman's Mustard and water; let stand 10 minutes. Boil vinegar in small saucepan until reduced to 1 Tbs. Stir in heavy cream, bouillon, corn starch and salt. Cook and stir until thickened. Add butter and mustard mixture. Serve with beef, pork, lamb and vegetables.

Basic Bordelaise Sauce

This recipe from the permanent file at Holland House® test kitchens will leave guests thinking you spent hours at the stove.

- 3 Tbs. butter
- ¼ cup diced onions
- 2 Tbs. flour
- 1 cup beef bouillon
- ½ cup Holland House® Red Cooking Wine
- 1 Tbs. chopped parsley
- 1 clove garlic, crushed

Heat butter in large skillet. Sauté onions in butter until golden; add flour and blend thoroughly. Add bouillon and stir until smooth. Blend in Holland House® Red Cooking Wine, parsley and garlic. Delicious on steak, roast beef and chops.

Creole Sauce

Louisiana housewives used to spend a whole day preparing Creole Sauce. Heinz® test-kitchen cooks make it quick, simple and simply delicious with this easy recipe.

- 1 large onion, thinly sliced
- ¼ cup chopped green pepper
- 2 Tbs. butter or margarine
- ½ cup Heinz® Tomato Ketchup
- ½ cup water
- 1 Tbs. Heinz® Worcestershire Sauce
- ½ tsp. salt
- Dash pepper

In saucepan, sauté onion and green pepper in butter until tender. Stir in ketchup, water, Worcestershire Sauce, salt and pepper. Simmer, uncovered, 10 minutes, stirring occasionally. Serve over baked, broiled or fried fish, omelets or other meat or chicken dishes. Makes 1½ cups sauce.

Slimmed-Down Pasta Sauce

For weight-watchers who are also pasta lovers, this sauce is the answer to a prayer; an extremely popular recipe from Mueller's.®

- 1 24-oz. can tomato juice
- 1 6-oz. can tomato paste
- ½ cup grated carrot
- 2 large cloves garlic, mashed
- 1 tsp. oregano leaves, crushed
- 1 tsp. onion salt
- 1 medium bay leaf
- Dash pepper

To make basic sauce, combine all ingredients in saucepan. Simmer 30 minutes, stirring occasionally. Remove bay leaf. Makes about 3½ cups sauce (300 calories total).

Variations:

Ground Beef: In saucepan brown ½ lb. lean ground beef (10% fat); add basic sauce ingredients and proceed as directed. Makes about 4⅓ cups sauce.

Mushroom: Add 1 cup sliced fresh mushrooms, or a 4-oz. can sliced mushrooms (with liquid) to basic sauce ingredients; proceed as directed. Makes about 4⅔ cups sauce.

Easy Meat Sauce

Lipton® featured this quick spaghetti sauce on their Onion Soup Mix package back in the 1960's. It was popular then and is even more so today.

- 1 lb. ground beef
- 1 clove garlic, finely chopped
- 1 envelope Lipton® Onion Soup mix
- ¼ tsp. oregano
- 1 28-oz. can tomato puree
- 1 cup water

In large saucepan, brown ground beef with garlic; stir in Lipton® Onion Soup mix, oregano, tomato puree and water. Simmer covered, stirring occasionally, about 30 minutes. Serve over hot noodles, spaghetti or rice. Makes about 5 cups sauce.

San Clemente Ham Sauce

The great cooks at the Sun-Maid® test kitchen tell me this is their all-time favorite sauce recipe.

- ½ cup Sun-Maid® Seedless Raisins
- ½ cup Sun-Maid® Golden Seedless Raisins
- ¼ cup brown sugar
- 1½ Tbs. corn starch
- ¼ tsp. salt
- ½ tsp. dry mustard
- Generous dash cloves
- 2 Tbs. vinegar
- 2 Tbs. ham drippings or butter
- 1 cup water
- ½ cup orange or pineapple juice
- ¼ cup Chablis

Bring all ingredients to a boil and simmer 5 minutes. Makes 2 cups sauce.

Cranberry Wine Sauce

Armour® put this American original on their Gold Star Boneless Turkey label a few years ago. It's superb.

1 16-oz. can whole berry cranberry sauce
¼ cup Burgundy wine
2 Tbs. brown sugar, packed
1 Tbs. prepared mustard
¼ tsp. onion salt

In saucepan, combine all ingredients. Simmer, uncovered, 5 minutes. Serve warm with sliced turkey. To serve with cold sliced turkey, chill sauce and spoon over turkey. Makes 2½ cups.

Basic Newburg Sauce

This is a basic cream-based sauce from the label of Holland House® Cooking Sherry that has so many uses it just can't be left out of this book. Serve it over shrimp or lobster as suggested below, or try it served over vegetables, leftover turkey or chicken, or use it instead of Hollandaise for Eggs Benedict—all lovely ideas, each as good as the other.

2 Tbs. butter
1 Tbs. flour
1 cup heavy cream
1 egg yolk
Salt and pepper to taste
2 Tbs. Holland House® Sherry Cooking Wine

Heat butter in large skillet. Sprinkle flour into butter and blend thoroughly. Gradually add heavy cream to mixture and cook, stirring constantly until thick and smooth (do not boil). Pour mixture over well-beaten egg yolk, stirring constantly with spoon or whisk. Salt and pepper to taste.

For Seafood Newburg:
Add to Newburg sauce 1 lb. cooked shrimp or lobster meat, seasoned by tossing with 2 Tbs. Holland House® Sherry Cooking Wine. Heat through and serve over rice or toast. Makes 4 average servings.
Cook over boiling water for 1 to 2 minutes, stirring constantly. Stir in cooking wine.

Basic Barbecue Sauce

A classic for sure. This simple, but very versatile and utterly delicious sauce recipe has been featured on the Grandma's® Molasses label for over 10 years.

1 cup Grandma's® Molasses
1 cup prepared mustard
1 cup vinegar

Mix molasses and mustard; stir in vinegar. Cover and refrigerate. Makes 3 cups.

Variations:

Tomato Barbecue Sauce: Add 1 cup ketchup to Basic Barbecue Sauce. Yields 1 quart.

Herb Barbecue Sauce: Add ¼ tsp. each, marjoram, oregano and thyme to 1 cup Basic Barbecue Sauce. Yields 1 cup.

For Oven-Broiled Chicken: Brush sauce on chicken parts, broil until tender, brush again.

For Barbecue Hamburger: Flavor, knead sauce into meat, brush on burgers, brown.

For Baked Glazed Ham: Brush with sauce during last half-hour of baking.

Lipton® Onion Butter

The Lipton® people printed this "terrific-idea" recipe on their Onion Soup mix packages years ago. It has become a classic, so don't wait—make it up today to have on hand when you want to make something especially good.

1 envelope Lipton® Onion Soup mix
1 8-oz. container whipped butter, or
½ lb. butter or margarine, softened

Thoroughly blend Lipton® Onion Soup mix with butter. Store covered in refrigerator. Makes about 1¼ cups.

Onion-Buttered Bread: Spread Onion Butter between slices of French® or Italian bread; wrap in foil and heat in 375°F. oven 15 to 20 minutes.

Onion-Buttered Baked Potatoes: Top a hot, split baked potato with 1 to 2 Tbs. Onion Butter.

Onion-Buttered Whipped Potatoes: Add ¼ cup Onion Butter and ¼ cup milk to 4 medium-cooked potatoes; beat until light and fluffy.

For Instant Potatoes: Prepare instant mashed potatoes according to package directions, using twice as much Onion Butter for butter.

Onion-Buttered Noodles: Toss ½ lb. cooked and drained noodles with ¼ cup Onion Butter.

Onion-Buttered Vegetables: Add 2 Tbs. Onion Butter to a cooked and drained 10-oz. package frozen vegetable.

Onion-Buttered Corn-on-the-Cob: Spread Onion Butter on hot cooked ears of corn; or spread on uncooked corn, then wrap in foil and toast on outdoor grill or in 400°F. oven about 30 minutes.

Onion-Buttered Sandwiches: Use softened Onion Butter to spread on bread slices when making sandwiches. Especially good with roast beef, cheese, lettuce and tomatoes.

Onion-Buttered Popcorn: Toss 2½ quarts popped popcorn with ½ cup melted Onion Butter.

Onion-Buttered Crescents: Separate one 8-oz. package refrigerated crescent dinner rolls into 8 triangles. Spread with Onion Butter. Roll up and bake according to package directions.

Macaroni & Beans Italiano

This is a hearty dish, the kind I like to serve on a cold winter night. It's a meatless recipe that meat lovers will love when some crusty homemade bread is served on the side. From the Heinz® permanent file of "most-often-requested."

- ½ cup chopped onion
- ½ cup chopped green pepper
- 1 medium zucchini, cut into ⅛-inch slices
- 3 Tbs. margarine or olive oil
- ¾ cup Heinz® Tomato Ketchup
- ¾ cup water
- 1 tsp. salt
- ½ tsp. oregano leaves
- ¼ tsp. garlic salt
- ⅛ tsp. pepper
- 1 1-lb. can Heinz® Vegetarian Beans in Tomato Sauce
- 1½ cups cooked macaroni
- Grated Parmesan cheese

Sauté first 3 ingredients in margarine until tender. Stir in ketchup and next 5 ingredients. Combine with beans and macaroni in a 1½-quart casserole. Bake in 375°F. oven, 35 to 40 minutes. Stir occasionally. Serve with Parmesan cheese. Makes 4 to 5 servings (about 4½ cups).

At-Ease Macaroni and Cheese

An "Elsie extra" from Borden's®—old-fashioned (remember how you loved it?) macaroni and cheese. This version is made especially good with sour cream.

- 2 Tbs. Borden® Country Store Butter
- 2 Tbs. flour
- ½ tsp. salt
- Dash pepper
- ½ cup Borden® Milk
- 1½ cups (6 ozs.) shredded Cheddar cheese
- 1 8-oz. container Borden® Sour Cream
- 1 cup uncooked macaroni, cooked and drained (2 cups cooked)

In medium saucepan, melt Butter; blend in flour, salt and pepper. Gradually stir in Milk and cheese; cook and stir over medium heat until thickened and smooth. Stir in Sour Cream and macaroni; heat through (do not boil). Garnish as desired. Refrigerate leftovers. Makes 4 to 6 servings.

Spinach Fettucine

Here's a delicious spin-off from classic Fettucine Alfredo adapted by the good cooks at Mueller's® test kitchens. A meatless main-course recipe, it is currently very popular and destined to remain so.

- ½ lb. fresh spinach
- 1 clove garlic, mashed
- 2 Tbs. chopped onion
- ½ cup butter or margarine
- 8 ozs. (5½ to 6 cups) Mueller's® Medium Egg Noodles
- ½ cup heavy cream
- 1 cup grated Parmesan cheese
- Pepper

Remove and discard tough stems from spinach; tear or coarsely chop leaves. In pan, cook garlic and onion in half the butter until golden. Add spinach; cover and cook until just wilted. Meanwhile, cook noodles as directed on package; drain and mix with remaining butter. Then toss with cream, cheese and spinach. Pass the pepper mill or shaker. Makes 3 to 4 servings.

Fettucine Romano

Here is one of the easiest pasta recipes you will ever find and one of the most delicious. An Italian classic perfected at the Hunt-Wesson® test kitchens.

- 8 ozs. fettucine or wide egg noodles
- Boiling salted water
- ½ cup finely chopped onion
- ¼ cup butter
- 1 6-oz. can Hunt's® Tomato Paste
- 2 cups water
- ¼ cup grated Romano or Parmesan cheese
- ½ cup sour cream
- ¼ cup chopped fresh parsley

Cook fettucine in boiling, salted water until tender; drain well. Meanwhile, sauté onion in butter. Thoroughly blend in Hunt's® Tomato Paste and water; heat through. Pour over hot cooked fettucine and toss with Romano cheese. Fold in sour cream. Sprinkle with parsley. Makes 4 to 6 servings.

Layered Spinach Supreme

One of the first of the "no-time-to-cook" recipes from Bisquick.® It's still considered by most cooks to be one of the best.

1 cup Bisquick® Baking Mix
¼ cup milk
2 eggs
¼ cup finely chopped onion
1 10-oz. package frozen chopped spinach, thawed and drained
½ cup grated Parmesan cheese
4 ozs. Monterey Jack cheese, cut into about ½-inch cubes
1 12-oz. carton cottage cheese
½ tsp. salt
2 cloves garlic, crushed
2 eggs

Heat oven to 375°F. Grease rectangular baking dish, 12 × 7½ × 2 inches. Mix Bisquick® Baking Mix, milk, 2 eggs and the onion; beat vigorously 20 strokes. Spread in dish. Mix remaining ingredients; spoon evenly over batter in dish. Bake until set, about 30 minutes. Let stand 5 minutes before cutting. Makes 6 to 8 servings.

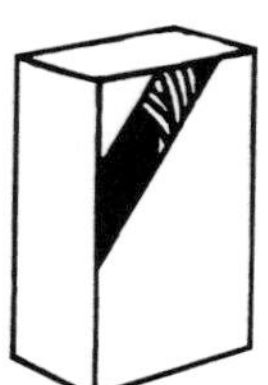

Gourmet French® Omelet

One of my own favorite omelets. It's quick to prepare and makes a light but satisfying meal any time of day or night. A Kraft® specialty.

2 2½-oz. jars sliced mushrooms, drained
3 Tbs. Parkay® Margarine
¾ cup (3 ozs.) shredded Cracker Barrel® Brand Sharp Natural Cheddar Cheese

6 eggs, beaten
⅓ cup milk
Salt and pepper
1 tsp. finely chopped chives

Sauté mushrooms in 1 Tbs. Margarine. Melt remaining margarine in 10-inch skillet over low heat. Combine eggs, milk and seasonings; pour into skillet. Cook slowly. As egg mixture sets, lift slightly with a spatula to allow uncooked portion to flow underneath. Cover omelet with ½ cup Cheese, mushrooms and chives; fold in half and sprinkle with remaining Cheese. Makes 3 to 4 servings.

Wheat Germ Vegetarian Torte

The most epicurian recipes come from the healthiest people. This recipe from the label on a jar of Kretschmer® Wheat Germ is fabulous. Bake it and see.

1 cup saltine cracker crumbs (about 26 crackers)
¾ cup Kretschmer® Regular Wheat Germ, divided
8 Tbs. butter or margarine, divided
2 medium 8 ozs. zucchini, sliced
1 medium onion, sliced
1 tsp. marjoram leaves, crushed
½ tsp. salt
¼ tsp. pepper
¼ tsp. tarragon leaves, crushed
1 cup grated Monterey Jack cheese
½ cup grated Parmesan cheese
2 eggs
⅓ cup milk
1 medium tomato, thinly sliced

Combine cracker crumbs, ¼ cup wheat germ and 6 Tbs. melted butter in small bowl. Stir well. Press evenly on bottom and about 1 inch up sides of 9-inch springform pan *or* on bottom and sides of 9-inch pie pan. Bake at 400°F. for 8 to

10 minutes until very lightly browned. Remove from oven. Sauté zucchini and onion in remaining 2 Tbs. butter until tender-crisp. Add seasonings to vegetable mixture. Stir well. Place half the vegetables in crumb crust. Sprinkle with about 3 Tbs. of the remaining wheat germ. Top with half the cheeses, remaining vegetables, then about 3 Tbs. wheat germ. Beat eggs and milk together. Pour into center of vegetable mixture. Arrange tomato slices on top and sprinkle with remaining cheeses and wheat germ. Bake at 325°F. for 40 to 45 minutes until hot and bubbly. Makes 6 servings.

French® Egg Nests

A Classic Creole recipe from Avery Island in Louisiana where Tabasco® pepper sauce has been made for over 75 years.

2 thick slices French® bread
3 Tbs. butter or margarine
2 eggs
Salt
Tabasco® pepper sauce
Grated Cheddar cheese

Take French® bread slices and hollow out the center of each. Dot with butter. Break egg into each hollow. Salt lightly and add 3 drops Tabasco® pepper sauce to each egg. Sprinkle with cheese. Bake in 325°F. oven until eggs are set. Serves 2.

Fish & Chips

I tell you those Crisco people know their deep-fried foods. This long-time "best ever" recipe pleases just about everybody. Some summer day serve it with a platter of tomatoes and cucumber slices, lemon-spiked iced tea and who knows, there may be fresh blueberry tart for dessert.

1 lb. fresh or frozen firm, white-fleshed fish fillets
1 lb. potatoes, peeled, (about 3 potatoes)
Crisco for deep frying
¼ cup flour
½ tsp. salt
1 egg yolk
2 Tbs. water
1 Tbs. Crisco, melted
1 egg white, stiffly beaten
¼ cup flour

Thaw fish, if frozen. Cut into serving-size pieces. Cut potatoes in uniform strips, slightly larger than for French® fries. To make chips: Deep fry potato strips until golden brown in Crisco heated to 375°F. (about 7–8 minutes). Remove, drain on paper towels, and keep warm. In medium bowl, combine first ¼ cup flour and salt. Make well in center; add egg yolk, water, and melted Crisco. Stir until batter is smooth. Fold in egg white. Dip fish in the remaining ¼ cup flour, then into batter. Deep fry fish until golden brown in Crisco heated to 375° (about 1½ minutes on each side.) Sprinkle fish with vinegar, if desired. Sprinkle fish and chips with salt. Makes 3–4 servings.

Fillet of Sole en Croute

Here's the sort of recipe you'd expect to find in an expensive restaurant. Very special and very elegant indeed; but surprisingly easy. An immediate hit when it appeared on the Pepperidge Farm Frozen Puff Pastry package.

4 small fillets of sole
Salt, pepper, thyme, tarragon
2 Tbs. butter or margarine
½ cup julienne onions
½ cup julienne mushrooms
½ cup julienne carrots
1 17¼-oz. package Pepperidge Farm Frozen "Bake It Fresh" Puff Pastry Sheets
1 egg, beaten

Sprinkle sole fillets lightly with salt, pepper, thyme and tarragon, and refrigerate. Melt butter in skillet; cut vegetables into narrow matchstick-like strips (julienne) and add to skillet. Season with salt and pepper and cook briefly, 3–5 minutes. Vegetables should remain crisp. Allow puff pastry sheets to thaw for 20 minutes, then unfold and cut each sheet into 4 squares. On a lightly floured surface, roll first square until it's slightly larger than the fillet. Place fillet in center of pastry, spoon ¼ cup of the julienne mixture on top. Roll second square of pastry only enough to cover sole fillet and border of the first sheet. Firmly press down edges to seal, trim excess with pastry wheel. If desired, use scraps to decorate pastry and attach with beaten egg. Repeat with remaining sole fillets and pastry. Place on baking sheet, brush top with beaten egg and bake in preheated 375°F. oven for 25–30 minutes or until golden brown. Makes 4 generous servings.

Teriyaki Fish Fillets

A California favorite from Kikkoman; light, lemony, refreshing. If you haven't already clipped and tried this one you must try it now.

⅓ cup Kikkoman Teriyaki Sauce
2 Tbs. lemon juice
1 Tbs. water
1 lb. fish fillets
⅓ cup thinly sliced green onions and tops

Combine teriyaki sauce with lemon juice and water. Place fish in single layer in shallow baking pan; pour teriyaki mixture over fish and marinate 5 minutes on each side. Bake fish in sauce in preheated 350°F. oven 10–15 minutes, or until fish flakes easily with fork. Remove fish onto serving platter, sprinkle with green onions and spoon sauce over all. Serve immediately. Makes 4 servings.

Batter-Fried Shrimp

Another Planters Peanut Oil winner, this is just the best recipe I've found for fried shrimp. The coating is crispy light, the shrimp cooked to pink perfection. The only thing wrong is that I have never been able to make enough.

2 lbs. uncooked shrimp, large
¾ cup unsifted flour
¾ cup water
1 egg, slightly beaten
1 Tbs. sugar
½ tsp. salt
Planters Peanut Oil

Peel shrimp leaving tails on; devein. Split shrimp part way through, butterfly fashion. Combine flour, water, egg, sugar and salt to make a batter. Dip shrimp into batter and fry in deep, hot (375°F.) Planters Peanut Oil until golden brown. Drain on paper towels. Makes about 6 servings.

Tuna Croquettes

Now let me tell you there is nothing, no nothing, that can match the incredible goodness of a perfectly fried croquette, crisp and crunchy on the outside, meltingly delicious on the inside, and who knows better how to make croquettes than the cooks at Criscol.

- 3 Tbs. Crisco
- ¼ cup flour
- ⅔ cup milk
- 2 Tbs. finely chopped onion
- 1 Tbs. snipped parsley
- 2 tsps. lemon juice
- ¼ tsp. salt
- Dash pepper
- Dash paprika
- 2 6½ or 7-oz. cans tuna, drained and flaked
- ⅔ cup fine dry bread crumbs
- 1 egg, beaten
- 1 8-oz. package frozen peas with cream sauce
- Crisco for deep frying

In saucepan, melt the 3 Tbs. Crisco. Blend in the flour. Add the milk. Cook and stir till thickened and bubbly. Add the onion, parsley, lemon juice, salt, pepper and paprika; stir in the tuna. Cover and chill thoroughly, about 3 hours. With wet hands, shape tuna mixture into 8 cones, using about ¼ cup for each. Roll in crumbs. Dip into a mixture of beaten egg and 2 Tbs. water; roll in crumbs again. Prepare peas with cream sauce according to package directions; keep hot. Meanwhile, fry a few croquettes at a time till brown and hot in deep Crisco heated to 350°F., about 3 minutes. Drain on paper toweling. Spoon pea sauce over croquettes. Makes 4 servings.

Tuna Creole in Rice Ring

Tuna again? It can be a company treat when you turn it into something special with a flavorful creole sauce and serve it in a buttery rice ring. A top request recipe ever

since it appeared on the Hunt's® Tomato Paste can about ten years ago.

- 1 green pepper, chopped
- ½ cup chopped onion
- ½ cup sliced celery
- 1 clove garlic, crushed
- 2 Tbs. pure vegetable oil
- 1 6-oz. can Hunt's® Tomato Paste
- 1¼ cups water
- 1 tsp. salt
- 1 tsp. dill weed
- 1 bay leaf
- Dash Tabasco
- 2 6½ to 7-oz. cans chunk style tuna, drained and flaked
- 4 cups hot cooked rice

Sauté vegetables and garlic until tender in oil. Add Hunt's® Tomato Paste, water and seasonings. Simmer 30 minutes, stirring occasionally. Stir in tuna; heat through. Pack hot cooked rice in buttered ring mold, turn out onto serving platter. Spoon tuna creole into center. Makes 4 servings.

Pasta, Pasta Americana!

Mueller's was the official supplier of pasta for the 1980 Olympic Winter games in Lake Placid. To celebrate they developed 80 new American-style recipes to be used on their packages. Here are four top winners.

Lake Placid Steak 'n' Peppers

- 1 lb. tender steak, very thinly sliced
- ¼ cup butter or margarine
- 1 large clove garlic, mashed
- 3 large onions, chopped
- 2 small green peppers, chopped
- ¼ cup dry sherry
- ¼ cup sliced pimiento
- 1 to 2 tsps. salt
- ½ tsp. pepper
- 8 oz. Mueller's Thin Spaghetti
- 2 Tbs. vegetable oil
- Grated Parmesan cheese

In large skillet brown meat in butter with garlic; remove meat to warm platter. Add onion and green pepper to skillet and cook until crisp-tender; add sherry, pimiento and seasonings; return meat to skillet. Meanwhile, cook spaghetti as directed on package; drain. Toss spaghetti with oil, then combine with meat-vegetable mixture. Top with Parmesan cheese. Makes 4–6 servings.

Chalet Casserole

- 8 oz. Mueller's Thin Spaghetti
- 2 cups meatless spaghetti sauce
- 4 oz. thinly sliced pepperoni
- 1 4-oz. can mushroom stems and pieces, undrained
- 1 Tbs. grated onion
- 2 slices (4 oz.) Mozzarella cheese, cut in half diagonally

Cook spaghetti as directed on package; drain. In 11 × 8 × 2-inch baking dish combine spaghetti with sauce, pepperoni, mushrooms with liquid, and onion; top with cheese. Bake at 350°F. about 20 minutes or until bubbling. Makes 4 servings.

Frank-ly Fabulous Spaghetti

- 1 lb. frankfurters, cut in 1-inch slices
- ½ cup chopped onion
- ¾ cup diced green pepper
- 2 Tbs. butter or margarine
- 2 8-oz. cans tomato sauce
- ½ tsp. chili powder
- ¼ tsp. ground cumin, if desired
- ⅓ cup sliced stuffed olives
- 8 oz. Mueller's Thin Spaghetti
- Grated Parmesan cheese

Cook frankfurters, onion and green pepper in butter until vegetables are tender. Stir in tomato sauce, chili powder and cumin. Simmer, covered, 20 minutes; stir occasionally. Add olives; heat. Meanwhile, cook spaghetti as directed on package; drain. Serve frankfurter sauce over spaghetti; sprinkle with Parmesan cheese. Makes 4–6 servings.

Unbelievable Lasagne

Lasagne originated in Italy, but you don't have to be Italian to make it. This short-cut method from Mueller's kitchens received its name (unbelievable) from the good American cooks who first tested the recipe. You don't have to pre-cook the lasagne and believe it or not it works!

- 4 to 5 cups spaghetti sauce
- 8 oz. lasagne
- 1 lb. Ricotta cheese
- 8 oz. Mozzarella cheese, shredded or thinly sliced
- 1 cup grated Parmesan cheese

In 13 × 9 × 2-inch baking pan, spread about 1 cup sauce; arrange a layer of uncooked lasagne; top with some sauce, Ricotta, Mozzarella, Parmesan and sauce. Repeat, gently pressing lasagne pieces into cheese mixture below. End with a final layer of lasagne; pour remaining sauce over, making sure all lasagne pieces are covered with sauce; top with remaining Mozzarella and Parmesan. (Do not be concerned with the empty space at the ends of the pan—during cooking the lasagne will expand and take up most of the area.) Bake at 350°F. for 45–55 minutes until lightly browned and bubbling. Allow to stand 15 minutes; cut in squares to serve. Serves 6–8.

Moon over Mostaccioli

We are told a romantically inclined member of the San Giorgio family came up with this intriguing name for what is surely one of the best pasta meals ever created.

- 2 Tbs. olive oil
- 2 Tbs. butter
- ½ cup finely chopped onion
- ½ cup finely chopped celery
- 1 medium green pepper, finely chopped
- ½ clove garlic, minced
- ¼ cup chopped stuffed olives
- ¼ cup chopped parsley
- 1 1-lb. jar San Giorgio Spaghetti Sauce with Meat
- 8 oz. (½ package) San Giorgio Mostaccioli Rigati (Pasta)
- ½ cup grated Cheddar cheese

Heat olive oil and butter in heavy saucepan. Sauté onion, celery, green pepper and garlic for 10 minutes. Add olives, parsley and sauce; simmer 10 minutes more. Meanwhile prepare mostaccioli according to package directions. Drain well. Toss with sauce in heated bowl. Sprinkle with Cheddar cheese. Serves 4.

Red Clam Sauce and Linguine

Traditional—and wonderful—a classic Italian dish that is on permanent file at the Hunt's® Tomato Paste test kitchens.

- 1 onion, chopped
- 1 clove garlic, minced
- 2 Tbs. olive oil
- 2 6½-oz. cans minced clams, drained
- 1 6-oz. can Hunt's® Tomato Paste
- 1 cup water
- 2 Tbs. lemon juice
- 1 Tbs. chopped fresh parsley
- 1 tsp. sugar
- ¼ tsp. rosemary

¼ tsp. ground thyme
8 oz. linguine or spaghetti, cooked and drained
Grated Parmesan cheese (optional)

Sauté onion and garlic in oil in skillet. Add clams and their juice, Hunt's® Tomato Paste, water, lemon juice, parsley, sugar, rosemary and thyme. Simmer, uncovered, 15 minutes. Serve over cooked linguine; sprinkle with Parmesan, if desired. Makes 4 servings.

Fettuccini Carbonara

San Giorgio printed this classic but easy recipe for Fettuccini on their box label a dozen years ago and it's a truly marvelous tasting, low-cost dinner any night of the week.

¼ lb. bacon
1 12-oz. box San Giorgio Fettuccini
¼ cup butter or margarine, softened
½ cup heavy cream, at room temperature
½ cup grated Parmesan cheese
2 eggs, slightly beaten
2 Tbs. snipped parsley

Sauté bacon until crisp; drain well and crumble. Cook Fettuccini according to package directions. Drain well and place in warm serving dish large enough for tossing. Add crumbled bacon, butter, heavy cream, grated cheese, eggs and snipped parsley; toss until Fettuccini is well coated. Makes 6 servings.

Salmon Quiche

Recommended for this book by a number of excellent cooks as the best salmon quiche ever. It's from Castle and Cook Inc. who produce Bumble Bee® Pink Salmon.

- 1 10-inch unbaked pie shell
- 1 15½-oz. can Bumble Bee® Pink Salmon
- 1 9-oz. package frozen chopped spinach
- 1½ cups shredded Monterey Jack cheese
- 1 3-oz. package cream cheese, softened
- ½ tsp. salt
- ½ tsp. thyme
- 4 eggs, lightly beaten
- 1 cup milk

Preheat oven to 375°F. Bake pie shell 10 minutes until partially set. Drain salmon. Mash bones. Cook spinach according to package directions. Drain well. Combine spinach, Monterey Jack cheese, cream cheese, salt and thyme. Arrange salmon and mashed bones into pie shell. Spoon spinach mixture on top. Combine eggs and milk. Pour over salmon and spinach. Bake in preheated oven 40–45 minutes. Let stand 10 minutes before serving. Makes 6–8 servings.

Mexican Quiche

A French® quiche with a Mexican Flavor? Of course that's what American cuisine is all about. We pick the best then combine them. The result? As delicious a dish as this "South of the Border" quiche from Pet-Ritz.®

- 1 Pet-Ritz® Regular Pie Crust Shell
- 1 4-oz. can Old El Paso Whole Chilies
- 6 slices bacon, cooked and drained
- 1 4-oz. cup Swiss cheese, shredded
- 3 eggs
- 1 cup light cream
- ¼ tsp. salt
- Dash ground nutmeg

Preheat oven and cookie sheet to 425°F. Drain chilies and dry with toweling. Remove rib and seeds. Chop in large pieces. Crumble bacon and mix with chopped chilies. Sprinkle Swiss cheese on bottom of unbaked pie shell, then chilies and bacon. Mix together eggs, cream, salt and nutmeg. Slowly pour over cheese mixture. (The pie will be very full, but should not spill over.) Place on cookie sheet in preheated oven and bake for 15 minutes. Reduce temperature to 350°F. and bake an additional 20–25 minutes or until knife inserted in the center comes out clean. Cool 10–15 minutes before serving. Serves 6–8.

Savory Fish Pie

A classic down-east recipe from Blue Bonnet Margarine—perfect for a one-dish supper.

- ½ tsp. peppercorns
- ¼ tsp. tarragon leaves
- 1 bay leaf
- 1½ lbs. flounder fillets
- ½ lb. yellow onions, sliced
- Water
- 1 Tbs. finely diced pimiento
- 3 Tbs. Blue Bonnet Margarine
- 3 Tbs. flour
- 2 tsps. dry mustard
- 1¼ tsp. salt
- ⅛ tsp. pepper
- ¾ cup milk
- 1 tsp. Worcestershire sauce
- ¼ cup chopped parsley
- 3 cups prepared mashed potatoes
- Paprika

Tie peppercorns, tarragon and bay leaf in cheesecloth. Place in a large saucepan with fillets and onions. Cover with water. Bring to a boil. Reduce heat; simmer until onions are tender. Drain; reserve ¾ cup stock. Arrange fish and onions in 2-quart oblong dish. Scatter diced pimiento over fish. Melt Blue Bonnet Margarine in a small heavy saucepan. Blend in flour, dry mustard, salt and pepper. Cook over low heat, stirring, until smooth and bubbly. Remove from heat and stir in milk and Worcestershire sauce. Return to heat and bring to a boil, stirring constantly. Cook 1 minute longer. Stir in parsley, spoon sauce over fish. Top with mashed potatoes. Sprinkle with paprika. Bake in a hot oven (400°F.) for 30–35 minutes, or until potatoes are lightly browned and edges are bubbly. Makes 6 servings.

Breakfast Sausage Apple Pie

Meat for dessert? Pie for breakfast? Why not? New Englanders often served mince-meat tarts for a main course at suppertime, apple pie with pork for breakfast. Back in Depression days this pie made a great inexpensive breakfast, lunch or supper dish. It still does. From Oscar Mayer's test kitchen.

1 lb. Oscar Mayer Pork Sausage Links
1 11-oz. package pie crust mix
1 1 lb. 4-oz. can apple pie filling
1 cup (4 oz.) shredded processed American cheese
½ cup brown sugar, firmly packed

Cook pork sausage links; drain on paper towel. Meanwhile, use ½ package pie crust mix to prepare single pastry for 9-inch pie pan. Line pan with pastry; flute edge and prick bottom and sides with fork. Bake 10 minutes in 375°F. oven. Pour pie filling into partially baked shell; arrange cooked sausage, spoke fashion, on pie filling; sprinkle with shredded cheese. For topping, combine brown sugar with remaining pie crust mix; sprinkle over pie. Return to oven and bake 25–35 minutes or until crust is golden brown. Serve warm. Makes 6 servings.

Italian Zucchini Crescent Pie

A new $40,000 Grand Prize Pillsbury Bake-Off® winner; a beautifully seasoned vegetable-and-cheese main course dish that received its just due. You'll love it.

4 cups thinly sliced, unpeeled zucchini
1 cup coarsely chopped onion
¼ cup margarine or butter
½ cup chopped parsley or 2 Tbs. parsley flakes
½ tsp. salt
½ tsp. pepper
¼ tsp. garlic powder
¼ tsp. basil leaves
¼ tsp. oregano leaves
2 eggs, well beaten
8 oz. (2 cups) shredded natural Muenster or Mozzarella cheese
8 oz. can Pillsbury Refrigerated Quick Crescent Dinner Rolls
2 tsp. Dijon or prepared mustard

Heat oven to 375°F. In 10-inch skillet, cook zucchini and onion in margarine until tender, about 10 minutes. Stir in parsley and seasonings. In large bowl, blend eggs and cheese. Stir in vegetable mixture. Separate dough into 8 triangles. Place in ungreased 11-inch quiche, or 10-inch pie pan or 12 × 8-inch baking dish; press over bottom and up sides to form crust. Spread crust with mustard. Pour vegetable mixture evenly into crust. Bake at 375°F. for 18–20 minutes or until knife inserted near center comes out clean. (If crust becomes too brown, cover with foil during last 10 minutes of baking.) Let stand 10 minutes before serving. Cut into wedges. To reheat: cover loosely with foil, heat at 375°F. for 12–15 minutes.

Ham Corn Bread Pie

If you grew up in Texas as I did, you'll remember corn bread pies. Served like today's pizza, they were a favorite teenage party fare. This updated version was dreamed up by the good cooks at Planters Peanut Oil Test Kitchens.

2 Tbs. Fleischmann's Margarine
1 cup onion slices
1 large clove garlic, minced
¼ tsp. chili powder
½ cup Planters Cocktail Peanuts, chopped
Generous dash pepper
1 10-oz. package corn bread mix
1 egg
½ cup milk
½ lb. sliced boiled ham
3 slices pasteurized processed American cheese, cut in half
2 pimiento-stuffed olives, sliced

Melt Fleishmann's Margarine in a large skillet. Add onions, garlic and chili powder. Cook over medium heat, stirring occasionally, until onions are tender. Remove from heat, stir in Planters Cocktail Peanuts and pepper. Prepare corn bread mix according to package directions, using egg and milk. Spread on bottom of 12-inch pizza pan. Arrange ham on corn bread; top with onion mixture. Bake in hot oven (425°F.) 10 minutes. Top with cheese. Bake 5 minutes longer, or until cheese is melted. Garnish with olive slices. Makes 6–8 servings.

Vegetable Nut Pie

When you want a hearty but meatless dish, try this vegetable nut pie. Hot from the oven it's positively superb. A smash-hit recipe ever since it first appeared in a Planters® cookbook.

- 1 9-inch pastry shell, unbaked
- 2 Tbs. Blue Bonnet® Margarine
- 1 cup chopped onion
- ½ cup chopped red bell pepper
- 4 cups coarsely chopped fresh spinach
- ¾ cup chopped Planters® Pecan Pieces or Planters® Pecan Chips
- 1¼ cups grated Swiss cheese
- 1¼ cups half-and-half
- 3 eggs
- ¾ tsp. salt
- ⅛ tsp. ground black pepper

Prebake pastry shell at 425°F. for 10 minutes. Melt Blue Bonnet® Margarine in a large skillet over medium heat. Add onion and red pepper; sauté until nearly tender. Stir in spinach and sauté until wilted. Sprinkle Planters® Pecan Pieces or Planters® Pecan Chips and cheese in bottom of pastry shell; spread spinach mixture over cheese layer. Beat together half-and-half, eggs, salt and pepper; pour into pie shell. Bake at 350°F. for 35 minutes, or until puffy and a knife inserted in center comes out clean. Do not overbake. Slice and serve hot. Makes 1 pie.

3.
Side Dishes: Vegetables, Potatoes, Beans, Pasta and Such

Do you know that for years I regarded fried tomatoes as in a league with spun sugar? Both were impossible for me to master and while the need was never pressing to concoct those spun-sugar fairy-tale desserts I had seen only in illustrations, last summer's bountiful harvest of tomatoes demanded I do something with all those red beauties. I determined to master fried tomatoes. After several soggy failures I had just about given up when I found a batch of recipes from the Pet Milk Company. Among them, oh happy day, was a recipe for fried tomatoes—and, wonder of wonders, it worked! These were the crispy-surfaced, luscious fried tomatoes of my dreams. I can tell you, I fried tomatoes just about every day until the first frost ended my tomato orgy. I even served them for Sunday breakfast, they were that good. Now I don't say you can get the same results with "store-bought" tomatoes but you can glorify even a lesser tomato with the Pet recipe. If ever I doubted that those home economists who test all the recipes for our food companies really know their business, I don't now. Their recipes *work!* That may sound very simple, but I've been cooking a long time and many a respected recipe doesn't work. I guess that's why I have enjoyed putting this book together. Every recipe I've tried has been a resounding success, and when you add the imagination and creativity that have gone into each one to its sure-fire accuracy—well now, that's a recipe.

Good side dishes are great budget stretchers, you know. Try Creamy Seasoned Noodles the next time you serve pot roast, or Corn 'n Pepper Fritters with oven-fried chicken. Campbell's Green Bean Bake is a great casserole to complement a thrifty meat loaf, and if you would add an elegant touch to a dinner party, try the easy Blender Hollandaise Sauce over steamed broccoli or asparagus.

I hope you will try all the side dishes here, simple or not so simple. You'll find they add great enjoyment and variety to every meal and some, such as Cheese-Stuffed Eggplant, are meals in themselves. Good eating, every one of them!

"PET" VEGETABLES

In 1932 the Pet Milk Company published their "Gold Cookbook." In those days, deep in the Great Depression, every cook was economy-minded, and recipes had to be thrifty as well as good. Here, from that cookbook of almost fifty years ago, are four all-time favorite ways with vegetables, as economical as they are great-tasting.

Fried Tomatoes (Batter Dipped Tomatoes)

- 4 medium tomatoes, half ripe
- ½ cup all-purpose flour
- 2½ tsps. salt
- 2½ tsps. sugar
- ¼ tsp. pepper
- ¾ cup Pet Evaporated Milk
- Oil for frying

Wash tomatoes, but do not peel. Cut into ¾-inch slices. Place on paper towels to drain. Combine flour, salt, sugar and pepper. Dust tomatoes in flour mixture on both sides. Add evaporated milk to remaining flour mixture to make a thick batter. Dip floured tomatoes in batter. Fry in hot oil ½-inch deep until golden brown on both sides. Makes 6 servings.

Creamed Spinach

Evaporated milk gives a mild flavor.

- 1 lb. fresh spinach
- 2 Tbs. all-purpose flour
- ½ cup Pet Evaporated Milk
- ¼ tsp. salt
- Few grains pepper

Wash spinach thoroughly. Shake water out of leaves. Tear leaves into bite-size pieces. Place in saucepan. Cover. Cook over low heat for 8 minutes or until tender. The water that clings to the leaves is enough to cook the spinach. Drain. Sprinkle flour over spinach. Stir to evenly coat leaves. Add evaporated milk, salt and pepper. Heat until sauce thickens. Makes 4 servings, ¼ cup each.

Carrots in Onion Sauce

¼ cup finely chopped onion
2 Tbs. oil
2 cups diced carrots, cooked and drained
⅓ cup Pet Evaporated Milk
¼ tsp. salt
Few grains pepper

Cook onion in hot oil over medium heat until limp. Stir in carrots, evaporate milk, salt, and pepper. Cook over low heat stirring gently until sauce coats the carrots and is slightly thickened. Serve hot. Makes 4 servings, ½ cup each.

Corn Pudding

2 cans (8¾ ounces each) corn
2 eggs, slightly beaten
¾ cup Pet Evaporated Milk
2 Tbs. margarine or butter, melted
1 tsp. salt
⅛ tsp. pepper

Mix well all ingredients. Pour into a greased 1½-quart baking dish. Bake at 350°F. for 45 minutes, until firm. Makes 6 servings, ½ cup each.

The Planters Peanut Oil cooks created these vegetable recipes. Each one is Italian-inspired. They will add great taste and good eating to any lunch, supper or dinner.

Broccoli Sauté

- 2 lbs. fresh broccoli
- ½ cup water
- ¼ cup Planters Peanut Oil
- 2 cloves garlic, minced
- 1 tsp. salt
- ⅛ tsp. pepper

Wash broccoli. Split ends of large stalks lengthwise into halves or quarters, depending on size. Place in large skillet. Sprinkle with water, Planters Peanut Oil, garlic, salt and pepper. Cover tightly; cook over very low heat 20 to 30 minutes, or until stalks are tender. Turn broccoli several times during cooking. Makes 4 servings.

Baked Eggplant Napoli

- ½ cup chopped onion
- 2 Tbs. Planters Peanut Oil
- 1 can (10½ ounces) tomato purée
- ⅔ cup water
- 1½ tsps. salt
- 1 tsp. oregano leaves
- Dash pepper
- 1 medium eggplant, peeled and thinly sliced
- 2 cups grated sharp Cheddar cheese

In a skillet sauté chopped onions in Planters Peanut Oil. Add tomato purée, water, salt, oregano and pepper. Bring to a boil and simmer for 15 minutes.

In a greased 2-quart baking dish alternate layers of sliced eggplant, tomato sauce and 1 cup grated cheese, starting with layer of eggplant and ending with layer of tomato sauce.

Bake in moderate oven (350°F.) for 1 hour. A few minutes before removing from oven, sprinkle remaining 1 cup grated cheese over top and continue heating until cheese melts. Makes 6 to 8 servings.

Zucchini Parmesan

¼ cup Planters Peanut Oil
8 medium zucchini, thinly sliced
⅔ cup coarsely chopped onion
2 Tbs. chopped parsley
1 large clove garlic, crushed or minced
1 Tbs. salt
¼ tsp. pepper
¼ tsp. oregano leaves
¼ tsp. rosemary leaves
4 cups peeled chopped tomatoes
½ cup grated Parmesan cheese

Heat Planters Peanut Oil in large skillet. Add zucchini, onion, parsley, garlic, salt, pepper, oregano and rosemary. Sauté mixture over medium heat, stirring often, until zucchini is tender, about 20 minutes. Toss in tomatoes and continue to sauté until tomatoes are thoroughly heated, about 5 minutes. Turn mixture into a serving dish; sprinkle with Parmesan cheese. Makes 8 to 10 servings.

Orange-Glazed Beets

This recipe has been around since the Twenties, and each time Stokely takes it off their Finest Cut Beets label, the outcry from customers makes them put it right back on again.

1 can (1 lb.) Cut Beets
1 Tbs. butter or margarine
2 tsps. flour
2 Tbs. brown sugar
½ cup orange juice

Heat beets in their own liquid. In small saucepan, melt butter. Remove from heat; add flour, brown sugar and orange juice. Return to heat, stirring constantly until thickened. Drain beets; add sauce to beets. Makes 4 to 5 servings.

Orange Carrots

Remember Orange-Glazed Carrots? I'll bet your mother made them from this recipe first printed in a Sunkist advertisement a generation ago.

- 1 lb. carrots
- ¾ cup water
- ¾ tsp. salt
- ½ tsp. fresh grated orange peel
- 1 Sunkist orange
- 2 Tbs. margarine or butter
- 2 to 3 Tbs. of your favorite syrup (cane, molasses, honey, pancake or brown sugar)

Wash and peel, scrub or scrape carrots. Slice crosswise into rounds or lengthwise into sticks. Bring water and salt to a boil in saucepan. Add carrots and cover pan. Cook over medium heat for 10 to 20 minutes, until tender. Drain well. Meanwhile grate ½ tsp. peel from orange. Peel orange and cut into bite-size pieces. Add orange pieces and peel, margarine and syrup to drained carrots. Place over low heat and stir gently until margarine is melted and oranges are heated. Serve at once. Makes 6 servings.

Note: For different flavor, leave out the syrup and add 1 to 2 Tbs. finely chopped green onions or chives.

Green Bean Bake

In the Sixties Campbell's kitchens introduced this all-time favorite Green Bean Casserole; it's an inspired combination of creamy sauce, green beans and crispy onion rings.

- 1 10¾-ounce can Campbell's Condensed Cream of Mushroom Soup
- ½ cup milk
- 1 tsp. soy sauce
- Dash of pepper
- 2 packages (9 ounces each) frozen green beans, cooked and drained
- 1 can (3½ ounces) French® fried onions

In 1½-quart casserole, stir soup, milk, soy, and pepper until smooth; mix in green beans and ½ can onions. Bake at 350°F. for 25 minutes; stir. Top with remaining onions. Bake 5 minutes more. Makes about 4 cups.

Blender Hollandaise Sauce

Sunkist introduced this fool-proof Hollandaise Sauce several years ago; it's guaranteed not to curdle and it's a sure-fire way to transform steamed broccoli, asparagus or grilled tomatoes into an epicurean dish.

- ½ cup butter or margarine (1 stick)
- 4 egg yolks
- 2–3 Tbs. fresh squeezed lemon juice
- ¼ tsp. salt
- Dash of pepper

Heat butter or margarine until bubbly. Meanwhile, place egg yolks, fresh lemon juice, salt and pepper in electric blender. Turn blender on and off quickly. Then turn to high speed and slowly add bubbly butter in a very thin but steady stream. Serve immediately over broccoli, asparagus, or grilled tomatoes. Also good on fish or for Eggs Benedict. Makes about 1 cup.

Corn 'N' Pepper Fritters

Planters Peanut Oil ran this recipe in an ad a few seasons back and I tried it then. I had to include it here for you because it's one of the best of its kind.

- 1 egg
- ½ cup milk
- 1 can (12 ounces) golden whole kernel corn with sweet peppers, undrained
- 1 Tbs. Planters Peanut Oil
- 1½ cups unsifted flour
- 1 Tbs. baking powder
- 1 tsp. salt
- Dash pepper
- Planters Peanut Oil

Beat egg in large bowl. Stir in milk, corn and 1 Tbs. Planters Peanut Oil. Add and beat in flour, baking powder, salt and pepper.

Drop by tablespoonfuls into deep or shallow hot (375°F.) Planters Peanut Oil. Fry until golden brown, 2 to 3 minutes on each side. Drain on paper towels. Serve hot. If desired, serve with syrup. Makes about 24 fritters.

Note: I like them best fried in deep oil. I think you will too.

Sweet Sour Shellie Beans

Do you know what Shellie Beans are? I didn't until I found this recipe on the Stokely Shellie Bean can. It's a great dish to serve with pork.

- 2 strips bacon
- ⅓ cup onion, finely diced
- 1 1-lb. can Shellie Beans
- 1 Tbs. sugar
- ⅛ tsp. salt
- Few grains pepper
- 2 Tbs. white distilled vinegar

Cut bacon in ½-inch pieces. Brown lightly with diced onion. Add liquid drained from Shellie Beans. Cook down to about

½ cupful. Add remaining ingredients and Shellie Beans. Heat and serve. Makes 4 servings.

Apple Kraut Bavarian

What a lovely supper dish, dreamed up for Stokely's Sauerkraut label a few years ago.

1 10-ounce package brown and serve sausage links
1 1-lb. can Stokely's Finest Bavarian Style Sauerkraut, drained
1 1 lb., 1-ounce can Stokely's Finest Applesauce

In large skillet, brown sausage links. Add remaining ingredients to skillet and heat to serving temperature. Delicious with mashed potatoes. Makes 4 servings.

Southern Cheese-Stuffed Eggplant

The lovely thing about this delicious recipe from Armour's Miss Wisconsin Cheddar Cheese package is that it can serve nicely as an extra good luncheon or supper main dish. It's quick and easy too!

2 eggplants, cut in half lengthwise
½ cup chopped onion
½ cup chopped green pepper
½ cup butter or margarine
2 tomatoes, peeled, chopped
1 tsp. salt
½ tsp. pepper
1 8-ounce package Medium Sharp Cheddar Cheese, shredded
1½ cups bread crumbs

Heat oven to 350°F. Scoop out interior of eggplants, leaving ¼-inch shell. Cube scooped-out interior; reserve. In large fry pan, cook onion and green pepper in ¼ cup butter or margarine on medium-low heat 5 minutes. Add tomatoes, salt, pepper and reserved cubed eggplant; cook 5 minutes. Drain liquid from vegetables. Stir in cheese and ½ cup bread crumbs. Spoon mixture into eggplant shells; place in greased 13 × 9-inch baking dish. Toss remaining bread crumbs with ¼ cup melted butter or margarine; sprinkle on top of stuffed eggplants. Bake at 350°F. for 30 minutes. Makes 8 servings.

Spaghetti With Zucchini Sauce

Vegetables and pasta that can solo as a main dish or complement sliced cold meat for a delicious, easy dinner. From Mueller's Spaghetti package.

- 1 medium onion, sliced
- ¼ cup olive oil
- 2 medium zucchini, sliced (about 6 cups)
- 3 cups diced tomatoes
- ½ tsp. salt
- 1 bay leaf
- ¼ tsp. pepper
- ¼ tsp. basil leaves
- ¼ tsp. oregano leaves
- 8 ounces Mueller's Spaghetti
- Grated Parmesan cheese

In large skillet or pot, sauté onion in hot oil until crisp-tender. Add zucchini, tomatoes, salt, bay leaf, pepper, basil and oregano. Simmer covered for 15 minutes; uncover and simmer 10 minutes longer. Discard bay leaf. Meanwhile, cook spaghetti as directed on package; drain. Serve spaghetti topped with zucchini sauce and grated Parmesan cheese. Makes 4 to 6 servings.

Grant Street Pilaf

A perfect side dish for chicken, lamb or pork from the Dole® Pineapple Chunks can.

- 1 20 ounce can Dole® Pineapple Chunks, in syrup
- 2 cups water
- 1 cup long-grain brown rice
- ½ tsp. rosemary
- 2 Tbs. butter
- 2 Tbs. soy sauce
- 1 tsp. grated fresh ginger root
- 2 Tbs. chopped green onion
- ¼ cup toasted slivered almonds

Drain pineapple syrup into saucepan. Add water and bring to boil. Stir in rice and rosemary. Cover and simmer 35 to 45 minutes, until rice is tender and liquid is absorbed. Mix in pineapple chunks and remaining ingredients and heat through. Makes 4 to 6 servings.

Mushroom Pilaf

This delicious side dish was the star of a recent Fleischmann's Margarine advertisement. It's a great accompaniment to chicken or lamb.

- 2 cups sliced mushrooms
- ½ cup chopped onion
- 2 cloves garlic, crushed
- 2 Tbs. chopped parsley
- 1 tsp. basil leaves, crushed
- ⅛ tsp. pepper
- 2 Tbs. Fleischmann's Margarine
- ⅔ cup uncooked converted rice
- 1⅓ cups water
- ⅓ cup chopped toasted blanced almonds

Sauté mushrooms, onion, garlic, parsley, basil and pepper in margarine about 5 minutes, stirring frequently. Stir in rice and water. Bring to a boil over high heat. Cover; reduce heat and simmer until liquid is absorbed and rice is tender, about 25 minutes. Stir in almonds. Makes 7 servings.

Campbell's Scalloped Potatoes

You'll never be disappointed by curdled scalloped potatoes when you use this never-fail Campbell's recipe.

- 1 10¾-ounce can Campbell's Condensed Cream of Celery or Mushroom Soup
- ⅓ to ½ cup milk
- ¼ cup chopped parsley
- Dash pepper
- 4 cups thinly sliced potatoes
- 1 small onion, thinly sliced
- 1 Tbs. butter or margarine
- Dash paprika

Combine soup, milk, parsley and pepper. In 1½-quart casserole, arrange alternate layers of potatoes, onion and sauce. Dot top with butter; sprinkle with paprika. Cover; bake at 375°F. for 1 hour. Uncover; bake 15 minutes more or until potatoes are done. Makes about 3½ cups.

Campfire Potatoes

The Purity Cheese Company tells us that these Campfire Potatoes have been a consumer favorite ever since the recipe first appeared on their Smokey Sharp cheese package a decade ago.

- ½ cup chopped onion
- 2 Tbs. butter
- 1 Tbs. flour
- ½ tsp. salt
- ⅛ tsp. pepper
- 1 cup (4 ounces) shredded Hoffman's Smokey Sharp
- ¾ cup milk
- 1 12-ounce package frozen shredded hash brown potatoes

Sauté onions in butter or margarine. Place in shallow one-quart baking dish or small skillet, brushed with butter. Add flour, salt and pepper. Mix well. Add cheese. Pour milk over cheese. Top with frozen potatoes. Cover. Bake at 350°F. for 30 to 35 minutes, or until potatoes are completely thawed. Mix well. Return to oven uncovered and bake 15 to 20 minutes, or until golden brown. Makes 4 servings.

Candied Sweet Potatoes

Southerners unite! This is the real thing—this recipe for sweet potatoes has remained a popular standby on the Karo Dark Corn Syrup label for years.

- 1 cup Karo Dark Corn Syrup
- ½ cup firmly packed dark brown sugar
- 2 Tbs. corn oil margarine
- 12 medium sweet potatoes, cooked, peeled, halved lengthwise

In small saucepan, heat corn syrup, brown sugar and margarine to boiling; reduce heat and simmer 5 minutes. Pour ½ cup of the syrup into 13 × 9 × 2-inch baking dish. Arrange potatoes, overlapping if necessary, in syrup. Top with remaining syrup. Bake in 350°F. oven, basting often, for 20 minutes, until well glazed. Makes 12 servings.

Creamy Seasoned Noodles

Here's an easy way to cook noodles using Good Season's Italian Salad Dressing Mix.

- 1 8-ounce package wide egg noodles or spaghetti
- 1 envelope Good Season's Italian Salad Dressing Mix
- ½ cup heavy cream or evaporated milk
- ¼ cup butter or margarine
- ¼ cup grated Parmesan cheese
- Chopped parsley, optional

Cook noodles as directed on package; drain well. Add remaining ingredients and toss lightly to blend thoroughly. Sprinkle with chopped parsley, if desired. Makes 4 cups or 8 servings.

Sautéed Wheatena

This unusual recipe is from the Wheatena box. Try it with lamb; it's delicious.

- 1 cup Wheatena
- 1 egg, beaten
- 1 tsp. salt
- ¼ cup butter or margarine
- 1 medium onion, diced
- 2 cups water

Combine Wheatena, egg and salt. In skillet, melt butter; sauté onion until golden. Add Wheatena mixture and water; mix well. Bring to boil; cover and cook over low heat until light in color, stirring occasionally. Cook about 10 to 12 minutes, until desired thickness. Makes about 5 to 6 servings.

Fried Wheatena

Down South we used to fry grits much like this. Try this variation without syrup as an accompaniment to roast chicken or duck.

- 1 cup Wheatena
- 3½ cups water
- 1 tsp. salt

Combine Wheatena, water and salt in large saucepan. Bring to rolling boil. Cook 5 minutes or until thick. Remove from heat; cool about 5 minutes. Pour into 9 × 5 × 3-inch loaf pan. Cover; chill until firm. Unmold; cut into 1-inch slices. Sauté, turning to brown on both sides. Serve hot with brown sugar or maple syrup. Makes 9 1-inch slices.

Note: Left-over Wheatena may also be used this way.

Boston Baked Beans

This genuine, old-time, real Baked Bean recipe is from the Grandma's Molasses label, where it was a fixture for years. This is the real thing, no instant nonsense allowed, so get out the bean pot, make up a batch of coleslaw and invite your friends for a Saturday-night feast.

- 1 lb. (2 cups) dried pea, marrow, Great Northern or navy beans
- 2 quarts water
- 1 onion, chopped
- ¼ lb. salt pork
- ¾ cup Grandma's Unsulphured Molasses
- 1 tsp. salt
- 1 tsp. dry mustard

Rinse beans in cold water and drain. Place in large saucepan and add water. Bring to a boil and boil for 2 minutes. Remove from heat, cover loosely and let stand for 1 hour. Return to heat and bring to a boil; cover and simmer gently over low heat for 1 hour, until beans are tender. Drain beans and reserve liquid. Turn beans into 2½-quart bean pot or casserole; add onion and mix lightly. Cut through surface of salt pork every ½ inch, making cuts about 1 inch deep. Bury pork in beans. Mix 2 cups reserved bean liquid with molasses, salt and dry mustard; pour over beans. Cover and bake in 300°F. oven for 5 to 6 hours. Check beans about once an hour and add additional bean liquid or water if the beans become dry; at the beginning of the cooking time the beans should be covered with liquid, and at the end of cooking the beans should be very moist and coated with syrupy liquid. Makes 8 servings.

Charleston Perloo with Mushrooms

What's the difference between Pilafs, Pilaus and Perloos? Down in Texas at the Uncle Ben's® Rice test kitchens they say there's no basic difference; a classic Pilaf, which calls for sautéing the rice and simmering in broth with regionally favorite foods and seasonings, is known by a variety of names in different countries. This very popular one was developed about 10 years ago from an old Charleston, South Carolina, recipe.

½ pound fresh mushrooms, sliced
1 clove garlic
1 Tbs. olive or vegetable oil
2 Tbs. butter or margarine
1 cup thinly sliced onion
1 cup Uncle Ben's® Converted Brand Rice
2¼ cups chicken broth
¼ cup dry white wine
1½ tsps. salt
¼ tsp. white pepper
¼ cup freshly grated Parmesan cheese
2 Tbs. chopped parsley

Sauté mushrooms and garlic in olive oil in 10-inch skillet until mushrooms are tender, but not brown. Remove and reserve mushrooms; discard garlic. Add butter to skillet. Sauté onion until tender. Add rice; cook, stirring constantly, 5 minutes. Add chicken broth, mushrooms, wine, salt and pepper. Bring to boil; reduce heat. Cover tightly and simmer 20 minutes. Remove from heat. Stir in cheese and parsley. Let stand, covered, until all liquid is absorbed, about 5 minutes. Makes 6 servings.

Thin and Crispy French® Fries

French® did I say? Perhaps by origin yes, but in this country no one vegetable is more universally loved than all-American crispy fries. Here's how to make the real thing. It's the famous Crisco recipe—on Crisco's label since 1938.

Use one or two medium-size potatoes per serving. Using knife or French-fry cutter, cut peeled potatoes into ¼-inch strips. Rinse or soak in cold water. Start heating enough Crisco Shortening to fill a 3-quart saucepan half full, or a deep fryer within ½ inch of the fill mark. Dry potato strips thoroughly on paper towel.

For extra quick French® fries: Heat deep Crisco Shortening to 365°F. For electric deep fryer, follow manufacturer's directions for amount of potato strips to fry at one time. For saucepan, cook 2–3 cups of potato strips at one time, adding slowly. Cook until potatoes are tender and lightly browned, about 10–15 minutes. Drain potatoes on paper towel. While frying remaining potatoes, keep fried ones warm in oven set at low temperature. Salt or season as desired. If desired, frozen French® fried potatoes can be used in place of fresh potatoes. For best results, fry about 10–15 minutes in Crisco Shortening using the above directions.

For extra crispy French® fries (for fresh potatoes only): Fry potatoes *first* time at 325°F. for about 3 minutes. Remove and drain on paper towel. Cool at least 15 minutes at room temperature. If desired, cool for up to 3 hours. To serve, re-heat Crisco to 365°F. and fry potato strips a *second* time for 6–8 minutes or until golden brown. Drain on paper towel.

Cheese 'n' Cream Potatoes

Appi Watkins gives the best parties in town; her buffets are famous and they always include her special potato casserole. It took me years to discover the recipe came from Betty Crocker.

- 1 package Betty Crocker® Sour Cream 'n' Chive Potatoes
- 2 cups milk
- 3 eggs
- ½ tsp. salt
- ¼ tsp. pepper
- 1 cup shredded Mozzarella cheese (about 4 oz.)

Heat oven to 350°F. Grease 1½-quart round casserole. Cover potatoes with boiling water in small bowl. Let stand uncovered 10 minutes; drain thoroughly. Beat milk and eggs with hand beater. Mix all ingredients in casserole.

Bake uncovered until potatoes are tender and top is golden brown, 45–50 minutes. Makes 6 servings.

Pennsylvania Dutch Potato Bake

At the Campbell test kitchens they tell me this is a very popular dish for buffet parties. Looks pretty and tastes grand, hot or at room temperature.

6 slices bacon
1 10¾-oz. can Campbell's Condensed Chicken Broth
2 Tbs. flour
¼ cup vinegar
2 Tbs. brown sugar
2 Tbs. diced pimiento
¼ cup diagonally sliced green onions
½ tsp. celery salt
¼ tsp. hot pepper sauce
6 cups cooked sliced potatoes

In skillet, cook bacon until crisp; remove. Pour off all but ¼ cup drippings. Gradually blend broth into flour until smooth; slowly stir into drippings. Add remaining ingredients except potatoes. Cook, stirring until thickened. In 1½-quart shallow baking dish (10 × 6 × 2 inches) arrange potatoes; pour broth mixture over potatoes. Cover; bake at 400°F. for 30 minutes. Garnish with bacon. Makes about 6 cups.

Pan-Fried Potatoes

Some of the best things you can eat are childishly simple to prepare—if you know how. You'll find the "know-how" for perfect pan-fried potatoes on the Crisco shortening label; but it's such a worthwhile thing to know I've included it here.

3 medium potatoes
Salt and pepper
⅓ cup Crisco

Wash and peel the potatoes. Cut potatoes in ⅛-inch slices. Season with salt and pepper. In a covered skillet, fry potatoes in hot Crisco over medium heat for 10 minutes. Turn potatoes carefully. Cook, uncovered, about 10 minutes longer, loosening slices of potatoes occasionally and browning all sides. Makes 4 servings.

Herbed Potatoes: Prepare pan-fried potatoes as above. The last 5 minutes of cooking, sprinkle the fried potatoes with 2 Tbs. finely chopped celery, 2 Tbs. snipped fresh parsley, 2 Tbs. finely chopped onion, and ½ tsp. dried oregano, crushed. Sprinkle potatoes with salt and pepper to taste. Makes 4 servings.

Twice-Baked Potatoes

I love them—so do just about another million Americans who found the recipe, as I did, on the Campbell Cheddar Cheese Soup label.

8 medium baking potatoes
2 Tbs. butter or margarine
¼ tsp. salt
1 can Campbell's Cheddar Cheese Soup
1 Tbs. chopped dried chives

Bake potatoes until done. Cut potatoes in half lengthwise; scoop out insides leaving a thin shell. With electric mixer, mash potatoes with butter and salt. Gradually add soup and chives; beat until light and fluffy. Spoon into shells. Sprinkle with paprika. Bake in 2½-quart shallow baking dish (13 × 9 × 2 inches) at 450°F. for 15 minutes or until hot. Makes 8 servings.

Freckle-Faced 'Taters

I've been told that salt and butter are the perfect topping for potatoes, but melted butter plus grated cheese and bread crumbs seasoned not only with salt but also with Tabasco and Worcestershire is something to keep in mind.

2 large potatoes, baked
½ cup grated Cheddar cheese
4 Tbs. butter or margarine
2 Tbs. milk
¼ tsp. Tabasco Pepper Sauce
⅛ tsp. salt
1 tsp. Worcestershire sauce
½ cup crushed croutons or bread crumbs

Quarter hot potatoes lengthwise and place in a bake-and-serve dish. Sprinkle grated cheese over potatoes. Melt butter in a skillet; add remaining ingredients, stirring until crushed croutons are moist. Crumble mixture over potatoes and place under broiler until cheese has browned. Makes 4 servings.

Spanish Rice

At Riviana Rice Company they tell me they put this recipe on the back of their box almost thirty years ago "just to

show potatoes they weren't so indispensable after all." I guess they did all right. It's now a Southern classic.

3 Tbs. bacon drippings
1 cup uncooked Riviana Rice
¾ cup chopped onion
½ cup chopped green pepper
½ cup chopped celery
1 14-oz. can stewed tomatoes
1 cup water
1½ tsps. salt
1 tsp. chili powder

Heat 2 Tbs. fat in large skillet; add rice. Brown lightly, stirring frequently. Add remaining 1 Tbs. fat, onion, green pepper and celery; cook until soft. Add remaining ingredients, cover pan tightly, and simmer for 20–30 minutes. If rice is then not sufficiently tender, add a little more water, cover, continue to cook until soft. Makes 6 servings (about ½ cup each).

Pilaf

Campbell put this Pilaf recipe on their beef broth can some fifteen years ago, and it's made millions of American meals "special" ever since.

½ cup fine noodles, broken in pieces
2 Tbs. butter or margarine
1 can Campbell's Beef Broth
⅓ cup water
½ cup raw long grain rice

In saucepan, brown noodles in butter; stir often. Add remaining ingredients. Bring to a boil; reduce heat. Cover; simmer 20–25 minutes, or until liquid is absorbed. Makes about 2½ cups.

Vegetables Sicily

A Parkay® Margarine vegetable recipe which has been used many times in my kitchen and never fails to please, no matter who's been invited to supper.

3 cups zucchini slices
1 medium onion, sliced
1 tsp. oregano leaves, crushed
½ tsp. salt
¼ tsp. pepper
⅓ cup Parkay® Margarine
1 medium tomato, cut into wedges

Sauté zucchini, onion, and seasoning in margarine. Add tomato; cook 5 minutes or until vegetables are tender. Makes 4–6 servings.

French-Style Vegetable Stew

From Heinz® the most marvelous vegetable dish. It originated in France, but it's right at home on American tables.

1 cup chopped onions
2 cloves garlic, minced
2 small zucchini, thinly sliced
1 medium green pepper, cut into thin strips
½ cup olive or salad oil
1 medium eggplant, pared, cut into strips (2 × ½-inch)
3 Tbs. flour
4 medium tomatoes, peeled, cut into eighths
¼ cup Heinz® Tomato Ketchup
1 Tbs. salt
1 tsp. Heinz® Apple Cider Vinegar
½ tsp. crushed oregano leaves
¼ tsp. pepper

In Dutch oven, sauté first four ingredients in oil until onion is transparent. Coat eggplant with flour; add with tomatoes to sautéed vegetables. Combine ketchup and remaining ingredients; pour over vegetables. Cover; simmer 30–35 minutes; stir occasionally, or until vegetables are tender. Makes 8–10 servings (about 7 cups).

NOTE: Zucchini may be peeled if skin is tough.

Sour Creamed Green Beans

You asked for that "other" green bean recipe, the one with sour cream. Well, there are dozens of variations on this theme, but here's one of the best from the Parkay® Margarine test kitchens.

1 onion, thinly sliced
Parkay® margarine
2 10-oz. packages frozen green beans, thawed, drained
1 cup dairy sour cream
¼ cup flour
1½ tsps. salt
¼ tsp. pepper
1 cup (4 oz.) shredded Kraft® sharp natural Cheddar cheese
1 cup soft bread crumbs

Sauté onion in ¼ cup margarine. Add to combined beans, sour cream, flour and seasonings; mix lightly. Pour into greased 1½-quart casserole. Sprinkle with cheese; top with crumbs tossed with ¼ cup melted margarine. Bake at 350°F. 25 minutes. Makes 4–6 servings.

Green Beans Polonaise

Is there anything elegant that can be done with a can of green beans? The cooks at Del Monte tell me there most certainly is and this is it.

1 16-oz. can Del Monte Whole or Cut Green Beans
3 Tbs. butter
1 clove garlic
2 Tbs. instant minced onion
3 Tbs. fine dry bread crumbs
Few drops lemon juice

In oven-proof dish, heat green beans in 300°F. oven. Melt butter over low heat. Set aside until milk solids have settled to bottom. Skim off clarified butter discarding solids. Rub skillet with garlic. Heat clarified butter until browned. Sauté onion and add bread crumbs and lemon juice. Cook until browned, being careful not to burn crumbs. Drain beans, keep warm. Top with buttered bread crumbs. Makes four servings.

Golden Capped Baked Tomatoes

Sun-ripened, home-grown tomatoes and this recipe from the R. T. French® Company can make your reputation next summer as the best cook in town.

6 medium-size tomatoes
Salt and pepper to taste
¼ cup mayonnaise
1 Tbs. French's® Prepared Mustard
1 tsp. French's® Minced Onion
½ tsp. sugar
2 Tbs. fine dry bread crumbs

Cut each tomato in half. Place cut side up in a shallow baking dish; sprinkle cut surface with salt and pepper. Combine the remaining ingredients. Spoon a portion on top of each tomato; spread to cover cut surface.* Bake in 400°F. oven 15 minutes

* Can be prepared in advance to this point. Refrigerate until ready to begin baking. Baking time may need to be increased slightly.

or until topping is lightly puffed and tomatoes are hot. Makes 6 servings.

Tomato Sour Cream Casserole

Daisy Doolin, mother of Elmer Doolin (the man who invented Fritos® Corn Chips), came up with this super recipe years ago. She made it with Fritos® Corn Chips. Now it's even zippier with Doritos® Tortilla Chips. Easy and filling, it's a great inexpensive dish.

- 1 medium onion, chopped
- 2 Tbs. salad oil
- 1 1-lb. 12-oz. can tomatoes
- 1 package Mexican style "sloppy joe" seasoning mix
- 1 4-oz. can green chilies, chopped
- 1 5½-oz. package Doritos® Nacho Cheese Tortilla Chips, slightly crushed
- ¾ pound Monterey Jack cheese, grated
- 1 cup sour cream
- ½ cup grated Cheddar cheese

Sauté onion in oil; add tomatoes, seasoning mix and green chilies. Simmer, uncovered, 10–15 minutes. In greased, deep 2-quart casserole, layer ingredients in the following order: sauce, crushed Doritos® Tortilla Chips, Monterey Jack cheese, sauce, Monterey Jack cheese. Top with sour cream. Bake at 325°F. for 30 minutes. Sprinkle with Cheddar cheese; bake 10 minutes longer. Makes 6–8 servings.

Elegant Puffed Broccoli

An original from Hellmann's® Best Foods who tell me it was one of the first recipes devised in their test kitchens to use this puffy broiled topping.

2 bunches broccoli, cut into spears or 2 10-oz. packages frozen broccoli spears, cooked, drained
2 egg whites, at room temperature
¼ tsp. salt
½ cup shredded Swiss cheese (2 oz.)
½ cup Hellmann's® Best Foods Real Mayonnaise

Arrange hot cooked broccoli in shallow 1½-quart pan or broiler proof serving dish. In small bowl with mixer at high speed beat egg whites and salt until stiff peaks form. Fold in cheese and mayonnaise; spoon evenly over broccoli. Broil 6 inches from source of heat 4 minutes or until golden brown. Serve immediately. Makes 6–8 servings.

Candy-Coated Carrots

Remember this sweet way to persuade you to eat your vegetables? The Tabasco® people tell me good cooks have been using their recipe for what will soon be four generations.

4 Tbs. butter or margarine
4 Tbs. brown sugar
¼ tsp. Tabasco® pepper sauce
⅛ tsp. salt
1 tsp. lemon juice
6–8 carrots, sliced and cooked

Place butter and brown sugar in a saucepan over medium heat, stir until combined. Add Tabasco and salt; mix well; add lemon juice. Remove from heat. Add hot, drained carrots and toss gently until coated evenly. Makes 4 servings.

Triple Corn Fritters

Back in 1960 the Green Giant test kitchens developed this super good version of an American classic. It's the best of the best; just perfect for a 1981 Sunday special breakfast or supper.

1⅓ cups Pillsbury's Best® All-Purpose or Unbleached Flour*
½ cup yellow cornmeal
1 Tbs. baking powder
2 tsps. sugar
1 tsp. salt
2 eggs, beaten
⅓ cup milk
2 Tbs. oil
1 8½-oz. can Green Giant Brand Golden Cream Style Corn
1 12-oz. can Green Giant Niblets Brand Golden Whole Kernel Corn, drained
Oil for deep frying

Lightly spoon flour into measuring cup; level off. In medium bowl, combine flour, cornmeal, baking powder, sugar and salt. In large bowl, combine eggs, milk, oil and cream style corn. Blend in dry ingredients, stirring just until moistened. Stir in whole kernel corn. In deep fat fryer or heavy saucepan drop batter by tablespoonfuls and fry in 2–3 inches hot fat (365°F.) for 2–3 minutes on each side or until golden brown. Drain on paper towel. Serve warm. Makes 28 fritters.

TIP: *Self-rising flour is not recommended.

Now-You-Like-'em Greens

And you will even if you never liked spinach before. It's this cream cheese sauce from McIlhenny Co. that does it.

3 lbs. (or 3 bunches) fresh spinach, cooked
¼ tsp. Tabasco® pepper sauce
½ tsp. salt
4 Tbs. butter or margarine
1 3-oz. package cream cheese
2 Tbs. milk
2 hard-cooked eggs, sliced or ⅔ cup bread crumbs.

To hot, drained spinach, add Tabasco, salt, butter, and cream cheese that has been softened with milk. Stir until butter has melted and ingredients are blended. Place in a casserole and bake for 10 minutes at 375°F. Garnish with egg slices or bread crumbs. Makes 6 servings.

New England Harvest Baked Beans

Several years ago this recipe won a contest sponsored by B & M Brick Oven Baked Beans. Chopped apples are the surprise ingredient and it tastes divine.

2 28-oz. cans B & M Brick Oven Baked Beans
½ cup ketchup or barbecue sauce
½ cup cider vinegar
½ cup maple syrup
¼ cup brown sugar
1 Tbs. dry mustard
2 cups baking apples (peeled, cored and cubed)
¼ to ½ lb. bacon

Preheat oven to 350°F. In a 3-quart baking dish, mix together B & M Brick Oven Baked Beans, ketchup, vinegar, maple syrup, brown sugar, dry mustard and baking apples. Arrange bacon slices over top of casserole. Bake uncovered, for 45 minutes. Makes 8 servings.

Beans Hawaiian

You don't have to be a vegetarian to enjoy this flavorful meatless bean recipe from Heinz®. For my taste, it's just perfect with cold sliced leftover baked ham.

2 1-lb. cans Heinz® Vegetarian Beans in Tomato Sauce
*1 8-oz. can pineapple chunks, drained
1–2 Tbs. light brown sugar
1½ tsps. Heinz® Mild Mustard
¼ tsp. salt
Dash ground cloves

Combine ingredients; pour into a 1-quart casserole. Bake, uncovered in 375°F. oven, 50–55 minutes or until beans are hot, stirring occasionally. Makes 4–6 servings (about 4 cups).

Rice à L'Orange

Here's a simple, but sensational recipe idea from Sunkist® Growers.

3 to 4 cups hot cooked rice
1 tsp. fresh grated orange peel
1 Sunkist® navel orange, peeled and cut in bite-size pieces
¼ cup chopped nuts, sliced green onions, sliced ripe olives *or* toasted sesame seed

To the rice, stir in orange peel and Sunkist® Orange and then add *one* of the last ingredients for extra flavor.

* 1 8½-oz. can pineapple slices, drained and cut into chunks may be substituted.

Orange Rice

Rice becomes party fare when done as is this pilaf from the Angostura® Bitters test kitchens.

- 1 6-oz. can frozen orange juice
- 2½ cups water
- ¼ tsp. ground saffron
- 1 Tbs. Angostura®
- 2 Tbs. butter
- 3 cups precooked rice

In a 2-quart saucepan mix orange juice with water, saffron, Angostura® and butter. Bring to a boil. Slowly stir in rice. Stir to blend well. Remove from heat, cover, and let stand for 10 minutes. Stir with a fork to fluff. Makes 8 servings.

Grecian Rice

Just about every would-be good cook who tasted this recipe wanted to serve it. The Blue Diamond® Almond Company used it in a booklet, but before that it appeared in national advertisements.

- 3 Tbs. butter or margarine
- ½ cup finely chopped onion
- ½ cup finely chopped green pepper
- 2 cloves garlic, minced or pressed
- 1 cup long grain rice
- 2 cups beef bouillon
- 1 tsp. cinnamon
- ½ tsp. salt
- ⅔ cup Blue Diamond® Chopped Natural Almonds
- ½ cup dark, seedless raisins

In large skillet melt butter; sauté onion, green pepper and garlic until barely tender. Add rice and cook, stirring often, until lightly toasted, about 4 to 6 minutes. Stir in bouillon, cinnamon and salt; cover and simmer 10 minutes. Stir in almonds and raisins; continue cooking, covered, another 5 minutes or until all liquid is absorbed. Makes 4 servings.

Guacamole Potatoes

The California avocado people ran this recipe in an ad a few years ago and it's been in my own permanent file ever since. I include it here because it's one of the best of the best of baked stuffed potatoes.

4 baking potatoes
1 California avocado
2 Tbs. sour cream
Dash salt and pepper
4 slices bacon, crisply cooked and crumbled

Scrub potatoes and rub skins with shortening. Prick skins with fork to allow steam to escape; bake in 375°F. oven for 1¼ to 1½ hours. Mash avocado with fork to chunky texture and mix in sour cream and seasonings. When potatoes are done, cut down the center, spoon in avocado mixture and sprinkle on crumbled bacon.

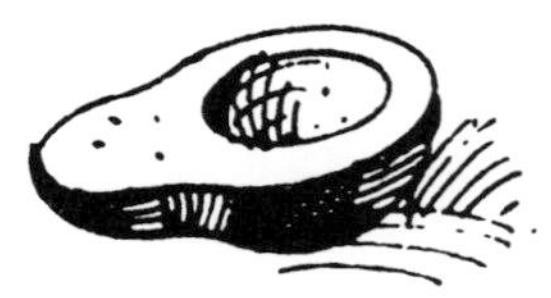

Saucy Skillet Potatoes

A positively inspired way to prepare potatoes for company from the Hellmann's® and Best Foods® Real Mayonnaise people. Everything but the final heating can be done ahead.

1 Tbs. margarine
1 cup chopped onions
½ cup Hellmann's® Best Foods® Real Mayonnaise
¼ tsp. pepper
4 medium potatoes, cooked, peeled, sliced (4 cups)

⅓ cup cider vinegar
1 Tbs. sugar
1¾ tsps. salt
1 Tbs. chopped parsley
1 Tbs. cooked crumbled bacon

In large skillet melt margarine over medium heat. Add onions; cook 2 to 3 minutes or until tender-crisp. Stir in next 5 ingredients. Add potatoes; cook, stirring constantly, 2 minutes or until hot (do not boil). Garnish with parsley and bacon. Makes 4 to 6 servings.

Sweet Potato Ring with Cashews

Heavenly molded sweet potatoes for a buffet party table featuring baked ham. I am told by the Planters® test kitchen staff that this recipe is a favorite of Southern cooks, but you don't have to be Southern to enjoy it.

¼ cup firmly packed light brown sugar
2 Tbs. Blue Bonnet® Margarine, melted
¼ cup chopped Planters® Cashew Halves
1 18-oz. can vacuum-packed sweet potatoes
1 cup milk
3 eggs
1 tsp. ground cinnamon
½ tsp. salt
¼ tsp. ground allspice

Combine brown sugar and Blue Bonnet® Margarine; spoon into bottom of a well-greased 1-quart ring mold. Arrange Planters® Cashew Halves in sugar mixture in mold. In electric blender or food processor combine sweet potatoes, milk, eggs, cinnamon, salt and allspice. Blend until smooth and creamy. Spoon into prepared ring mold. Place ring mold in pan of hot water and bake at 325°F. for 1 hour and 10 minutes, or until knife inserted in center comes out clean. Loosen edges with a knife; invert onto serving plate and serve immediately. Serves 6 to 8.

Sweet Potato Puffs

If you want to dress up sweet potatoes for company try this recipe from Blue Diamond® and the California Almond Grower Exchange. It's a classic from the 1950's.

- 3 large sweet potatoes
- ½ cup butter or margarine
- ½ cup milk
- ½ tsp. salt
- ¼ cup brown sugar, packed
- ⅛ tsp. pumpkin pie spice
- ¼ cup blanched slivered Blue Diamond® Almonds

Scrub potatoes; cut off ends and place in baking pan. Bake in 400°F. (hot) oven 1 hour. Cut potatoes lengthwise into halves and scoop pulp into a mixing bowl. Add half the butter, then milk and salt. Beat until light and fluffy. Fill shells with potato mixture; return to oven. Cream together remaining butter, sugar and pumpkin pie spice. Fold in Almonds. Place a dollop of the almond topping on each potato half. Return to oven and heat five minutes or until topping is melted. Makes 6 servings.

Easy Corn Puff

A family favorite and definitely a "classic." During the 1950's it was featured in a recipe booklet packed in the Bisquick® Baking Mix box. So good!

- 2 10-oz. packages frozen corn or chopped broccoli
- 1 cup Bisquick® Baking Mix
- 1 cup milk
- 2 eggs
- ½ tsp. salt
- 1 cup shredded Cheddar cheese (about 4 ozs).

Heat oven to 325°F. Butter 5-cup soufflé dish or 1½-quart round casserole. Cook corn as directed on package; drain. Beat Baking Mix, milk, eggs and salt with hand beater until smooth. Stir in corn and cheese. Pour into soufflé dish. Bake until knife inserted halfway between center and edge comes out clean, about 1 hour. Serve immediately. Makes 6 servings.

Corn Pudding

In the 1960's Stokely–Van Camp® introduced this all-time favorite "new" recipe for creamed corn. It's an inspired combination of crispy whole kernel and old-fashioned cream-style corn.

- 1 Tbs. butter or margarine, melted
- 3 eggs, well-beaten
- 1 17-oz can Whole Kernel Golden Corn, drained
- 1 17-oz can Stokely's Finest® Cream Style Golden Corn
- 2 Tbs. all-purpose flour
- 1 cup milk
- 1 tsp. sugar
- ½ tsp. salt
- Dash pepper

Preheat oven to 350°F. Combine all ingredients. Pour into greased 1½-quart casserole. Place casserole in pan of water. Bake, uncovered, 1 hour and 20 minutes, or until knife inserted in center comes out clean. Makes 6 servings.

Confetti Green Beans

So easy, so elegant. This Italian-style recipe was printed on the inside label of the Land O Lakes® carton. It's really delicious.

- ⅓ cup Land O Lakes® Unsalted Butter
- 1 10-oz. package frozen cut green beans, thawed, drained
- 1 8-oz. can whole kernel corn, drained
- ½ cup pitted, sliced (¼-inch) ripe olives
- 1 tsp. *each* basil leaves and oregano leaves
- ½ tsp. garlic powder
- 1 medium tomato, cut into 16 wedges

In heavy 2-quart saucepan melt Butter over medium heat (4 to 5 minutes). Add remaining ingredients *except* tomato. Cover; cook over medium heat, stirring occasionally, until vegetables are crisply tender (8 to 10 minutes). Add tomato wedges. Cover; let stand 1 minute or until tomatoes are heated through. Makes 4 1-cup servings.

Lemony Vegetable Sauté

This is one of my favorite vegetable combinations and everyone who tries it is delighted. It's very much like one my mother prepared, but this version, up-dated by Dole®, is just that little bit better.

½ lb. broccoli, cut into flowerettes
¼ cup oil
2 cups thinly sliced carrots
2 cups sliced Dole® Fresh Mushrooms
1 lemon, thinly sliced
¼ cup butter, melted
3 Tbs. sugar

Sauté broccoli in oil until tender-crisp. Remove. Stir in carrots and sauté until tender-crisp. Stir in mushrooms and sauté lightly. Return broccoli to skillet. Stir in lemon. Combine butter and sugar. Add to vegetables. Stir until vegetables are well glazed. Makes 4 to 6 servings.

Savory Baked Tomatoes

Here's the really delicious recipe from Pompeian® for baked stuffed tomatoes that people just keep asking for time and again.

- 4 large tomatoes
- ⅓ cup Pompeian® Olive Oil
- 1 small onion, chopped
- 1 pimiento, cut into strips
- 2 Tbs. minced ham
- ½ tsp. salt
- ⅛ tsp. pepper
- ¼ tsp. marjoram
- 1 Tbs. minced parsley
- 1 cup soft bread crumbs

Cut a 2-inch wide cap from the stem end of the tomatoes. Hollow out tomatoes, removing pulp and discard with the caps. Heat 4 Tbs. of olive oil in a skillet, add onion and sauté until tender. Stir in remaining ingredients, browning slightly. Spoon stuffing mixture into tomatoes. Place remaining 2 Tbs. olive oil into a shallow baking pan, arrange stuffed tomatoes in the pan, brush with a little of the oil. Bake at 350°F. for 40 minutes until cooked through. Makes 4 servings.

Creamed Cauliflower Casserole

An irresistible way to serve "good for you" vegetables. The recipe from the label of a classic convenience food—Pepperidge Farm® Stuffing Mix.

- 1 medium head cauliflower
- 3 Tbs. butter or margarine
- ¼ cup flour
- 2 cups milk
- ¾ tsp. salt
- ⅛ tsp. pepper
- 1 8-oz. package Pepperidge Farm® Herb Seasoned Stuffing Mix
- 1 cup water
- ½ cup butter or margarine, melted

Break cauliflower into small pieces and cook until just tender. Drain and place in a shallow 2-quart casserole. Melt butter in a medium saucepan. Stir in flour and cook together a few minutes, while stirring. Remove from heat and blend in milk. Bring to a boil, stirring constantly, and simmer until thickened. Pour over cauliflower in casserole. Combine the last three ingredients and spoon on top, pressing down if necessary. Bake at 350°F. for 30 minutes. Serves 8 to 10.

Note: Broccoli used in place of cauliflower makes a delicious change.

Peas à la Crème

This vegetable dish always seems very special to me, partially because my mother often served it at luncheons and dinner parties, in little individual tart shells. It's Stokely–Van Camp's® alternate to just plain creamed peas.

⅓ cup commercial sour cream
½ tsp. instant chicken flavored bouillon
½ tsp. lemon juice
Dash pepper
1 16-oz. can Peas
Fresh dill (optional)

Mix sour cream and bouillon in saucepan. Let stand 10 minutes to dissolve bouillon. Add lemon juice and pepper. Place over low heat to blend flavors; do not boil. Heat peas in their own liquid; drain. Place in serving dish; top with sauce, and garnish with fresh dill if desired. Makes 4 servings.

Broccoli au Gratin

Campbell's® way of making broccoli a party dish; a label recipe from my mother's time and one from *Campbell's® 100 Best Recipes* cookbook.

1 bunch broccoli (about 2 lbs.) or 1 small head cauliflower (or two 10-oz. frozen packages of either vegetable)
1 11-oz. can Campbell's® Condensed Cheddar Cheese soup
¼ cup milk
2 Tbs. buttered bread crumbs
4 slices bacon, cooked and crumbled

Cook vegatable; drain. Place in shallow baking dish (10 × 6 × 2 inches). Stir soup; blend in milk; pour over vegetable. Top with crumbs. Bake at 350°F. for 20 minutes or until hot. Garnish with bacon before serving. Makes 4 to 6 servings.

Cheese-Stuffed Zucchini

Even non-squash eaters will ask for seconds when you prepare this label recipe from Purity® Cheese.

8 medium zucchini, about 2¼ lbs.
1 package (8 ounces) Farmers Cheese, shredded
2 eggs, beaten
1 cup cooked rice
¼ cup finely chopped onion
¼ cup fine dry bread crumbs
1 Tbs. parsley flakes
½ tsp. salt
Seasoned salt
Paprika

Parboil zucchini for about 5 to 7 minutes. Cool. Cut in half lengthwise. Scoop out zucchini pulp, leaving shell. Place zucchini cut side down to drain. Chop pulp. Mix pulp with cheese, (reserving ½ cup) eggs, rice, onion, bread crumbs, parsley and salt. Sprinkle zucchini shells with seasoned salt; then stuff with cheese-rice mixture. Place in a greased 15½ × 10½ × 1-inch pan. Bake 350°F. for 20 to 25 minutes or until heated through. Last few minutes of baking top with remaining cheese. Makes 16 pieces.

Honey-Glazed Squash

A wintertime special at our house when I was a child and a classic recipe from the French® Company test kitchen.

2 or 3 acorn squash
Salt and pepper
¼ cup honey
2 Tbs. butter or margarine, softened at room temperature
1 Tbs. French's® Worcestershire Sauce
¼ cup raisins

Cut squash in half; remove seeds. Place, cut-side down, in shallow pan; add about ½ inch hot water to pan. Bake in 350°F. oven 40 to 50 minutes, until almost tender. Discard water; turn squash cut-side up. Sprinkle with salt and pepper. Combine honey, butter, Worcestershire Sauce and rasins; spoon into cavities of squash. Return to oven and bake 15 minutes, until tender. Makes 4 to 6 servings.

French-Fried Onions

You'll never know how really great-tasting French-fried onions can be until you've fried your own. The "how to" is from the Crisco® Oil permanent recipe file. It's perfect.

2 large Bermuda onions
⅔ cup milk
½ cup all-purpose enriched flour
½ teaspoon salt
Crisco® Oil for deep frying
Salt

Cut cleaned onions into ¼-inch slices. Separate into rings. Soak onion rings in milk and then dip in flour seasoned with ½ tsp. salt. Fry a few at a time in deep Crisco® Oil heated to 375°F. Cook until lightly browned, 2 to 3 minutes. Drain on paper towels. Sprinkle with salt. Makes about 4 servings.

Monterey Bay Chutney

I couldn't quite decide where to place this Sun-Maid® recipe; it's more a relish than a side dish, but it goes well with roast chicken, lamb chops or steak and it tastes so great that it just had to be included somewhere in the book.

1 cup Sun-Maid® Seedless Raisins
1 cup Sun-Maid® Golden Seedless Rasins
1 cup Sun-Maid® Currants
1 cup finely chopped onion
1 quart diced pared tart apples
1 tsp. salt
1½ tsps. powdered ginger
½ tsp. allspice
⅛ tsp. cloves
1 cup vinegar
1 cup dry white wine or water
½ cup sugar
¼ cup diced green pepper
¼ cup diced pimiento

Combine all ingredients, except green pepper and pimiento. Simmer 20 to 25 minutes, uncovered, until thickened. Add green pepper and pimiento. Cook 5 minutes longer. Cool. Makes about 1½ quarts.

4.

All-American Sauces

Sparkle—that's what a good sauce lends to the dish at hand. Now the French® have long been regarded as the masters of sauce-making but they had best look to their laurels, for here are real American-made, American-born, sauces to transfer so-so dishes into super ones. For example, if you would make the most of leftover meat, try one of the trio of sauces from Pepperidge Farm; turn those fresh-cooked, but dull, green beans or broccoli into a treat with Tabasco's special cream and mayonnaise sauce, or surprise yourself with a barbecue sauce made with strained baby food—that's right, baby food!

All our sauces are "asked for" specials featured by food companies on their labels and in their advertising. They are indeed "tried and true," easy, expert and extra special. And why not? All the skill and resources of trained and talented cooks went into their creation, and each is just that, a creation in its own right.

Continental Lemon Sauce

This has been dressing up vegetables, broiled fish, even poached eggs since 1965; as spectacularly good as hollandaise but a lot easier. It's from Hellmann's® Best Foods.

1 cup Hellmann's® Best Foods Real Mayonnaise
2 eggs
3 Tbs. lemon juice
½ tsp. salt
½ tsp. dry mustard

In small saucepan with wire whisk beat all ingredients until smooth. Stirring constantly, cook over medium-low heat until thick (do not boil). Serve over vegetables, seafood or poached eggs. Sprinkle with paprika. Makes 1⅔ cups.

Burgundy Steak Sauce à la Worcester

You don't have to serve a sirloin steak to enjoy this sauce, though it's nice. Try it over plain grilled hamburger. Fabulous!

2 Tbs. butter or margarine
¼ cup chopped onion
2 10½-oz. cans beef gravy
3 Tbs. Burgundy or other dry red wine
4 tsp. Lea & Perrins® Worcestershire Sauce
2 Tbs. chopped parsley

In a small saucepan melt butter. Add onion; sauté for 3 minutes. Stir in gravy, wine and Lea & Perrins®. Cook and stir until hot, about 2 minutes. Stir in parsley. Serve hot over steak or hamburgers. Makes approximately 3 cups.

Hunt's® Hawaiian Sauce

A very popular sauce with a very special flavor. Another American sauce original from Hunt's®.

¼ cup light brown sugar, firmly packed
2 tsps. cornstarch
1 8-oz. can Hunt's® Tomato Sauce
1 8½-oz. can crushed pineapple, undrained
1 Tbs. lemon juice
1 Tbs. minced crystallized ginger
¼ tsp. onion salt
¼ tsp. garlic salt
⅛ tsp. pepper

Blend brown sugar and cornstarch in 1-quart saucepan. Add remaining ingredients; blend thoroughly. Bring to a boil, stirring. Lower heat; cover, simmer gently 15–20 minutes. Stir occasionally. Use as a basting or serving sauce for chicken, ribs, meatballs. Makes 2 cups.

Hunt's® Quick Spaghetti Sauce

A very special sauce from Hunt's® Tomato Sauce Cookbook which is a collection of all-time favorites from Hunt's® Products labels. The book was compiled in response to consumers who complained "they were running out of space to store the cans" or "never got to copy the recipe before the can was thrown away."

- ½ lb. ground beef
- 3 8-oz. cans Hunt's® Tomato Sauce
- ½ cup water
- 1 4-oz. can sliced mushrooms, drained
- 2 Tbs. minced onion flakes
- 1½ tsp. light brown sugar, firmly packed
- ¾ tsp. oregano
- ½ tsp. basil
- ½ tsp. garlic salt
- ⅛ tsp. marjoram

Sauté ground beef in skillet; drain. Add remaining ingredients. Heat to boiling. Simmer 10 minutes. Stir occasionally. Serve over hot cooked spaghetti or other pasta. Makes 4 servings.

Come-and-Get-It Sauce for Vegetables

This is such an elegant but easy way to sauce a vegetable you'll wonder why you didn't think of it yourself. The Tabasco Pepper Sauce people did way back in 1950.

- 1 cup sour cream
- ¼ cup mayonnaise
- 2 Tbs. lemon juice
- ½ tsp. salt
- ¼ tsp. Tabasco Pepper Sauce

Combine all ingredients in a saucepan and heat gently; do not allow to boil. Spoon over vegetable when serving, or place vegetable in a casserole, top with sauce, sprinkle with bread crumbs, and place under broiler until crumbs are brown, 1–2 minutes. Ideal with cooked fresh asparagus, or broccoli, cabbage, cauliflower, green beans, etc. Sauce for 4–6 servings.

THREE SUPER SAUCES FROM PEPPERIDGE FARM

Pepperidge Farm developed these special sauces for hot sandwiches to make the most of their soft Family Rolls and leftover meats. Just split and heat rolls, cover with room-temperature sliced meat, top with bubbly hot sauce and serve at once.

Beef Barbecue Sauce

2 Tbs. butter or margarine
1 large onion, chopped
1 cup chili sauce
½ cup beer
½ cup sliced stuffed olives

Combine all ingredients in a saucepan and simmer for 5 minutes or until flavors are blended. Makes 1½ cups sauce.

Apple and Raisin Sauce for Ham

1 cup apple sauce
½ cup apple butter
½ cup raisins
½ cup maple syrup

Combine all ingredients in a saucepan and simmer until bubbly. Makes 2¼ cups.

Curried Sauce for Turkey or Chicken

¼ cup butter or margarine
1 clove garlic, chopped

1 onion, chopped
1 apple, peeled, cored and chopped
1 tsp. curry powder
¼ cup flour
1 cup chicken broth
1 cup (½ pint) light cream
Salt and pepper

In a saucepan, melt butter and sauté garlic, onion and apple for 5 minutes. Stir in curry powder and sauté for 1 minute more. Stir in flour and gradually add chicken broth and cream. Stir over low heat until sauce bubbles and thickens. Season to taste and add salt and pepper. Serve with cooked sliced turkey or chicken. Makes 2 cups.

Barbecue Sauce for Hot Dogs

Best recipes sometimes come from the most surprising places. This one from the Gerber people who, as I'm sure you know, make excellent baby food.

1 7¾-oz. jar Gerber Junior Peach Cobbler
⅓ cup ketchup
⅓ cup vinegar
⅓ cup brown sugar
1 clove garlic, minced
1 Tbs. Worcestershire sauce
½ tsp. ginger
¼ tsp. mace
1 tsp. onion salt

Combine all ingredients thoroughly. Score hot dogs diagonally on three sides. Barbecue, basting with sauce about three times while cooking. Makes 1½ cups sauce (enough for 2 lbs. of hot dogs).

Variations: Use on pork or chicken. Use heated sauce in chafing dish with sliced hot dogs.

Worcestershire Butter Sauce

Simple, but simply elegant. It's sauces like this that separate the chefs from the cooks.

½ cup butter or margarine
1 Tbs. chopped parsley
2 Tbs. lemon juice
1½ tsp. Lea & Perrins® Worcestershire Sauce
⅛ tsp. salt

In a small saucepan melt butter. Stir in remaining ingredients. Heat thoroughly. Serve over fish or vegetables.

Texas Barbecue Sauce

English Lea & Perrins® Worcestershire Sauce goes western for the best barbecue you'll ever eat.

1 5-oz. bottle Lea & Perrins® Worcestershire Sauce
2 cups water
1 cup cider vinegar
¾ cup lemon juice
¼ cup oil
¼ cup firmly packed brown sugar
2 tsps. salt
1 tsp. garlic salt
½ tsp. ground black pepper

In a medium saucepan combine all ingredients. Bring to boiling point. Reduce heat and simmer, uncovered for 10 minutes. Cool. Pour into tightly covered container. This sauce will keep refrigerated for several weeks. Use for chicken, hamburgers or steak. Makes 4 cups.

Horseradish Sauce

Now I will tell you how to make a beef eater happy and still keep your budget in line. Cook up some inexpensive

beef short ribs, then serve them with this horseradish sauce from Hellmann's® Best Foods. Or serve with sliced meats, such as tongue, ham or cold cuts.

1½ cups Hellmann's® Best Foods Real Mayonnaise
¼ cup prepared horseradish, drained
2 Tbs. light corn syrup
2 Tbs. dry sherry or tarragon vinegar
2 tsps. prepared mustard
¼ tsp. hot pepper sauce
⅛ tsp. salt

In small bowl stir together all ingredients. Cover; chill. Makes 2 cups.

In 1921 the Mazola Company produced a cookbook featuring Mazola Oil. It was endorsed by Oscar of the Waldorf—a famous chef of that time. In it were two of his own original sauces. Today these sauces are classics; used by good cooks all over the world.

Delmonico Sauce

½ cup plain French® dressing
1 tsp. tomato ketchup
1 tsp. Worcestershire sauce
¼ tsp. finely chopped green peppers
1 hard-boiled egg finely chopped or rubbed through a sieve.

Mix all ingredients and serve on freshly cooked broccoli or green beans, or use as a superb salad dressing on crisp greens.

Tartar Sauce

1 cup of mayonnaise
2 Tbs. of capers
2 Tbs. of olives
2 Tbs. of gherkins
1 Tbs. of parsley
¼ tsp. of onion juice or finely chopped shallots or white onions

Chop capers, olives, gherkins, and parsley very fine. Fold into the mayonnaise and serve cold. Serve with fried fish or cold seafood.

Seafood Cocktail Sauce

Another American original. This recipe was perfected by Creole cooks on Avery Island in Louisiana where they make Tabasco Pepper Sauce.

1 Tbs. prepared horseradish
1 Tbs. Worcestershire sauce
3 Tbs. ketchup
¼ tsp. Tabasco Pepper Sauce
1 Tbs. lemon juice
¼ tsp. salt

Mix ingredients thoroughly. Makes 4 very small servings.

5.

Salads and Their Dressings

I'll confess I love salads, perhaps because they are all too often culinary orphans and like all neglected orphans they flower with a little imagination and a bit of T.L.C.

A salad can make a meal. Pick one of the casserole dishes in this book, or any hearty main course, add a salad, and dinner is served; or the salad can *be* the meal. Take a Caesar salad, add crunchy rolls, a good dessert and coffee; who could ask for more for a perfect lunch or supper?

Salads are doubly important to you and your family because they provide the fresh uncooked fruits and vegetables we all need. There's been a lot of talk lately about the need for roughage in our diets. The surest and most pleasant way to consume sufficient roughage is to eat a generous serving of salad at least once a day. Fresh salad vegetables and fruits also provide important vitamins and minerals. Moreover, every healthy person requires some unsaturated fats, and the most flavorful way to add them to your diet is with a zesty salad dressing. A good salad rounds out the meal, adding contrasting flavor and texture to the main dish, complementing and enhancing the meat, chicken or fish you may be serving—deliciously! In fact, if your family doesn't eat salad, it's not because they don't like salads, but because the salad lacked inspiration. Look through these pages for the best-ever salads and dressings.

Included are the old favorites, such as Perfection and Under the Sea salads, along with a bevy of new ideas, plus a collection of salad dressings that will turn anyone into a salad buff. I've tried every one and I would be hard pressed to pick the best. Every one is a triumph of flavor, a great addition to any cook's repertoire. Perhaps, too, you will find, as I did, that these recipes will lead to other new ideas, fruits and vegetable combinations you hadn't thought of before, or new ways to use a dressing you particularly liked. I hope so, for salad making is fun, easy, quick, and a great way to add sparkling new flavor at low cost to every meal you serve.

Caesar Salad

The Caesar Salad was created at Caesar's Bar and Grill in Tijuana, Mexico, just South of the Border near the fragrant lemon groves of California. Caesar's famous salad has been acclaimed by epicures the world over. The Sunkist Lemon people printed this classic in their advertising a decade ago. It's a year-round favorite.

- 1 clove garlic, crushed
- ⅔ cup olive oil
- 4 quarts romaine lettuce, chilled, torn (about 3 medium heads)
- 1 tsp. salt
- Freshly ground pepper
- 1 Tbs. Worcestershire sauce
- 1 egg
- 3 to 4 Tbs. fresh squeezed lemon juice
- 2 Tbs. wine vinegar
- 6 to 8 anchovy fillets, chopped, optional
- ½ cup grated Parmesan cheese
- 1 cup croutons

Add garlic to oil; let stand overnight. Discard garlic. Place romaine in large salad bowl. Sprinkle with salt, pepper and Worcestershire sauce. Coddle egg for 1½ minutes; break into middle of salad. Pour lemon juice and wine vinegar over egg. Toss lightly to mix well. Add remaining ingredients, tossing after each addition. Adjust seasonings if necessary. Serve immediately. Makes 8 servings.

Cannellini Chef's Salad

From Progresso Foods, a meal-sized salad to serve with Italian bread and a glass of Chianti.

- 2 cans (20 ounces each) Progresso Cannellini Beans
- ⅓ cup olive oil
- 3 Tbs. wine vinegar
- 3 quarts torn iceberg lettuce
- ¼ lb. sliced ham, slivered
- 2 ounces sliced salami, slivered

- 1 clove garlic, minced
- 2 tsps. oregano leaves, crumbled
- 1 tsp. salt
- ¼ tsp. ground black pepper
- ¼ lb. Mozzarella cheese, slivered
- ¼ cup sliced roasted peppers

Drain cannellini beans thoroughly. Meanwhile, in a medium bowl mix together oil, vinegar, garlic, oregano, salt and black pepper. Stir in cannellini beans. Place lettuce in a very large bowl. Spoon beans in a circle close to side of bowl. Arrange ham, salami, cheese and roasted peppers in any desired pattern over the lettuce. Toss just before serving. Makes 6 portions.

Salmon Salad on Avocado Half Shells

A delicious new way to serve canned salmon, from the Avocado Advisory Board's advertising pages.

- 3 California avocados
- Lettuce
- 1 15½-ounce can or 2 7¾-ounce cans salmon, chilled
- 2 Tbs. sliced green onion
- ½ cup sliced celery
- Lemon-Parsley Dressing

Halve, pit and peel avocados, arrange on lettuce-lined plates. Drain salmon and separate into chunks with a fork. Toss salmon lightly with celery and green onions. Fill avocados with salmon mixture. Drizzle with Lemon-Parsley Dressing.

Lemon-Parsley Dressing: Combine ⅔ cup oil, 3 Tbs. lemon juice, one clove of minced garlic, ¼ tsp. dry mustard, ½ tsp. salt, ⅛ tsp. pepper and 1 Tbs. minced parsley in jar. Cover and shake until blended. Makes approximately 1 cup dressing.

Sunkist Onion and Orange Salad

This was a Hollywood favorite back in the days when Greta Garbo was queen of the film capital. It was and still is one of the best salads ever devised.

- 1 large mild flavored onion
- 2 large Sunkist Oranges, peeled
- ¼ tsp. salt
- ⅛ tsp. oregano, crushed
- ¼ cup salad oil
- 1 Tbs. fresh squeezed orange juice
- 1 Tbs. fresh squeezed lemon juice
- Lettuce
- 2 Tbs. ripe black olives, sliced
- Coarsely ground black pepper

Cut onion into 8 thin slices and oranges into 6 slices each. Place in glass dish; marinate for 15 minutes in mixture of salt, oregano, oil, orange and lemon juice. Arrange in a row on individual beds of crisp lettuce, alternating 3 orange slices and 2 onion slices per serving. Top with sliced olives and spoon over remaining marinade. Add a generous sprinkling of fresh ground pepper. Makes 4 servings.

Under-The-Sea-Salad

This recipe is pre–World War II vintage, and the Jell-O® people tell us it remains a consistent favorite to this day.

- 1 16-ounce can pear halves
- 1 3-ounce package Jell-O® Lime Gelatin
- ¼ tsp. salt
- 1 cup boiling water
- 1 Tbs. lemon juice
- 2 3-ounce packages cream cheese
- ⅛ tsp. cinnamon
- Chicory or watercress
- Mayonnaise, optional

Drain pears, reserving ¾ cup of the syrup. Dice pears and set aside. Dissolve Jell-O® and salt in boiling water. Add reserved syrup and lemon juice. Pour 1¼ cups into an 8 × 4-inch loaf pan. Chill until set but not firm, about 1 hour. Meanwhile, soften cheese until creamy. Very slowly blend in remaining gelatin, beating until smooth. Blend in pears. Spoon into pan. Chill until firm, about 4 hours. Unmold and garnish with chicory or watercress. Serve with mayonnaise, if desired. Makes about 3½ cups or 6 servings.

Note: Recipe may be doubled, using a 9 × 5-inch loaf pan. Recipe may be chilled in a 4-cup mold.

Cool 'N Creamy Coleslaw

If you are tired of "just coleslaw" whip up this special molded version. It's been a favorite since the recipe appeared on the Knox Gelatine package decades ago.

- 2 envelopes Knox Unflavored Gelatine
- 2 Tbs. sugar
- 1¾ cups boiling water
- 1⅓ cups mayonnaise
- ¼ cup lemon juice
- 4 cups shredded cabbage
- 1 cup shredded carrots
- ¼ cup finely chopped onion

In large bowl, mix Knox Unflavored Gelatine and sugar; add boiling water and stir until gelatin is completely dissolved. With wire whisk or rotary beater, blend in mayonnaise and lemon juice; chill until mixture is consistency of unbeaten egg whites. Stir in cabbage, carrots, and onion; pour into 11 × 7-inch pan and chill until firm. To serve, cut into squares. Makes about 8 servings.

Cranberry Apple Waldorf

Back in the Thirties Christmas wasn't Christmas at our house without this molded cranberry salad. The recipe was on the Knox Gelatine box for years and it's still festive and delicious.

- 3 envelopes Knox Unflavored Gelatine
- ⅓ cup sugar
- 1 cup boiling water
- 3½ cups cranberry juice cocktail
- 1 cup chopped apple
- ½ cup chopped celery
- ⅓ cup chopped walnuts

In large bowl, mix Knox Unflavored Gelatine and sugar; add boiling water and stir until gelatin is completely dissolved. Add cranberry juice; chill until mixture is consistency of unbeaten egg whites. Fold in apple, celery and walnuts; pour into 8- or 9-inch square pan and chill until firm. To serve, cut into squares, serve as a relish. Makes about 8 servings.

Perfection Salad

Birth of a classic recipe . . . In *1905*, Charles Knox ran a cookery contest, and Fannie Farmer was one of the judges. Third prize, a sewing machine, was awarded to Mrs. John E. Cooke of New Castle, Pennsylvania, who submitted a recipe she called Perfection Salad. The recipe was widely distributed and was greeted with such enthusiasm it is now considered an American classic.

- 1 envelope Knox Unflavored Gelatine
- ¼ cup sugar
- ½ tsp. salt
- 1¼ cups water, divided
- ¼ cup vinegar
- 1 Tbs. lemon juice
- ½ cup shredded cabbage, red or green
- 1 cup chopped celery
- 1 pimiento, cut in small pieces, or 2 Tbs. chopped sweet red or green pepper

Mix Knox Unflavored Gelatine, sugar and salt thoroughly in a small saucepan. Add ½ cup of water. Place over low heat, stirring constantly until gelatin is dissolved. Remove from heat and stir in remaining ¾ cup of water, vinegar and lemon juice. Chill mixture to unbeaten egg white consistency. Fold in shredded cabbage, celery and pimiento or pepper. Turn in a 2-cup mold or individual molds and chill until firm. Unmold on serving plate and garnish with salad greens. Serve with favorite salad dressing.

Variations:

Pineapple Perfection Salad: Substitute ¾ cup canned pineapple juice for ¾ cup of the water. Reduce sugar to 2 Tbs.

Olive Perfection Salad: Substitute ½ cup chopped ripe olives for the pimiento.

Peanut Perfection: Substitute ½ cup chopped peanuts for the celery.

Cucumber and Onion Perfection: Substitute ½ cup chopped cucumbers and 1 small onion, chopped, for the celery.

Cauliflower Perfection Salad: Substitute ½ cup finely cut crisp raw cauliflower and 2 Tbs. chopped green pepper for ½ cup of the chopped celery.

Jell-O® Artichoke Salad

A beautifully molded salad to grace the most elegant buffet table. Dreamed up by the cooks in General Foods kitchens.

1 9-ounce package Birds Eye® Deluxe Artichoke Hearts
1 cup (about ¼ lb.) sliced fresh mushrooms
1 cup prepared Good Seasons Italian Salad Dressing
1 3-ounce package Jell-O® (Lemon or Lime)
1 cup boiling water
2 tsps. vinegar
¾ cup cold water
1 Tbs. sliced pimiento

Cook artichoke hearts as directed on package. Drain and combine with mushrooms in a bowl. Pour dressing over vegetables and allow to marinate at least 1 hour. Drain, reserving marinade. Dissolve Jello-O® in boiling water. Add vinegar and cold water. Chill until thickened. Fold in the drained mushrooms and artichoke hearts, and pimiento. Pour into a 4-cup mold. Chill until firm, about 4 hours. Makes 3⅓ cups or 6 salads.

Note: If desired, reserved marinade can be combined with mayonnaise and used as a dressing for the salad.

Jell-O® Molded Vegetable Relish

A zippy relish that is really a salad, especially nice for a summer luncheon mainstay. Start with a soup, end with a special dessert, and it's a party!

1 3-ounce package Jello-O® (Lemon or Lime) Gelatin
¾ tsp. salt
1 cup boiling water
¾ cup cold water
2 Tbs. vinegar
2 tsps. grated onion
Dash of pepper
Vegetable combinations*

Dissolve Jell-O® and salt in boiling water. Add cold water, vinegar, grated onion, and pepper. Chill until thickened. Fold in your choice of vegetable combination. Pour into individual molds for salad or small molds for relish. Chill until firm, about 3 hours. Unmold. For salad, serve with crisp lettuce and garnish with mayonnaise, if desired. Makes about 3 cups or 6 salad servings or 8 relish servings.

**Vegetable Combinations:*

½ cup each finely chopped cabbage, celery, and carrots, and 3 Tbs. finely chopped green pepper.

¾ cup each finely chopped cabbage and celery, ¼ cup finely chopped green pepper, and 2 Tbs. diced pimiento.

¾ cup each finely chopped cabbage and celery, ½ cup chopped pickle, and 2 Tbs. diced pimiento.

¾ cup each drained cooked peas and diced celery and ½ cup finely chopped cabbage.

1 cup finely chopped cabbage, ½ cup sliced stuffed olives; omit salt.

⅔ cup grated carrots and ¼ cup finely chopped green pepper.

Summer Salad

A great salad for a summer lunch or supper, the recipe first appeared on the back of Armour's Golden Star Ham and I've been serving it ever since. Try it with hot orange muffins and iced tea—it's beautiful!

Leaf lettuce
1 29-ounce can peach halves, drained
1 17-ounce can pear halves, drained
1 14¼-ounce can sliced pineapple, drained
1 lb. Armour Golden Star Ham, thinly sliced
Cream cheese
Chopped walnuts
Canned blueberries
Whole strawberries

Dressing: ¾ cup dairy sour cream, 1 Tbs. horseradish mustard, 2 tsps. sugar, 1 tsp. lemon juice. Combine ingredients; chill. Serve with salad.

Salad: Line platter with lettuce; arrange peaches, pears, pineapple slices and ham on lettuce. Roll cream cheese into balls; roll in walnuts. Arrange cream cheese balls with pineapple. Fill each peach half with blueberries; garnish each pear half with a strawberry. Makes 4 servings.

Poppy Seed Dressing

Sunkist Lemon Growers suggest this creamy-smooth dressing for fruit salad.

- ½ cup sugar
- 1 tsp. salt
- 1 tsp. dry mustard
- 1 tsp. fresh grated lemon peel
- 1 tsp. finely minced onion
- ⅓ cup fresh squeezed lemon juice
- ¾ cup salad oil
- Few drops red food coloring
- 1 Tbs. poppy seeds

Combine all ingredients except food coloring and poppy seeds in electric blender or covered container. Cover and blend or shake until thoroughly mixed. Tint mixture to a delicate pink color with a drop or two of red food coloring. Stir in poppy seeds. Chill before serving with fresh fruits in season. Makes 1½ cups.

Old-Fashioned Potato Salad

This is the real thing! Apparently customers agree. They have been asking for the recipe since it originally appeared.

- 1 cup Hellmann's (or Best Foods) Real Mayonnaise
- 1 cup minced onion
- 3 Tbs. white vinegar
- 2 tsps. salt
- ¼ tsp. pepper
- 2 hard-cooked eggs, chopped
- 3 lbs. potatoes, cooked, peeled, cubed (about 6 cups)
- 2 cups sliced celery

In large bowl stir together mayonnaise, onion, vinegar, salt, pepper and eggs. Add potatoes and celery; toss to coat well. Cover; refrigerate for at least 4 hours. If desired, sprinkle with paprika. Makes about 8 cups.

Avocado Dressing for Fruit Salads

The fruit salad dressing supreme, this recipe first appeared in the Avocado Advisory Board's advertising in 1965. It's been an "asked-for" special ever since. It gives an added dimension to a favorite fruit salad, making it more of a "meal." Serve with hot honey buns and loads of fresh coffee.

3 avocados, puréed
1 cup sour cream
1½ tsps. salt
2 Tbs. lime juice

Combine all ingredients and chill 30 minutes. Serve with green or fruit salad. Makes 3 cups.

Tomato French® Dressing

Here it is! That classic French® Dressing recipe that appeared on Campbell's Tomato Soup cans back before World War II. It's a "secret" recipe of many great cooks.

1 10¾-ounce can Campbell's Condensed Tomato Soup
½ cup salad oil
¼ cup vinegar
½ tsp. dry mustard

In covered jar or shaker, combine ingredients; shake well before using. (Or mix in an electric blender.) Makes about 1½ cups.

Variations: To 1 recipe of Tomato French® Dressing add any one of the following:

4 slices bacon, cooked and crumbled
¼ cup crumbled blue cheese
1 medium clove garlic, minced
¼ cup sweet pickle relish

HELLMANN'S (OR BEST FOODS) FOUR BEST

A few years ago a series of recipes was featured in the Hellmann's advertising. Here are four of the best, two of which include Dannon Yogurt. I think you will enjoy them all.

Pecan Dressing

⅓ cup Hellmann's (or Best Foods) Real Mayonnaise
⅓ cup chopped pecans
¼ cup Karo Light Corn Syrup
1 cup (8 ounces) Dannon Plain Yogurt

Stir together first 3 ingredients. Fold in yogurt. Chill. Serve over fruit. Makes 1½ cups.

Thousand Island Dressing

⅓ cup Hellmann's (or Best Foods) Real Mayonnaise
1 hard-cooked egg, finely chopped
½ cup chili sauce
1 Tbs. chopped pimiento-stuffed olive
1 Tbs. chopped dill pickle
1 tsp. grated onion
1 8-ounce cup Dannon Plain Yogurt

Stir together first 6 ingredients. Fold in yogurt. Chill. Makes 2 cups.

California-Style Blue Cheese Dressing

- 1 cup Hellmann's (or Best Foods) Real Mayonnaise
- 1 4-ounce package blue cheese, crumbled (1 cup)
- ¼ cup dry white wine
- 1 Tbs. grated onion
- 4 to 5 drops hot pepper sauce

Combine all ingredients. Cover; chill 1 hour. Serve over fresh-cooked chilled vegetables or tossed salad. Makes 1⅔ cups.

Russian Dressing

- ½ cup Hellmann's (or Best Foods) Real Mayonnaise
- ⅓ cup chili sauce
- 2 Tbs. milk
- 1 Tbs. sweet relish

Combine all ingredients. Cover; chill 1 hour. Serve over greens. Makes 1 cup.

Low Calorie Blue Cheese Dressing

The Tabasco people ran this recipe in an ad a few years ago and I tried it then. I had to include it here because (weight watchers take note) it's one of the best.

- 1 8-oz. can tomato sauce
- 2 Tbs. ketchup
- 4 tsps. lemon juice
- 1 tsp. grated onion
- ¼ tsp. Tabasco Hot Pepper Sauce
- ½ tsp. salt
- ¼ cup crumbled blue cheese

Blend together all ingredients except blue cheese. Stir in blue cheese. Serve with salad greens. Makes 1⅓ cups (25 calories per Tbs.).

Peanut Butter Dressing

One of the most popular recipes from the Skippy® Peanut Butter kitchens is this one for fruit salad dressing.

½ cup Skippy® Super Chunk Peanut Butter
½ cup Karo Dark corn syrup
½ cup milk

In small bowl stir together peanut butter and corn syrup until blended. Stir in milk. Cover; refrigerate. Serve over fresh fruit. Makes about 1⅓ cups.

Macaroni Supper Salad

I bet you never thought of putting Hunt's® Tomato Sauce in a salad, but what goes better than tomato sauce with macaroni?

1 8-oz. pkg. small shell macaroni
2 cups diced cooked ham or luncheon meat
½ cup coarsely grated raw carrot
¼ cup chopped onion
¼ cup chopped green pepper
1 tsp. salt
1 cup mayonnaise or salad dressing
1 8-oz. can Hunt's® Tomato Sauce

Cook, drain and rinse macaroni according to package directions. Mix with ham, carrots, onion, green pepper and salt in large bowl. Blend mayonnaise and Hunt's® Sauce in small bowl. Pour over salad ingredients; toss lightly to mix. Chill thoroughly. Serve on crisp salad greens. Makes 6 servings.

Chutney Ham Salad

Highly recommended by trustworthy friends who are also trustworthy cooks who obtained the recipe from the trusty people at Dole's® test kitchens.

1 1-lb. 4-oz. can Dole® Chunk Pineapple in Juice
2 cups diced ham
1 cup shredded Cheddar cheese
Crisp salad greens
1 cup dairy sour cream
3 Tbs. chutney

Drain pineapple, reserving 2 Tbs. juice. Arrange pineapple, ham and cheese onto each of four salad plates lined with crisp salad greens. For dressing, combine sour cream, reserved juice and chutney. Spoon over each salad to serve. Makes 4 servings.

Sesame Salmon Boats

Add another great and different main course salad to your collection. It makes very good use of Bumble Bee® Red Salmon. If you like salmon, you'll be pleased.

1 7¾-oz. can Bumble Bee® Red Salmon
1 avocado
Crisp salad greens
Lemon juice
¼ cup mayonnaise
¼ tsp. dill weed
¼ tsp. garlic salt
2 tsps. toasted sesame seeds

Drain salmon. Remove skin, if desired. Mash bones. Halve avocado; remove seed. Place each half on a salad plate lined with crisp salad greens. Sprinkle with lemon juice. Combine mayonnaise, dill weed, garlic salt and 1 tsp. sesame seeds. Fold in salmon and mashed bones. Spoon into avocado halves. Sprinkle with remaining sesame seeds to serve. Makes 2 servings.

Crisp and Crunchy Tuna

Dole® Pineapple and Bumble Bee® Tuna make all-American tuna salad a star-spangled special.

1 1-lb. 4-oz. can Dole® Sliced Pineapple in Juice
1 7-oz. can Bumble Bee® Solid White Albacore Tuna, drained
1 11 oz. can mandarin orange segments, drained
1 medium cucumber, peeled, scored and sliced
¼ cup chopped green onion
Crisp salad greens
1 cup mayonnaise
1 Tbs. lemon juice
¼ tsp. curry powder

Drain pineapple, reserving 2 Tbs. juice. Break large chunks of tuna with a spoon. Toss tuna, oranges, cucumber and green onion. Spoon onto each of 5 salad plates lined with crisp salad greens. Arrange 2 slices pineapple over each. Combine reserved juice, mayonnaise, lemon juice and curry. Spoon over each salad to serve. Makes 5 servings.

Italian Bean Salad

The seasoning is Italian, but it's one of America's favorite salads—from Hellmann's® Best Foods.

1 6-oz. envelope Italian dressing mix
¼ cup cider vinegar
1 9-oz. package frozen Italian green beans, cooked, drained

1 16-oz. can chick peas, drained
1 7-oz. can pitted ripe olives, drained
1 cup sliced celery
1 small red onion, thinly sliced
½ cup Hellmann's® Best Foods Real Mayonnaise

In medium bowl stir together dressing mix and vinegar. Add next 5 ingredients; toss to coat well. Cover; chill overnight. Just before serving, toss salad with Real Mayonnaise. Makes 6–8 servings.

All-American Macaroni Salad

What backporch supper was ever complete without it? Cold cuts, ice, and coconut cake for dessert. Memories are made of such menus.

½ cup Hellmann's® Best Foods Real Mayonnaise
1 tsp. prepared mustard
¼ tsp. salt
⅛ tsp. pepper
1 cup elbow macaroni (4 oz.), cooked, drained
½ lb. frankfurters, sliced
¼ cup cubed processed American cheese
¼ cup sliced green onions (optional)

In large bowl stir together first 4 ingredients. Add remaining ingredients; toss to coat well. Cover; chill at least 2 hours. Makes 4 cups.

California Sliced Vegetable Salad

This Hollywood-style salad was the star of a recent Lea & Perrins® Worcestershire Sauce advertisement. It's a beautiful addition to any menu.

2 ripe avocados, peeled, pitted, and sliced
2 ripe tomatoes, sliced
1 red onion, thinly sliced
⅓ cup oil
1 Tbs. Lea & Perrins® Worcestershire Sauce
1 Tbs. lemon juice
1 tsp. basil leaves, crumbled
1 tsp. salt
½ tsp. sugar
2 Tbs. chopped parsley

On a shallow platter alternately arrange avocado, tomato and onion slices, one slice overlapping the next. In a small container combine remaining ingredients except parsley. Mix well. Pour over vegetables. Cover and refrigerate for 1 hour. Sprinkle with parsley and serve. Makes 6 servings.

Corn 'n' Cucumbers

Even in the dead of winter you'll find the ingredients for this salad very easy to come by. It features Del Monte canned kernel corn, thinly sliced cucumbers and a tangy sauce.

2 medium cucumbers
½ medium onion
1 17-oz. can Del Monte Whole Kernel Family Style Corn
½ cup white distilled vinegar
2 Tbs. sugar
2 Tbs. water
1 tsp. dill weed
¼ tsp. pepper
Dash cayenne pepper
Parsley sprigs

Peel and thinly slice cucumbers and onion. Drain corn, reserving liquid for other recipe uses. Combine all other ingredients except parsley. Pour over cucumbers, onion and corn in salad bowl. Chill. Toss and garnish with parsley sprigs.

Country-Style Cole Slaw

This cole slaw reminds me of Mary Eisenman. Mary lived next door to me in Shreveport, Louisiana, and was famous for her cold fried chicken and cole slaw Sunday night suppers. She probably got the cole slaw recipe from Hellmann's® Best Foods as I did.

½ cup Hellmann's® Best Foods Real Mayonnaise
2 Tbs. sugar
2 Tbs. cider vinegar
¾ tsp. salt
¼ tsp. dry mustard
⅛ tsp. celery seeds
4 cups coarsely shredded cabbage
¾ cup coarsely shredded carrots
½ cup diced green pepper
2 Tbs. sliced green onions

In medium bowl stir together first 6 ingredients. Add remaining ingredients; toss to coat well. Cover; chill at least 2 hours. Makes 4 cups.

Acapulco Salad

This is a special salad, very special indeed. Served with your own homemade enchiladas and ice cold beer, it's not just supper, it's a fiesta.

1 2¼-oz. can sliced ripe olives
1 8½-oz. can garbanzo beans
1 8¾-oz. can Del Monte Whole Kernel Family Style Corn
½ head iceberg lettuce
1 bunch radishes
Bottled green goddess dressing
Garlic salt and pepper to taste
Shredded cheddar cheese

Drain olives, garbanzo beans and corn. Using sharp knife, shred lettuce, and thinly slice radishes. Toss ingredients with dressing. Garnish with garlic salt, pepper and cheddar cheese.

Ensalada Verde

This is an all-green salad—verdant and cool—in a Spanish marinade and with a garlic salsa.

2 avocados, peeled, pitted and sliced
½ cup olive or salad oil
2 Tbs. vinegar
1 clove garlic, halved
1 tsp. each: dry mustard, salt
¼ tsp. pepper
1 cup pimiento-stuffed olives
1 package each: frozen Italian green beans, French-style green beans, green peas, asparagus spears—all cooked and drained
1 large cucumber, peeled and thinly sliced
Salsa Aioli (opposite)

Combine for marinade: oil, vinegar and seasonings. Beat or shake well. Arrange avocados, olives and vegetables in serving dish. Pour marinade over vegetables and chill several hours. Makes 6–8 servings.

Salsa Aioli: Crush 6 cloves garlic; beat in 2 egg yolks. With fork or wire whisk, slowly beat in 1 cup olive oil and juice of 1 lemon. Add salt and pepper to taste. Makes about 1 cup.

Avocado and Mushroom Salad

This elegancy of avocados and raw white mushrooms is marinated in wine, greened with parsley and spiced with fresh pepper. A lovely accompaniment to a rich main dish.

- ⅓ cup olive oil
- 1 Tbs. white wine vinegar or white wine
- 1 Tbs. chopped parsley
- 1 clove garlic, halved
- 1 tsp. salt
- Fresh ground black pepper
- Juice of 1 lemon
- 2 avocados, peeled, pitted and thinly sliced
- ½ lb. mushrooms, thinly sliced
- Parsley, for garnish

Combine and chill for marinade: oil, vinegar, seasonings and lemon juice. Layer sliced avocados and mushrooms on platter. Marinate in dressing 1 hour. Makes 6–8 servings.

Waldorf Salad à la Russe

Waldorf salad goes Russian with the addition of sour cream and Wish-Bone® Russian Dressing.

¼ cup Wish-Bone® Russian Dressing
¼ cup dairy sour cream
1 cup diced apple
1 cup diced celery
½ cup chopped walnuts

In medium bowl, blend Wish-Bone® Russian Dressing with sour cream. Add apple, celery and walnuts; toss together. If desired, serve in lettuce cups. Makes about 4 servings.

Garden Fresh Salad

The "can't-be-improved," original, creamy smooth gelatine salad with crunchy vegetables. It's from the Knox Unflavored Gelatine package and surely belongs in every good cook's recipe file.

2 envelopes Knox Unflavored Gelatine
2 Tbs. sugar
1½ cups boiling water
1 cup mayonnaise
¼ cup Wish-Bone® Italian Dressing
3 Tbs. lemon juice
Suggested Vegetables*

In large bowl, mix Unflavored Gelatine with sugar; add boiling water and stir until Gelatine is completely dissolved. With wire whisk or rotary beater, blend in mayonnaise, Italian

*Suggested Vegetables: Use any combination of the following to equal 2 cups; Chopped tomato, celery, radishes, mushrooms, asparagus or cucumbers.

dressing and lemon juice; chill, stirring occasionally, until mixture is the consistency of unbeaten egg whites. Fold in suggested Vegetables. Turn into 8-inch round or square baking pan; chill until firm. To serve, cut into wedges or squares. Makes about 8 servings.

Summer Salad with Sour Cream Dressing

This is one of those especially Southern salad ideas that was handed down from one generation to the next and then passed on from friend to friend until no one quite remembers the original recipe. This version was perfected by the good cooks at the Tabasco Pepper Sauce kitchens.

2 tsps. unflavored gelatin
Sour Cream Dressing (page 272)
¼ cup cold water
2 cups cottage cheese
1 cup (¼ pound) crumbled blue cheese
½ cup mayonnaise
2 Tbs. minced scallion
1 tsp. Tabasco Red Hot Pepper Sauce
½ cup heavy cream, whipped
3 cups cut-up fresh fruit in season
(melon balls, strawberries, pear strips, citrus sections, etc.)
6 lettuce cups

Sprinkle gelatin over water; stir over hot water until gelatin is dissolved. Combine cheeses; blend in gelatin. Stir mayonnaise, scallion and Tabasco into cheese mixture until all ingredients are thoroughly blended. Fold whipped cream into cheese. Pour into lightly oiled quart mold. Chill until firm, about 4 hours. Carefully unmold cheese salad onto plate. Surround mold with individual fruit salads in lettuce cups. Serve with Sour Cream Dressing.

Sour Cream Dressing:

1 cup sour cream
1 Tbs. mayonnaise
¼ tsp. Tabasco Red Hot Pepper Sauce

Combine all ingredients. Refrigerate until ready to serve. Makes 6 servings.

Salmon Dill Mousse

A buffet party special salad. It's been a favorite recipe since Jell-O® first introduced it back in the 1930's.

2 3-oz. packages or 1 6-oz. package Jell-O® Lemon Gelatin
2 cups boiling water
1 cup cold water
3 Tbs. lemon juice
1 1-lb. can pink salmon, drained and flaked
½ cup sour cream
¼ cup mayonnaise
2 Tbs. minced onions
1½ tsp. dill weed

Dissolve gelatin in boiling water. Add cold water and lemon juice. Chill until thickened. Mix salmon with remaining ingredients. Blend into thickened gelatin. Pour into an 8 × 4-inch loaf pan. Chill until firm—about 4 hours. Unmold. Garnish with dill and thinly sliced cucumber, if desired. Makes 5⅓ cups or 6–8 servings.

Beets in a Mustard Ring

This buffet supper salad mold recipe was created by special request from a Midwest consumer who asked Standard Brands Test Kitchens for "a mustard ring mold like the one that was always served at church suppers when I was a girl."

4 eggs
¼ cup white vinegar
¼ cup sugar
1 Tbs. dry mustard
½ tsp. salt
1 3-oz. package Royal Lemon Gelatin
¾ cup boiling water
1 cup heavy cream, whipped
Small whole pickled beets

Break eggs in top of double boiler and beat until foamy. Add vinegar, sugar, dry mustard and salt; blend well. Dissolve Royal Lemon Gelatin in boiling water, add to egg mixture and cook over simmering water, stirring frequently, until mixture is of custard consistency. Cool. Fold whipped cream into cooled mixture. Pour into a 5-cup ring mold and chill until firm. To serve, unmold and fill center with pickled beets. Makes 8–10 servings.

California Fruit Salad Rosé

From Knox Unflavored Gelatine this is a delicate combination of wine and fruit that's extra easy to prepare. It's been featured on their package since 1965.

1 envelope Knox Unflavored Gelatine
2 Tbs. sugar
¾ cup boiling water
1¼ cups rosé wine
1 cup thinly sliced peaches
½ cup sliced bananas
½ cup sliced strawberries

In medium bowl, mix Unflavored Gelatine with sugar; add boiling water and stir until Gelatine is completely dissolved. Stir in wine. Chill, stirring occasionally, until mixture is consistency of unbeaten egg whites. Fold in peaches, bananas and strawberries. Turn into 4-cup mold or bowl and chill until firm. Makes about 6 servings.

Iberia French® Dressing

It's the bit of sugar and the peppery hot Tabasco that give this time-honored French® dressing its American accent.

⅔ cup salad oil
⅓ cup lemon juice or vinegar
½ tsp. Tabasco Pepper Sauce
1 tsp. each salt, paprika, dry mustard
½ tsp. sugar

Combine ingredients and shake well in covered jar. Shake well before using. Makes 1 cup dressing.

Variations: To ½ cup Iberia French® Dressing add:

Roquefort Dressing: 1–2 Tbs. Roquefort cheese, crumbled.

Chive Dressing: 1–2 Tbs. chopped chives or green onion.

Herb Dressing: 2 tsps. chopped parsley, ⅛ tsp. thyme, ½ tsp. oregano.

Creole Dressing: ¼ cup ketchup, ½ tsp. Worcestershire sauce.

Vinaigrette Dressing: 1 hard-cooked egg, chopped, 2 Tbs. chopped green pepper, 1 Tbs. grated onion.

Hot Dan's Dressing

The R. T. French® Company printed this creamy hot sauce on the mustard jar several years ago; it's a sure-fire way to transform potato salad, cole slaw and deviled eggs into an epicurean feast.

¼ cup French's® Prepared Mustard
2 Tbs. sugar
2 Tbs. vinegar
2 Tbs. half-and-half or undiluted evaporated milk
¼ tsp. salt

Combine all ingredients; beat with rotary beater until light and fluffy. Makes ½ cup.

YOGURT DRESSINGS

I can't track down just exactly who dreamed up yogurt dressing, but I'm told this winning combination originated in California. Dannon was the first to print the recipe. It's another American original that has become a national favorite.

Fruit Yogurt Dressing

Cool, creamy Yogurt Dressing is perfect for fruit salad.

½ cup Hellmann's® Best Foods Real Mayonnaise
1 8-oz. container flavored Dannon Yogurt

Fold mayonnaise into yogurt. Cover; chill. Makes 1½ cups.

Blue Cheese Dressing

Very special on sliced tomatoes or as a dip with raw vegetables.

⅓ cup mayonnaise
⅓ cup crumbled blue cheese
1 cup plain Dannon Yogurt

In small bowl, mix mayonnaise and blue cheese. Fold in yogurt. Cover and chill until serving time. Makes about 1½ cups.

Family French® Dressing

This is that well beloved French® dressing from Heinz® that originated back in the 1920's. Your mother, no doubt, made it; mine did, and I still love it. So will you.

½ cup Heinz® Tomato Ketchup
½ cup salad oil
¼ cup Heinz® Apple Cider Vinegar
2 tsps. confectioners' sugar
1 clove garlic, split
¼ tsp. salt
Dash pepper

Combine ingredients in jar. Cover; shake vigorously. Chill to blend flavors. Remove garlic; shake again before serving. Makes 1¼ cups.

Green Goddess Dressing

This creamy mixture dresses cold seafood as well as green salads.

- 1 cup Hellmann's® Best Foods Real Mayonnaise
- ½ cup parsley sprigs
- 2 green onions, cut up
- 2 Tbs. tarragon vinegar
- 2 tsps. sugar
- ¼ tsp. salt
- ¼ tsp. dry mustard
- ⅛ tsp. garlic powder
- ⅛ tsp. pepper
- ½ cup plain yogurt

Place first 9 ingredients in blender container; cover. Blend until smooth. Fold in yogurt. Cover; chill. Makes 1½ cups.

Louis Dressing

A California original. Great over cooked shrimp, tomato slices or hard cooked eggs.

- 1 cup Hellmann's® Best Foods Real Mayonnaise
- ½ cup spinach leaves
- 5 watercress sprigs
- ½ small onion
- 1 small clove garlic
- 1 Tbs. lemon juice
- 1½ tsps. sugar

Place all ingredients in blender container; cover. Blend until smooth. Cover; chill. Makes 1¼ cups.

Cucumber Parsley Dressing

A delicious idea for green salads or cold fish; a Hollywood favorite back in the 1930's adapted by the Dannon® Yogurt people.

- ½ cup mayonnaise
- 1 cup peeled, seeded and chopped cucumber
- 1 cup chopped parsley
- 1 clove garlic, minced
- ½ tsp. salt
- ⅛ tsp. ground black pepper
- 1 cup Dannon® Plain Yogurt

Stir together first 6 ingredients. Stir in Dannon® Yogurt. Chill. Makes about 2 cups.

Remoulade Dressing

- 1 cup Hellmann's® Best Foods Real Mayonnaise
- 4 sprigs parsley
- 2 Tbs. chili sauce
- 2 Tbs. capers
- 2 Tbs. milk
- 2 tsps. prepared mustard
- 1 small clove garlic

Place ingredients in blender container; cover. Blend until smooth. Cover; chill. Makes 1¼ cups.

Tangy Coconut Salad Dressing for Fruit, Ham or Chicken Salads

The Holland House® Cream of Coconut label says this lovely and different salad dressing is equally good on fresh fruit salad or on a salad of ham or chicken. I can't decide which I like best.

- ½ cup corn oil
- ½ cup of Coco Casa® Cream of Coconut
- 1 6-oz. can frozen concentrated orange juice, thawed and undiluted
- ¼ tsp. curry powder
- ½ tsp. salt

In a bowl, combine all ingredients and beat until smooth and thick. Chill until ready to serve. Beat again and toss with salad when ready to serve. Makes 1¾ cups.

Honey Dressing

The good cooks at Kraft® suggest this creamy-smooth dressing for fruit salad.

- ¾ cup Kraft® Real Mayonnaise
- ⅓ cup honey
- 1 Tbs. grated lemon rind
- ¾ tsp. lemon juice
- ¼ tsp. ginger

Combine Mayonnaise, honey, lemon rind, lemon juice and ginger; mix well. Chill. Makes 1 cup.

California Tossed Salad

Beautiful, just beautiful, is what I call this salad. First served many years ago in the executive restaurant at MGM Studios in Hollywood, it was adapted for a national ad by the Diamond® Walnut Company.

- ½ cup large pieces Diamond® Walnuts
- ⅓ cup salad oil
- 1 tsp. seasoned salt
- 3 Tbs. lemon juice
- 1 tsp. granulated sugar
- ¼ tsp. marjoram, crumbled
- ¼ tsp. dill weed
- 1½ quarts torn mixed salad greens
- 6 ozs. cooked shrimp or prawns (or 1 5-oz. can drained)
- 1 large tomato, cut in wedges
- ¼ cup radish slices
- ¼ cup ripe olive slices
- 2 Tbsp. chopped chives or green onion
- ¼ cup cheese cubes

Toast walnuts lightly in small skillet over low heat with 1 tsp. oil, stirring frequently, about 5 minutes. Remove from heat; sprinkle with ¼ tsp. seasoned salt. Cool. Beat together remaining oil, salt, lemon juice, sugar, marjoram and dill weed. In large bowl, combine greens, shrimp, tomato, radish, olives and chives. Stir dressing; pour over salad. Toss until evenly coated. Add walnuts; toss again. Sprinkle with cheese. Serve at once. Makes 2 quarts salad, 4 large servings.

Crescent City Salad

Gulf shrimp and "creole" tomato chunks in a caraway-flavored dressing are featured in this New Orleans–style salad from Heinz®.

- ⅔ cup salad oil
- ⅓ cup Heinz® Wine Vinegar
- 2 Tbs. chopped parsley
- 1 clove garlic, minced
- ½ tsp. caraway seeds
- ½ tsp. salt
- ½ lb. fresh mushrooms, sliced
- 6 cups torn salad greens, chilled
- ½ lb. cooked shrimp
- 1 cup tomato chunks
- ½ cup chopped onion

Combine first 6 ingredients in jar. Cover; shake vigorously. Add mushrooms; chill to blend flavors. Shake again before tossing with salad greens, shrimp, tomatoes and onion. Makes 8 servings (about 8 cups).

Cold Salmon & Cucumber Salad

A delicious new way to turn canned salmon into a spectacular cold main-course entrée. It's from the Dannon® Yogurt advertising pages.

- 2 envelopes unflavored gelatin
- 1½ cups chicken broth
- ½ cup mayonnaise
- 2 Tbs. lemon juice
- 2 cups Dannon® Plain Yogurt
- 2 Tbs. minced onion
- 2 Tbs. chopped dill
- 1 1-lb. can salmon, drained with skin and bones removed
- 2 cucumbers peeled, chopped and seeds removed
- Salt to taste

Stir gelatin and chicken broth over low heat until gelatin is dissolved. Beat in mayonnaise and lemon juice. Chill until the mixture is thick and syrupy. Fold in yogurt, dill, onion, cucumbers and salmon. Pour into mold. Chill until set. Unmold, garnish with hard-boiled eggs, parsley, tomatoes and put on a bed of cooked rice or lettuce. Serves 4 to 6.

Ivan's Potato Salad

I found this recipe over 10 years ago in a folder that came in a box holding a jar of Romanoff® Icelandic Lumpfish Caviar. It's a sensational salad, not nearly as expensive as it looks and positively delicious. You'll be asked for the recipe. I guarantee it, every time it's served.

10 medium potatoes, peeled and thinly sliced (6 cups)
6 Tbs. oil
3 Tbs. vinegar
3 Tbs. lemon juice
¼ cup chopped onion
¼ tsp. powdered dill
Dash of salt and pepper
4 hard-cooked eggs, chopped
¼ cup mayonnaise
3 Tbs. (½ oz.) Romanoff® Caviar
Additional Caviar for garnish

Cook potatoes in boiling salted water until barely tender, about eight minutes. Drain. In large bowl, combine oil, vinegar, lemon juice, onion, dill, salt and pepper. Add potatoes; toss to coat. Mash eggs with mayonnaise. Gently stir in Caviar and fold into potatoes. Cover; keep cold. At serving time, garnish with additional Caviar. Makes 8 generous servings.

Mexican Macaroni Salad

A hearty meatless main-course salad high in protein; a favorite luncheon special at the Hellmann's® and Best Foods® Executive Dining Room.

1 cup Hellmann's® Best Foods® Real Mayonnaise
⅓ cup skim milk
6 drops hot pepper sauce
1 8-oz. package elbow macaroni, cooked, drained

- 2 tsps. instant chopped onion
- 1 tsp. salt
- 1 tsp. chili powder
- ⅛ tsp. garlic powder
- 1 16-oz. can red kidney beans, well drained
- 1 cup diced part-skim Mozzarella cheese (4 ozs.)

In large bowl stir together first 7 ingredients. Add remaining ingredients; toss to coat well. Cover; chill at least 2 hours. Makes 8 1-cup servings.

Southwestern Noodle Salad

An unusual approach to the traditional macaroni salad from the test kitchens of the French® Company. Make it two or three days ahead, but do taste before serving since it may need a dash more salt and an extra splash of vinegar.

- 1 lb. medium to small shell macaroni, cooked al dente, thoroughly drained
- ⅔ cup cider vinegar
- ¼ cup vegetable oil
- 1 cup minced celery (about 2 stalks)
- ½ cup chopped (about ½ large) green pepper
- 6 green onions, minced
- 1 2-oz. jar chopped pimiento, drained
- 3 generous dashes French® Company Worcestershire sauce
- 3 dashes hot pepper sauce
- 1 Tbs. minced, roasted green chili pepper
- 1 tsp. salt
- ½ tsp. freshly ground pepper
- 1 15-oz. can black-eyed peas, drained
- 1 12-oz. can corn, drained
- ½ cup pitted black olives, drained and chopped
- 1 2-oz. jar green olives with pimiento, drained and chopped
- ⅓ cup mayonnaise (about)

Place macaroni in large bowl. Pour vinegar over and let stand while preparing other ingredients. Add all other ingredients to macaroni and mix well. Cover and refrigerate 2 to 3 days. Taste for seasoning before serving. Makes 12 servings.

Four-Layer Vegetable Salad

One of the best salad ideas ever from Land O Lakes®. You make the dressing in the salad bowl, layer on the salad and refrigerate until ready to toss and serve. Super easy, super good.

Dressing

- ½ cup Land O Lakes® Sour Cream
- ½ cup salad dressing or mayonnaise
- 1 Tbs. prepared mustard
- ½ tsp. dill weed

Salad

- ¼ cup chopped green onion
- ¼ cup chopped celery
- ¼ cup chopped green pepper
- 1 cup frozen peas, thawed and drained
- 5 cups torn head lettuce (½ to ¾ head)
- 1 cup (4 ozs.) shredded Land O Lakes® Medium Natural Cheddar Cheese
- 5 slices bacon, fried and finely crumbled

Combine all dressing ingredients in large bowl; blend well. Layer onion, celery, green pepper, peas and lettuce over dressing. Sprinkle with Cheese and top with bacon. Cover and refrigerate overnight or at least 4 hours. Toss before serving. Makes 6 1-cup servings.

Tangy Bean Salad

An over-popular historic curiosity, this is the first of many versions of Three-Bean Salad and a Stokely–Van Camp® original.

- ½ cup white vinegar
- ½ cup sugar
- ½ cup vegetable oil
- ½ cup chopped onion
- ½ cup chopped green pepper
- 1 16-oz. can Cut Green Beans, drained
- 1 15½-oz. can Cut Wax Beans, drained
- 1 15-oz. can Dark Red Kidney Beans, drained
- Red onion rings (optional)

Combine vinegar, sugar, oil, onion, and green pepper in large bowl and mix well. Drain all Beans and add to dressing. Toss gently and marinate in refrigerator for at least 4 hours or overnight. Serve in bowl lined with lettuce. May be garnished with onion rings. Makes 10 servings.

Cool Corn Salad

The perfect picnic salad developed by Stokely–Van Camp® cooks back when they first introduced canned whole kernel corn. It's a recipe people have asked for ever since that time.

- ¼ cup commercial sour cream
- ¼ cup mayonnaise
- 1 Tbs. prepared mustard
- 2 tsps. white vinegar
- 1 tsp. sugar
- ¼ tsp. salt
- ⅛ tsp. pepper
- 1 17-oz. can Whole Kernel Golden Corn, drained
- 1 2-oz. jar Sliced Pimientos, drained and diced
- 2 carrots, peeled and grated
- ½ cup diced onion

In medium-size bowl, make dressing by combining sour cream, mayonnaise, mustard, vinegar, sugar, salt, and pepper. Add remaining ingredients and toss to blend. Cover and refrigerate at least 1 hour. Makes 4 to 6 servings.

Studio City Special

Remember carrot-raisin salad? Here it is, made elegant by Sun-Maid®, the raisin people.

- 2 cups grated carrot (4 large carrots)
- ½ cup Sun-Maid® Seedless Raisins
- 1 13¼-oz. can pineapple tidbits, drained
- ½ cup mayonnaise
- 1 Tbs. instant minced onion
- 1 tsp. prepared mustard
- ⅛ tsp. salt
- ½ tsp. celery seed

Pare and cut carrots into chunks. Whirl (dry) in blender until grated. Combine all ingredients. Serve in lettuce cups. Makes 4 servings.

Tart Cranberry Mold

This just might be the recipe you've been trying to track down. It's that tart-sweet cranberry mold your mother or perhaps her best friend always served with the Thanksgiving turkey. There are dozens of variations, but this one from Heinz® is, in my opinion, the best. Certainly it's one of the first and appeared in a booklet printed back in 1946.

- 1 3-oz package lemon-flavored gelatin
- ⅓ cup chopped Heinz® Sweet Pickles

1½ cups boiling water
1½ cups raw cranberries
½ medium orange, seeded, unpeeled
3 Tbs. sugar
2 cups prepared whipped-topping mix

Dissolve gelatin in boiling water; chill until slightly thickened. Meanwhile, put cranberries and orange through food chopper using fine blade. Stir in pickles and sugar. Fold cranberry mixture into thickened gelatin; then gently fold in whipped-topping mix. Pour into a 1-quart (or 8½-cup) molds. Chill until firm. Unmold on lettuce or endive. Makes 8 servings.

California Salad Dressing

This easy to prepare homemade salad dressing has been a favorite for years in The R. T. French® Company consumer services kitchens.

1 envelope French's® Sour Cream Sauce Mix
½ cup milk
1 cup mayonnaise
2 Tbs. French's® Parsley Flakes
2 Tbs. vinegar
2 Tbs. anchovy paste, if desired
½ tsp. French's® Garlic Salt
⅛ tsp. French's® Pepper
Salad greens

Prepare Sour Cream Sauce with milk as directed on envelope. Stir in mayonnaise, Parsley Flakes, vinegar, anchovy paste, Garlic Salt and Pepper. Serve with salad greens. Makes 2 cups dressing.

Note: If preferred, toss salad with crisp croutons and tiny cooked shrimp just before adding dressing.

Yogurt "Mayonnaise"

Requests for this recipe have been pouring in ever since it was developed at The Dannon® test kitchens in the 1960's.

- 1 cup Dannon® Plain Yogurt
- 2 Tbs. butter
- 4 Tbs. flour
- 1 cup milk
- 1 egg yolk
- 2 Tbs. lemon juice
- ½ tsp. dry mustard
- ½ tsp. salt

Melt the butter in a skillet and stir in flour. Add milk all at once and stir over medium heat until thick. Remove from heat and beat in egg yolk, lemon juice, mustard and salt. Stir in yogurt and cool. Makes approximately 2 cups.

Chicken Salad Habañera

Here's the chicken salad that will make everyone dance with joy. The California Olive Industry says so, and I believe it. Try it and see for yourself.

- 1½ cups boned, cooked chicken, in thin strips
- 1 cup California ripe olives, sliced in wedges
- 1 California avocado, cut into crescents
- ⅓ cup green pepper strips
- ¼ cup red onion, finely chopped
- 2 to 3 Tbs. pimiento, in thin strips
- 4 cups lettuce, shredded
- Dressing (opposite)

Combine ingredients; hold aside avocado. Cover and chill. Combine dressing ingredients in a jar and shake well. Refrigerate. Just before serving add avocados, shake dressing (opposite) and pour over salad. Toss lightly; serve on bed of shredded lettuce. Serves 4.

Dressing

⅓ cup salad oil
¼ cup red wine vinegar
¼ cup lemon juice
1 Tbs. sugar
1 tsp. salt
½ tsp. pepper
⅛ to ¼ tsp. fresh garlic, minced

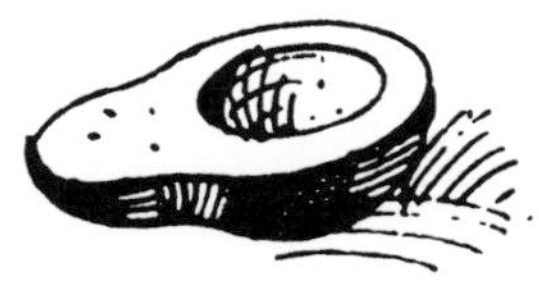

New Delhi Chicken Salad

Swanson® introduced this "different from everyday" salad several years ago. It's an inspired combination of crisp apples and tender chunks of chicken punctuated by the heady flavors of Indian condiments and spices.

¼ cup mayonnaise
¼ cup sour cream
2 Tbs. finely chopped chutney
2 tsps. lemon juice
½ tsp. curry powder
¼ tsp. salt
2 5-oz. cans Swanson® Chunk Chicken
1 small apple, diced (about ½ cup)
½ cup chopped celery
2 Tbs. toasted slivered almonds
4 slices pineapple

In bowl, combine mayonnaise, sour cream, chutney, lemon juice, curry and salt. Toss lightly with Chicken, apple, celery and almonds. Chill. Serve on pineapple slices. Garnish with additional almonds if desired. Makes about 2½ cups; 4 servings.

Chicken Salad Supreme

A justly popular main-course salad that's a fine blend of ingredients with just the right amount of tangy, well-balanced dressing. A fine French® chef perfected this recipe for Grey Poupon® Dijon Mustard.

- ¾ cup mayonnaise
- 3 Tbs. Grey Poupon® Dijon Mustard
- 2 cups cooked chicken, cubed
- 2 Tbs. each, chopped pimiento and pickle relish
- ¾ cup chopped celery
- ½ cup slivered toasted almonds
- 2 hard-cooked eggs, diced
- 1 Tbs. minced onion

Combine mayonnaise and mustard. Toss dressing lightly with remaining ingredients. Chill. If desired, serve on a bed of greens. Serves 4.

Heavenly Turkey Macaroni Salad

This Mueller's® brainstorm for using up that leftover roast turkey can be made a day or so ahead of time and still taste perfectly wonderful. Just toss it again shortly before serving. Serve it as a main course luncheon dish or take it in a cooler on a picnic.

- 8 ozs. (2 cups) Mueller's® Elbow Macaroni
- 1 cup mayonnaise
- ¼ cup light cream
- 1 cup sliced celery
- 1 Tbs. minced scallions
- 1 Tbs. minced crystallized ginger, if desired
- 1 tsp. salt
- Dash pepper
- 2 cups diced cooked turkey
- 1 cup seedless grapes, cut in half
- ½ cup coarsely chopped walnuts
- Salad greens
- Jellied cranberry sauce

Cook Mueller's® Elbow Macaroni as directed on package; drain. Rinse with cold water; drain again. Meanwhile, in large salad bowl combine mayonnaise, cream, celery, scallions, ginger, salt and pepper. Add macaroni, turkey, grapes and walnuts; mix lightly. Serve on greens; garnish with cubes of cranberry sauce. May also be garnished with additional grapes and walnuts, if desired. Makes 6 servings.

Deviled Ham Stuffed Tomatoes

Though there is no end of stuffed tomato recipes here's one that's a must. It comes from the Underwood® Deviled Ham people. Use sun-ripened, fresh from the garden tomatoes and serve with hot blueberry muffins and ice tea!

- 2 4½-oz. cans Underwood® Deviled Ham
- 1 cup (4 ozs.) shredded Swiss cheese
- ½ cup chopped pimiento-stuffed olives
- 2 Tbs. chopped onion
- 4 medium tomatoes, cut into quarters, to within ¼ inch of bottom

In a bowl, mix together deviled ham, cheese, olives and onion. Spoon mixture into center of tomatoes. Chill. Makes 4 servings.

Celebration Salad

The seasoning in this salad is superb; the recipe is from a Mueller's® Elbow Macaroni package and is one of the best ever.

- Cooked asparagus spears
- Bottled Italian dressing
- ½ tsp. prepared horseradish
- ¼ tsp. dry mustard
- 2 Tbs. sliced scallions

- 8 ozs. (2 cups) Mueller's® Elbow Macaroni
- ¾ cup mayonnaise
- 2 Tbs. ketchup
- 2 cups slivered cooked ham
- 1 cup sliced celery
- Watercress
- Cherry tomatoes

Marinate asparagus in Italian dressing overnight, or at least 3 to 4 hours. Cook Mueller's® Elbow Macaroni as directed on package; drain. Rinse with cold water; drain again. In bowl blend mayonnaise, ketchup, horseradish, mustard and scallions; toss in macaroni, ham and celery. To serve, arrange asparagus spears on platter; top with macaroni salad. Garnish with watercress and cherry tomatoes. Makes 6 servings.

Salad Oscar

The contrast of piping hot sausages and dressing on cold lettuce and vegetables sparked with crisp croutons is positively sensational. Just do serve right away or the lettuce will wilt. A plus-extra good recipe from the plus-extra good cooks at Oscar Mayer®.

- 1 12-oz. package Oscar Mayer® Cheese Smokies (links)
- 1 small head lettuce, (about 1 lb.)
- ½ medium green pepper, sliced into rings
- 2 slices onion, separated into rings
- 1 medium tomato, cut into wedges
- ¼ cup sliced fresh mushrooms, caulifllowerettes or ripe olives
- ¾ cup creamy French® dressing
- ½ cup flavored croutons

Cut links into ½-inch slices; set aside. Wash lettuce; use darker green leaves to line individual serving plates. Tear remaining lettuce into bite-size pieces. Arrange lettuce pieces and remaining vegetables on lettuce-lined plates. In saucepan combine smoked sausage links with French® dressing; heat to boiling, stirring often. Reduce heat to low; cover; heat 5 minutes. Top salad with smoked sausage link mixture and croutons. Serve immediately. Makes 2 to 4 servings.

6.
Soups to Make the Pot Smile

"It's a day to make the pot smile," my mother used to say, and it was; a cold, frosty day in late fall or deep into winter; a perfect day for the slowly simmered, rich and hearty soup she liked to prepare. Such soups do have a way of stirring you to life but the idea that all good soup must take hours to prepare can be laid to rest right here and now. Soup need not always be a day-long project. Here are quick-cooking soups to make, not just the pot, but you and your family smile with satisfaction from first spoonful to last.

A good soup can make the meal. In fact, with some homemade bread and a salad or some fresh fruit and cheese for dessert it can be the meal, one of the finest you can possibly prepare. Just try Frank Morgan's Pirate Bean Soup (page 307) with thin slices of lightly buttered Russian Black Bread (page 358) or the Italian Pasta Pot (page 305) with freshly baked Pita Bread (page 362) and you'll see what I mean.

On the other hand there are a great many types of soup—delicate as well as hearty—and they all have their place. Nothing pleases me so much as a fine China cup filled with classic Purée Mongole at the start of an elegant dinner. I think Spanish Bisque the all-time perfect soup for a summer lucheon, and when it comes to singing out the old, kissing in the new, nothing, but nothing, will take the place of a great New Year's Eve oyster stew—the perfect soup to serve with champagne.

You'll find these all here and quite a few more. The nice thing is that whatever you make you can be sure of success. Each recipe has been tested and retested so that you can relax and enjoy both the making and serving as well as the eating.

Danish Tomato Soup

Ungarnished hot consommé looks so forlorn, and plain tomato soup, no matter if it is red, ought to have a little something to dress it up. It does with this elegant version from the Blue Diamond® Almond Growers.

1 10½-oz. can condensed tomato soup
1 can milk
⅛ tsp. dill weed
Sour cream and toasted blanched slivered almonds for garnish

Combine and heat ingredients through. To serve, garnish with a dollop of dairy sour cream and plenty of toasted blanched slivered almonds. Makes 3 servings.

Easy French® Onion Soup

If this easy onion soup recipe and its deluxe variation from *Bon Appetit* magazine aren't in your file, they should be. Here they are if you missed them; French's® Worcestershire Sauce creations and among the best of their kind.

2 Tbs. butter or margarine
1 large onion, sliced
½ tsp. sugar
1 10½-oz. can beef bouillon
1¼ cups water
2 Tbs. French's® Worcestershire Sauce

Melt butter in medium-size saucepan. Add onion and sugar; cook and stir 5 to 10 minutes until lightly browned. Add bouillon, water and Worcestershire Sauce; simmer 10 to 15 minutes.

Deluxe French® Onion Soup

4 slices French® or pumpernickel bread
Easy French® Onion Soup (above)
½ cup Swiss cheese, shredded
1 Tbs. Parmesan cheese, grated

Arrange bread on baking sheet; bake in 300°F. oven 20 to 30 minutes, until crisp and dry. Spoon soup into 4 oven-proof serving dishes; top each with 1 slice bread and sprinkle generously with cheese mixture. Place under broiler 2 to 3 minutes to melt cheese. For soup bowls which are not oven-proof, toast bread as directed. Add cheese and broil, then place on hot soup. Makes 4 servings.

Spanish Bisque

First served at the elegant Beverly Wilshire Hotel in Beverly Hills, California. An exclusive recipe that was *not* available until someone wrote the Avocado Advisory Board who then sent a home economist from their test kitchen to taste, and duplicate the special soup. It was well worth the trip!

2 avocados
1⅔ cups (13¾-oz. can) chicken broth
3 Tbs. lemon juice
¾ tsp. salt
Dash cayenne
Dash garlic powder
1 cup light cream
Garniture (opposite)

Puree avocados with broth, lemon juice and seasonings. Blend in cream; cover and chill. Serve with your choice of the garnishes below. Makes 6 to 8 servings.

Garnishes: Crumbled crisp bacon, chopped toasted almonds, buttered croutons, chili relish (mix 2 Tbs. minced onion with 2 canned green chili peppers, chopped, and 3 canned pimientos, chopped), diced ham, slivered prosciutto, finely chopped hard-cooked egg or chopped anchovy fillets.

Gazpacho Soup

A "where-did-you-get-the-recipe?" soup. Some cooks won't tell, but this really great, smash-hit gazpacho recipe can be found on the label of a Snap-E-Tom® Bloody Thomas Mix can.

- 1 10-oz. can Snap-E-Tom® Tomato Cocktail (or 2 6-oz. cans)
- ½ medium cucumber, chopped
- 1 medium tomato, chopped
- 1 Tbs. sugar
- ¼ cup red wine vinegar
- ¼ cup salad oil
- 2 10-oz. cans Snap-E-Tom® Tomato Cocktail (or 3 6-oz. cans)
- 1 medium tomato, finely chopped
- ½ medium cucumber, finely chopped
- 1 small onion, finely chopped

Blend together in blender the first 6 ingredients. Add these to the last 4 ingredients and chill. Serve very cold with at least 2 of the following garnishes: croutons, chopped hard-boiled egg whites, chopped green bell pepper, chopped fresh onion. Makes 6 servings.

Spicy Jellied Consommé

On the subject of chilled soups, this one gives a different twist to your taste buds. It's those few drops of Angostura® that add the subtle, exotic flavor.

- 2 Tbs. minced chives
- ¾ tsp. Angostura®
- 1 can consommé

Add chives and Angostura® to each can of consommé. Chill until jelled, beat slightly with fork. Serve in cups.

Leek and Potato Soup

You'll find this recipe on the back of a package of Frieda's® Finest Leeks. It's in the produce department and yes, there is a Frieda. She's a versatile and talented woman who runs her own business and is a great cook besides. This is her own recipe for vichyssoise, or Leek and Potato soup if you prefer.

- 4 leeks, white parts only
- 3 Tbs. butter
- 3 potatoes
- 1 tsp. salt
- 1 quart chicken stock
- 1½ pints rich milk
- 1 pint heavy cream (half-and-half)
- Chopped chives

Slice leeks thinly; peel and slice potatoes. Cook leeks in butter until limp. Transfer them to the soup pot and add the potatoes. Add salt and broth; let simmer until potatoes are very tender. Put contents of pot through a sieve; return mixture to soup pot and add milk. Let simmer a few minutes. Correct seasoning and add a little ground white pepper if you like. Chill in the refrigerator. Just before serving, beat in the cream. Serve in chilled bowls and sprinkle the top with chopped chives. Serves 6.

Potage Senegalese

From *Campbell's® Best Recipes* cookbook. In my opinion it's very good served hot, but positively fabulous when well chilled, then ladled into icy-cold bowls.

1 10¾-oz. can Campbell's Condensed Cream of Chicken Soup
1 soup can water
½ cup light cream
¼ cup applesauce
2 Tbs. shredded coconut
1 tsp. curry powder
½ tsp. garlic salt
½ tsp. onion powder
1 avocado, sliced

In saucepan, combine all ingredients except avocado. Heat; stir occasionally. Top each serving with avocado. Makes about 3½ cups.

For chilled soup: Prepare recipe as above; chill 6 hours. Serve in chilled bowls.

Corn Chowder

They tell me at Stokely–Van Camp® this chowder is their "best ever" for a cold winter's day.

3 Tbs. butter or margarine
1 cup diced cooked ham
½ cup chopped onion
½ cup shopped celery
½ cup chopped green or red pepper
2 cups chicken broth
1 cup diced potatoes
⅛ tsp. pepper
1½ cups milk
½ cup heavy cream
1 17-oz. can Whole Kernel Golden Corn
1 2-oz. jar Sliced Pimientos, drained
Paprika

Melt butter in large saucepan. Sauté ham 5 minutes and set aside. Sauté onion, celery and green pepper until onion is transparent. Add chicken broth, potatoes, and pepper. Cover and cook over moderate heat about 20 minutes, or until potatoes are just tender. Add milk, cream, corn, reserved ham and pimientos. Reduce heat and cook until thoroughly heated. Do not boil. Spoon into bowls and garnish each serving with paprika. Makes 6 servings.

Golden Cheese Soup

This is what I call a light-hearty soup—light, but with hearty flavor. It's a Land O Lakes® recipe from their Process American Cheese package. A "just right" soup for a chilly night.

- ¼ cup Land O Lakes® Sweet Cream Butter
- ½ cup shredded carrot
- ⅓ cup all-purpose flour
- 1 Tbs. instant minced onion or 3 Tbs. fresh chopped onion
- 1 tsp. instant chicken bouillon
- ¼ tsp. salt
- ¼ tsp. dry mustard
- ¼ tsp. curry powder, if desired
- ⅛ tsp. pepper
- 3 cups milk
- ¼ tsp. hot pepper sauce
- 2 cups (8 ozs.) shredded Land O Lakes® Process American Cheese
- ½ cup beer

In heavy 2-quart saucepan melt butter over medium heat. Sauté carrots in melted butter until tender (5 to 7 minutes). Remove from heat; stir in flour, onion, bouillon and seasonings until well combined. Slowly stir in milk and hot pepper sauce until smooth. Return to heat. Add cheese. Cook over medium heat, stirring frequently, until mixture thickens and comes to a boil. Boil gently for 1 minute, stirring constantly.

Reduce heat; add beer and heat through. Serve immediately. Garnish with popcorn. Makes 4 servings.

Tip: If using fresh onion, sauté with carrot until tender. To reheat or thin soup, add more beer or milk.

Purée Mongole

This elegant classic was developed at the Campbell's® Soup test kitchen way back, even before your mother's time, but it's still very much in fashion.

1 11¼-oz. can Campbell's® Condensed Green Pea Soup
1 10¾-oz. can Campbell's® Condensed Tomato Soup
1 cup milk
1 cup water
Dash curry powder, optional

In saucepan, stir Green Pea Soup until smooth; gradually blend in remaining ingredients. Heat; stir occasionally. Do not boil. Makes about 4½ cups.

Oyster Bisque

Oyster Bisque has always been a New Year's Eve tradition at our house, but no one was ever quite as satisfied as with the results I obtained from this recipe about 10 years ago from the Tabasco® pepper sauce people.

1 dozen (1 pint) shucked large raw oysters
1 cup oyster liquor
3 cups milk
1 bay leaf
⅓ cup butter or margarine, melted
⅓ cup flour

- 1 cup heavy cream
- 1 slice onion
- 2 stalks celery
- 1 sprig parsley
- 1¾ tsps. salt
- ½ tsp. Tabasco® pepper sauce
- Chopped chives

Drain oysters; reserve 1 cup liquor. Dice oysters into saucepan and add liquor; slowly bring oysters to boiling point; remove. In same saucepan scald milk and cream with onion, celery, parsley and bay leaf; strain. Blend butter with flour, salt and Tabasco® pepper sauce. Slowly stir in scalded milk; stir over low heat until thickened. Add oysters and cooking liquid; heat to serving temperature. Garnish with chopped chives. Makes 6 to 8 servings.

Seafood Bisque

A new idea whose time has come; a delicious "quickly" soup from Birds-Eye® destined to become a cross-country favorite.

- 1 8-oz. package Birds-Eye® Green Peas with Cream Sauce
- 1 cup milk
- 1 cup half-and-half
- 1 7¾-oz. can red salmon, flaked*
- 1 Tbs. ketchup

Combine vegetable, milk and half-and-half in saucepan. Bring to a full boil over medium-high heat, stirring occasionally. Remove from heat and stir until sauce is smooth. Add salmon and ketchup. Cover; simmer 5 minutes. Makes 3 servings.

* Or use 1 7-oz. can tuna, drained and flaked

Seafood Gumbo

After much debate, this is one of the ten soup recipes rated highest in favor at the Hunt-Wesson® test kitchen.

- 1 clove garlic, minced
- 1 large onion, chopped
- ½ green pepper, diced
- ¼ cup Wesson Oil
- 1 14½-oz. can Hunt's® Whole Tomatoes
- 1 6-oz. can Hunt's® Tomato Paste
- 3 cups water
- 1 Tbs. Worcestershire sauce
- 2 tsp. salt
- 1 bay leaf
- ½ tsp. chili powder
- ½ tsp. crushed basil leaves
- ½ lb. crab meat
- ½ lb. raw shrimp, shelled and cleaned
- ½ lb. fresh haddock or halibut, cut in chunks
- 1 10-oz. pkg. frozen sliced okra, partially thawed
- 3 cups hot cooked rice

In a Dutch oven, sauté garlic, onion and green pepper in hot oil, stirring until tender. Add remaining ingredients except seafood, okra and rice. Simmer, uncovered, 45 minutes; remove bay leaf. Add crab, shrimp, haddock and okra; cover and simmer 10 to 12 minutes. Serve in soup bowls over rice. Makes 8 servings.

Italian Pasta Pot

***Viva La Roma!* Trust Campbell's®, the soup people, to top even themselves. Serve an Italian antipasto, some crusty bread, red wine, then fresh fruit and cheese for dessert. Your supper party will be the talk of the crowd.**

- ½ cup chopped green pepper
- 1 large clove garlic, minced
- ¼ tsp. rosemary leaves, crushed
- 3 soup cans water
- 1 about 16-oz can chick peas, drained

2 Tbs. olive oil
3 10¾-oz. cans Campbell's® Tomato Soup
1 cup cooked small shell macaroni
2 tsps. chopped anchovy fillets

In large saucepan, cook pepper with garlic and rosemary in oil until tender. Stir in soup and water. Add remaining ingredients. Heat; stir occasionally. Garnish with grated Parmesan cheese, if desired. Makes about 9½ cups, 6 to 8 servings.

Zuppa Pasta Fagiola

This recipe, from Mueller's,® makes a lot of soup. If there are only two or three of you, make it all up to the point of adding the pasta. Freeze half and add ½ cup pasta to the remainder and continue to cook until tender. And there you have it, two superb supper soups. Served with good bread and cheese, each portion is a meal in itself.

¾ pound dried white kidney or lima beans
Water
Ham shank (about 2 lbs) or ham bone
2 cloves garlic, minced
4 medium firm tomatoes, peeled and chopped
½ tsp. pepper
¼ tsp. rubbed sage
¼ tsp. thyme leaves
6 cups water
¼ cup olive oil
1 cup dry white wine
1 tsp. salt
¼ tsp. pepper
2 ozs. (1 cup) Mueller's® Twist Macaroni

Soak beans in water overnight; drain. Remove skin and excess fat from ham shank. In large kettle combine beans, ham shank, garlic, 2 of the chopped tomatoes, ½ tsp. pepper, sage, thyme and 6 cups of water. Bring to a boil; cover and simmer gently 2 hours, or until beans are tender. Remove shank from kettle; dice meat and return to kettle. While beans are cooking, combine olive oil, the remaining 2 chopped tomatoes, wine, salt and ¼ tsp. pepper in medium saucepan. Simmer, uncovered, 20 minutes. Pour into bean mixture. Bring to a boil; add Macaroni and continue to cook 9 to 12 minutes or until macaroni is tender. Serve in large soup bowls. 8 to 10 servings.

Pirate Bean Soup

Actor Frank Morgan (remember him as the wizard in the *Wizard of Oz*?) developed this recipe for his brother Ralph's import business. It soon became a favorite with his show biz pals whose children and childrens' children wrote Angostura® asking if they could possibly obtain the original recipe. Indeed they can. It's in this company's permanent file of "all-time best."

2½ cups dried pea beans
1 onion, sliced
1 tsp. bacon fat
1 tsp. salt
⅛ tsp. pepper
½ cup ketchup
1 Tbs. Angostura®

Wash beans thoroughly, cover with cold water and soak overnight. Add water to make about 4 cups and simmer for one hour. Sauté onion in bacon fat until golden. Add onion, salt and pepper to beans and continue simmering for another two hours. Just before removing from fire, add ketchup and Angostura®, and stir well. Makes 6 servings.

Frankfurter Creole Chowder

Considered one of the best of the best-tasting "budget-minded" soups at Campbell's®.

- 1 lb. frankfurters, cut in ½-inch slices
- ¼ tsp. basil or thyme leaves, crushed
- 2 Tbs. butter or margarine
- 1 11½-oz. can Campbell's® Condensed Split Pea with Ham Soup
- 1 10¾-oz. can Campbell's® Condensed Cream of Potato Soup
- ½ soup can water
- 1 can (about 8 ozs.) tomatoes, cut up
- 1 can (about 8 ozs.) whole kernel corn, undrained

In large saucepan, brown frankfurters with basil in butter. Add soups; gradually stir in water. Add remaining ingredients. Heat; stir occasionally. Makes about 6 cups.

7.

Sandwiches

We eat sandwiches for lunch, pack them in school boxes, serve them at parties, make a meal of them; in short, we love sandwiches.

Fortunately, our food companies are just as fond of sandwiches as the customers, for their test kitchens continue to come up with fresh variations on old favorites as well as totally new combinations of sandwich "fixin's." Included here are the very special favorites, the asked-for recipes—sandwiches so popular the recipes are kept in permanent files to be sent out over and over to the customers who apparently never get enough good sandwich ideas.

I hope you will give the sandwich meal its just due; a good sandwich can, and should be, a meal in itself. Add a beverage, perhaps a good dessert and you have the makings of a perfect lunch or supper.

Now a few tips from the experts that I pass onto you with pleasure: A thin layer of softened butter, spread on cold, almost frozen bread, keeps a moist filling from making a soggy sandwich. Varied breads add to sandwich pleasure; homey-tasting whole wheat makes a great ham sandwich, English muffins are a pleasant change for hamburgers, and all sorts of buns can replace ordinary breads. Don't forget the relishes—pickles of course, for most sandwiches, but sometimes a sweet touch is great, too. Watermelons pickled with ham or tongue, cranberry sauce for turkey or chicken, and a couple of plump ripe olives added to a hamburger taste delicious. Sandwiches are also good garnished with cherry tomatoes or sticks of crisp cucumber and celery. The idea is to serve your sandwiches with imagination, with *verve!* That's what makes the difference.

Peanut Butter 'n' Bacon Sandwich

Not for the kindergarten crowd; Lea & Perrins® developed this peanut butter sandwich for gourmets.

- ¼ cup peanut butter
- 2 strips crisp bacon, crumbled
- 2 tsps. Lea & Perrins® Worcestershire Sauce
- 2 tsps. instant minced onion
- 2 slices bread

Combine all ingredients. Spread on slice of bread. Top with second slice. Makes 1 sandwich.

Egg Salad Filling

"Can you give me a recipe for a really tasty egg salad filling?" Requests like this were so frequent at the French's® Mustard test kitchens that they developed this recipe. It's just the right amount of mustard plus the celery salt that turns the trick.

- 4 hard-cooked eggs, finely chopped
- ¼ cup finely chopped celery
- 1 Tbs. French's® Prepared Mustard
- 2 Tbs. mayonnaise
- 1 Tbs. parsley flakes
- ¼ tsp. celery salt
- 1 tsp. sugar

Combine ingredients and mix thoroughly. Makes enough filling for 4–6 sandwiches.

Balboa Party Burgers

A Kraft® "classic" and a very fancy burger. If there were a contest for the best possible burger, this would be my choice.

- ½ cup Kraft® Real Mayonnaise
- ½ cup dairy sour cream
- ½ cup finely chopped onion
- 2 Tbs. chopped parsley
- 2 lbs. ground beef
- Salt and pepper
- 1 cup (4 ozs.) shredded Kraft® Sharp Cheddar Cheese
- 6 rye bread slices, toasted
- Soft margarine
- Lettuce
- 2 large tomatoes, sliced

Combine mayonnaise, sour cream, onion and parsley; mix well. Shape meat into six oval patties. Broil on both sides to desired doneness. Season with salt and pepper. Top patties with sauce and cheese; broil until cheese is melted. Spread toast with margarine; top with lettuce, tomato and patties. Makes 6 servings.

Hamburgers Rancheros

Ever since the West was won, campfire cooks have known how good a spicy tomato sauce tasted over broiled meat. Here's an updated version with a special touch from Del Monte.

- 4 slices bacon, snipped
- 1 15-oz. can Del Monte Tomato Sauce
- ½ tsp. chili powder
- ½ tsp. garlic powder
- 2 Tbs. instant minced onion

¼ tsp. salt
¼ tsp. pepper
15 pitted green olives
1½ lbs. ground beef

Cook bacon and drain. Reserve 2 Tbs. drippings. Mix together in saucepan: tomato sauce, chili powder, garlic powder, onion, salt and pepper. Simmer 15 minutes. Halve the olives. Form beef into 4 patties and broil. Top with sauce, olives and bacon pieces.

Boston Burgers

Remember these? A 1930's favorite from Kraft® and a real budget stretcher that tastes just as great now as way back then.

½ lb. ground beef
¼ cup chopped onion
1 22-oz. can baked beans
¼ cup chili sauce
½ tsp. salt
Dash of pepper
8 hamburger buns, split, toasted
1 4-oz. pkg. Kraft® Shredded Sharp Cheddar Cheese

Brown meat; drain. Add onion; cook until tender. Stir in beans, chili sauce and seasonings. Cover; simmer 20 minutes. Fill buns with meat mixture and cheese. Makes 8 sandwiches.

Piñata Burgers

Pita (pocket) bread sandwiches were big news in the 1970s. This one, from the R. T. French® Company, is a smash hit every time it's served.

- ½ ripe avocado, diced or ½ cup chopped zucchini
- 1 medium-sized tomato, chopped
- 3–4 Tbs. French's® Worcestershire Sauce
- 1 Tbs. salad oil
- 1 tsp. lemon juice or vinegar
- 1 tsp. French's® Parsley Flakes
- 1¼ tsps. French's® Onion Salt
- 2 lbs. ground beef
- 6 small loaves pita (pocket) bread

Combine avocado, tomato, 1 Tbs. of the Worcestershire sauce, oil, lemon juice, parsley flakes, and ¼ tsp. of onion salt. Mix remaining 2 or 3 Tbs. Worcestershire and 1 tsp. of onion salt with the ground beef; form into 12 thin patties.* Place a spoonful of drained avocado mixture in center of 6 patties; top with remaining 6 patties and press edges together with a fork to seal. Grill over hot coals for about 10 minutes, turning once. Brush with liquid drained from avocado mixture while grilling. Slit outer edge of pita bread half way around and insert burger. Makes 6 servings.

Tuna Bunwiches

Americans have been eating tuna sandwiches since way back when tuna was first put into cans. It's not what you call new—but a tuna bunwich with chopped peanuts and cream cheese and French's® Prepared Mustard—now that's news!

* *Hint:* To easily form thin patties of uniform size, place a large square piece of plastic wrap over the inside of a plastic 1-lb. coffee can lid. Press enough ground beef into the lid to completely fill it, packing firmly. Carefully lift out the plastic wrap and place formed patty on a platter. Repeat process for each patty.

1 3-oz. package cream cheese, softened
2 Tbs. French's® Prepared Mustard
1 7-oz. can tuna, drained
½ cup finely chopped celery
¼ cup chopped peanuts
6 hamburger rolls
Tomato slices
Lettuce

Beat together cream cheese and mustard until smooth; stir in tuna, celery, and peanuts. Spread on rolls; top with tomato and lettuce. Makes 6 servings.

Scotchburgers

New Pepperidge Farm Puff Pastry Sheets, an old recipe for "penny pies" sold on the streets of Aberdeen, Scotland, as far back as the eighteenth century, add up to a great new hot or cold sandwich idea.

1 17¼-oz. package Pepperidge Farm Frozen "Bake It Fresh" Puff Pastry Sheets
2 lbs. lean ground beef
½ cup chopped celery
2 Tbs. instant minced onion
¼ cup chopped parsley
¼ tsp. sage
¼ tsp. salt
⅛ tsp. pepper
1 cup Pepperidge Farm Corn Bread Stuffing
¼ cup plain yogurt or sour cream
1 egg, beaten

Thaw pastry 20 minutes, then unfold sheets. Cut each sheet into 4 squares. In a large mixing bowl, thoroughly mix beef, celery, onion, parsley, sage, salt, pepper and stuffing. Stir in yogurt or sour cream until mixture is bound together. Shape mixture into 8 generous size meat patties. Broil patties on each side for 3–4 minutes or until brown. Cool. Drain on paper towels. On a lightly floured board, roll out each square of pastry about 1½ inches larger than meat patties. Set the patties in center of square and fold pastry over meat, sealing edges in the center. Place seam side down on a baking sheet and brush with beaten egg. Bake in preheated oven (400°F.) for 20 minutes. Serve hot or cold. Makes 8 servings.

Sausage and Pepper Filled Deli Rolls

Pepperidge Farm kitchens adapted this Italian hero-style sandwich for their packaged Deli rolls. Serve them with a jug of red wine and you'll think you're in Italy.

1½ lbs. sweet Italian sausage
1 clove garlic, chopped
2 red onions, sliced thinly
2 red peppers, seeded and cut into thin strips
2 green peppers, seeded and cut into thin strips
3 tomatoes, chopped
1 tsp. oregano
Salt and pepper
1 11-oz. package Pepperidge Farm Deli Rolls

Slice sausages in ½-inch thick crosswise slices. Fry sausage in a skillet until brown and cooked; remove from skillet. Add garlic, onions and peppers to pan drippings. Sauté for 5–6 minutes or until vegetables are tender but still crisp. Add tomatoes and oregano and simmer 5–6 minutes or until tomatoes are cooked. Season to taste with salt and pepper. Split roll and fill with sausage filling. Serve at once with plenty of napkins. Makes 6 servings.

The Original Brunch-wich

This super flavorful hot sandwich was the star of a recent series of advertisements from Underwood. It's just perfect for a festive brunch or luncheon party.

1 4½-oz. can Underwood Deviled Ham
2 English muffins, split, toasted
4 eggs, poached
4 slices, your favorite cheese

Spread deviled ham on each muffin half; top with poached egg. Lay cheese slice over each muffin. Broil 3–4 minutes until cheese is melted. Makes 4 servings.

Pizza Brunch-wich

Another brunch-wich from Underwood? I just couldn't resist it—you won't either when you bite into this combination.

1 4½-oz. can Underwood Deviled Ham
2 English muffins, split, toasted
4 eggs
¼ cup water
2 Tbs. butter or margarine
½ cup spaghetti sauce
2 slices Mozzarella cheese, halved

Spread deviled ham on each toasted muffin half. In small bowl, beat eggs with water. In medium skillet, melt butter; add eggs and cook, stirring constantly, until eggs are set. Spoon eggs over muffins. Top with spaghetti sauce. Place ½ slice of cheese over sauce. Broil 3–4 minutes or until cheese melts. Makes 4 servings.

Grilled Ham Salad 'n' Cheese

An American favorite since way back when drugstores had lunch counters. This version from Miracle Whip Salad Dressing is special, very special indeed.

2 cups finely chopped ham
⅓ cup Miracle Whip Salad Dressing
¼ cup sweet pickle relish
16 slices white bread
Kraft® Pure Prepared Mustard
16 Kraft® American Singles Pasteurized Processed Cheese Food
Soft Parkay® Margarine

Combine meat, salad dressing and pickle relish; mix lightly. For each sandwich, spread two bread slices with mustard; cover one bread slice with one cheese food slice, ham mixture, second cheese food slice and second bread slice. Spread outside of sandwich with margarine; grill until lightly browned on both sides. Makes 8 sandwiches.

The California Club

It was 1933, Fred Astaire movies and bathtub gin martinis were "in" when Paul Evins, chef at a famous country club, invented the "club" sandwich. It's been a hit ever since and this version from the Avocado Growers is the best yet.

4 avocados, sliced
1 cup mayonnaise
¼ cup chili sauce
24 slices white toast
Lettuce
2 large tomatoes, sliced
8 slices cooked turkey
1 lb. bacon, cooked crisp
Salt and pepper
Pimiento-stuffed olives

Blend mayonnaise and chili sauce; spread on toast. Assemble 8 double-decker sandwiches with avocado and remaining ingredients. Add salt and pepper to taste. Quarter sandwiches; secure with cocktail picks and garnish with olives. Makes 8 sandwiches.

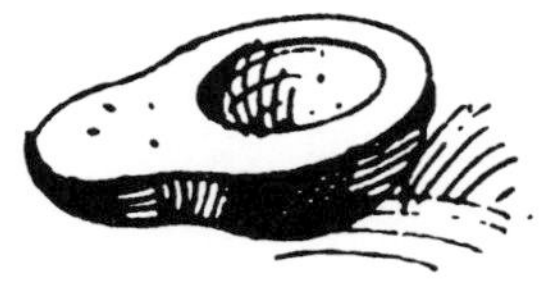

Open-Face Reubens

Corned beef on rye with Swiss cheese, onion rings, sauerkraut and a tangy dressing to top it all. Delicatessen fans, this is it!

Rye bread slices, toasted
Sauerkraut
Corned beef slices
Swiss cheese slices
Onion rings
Kraft® Thousand Island dressing

Cover toast with sauerkraut, meat, cheese and onions. Serve open-style with dressing.

Coney Islands

Get your Coney Island Red Hots! Get your red hots here! Campbell soup takes you back to Nathan's Pier restaurant on Coney Island in New York when hot dogs topped with spicy sauce and chopped onions went for ten cents each or three for a quarter.

4 frankfurters, split lengthwise
1 Tbs. butter or margarine
1 can Campbell's Chili Beef Soup
⅓ cup water
4 frankfurter buns, split and toasted
Chopped onion

In skillet, brown frankfurters in butter. Add soup, water. Heat; stir. Place frankfurters in buns; spoon chili over. Garnish with onion. Makes 4 sandwiches.

Spring Salad Sandwich

Make this meatless creation from Lea & Perrins® for a gourmet vegetarian or for anyone who enjoys a great sandwich.

1 8-oz. package cream cheese, softened
¼ cup dairy sour cream
¼ cup chopped celery
¼ cup grated carrot
2 Tbs. chopped radishes
2 Tbs. minced scallions
1 tsp. Lea & Perrins® Worcestershire Sauce
8 slices pumpernickel bread

In a small bowl thoroughly combine cream cheese, sour cream, celery, carrot, radishes, scallions and Lea & Perrins®. Spread a heaping ⅓ cup on each of 4 slices of bread. Top with remaining bread and cut in half. Makes 4 sandwiches.

Sausage en Croute

Here's a "sandwich" that's just made to star at your next brunch party. Created by Pepperidge Farm when they introduced their new Frozen Puff Pastry Sheets.

- 1 sheet Pepperidge Farm Frozen "Bake It Fresh" Puff Pastry
- 1 lb. pork sausage
- ½ cup chopped onion
- ⅓ cup chopped green pepper
- 1 large tomato, diced
- 1 cup shredded Swiss cheese
- 3 Tbs. chopped parsley

Thaw puff pastry sheet 20 minutes. Meanwhile, in a skillet, brown sausage stirring to break into bits. Add onion and green pepper and cook until tender. Remove from heat and pour off drippings. Add tomato, cheese and parsley. Unfold and roll out pastry on lightly floured board to 14 × 10-inch rectangle. Transfer to baking sheet lined with brown paper. Spread sausage mixture on pastry. Roll up from long side jelly roll fashion. Pinch edges to seal. Form into circle, pinch together. Cut ⅔ way through roll at 1½ inch intervals and turn pieces up with cut side showing. Bake at 425°F. for 20 minutes or until golden. Makes 6–8 servings.

8.
All Manner of Breads

When a friend opened her house for guests recently, she put a loaf of homemade bread in the oven just before the stream of visitors began to arrive. Her house is pretty, but that aroma of freshly baked bread transformed it into a home with all the warmth and charm that means. This is not to say you should bake your own bread just for fragrance, but it's a fact that nothing smells quite so good or tastes quite so great as freshly baked bread, and nothing else spells home in quite the same delicious way.

However, all the romantic prose in the world will not improve a heavy, tasteless loaf or a dry and crumbly muffin. It's all very well to carry on about the joy of homemade breads, but the price of ingredients being what they are, few cooks can afford failures and, until recently, homemade bread was a "chancy" thing. No longer. The "guess" has been taken out of bread-making by the flour millers, the yeast makers, and producers of shortening and grains—in fact, all the companies who employ the best cooks in the business to perfect bread, muffins, rolls and biscuits that are a joy to make as well as to eat.

I've made sure especially to include all those lovely "special" breads; old-fashioned gingerbread, Swedish tea ring, oatmeal muffins, a hearty whole wheat loaf and, of course, that all-time most-requested recipe, baking powder biscuits. There are yeast breads and quick breads, new-method breads that are double quick to make. Every one is easy, in fact, fail proof. Our test-kitchen experts have seen to that.

Quick Buckwheat Cakes

Old-fashioned buckwheat pancakes from the back of Elam's Pure Buckwheat Flour box, so special they deserve special treatment. Try real maple syrup and sweet butter or fresh berries and sour cream. Make lots of coffee!

- 2 cups Pure Buckwheat Flour
- 1 tsp. baking powder
- ¾ tsp. salt
- ½ tsp. baking soda
- 2½ cups milk
- ¼ cup cooking oil or melted shortening

Combine first four ingredients in bowl; mix well. Add milk and oil or melted shortening; stir until smooth. Stir batter down before using each time. For each pancake, pour about ¼ cup batter onto hot, lightly greased griddle. Bake until top is covered with bubbles and edges look cooked. Turn and brown second side. Makes about 16 cakes, 4 inches in diameter.

Buttermilk Cakes: Follow recipe for Quick Buckwheat Cakes above and change as follows: Increase baking soda to 1½ tsps. Substitute 3 cups buttermilk or sour milk for 2½ cups sweet milk. Makes about 18 cakes, 4½ inches in diameter, 6 servings of 3 pancakes each.

Banana Bran Bread

Elam's have been printing this recipe for Banana Bread on their Bran package for over a decade. It's a classic the customers won't let them drop.

- ⅓ cup shortening
- ⅔ cup honey
- ¾ cup Bran
- 2 eggs
- 1 cup ripe banana pulp
- 1½ cups all-purpose flour
- 2¼ tsps. baking powder
- ½ tsp. salt

Thoroughly blend the first five ingredients in a bowl. Sift together and add flour, baking powder and salt. Pour into a greased 8½ × 4½ × 2½-inch loaf pan. Bake at 350°F. for 1 hour, until done. Cool on wire rack. Makes 1 loaf.

Our Best Bran Muffins

Your mother probably made muffins from this old-timer. The recipe for Best Bran Muffins first appeared on Kellogg's All-Bran cereal box in 1926.

- 1¼ cups all-purpose flour
- 3 tsps. baking powder
- ½ tsp. salt
- ½ cup sugar
- 1½ cups Kellogg's All-Bran cereal or Bran Buds cereal
- 1¼ cups milk
- 1 egg
- ⅓ cup shortening or vegetable oil

Stir together flour, baking powder, salt and sugar. Set aside. Measure All-Bran cereal and milk into large mixing bowl. Stir to combine. Let stand 1 to 2 minutes, until cereal is softened. Add egg and shortening. Beat well. Add flour mixture, stirring only until combined. Portion batter evenly into 12 greased 2½-inch muffin-pan cups. Bake in 400°F. oven for about 25 minutes or until lightly browned. Makes 12 muffins.

Variations: 3 cups Kellogg's Raisin Bran cereal or 2½ cups Kellogg's 40% Bran Flakes cereal may be substituted for All-Bran cereal.

Pumpkin Bread

This is a long-time favorite recipe from Del Monte, especially good to have on hand for holiday entertaining. Extra easy too! It's been on their pumpkin can label since 1969.

- 3 cups sugar
- 1 cup salad oil
- 4 eggs, beaten
- 1 16-ounce can Del Monte Pumpkin
- 3½ cups sifted flour
- 2 tsps. baking soda
- 2 tsps. salt
- 1 tsp. baking powder
- 1 tsp. nutmeg
- 1 tsp. allspice
- 1 tsp. cinnamon
- ½ tsp. ground cloves
- ⅔ cup water

Cream sugar and oil. Add eggs and pumpkin; mix well. Sift together flour, baking soda, salt, baking powder, nutmeg, allspice, cinnamon and cloves. Add to pumpkin mixture alternately with water. Mix well after each addition. Pour into 2 well-greased and floured 9 × 5-inch loaf pans. Bake at 350°F. for 1½ hours, until loaves test done. Let stand for 10 minutes. Remove from pans to cool. Makes 2 loaves.

Super Wheat Germ Zucchini Bread

Super good-tasting and super-good for you. This Wheat Germ Zucchini Bread made its debut on the Kretschmer jar in 1977. Its flavor comes from the honest taste of wheat. Try it hot, spread with soft butter for a special "coffee-break" treat.

1¼ cups Kretschmer Wheat Germ, regular
3 cups flour
3 tsps. baking powder
1 tsp. salt
2 tsps. cinnamon
1 cup chopped nuts
2 eggs
1¾ cups sugar
2 tsps. vanilla
⅔ cup cooking oil
3 cups (about 3 medium-size) grated zucchini

Mix together wheat germ, flour, baking powder, salt, cinnamon and nuts. Beat eggs until light-colored and fluffy. Beat in sugar, vanilla and oil. Stir in zucchini. Gradually stir in wheat-germ mixture. Turn into 2 greased and floured 8½ × 4½ × 2½-inch loaf pans. Bake in 350°F. oven for 1 hour, until a pick inserted into center comes out clean. If using glass pans, bake at 325°F. Cool for 5 to 10 minutes. Remove from pans and cool on rack. Makes 2 loaves.

Dilly Casserole Bread

The most memorable bread recipe from all of the Pillsbury Bake-Off Contests! The soft moist texture, the delicate dill and onion flavor and its easy preparation truly make it a prize-winner.

1 pkg. active dry yeast
¼ cup very warm water (105°F. to 115°F.)
1 cup creamed cottage cheese
2 Tbs. sugar
1 Tbs. instant minced onion
¼ tsp. soda
1 Tbs. margarine or butter
1 egg
2½ cups Pillsbury's Best All Purpose or Unbleached Flour*

* For use with Pillsbury's Best Self-Rising Flour, omit salt and soda.

2 tsps. dill seed
1 tsp. salt

Margarine or butter, softened
Salt

In large bowl, soften yeast in warm water. In small saucepan, heat cottage cheese to lukewarm. Combine cottage cheese, sugar, onion, dill seed, 1 tsp. salt, soda, margarine and egg with softened yeast. Lightly spoon flour into measuring cup; level off; add 1½ cups flour. Beat for 2 minutes at medium speed. By hand, stir in remaining 1 cup flour. Mix thoroughly. Cover; let rise in warm place until light and doubled in size, 50 to 60 minutes.

Generously grease (not oil) 8-inch round 1½- or 2-qt. casserole. Stir down dough; turn into greased casserole. Let rise in warm place until light and doubled in size, 30 to 40 minutes. Heat oven to 350°F. Bake for 40 to 50 minutes, until golden brown. Immediately remove from pan. Brush with soft margarine and sprinkle with salt. Makes 1 loaf.

In High Altitude: Above 3500 feet, bake at 357°F. for 35 to 40 minutes.

Wheat Germ White Bread

An old-fashioned nutty-flavored wheat germ bread from the label of Elam's Unbleached White Flour with Wheat Germ. Just try a slice spread with sweet butter!

- 1¼ cup milk, scalded
- 1½ Tbs. honey
- 1¼ tsp. salt
- 2 tsps. cooking oil, soft shortening or butter
- 1 ¼-ounce package active dry yeast
- ¼ cup warm water (105–115°F.)
- 3⅓ cups (about) Unbleached White Flour with Wheat Germ

Combine first 4 ingredients in bowl; mix and cool to lukewarm. Dissolve yeast in warm water. Stir into milk mixture. Stir a small amount of flour into liquids at a time, adding flour as needed to make a stiff dough. Beat well after each addition. Turn dough onto lightly floured board; knead until dough is smooth and elastic. Place dough in well-greased bowl; turn dough to grease top and cover with damp towel. Let rise in warm place until double in size. Punch down; let rise again until double in size. Punch down; let rest for 10 minutes. Shape dough into loaf. Place in greased 9 × 5 × 3-inch loaf pan; brush top of loaf with soft shortening, butter or cooking oil. Cover; let rise until almost double in size. Bake in moderate oven (375°F.) until done, about 40 minutes. Makes 1 large loaf.

Note: If desired, above recipe may be doubled and shaped into 3 loaves; place in 3 greased 8½ × 4½ × 2⅝-inch loaf pans. Reduce baking time to 35 minutes.

Basic Sweet Dough

For coffee cakes, cinnamon buns or just faintly sweet dinner rolls, this recipe from the box of Elam's Unbleached White Flour with Wheat Germ can't be beaten for flavor and texture.

½ cup milk, scalded
⅓ cup honey or sugar
1½ tsps. salt
¼ cup butter
1 egg, beaten slightly
½ tsp. grated lemon rind
1 ¼-ounce package active dry yeast
¼ cup warm water (105–115°F.)
2¾ cups (about) Unbleached White Flour with Wheat Germ

Combine first 4 ingredients in bowl; mix and cool to lukewarm. Stir in egg and lemon rind. Dissolve yeast in warm water. Stir into milk mixture. Stir flour into liquids, a little at a time, adding flour as needed to make a stiff dough. Beat well after each addition. Turn dough onto lightly floured board; knead until dough is smooth and elastic. Place dough in well-greased bowl; turn dough to grease top. Cover with damp towel; let rise in warm place until double in size. Punch down; let rest for 10 minutes. Prepare as directed for one of the sweet breads listed below.

Cinnamon Rolls: Roll sweet dough into an 8 × 10-inch rectangle; brush 2 Tbs. melted butter over dough. Combine and mix ½ cup sugar or turbinado and 2 tsps. cinnamon; sprinkle evenly over dough. Roll up as for jelly roll, starting with long side. Cut roll crosswise into slices 1 inch thick. Place, cut side down, in greased 13 × 9 × 2-inch baking pan. Cover; let rise in warm place until double in size. Bake in moderate oven (350°F.) about 30 minutes, until done and browned. Frost with a confectioners' sugar icing, if desired. Makes 18 rolls.

Butterscotch Pecan Rolls: Melt 3 Tbs. butter in saucepan; add ⅓ cup brown sugar, packed, and ¼ cup honey or corn syrup. Place over low heat until sugar melts and mixture is smooth. Pour into buttered 13 × 9× 2-inch baking pan; spread in even layer over bottom of pan. Sprinkle ⅓ cup coarsely chopped pecans over butterscotch mixture. Proceed as for Cinnamon Rolls above, except substitute ¾ cup (packed) light brown sugar for granulated sugar or turbinado and omit cinnamon. Sprinkle ⅓ cup chopped pecans over sugar before rolling. Immediately upon removing from oven, invert pan on rack over a sheet of aluminum foil or a buttered baking sheet. Let stand 1 or 2 minutes before removing from pan. Makes 18 rolls.

Coffee Cake: Prepare Basic Sweet Dough using above recipe and change as follows: Increase honey or sugar to ½ cup. Roll dough into a 14 × 10 inch-rectangle. Brush 1 Tbs. melted butter over surface. Combine and mix ¼ cup brown sugar, packed, 2 tsps. cinnamon, ¾ cup chopped pecans and 1 cup raisins or coarsely chopped mixed candied fruit.* Sprinkle evenly over dough. Roll up as for jelly roll, starting with long side. Seal long edge. Form into a ring, seam side down, on greased baking sheet. Fasten ends together by moistening and pinching edges together. Using scissors cut two-thirds of the way through the ring to center at 1½-inch intervals. Turn each section slightly to one side. Cover; let rise until double in size. Bake in moderate oven (350°F.) until done and browned, about 30 minutes. (Cover loosely with aluminum foil if ring browns too quickly.) If desired, drizzle favorite confectioners' sugar icing over ring while warm. Makes 1 large coffee ring.

Parkerhouse Rolls

These rolls were originally created by the chef of Boston's famed Parker House Hotel in 1905.

* If using candied fruit, substitute finely shredded orange rind for cinnamon.

Prepare one recipe of Wheat Germ Hot Rolls dough. Instead of dividing dough and shaping into balls, roll it ½-inch thick on a lightly floured board. Cut into rounds, using a floured 2½- or 3-inch cookie cutter. Brush tops of rounds with melted butter. Using back of dinner knife blade make an indentation across each round of dough to one side of center and fold round in half. Press edges together lightly. Arrange rolls close together in rows on greased baking sheet. Brush tops with melted butter. Cover; let rise until double in size. Bake in moderate oven (375°F.) until done and brown, 15 to 18 minutes. Brush tops with melted butter. Makes 20 to 24 rolls.

Stollen

Real honest-to-goodness stollen, not just coffee cake; here's the European recipe faithfully tested by the Blue Diamond Almond test kitchens. Perfect for Sunday brunch or a special holiday breakfast.

- 1 package dry yeast
- ¼ cup lukewarm water
- ⅔ cup milk
- ½ cup butter or margarine
- ¼ cup sugar
- 1 egg
- ½ tsp. almond extract
- ½ tsp. salt
- 3¼ to 3½ cups sifted all-purpose flour
- ¾ cup Blue Diamond Blanched Slivered Almonds, toasted
- 1 cup golden raisins
- ½ cup halved candied cherries
- Confectioners' sugar icing

Dissolve yeast in water. Scald milk; add butter and sugar and stir until sugar is dissolved. Cool to lukewarm. Beat egg and add to milk mixture with yeast, almond extract and salt. Stir in 2 cups flour and beat until smooth. Stir in almonds, raisins and cherries. Add remaining flour, and mix until smooth. Cover and let rise in warm place until doubled in bulk, about 1½ hours. Punch down; knead lightly, and pat to 12-inch circle. Fold in half and press edges together firmly. Place on greased baking sheet. Brush top with melted butter. Let rise ½ hour in warm place. Bake in moderate (350°F.) oven for about 30 minutes. Spread top with icing while warm. Makes 1 large loaf.

Crumb Coffee Cake

I like this best made with pecans and served warm with lots of hot, fresh coffee! From the Domino Sugar carton back in 1968.

Topping:

- ⅓ cup firmly packed Domino Light Brown Sugar
- 3 Tbs. all-purpose flour
- 1 tsp. cinnamon
- 2 scant Tbs. soft butter or margarine
- ½ cup chopped nuts, optional

Combine brown sugar, flour and cinnamon in small mixing bowl. With pastry blender, blend butter into mixture thoroughly. Add nuts. Set aside.

Cake:

- 2 cups sifted all-purpose flour
- 2¼ tsps. double-acting baking powder
- ¾ cup Domino Superfine Sugar
- ¾ tsp. salt
- 2 eggs, well beaten
- ½ cup milk
- ½ cup salad oil

Sift together flour, baking powder, sugar and salt into mixing bowl. Combine beaten eggs, milk and oil. Stir liquid ingredients into dry ingredients until barely blended. Turn batter into greased 9-inch square cake pan. Spoon crumb topping over batter. Bake in 400°F. oven for 25 to 30 minutes, until done. Makes 9 3-inch squares.

Homemade Crisco Quick Bread Mix

And here's that "most asked for" quick bread mix from Crisco. (See following recipe also.)

10 cups sifted flour
⅓ cup baking powder
¼ cup sugar
1 Tbs. salt
2 cups Crisco

In large bowl, combine the flour, baking powder, sugar and salt. Cut Crisco into dry ingredients with pastry blender till mixture resembles coarse meal. Store in covered container up to 6 weeks at room temperature. For longer storage, place in freezer. To measure, spoon mix into measuring cup; level with spatula. Makes 12 cups.

Sally Lunn

The lovely thing about this old-fashioned favorite from the Fleischmann Yeast package is that no kneading is required.

½ cup warm water (105–115°F.)
1 package Fleischmann's Active Dry Yeast
1 cup warm milk
½ cup (1 stick) softened Fleischmann's Margarine

¼ cup sugar
2 tsps. salt
3 eggs, well beaten (at room temperature)
5½–6 cups unsifted flour

Measure warm water into large warm bowl. Sprinkle in Fleischmann's Yeast; stir until dissolved. Add milk, Fleischmann's Margarine, sugar, salt and eggs. Stir in 3 cups flour. Beat until well-blended, about 1 minute. Stir in enough remaining flour to make a soft dough. Cover; let rise in warm place, free from draft, until doubled in bulk, about 1 hour.

Stir down; spoon into well-greased and floured 10-inch tube pan or 2 well-greased 9 × 5 × 3-inch loaf pans. Cover; let rise in warm place, free from draft, until doubled in bulk, about 1 hour.

Bake large loaf at 400°F. about 30 minutes, or until done. Bake small loaves at 375°F. about 30 minutes, or until done. Remove from pans and cool on wire racks.

Sixty-Minute Rolls

Hot from the oven freshly made rolls for Sunday brunch, or any night supper. A rapid mix recipe from the Fleischmann's Yeast package. You'll love it.

3½ to 4½ cups unsifted flour
3 Tbs. sugar
1 tsp. salt
2 packages Fleischmann's Active Dry Yeast
1 cup milk
½ cup water
¼ cup (½ stick) Fleischmann's Margarine

In a large bowl thoroughly mix 1½ cups flour, sugar, salt, and undissolved Fleischmann's Active Dry Yeast. Combine milk, water and Fleischmann's Margarine in a saucepan. Heat over low heat until liquids are very warm (120–130°F.). Margarine does not need to melt. Gradually add to dry ingredients and beat 2 minutes at medium speed of electric mixer, scraping bowl occasionally. Add ½ cup flour. Beat at high speed 2 minutes, scraping bowl occasionally. Stir in enough additional flour to make a soft dough. Turn out onto lightly floured board; knead until smooth and elastic, about 5 minutes. Place in greased bowl, turning dough to grease top. Cover; place bowl in pan of water of about 98°F. Let rise 15 minutes. Turn dough out onto floured board. Divide in half and shape as Curlicues or Lucky Clovers (below). Cover; let rise in warm place, free from draft (about 90°F.), 15 minutes. Bake at 425°F. about 12 minutes, or until done. Remove from baking sheets and cool on wire racks.

Variations:

Curlicues: Roll out each half to a 12 × 9-inch rectangle. Cut into 12 equal strips (about 1-inch wide). Hold one end of strip firmly and wind closely to form coil. Tuck end firmly underneath. Place on greased baking sheets about 2 inches apart.

Lucky Clovers: Form each half into a 12-inch roll. Cut into 12 equal pieces. Form into balls; place in greased muffin pans 2¾ × 1¼ inches. With scissors, cut each ball in half, then into quarters, cutting through almost to bottom of rolls.

Frozen Dinner Rolls

Here's the very first recipe from Fleischmann's Yeast Company for your own freeze now, bake later, rolls. It's still one of their most popular.

5½ to 6½ cups unsifted flour
½ cup sugar
1½ tsps. salt
2 packages Fleischmann's Active Dry Yeast
1¼ cups water
½ cup milk
⅓ cup Fleischmann's Margarine
2 eggs (at room temperature)

In a large bowl thoroughly mix 2 cups flour, sugar, salt, and undissolved Fleischmann's Active Dry Yeast.

Combine water, milk and Fleischmann's Margarine in a saucepan. Heat over low heat until liquids are very warm (120–130°F.). Margarine does not need to melt. Gradually add to dry ingredients and beat 2 minutes at medium speed of electric mixer, scraping bowl occasionally. Add eggs and ½ cup flour. Beat at high speed 2 minutes, scraping bowl occasionally. Stir in enough additional flour to make a soft dough. Turn out onto lightly floured board; knead until smooth and elastic, about 8–10 minutes. Cover with plastic wrap, then a towel, let rest 20 minutes.

Punch dough down. Shape into desired shapes for dinner rolls. Place on greased baking sheets.* Cover with plastic wrap and foil, sealing well. Freeze until firm. Transfer to plastic bags. Freeze up to 4 weeks.

Remove from freezer; place on greased baking sheets. Cover; let rise in warm place, free from draft, until doubled in

* Editor's note: These can be baked immediately, if desired.

bulk, about 1½ hours. Bake at 350°F. 15 minutes, or until golden brown and done. Remove from baking sheets and cool on wire racks.

Quick Mix Biscuits

2 cups Homemade Crisco Quick Bread Mix
½ cup milk

Preheat oven to 425°F. In bowl, make a well in the Crisco Quick Bread Mix; add milk all at once. Stir quickly with fork just till blended. Transfer dough to a lightly floured surface. Knead gently 8–10 times. Roll dough ½–¾ inch thick. Cut with floured biscuit cutter. Bake on ungreased baking sheet at 425°F. about 12–15 minutes. Makes 8–10 biscuits.

Giant Popovers

The Planters Peanut Company tells me they receive steady requests for this recipe and have for years.

6 eggs
¼ cup Planters Peanut Oil
2 cups milk
1¾ cups unsifted flour
1½ tsps. salt

In large bowl, combine eggs and Planters Peanut Oil; beat slightly. Gradually beat in milk, flour and salt. Pour batter into 10 well-oiled custard cups. Place custard cups on baking sheet. Bake in moderate oven (375°F.) 1 hour, or until firm and brown. If desired, remove popovers from oven after 45 minutes, cut slit in the side of each to let steam escape, quickly return to oven for last 15 minutes. Makes 10 large popovers.

Pioneer Corn Bread

This authentic, old-timey corn bread from Elam's is the best you'll ever bake. Served with corn syrup and lots of melty soft butter, it's a treat you'll long remember.

2 cups Stone Ground Yellow Corn Meal
2 tsps. baking powder
1 tsp. soda
1 tsp. salt
1 egg, beaten slightly
1 cup buttermilk
¼ cup cooking oil or melted shortening

Combine first four ingredients in bowl; mix well. Add buttermilk, egg and oil or melted shortening. Stir just until dry ingredients are moistened; do not beat. Pour into well-greased 8-inch square baking pan dusted with Yellow Corn Meal. Bake in hot oven (425°F.) 20 minutes or until done and a light golden brown. Makes 16 pieces, 2 inches square.

Variations: Follow recipe for Pioneer Corn Bread above and change as suggested below:

Sweet Milk Corn Bread: Substitute sweet milk for buttermilk. Increase baking powder to 3 tsps. and omit soda.

Muffins: Fill well-greased medium size muffin cups ⅔ full. Reduce baking time to 12–15 minutes or until done and a light golden brown. Makes 12 2½ × 1⅛-inch muffins.

Oatmeal Muffins

Your mother may have made these muffins; if so you'll remember how good they tasted, hot from the oven, lavish with sweet butter and homemade jam.

3 cups Scotch Style Oatmeal
3 Tbs. sugar
3 tsps. baking powder
¾ tsp. salt
1½ cups milk
1 egg, beaten
3 Tbs. cooking oil or melted shortening

Combine first 4 ingredients in bowl; mix. Combine milk, egg and oil or melted shortening; beat slightly. Add liquids to dry ingredients; stir just until dry ingredients are moistened. Fill greased muffin cups (2½ × 1¼ inches) about ⅞ full using an equal amount of batter in each cup. Bake in hot oven (425°F.) until done and lightly browned, 20–25 minutes. Makes 12 muffins.

Two-Hour Nut Roll

Super great tasting but super quick to make. This beautiful coffee cake with its old world flavor was one of the first new rapid-mix method recipes from Fleischmann's Yeast.

6–7 cups unsifted flour
3 Tbs. sugar
1 tsp. salt
2 packages Fleischmann's Active Dry Yeast
1 cup dairy sour cream
½ cup water
1 cup (2 sticks) Fleischmann's Margarine
3 eggs (at room temperature)

In a large bowl thoroughly mix 2 cups flour, sugar, salt and dissolved Fleischmann's Active Dry Yeast. Combine sour cream, water and Fleischmann's Margarine in a saucepan. Heat over low heat until liquids are very warm (120–130°F.).

Margarine does not need to melt. Gradually add to dry ingredients and beat 2 minutes at medium speed of electric mixer, scraping bowl occasionally. Add eggs and 1 cup flour. Beat at high speed 2 minutes, scraping bowl occasionally. Stir in enough additional flour to make a soft dough. Turn out onto lightly floured board; knead a few times to form a ball. Cover and let rest 10 minutes.

Divide dough into 4 equal pieces. Roll out each piece into a 14 × 12-inch rectangle. Spread each with one-fourth of either of the nut fillings (below). Roll each up from long side, as for jelly roll. Seal edges. Place on greased baking sheets, sealed edges down. Cover; let rise in warm place, free from draft, until doubled in bulk, about 1 hour. Bake at 350°F. about 35 minutes, or until done. Remove from baking sheets and cool on wire racks. When cool, if desired, drizzle with confectioners' sugar frosting.

Maple Walnut Filling: Melt ¾ cup (1½ sticks) Fleischmann's Margarine over low heat. Stir in ½ cup sugar and 3 Tbs. imitation maple flavor. Add 5 cups ground Planters or Southern Belle English Walnuts; blend well.

Pecan Filling: Melt 1 cup (2 sticks) Fleischmann's Margarine over low heat. Stir in ½ cup sugar and ¼ cup vanilla extract. Add 7 cups (4 6-oz. cans) ground Planters or Southern Belle Pecans; blend well.

Swedish Tea Ring

Around Christmas time this is the most requested recipe at the Parkay® Margarine test kitchens. It's just perfect for Christmas morning breakfast.

Editor's note: These freeze well if you can't eat them all at once.

2½–3	cups flour	¼	cup Parkay® Margarine, melted
¼	cup sugar	½	cup raisins
1	pkg. active dry yeast	¼	cup granulated sugar
1	tsp. salt	¼	cup packed brown sugar
½	cup milk	¼	cup chopped nuts
¼	cup water	1	tsp. cinnamon
	Parkay® margarine		Vanilla Drizzle (below)
1	egg		

In large mixing bowl, combine 1 cup flour, sugar, yeast and salt. Heat milk, water and ⅓ cup margarine over low heat until warm. Add to flour mixture; beat 3 minutes at medium speed of electric mixer. Add ½ cup flour and egg; beat 2 minutes at high speed. Stir in enough remaining flour to form a soft dough. On lightly floured surface, knead dough until smooth and elastic. Place in greased bowl; brush with melted margarine. Cover; let rise in warm place until double in volume, about 1½ hours. Punch down dough; let rest 10 minutes.

On lightly floured surface, roll out dough to 15 × 10-inch rectangle. Brush with margarine; sprinkle with combined raisins, sugars, nuts and cinnamon. Roll up, starting at long end; seal long end. Place on greased cookie sheet. Join ends to form ring; seal ends. With scissors, cut two-thirds of the way through ring at 1-inch intervals; turn each section on its side. Let rise until double in volume, about 45 minutes. Bake at 350°F., 25–30 minutes. Drizzle with Vanilla Drizzle.

Vanilla Drizzle

1 cup sifted confectioners' sugar
1 Tbs. milk
1 tsp. vanilla

Combine ingredients; mix well.

Orange Juice Muffins with Honey Spread

These muffins were always called Adele's favorite in our house. If you had the recipe but lost it, for goodness sake, don't lose it again.

- 2 cups Bisquick® Baking Mix
- 2 Tbs. sugar
- 1 egg
- 1 tsp. grated orange peel
- ⅔ cup orange juice
- 2 Tbs. sugar
- ¼ tsp. ground cinnamon
- ⅛ tsp. ground nutmeg
- Honey Spread (below)

Heat oven to 400°F. Grease bottoms only of 12 medium muffin cups. Mix baking mix, 2 Tbs. sugar, the egg, orange peel and orange juice; beat vigorously 30 seconds. Fill muffin cups about ⅔ full. Mix 2 Tbs. sugar, the cinnamon and nutmeg. Sprinkle each muffin with about ½ tsp. sugar mixture. Bake 15 minutes. Serve with Honey Spread. 12 muffins.

Honey Spread: Beat ½ cup margarine or butter, softened, and ½ cup honey until fluffy.

Raisin Muffins

Old-fashioned muffins with a "down-home" taste.

- 1 egg, slightly beaten
- 1 cup milk
- 3 Tbs. vegetable oil
- ⅓ cup raisins
- 1¾ cups Bran Chex® cereal
- 1 cup sifted all-purpose flour
- ⅓ cup sugar
- 2 tsps. baking powder
- ½ tsp. salt
- ½ tsp. cinnamon

Preheat oven to 400°F. Grease twelve (2½-inch) muffin cups. Combine egg, milk, oil, raisins and Bran Chex®. Let stand 10 minutes. Meanwhile, sift together dry ingredients. Stir Bran Chex® cereal mixture to blend. Add all at once to dry ingredients. Stir only until moistened. Fill muffin cups ⅔ full. Bake 20 minutes or until lightly browned. Makes 12 muffins.

Blueberry Muffins

An old-fashioned, not-too-sweet berry muffin, from the Parkay® Margarine test kitchens. Just try them, still warm from the oven, with steaming hot mugs of freshly made coffee.

- 2 cups flour
- ⅓ cup sugar
- 2 tsps. baking powder
- ½ tsp. salt
- 1 egg, slightly beaten
- ¾ cup milk
- ½ cup Parkay® Margarine, melted
- 1 cup fresh blueberries

Combine dry ingredients. Add combined egg, milk and margarine, mixing just until moistened. Fold in blueberries. Spoon into greased and floured medium-size muffin pan, filling each cup ⅔ full. Bake at 425°F., 20–25 minutes or until golden brown. Makes 1 dozen muffins.

Variations: Substitute for fresh blueberries 1 cup:
Well-drained, thawed frozen blueberries or cranberries
Well-drained pitted dark sweet cherries
Fresh cranberries

Harvest Tea Loaf

Bake this, set out the creamy butter, brew a pot of tea and ask your mother-in-law over—it's that good. A surprise recipe from Gerber Baby Foods.

¾ cup sugar
⅓ cup shortening
2 eggs
1 7½-oz. jar Junior Gerber Squash
1½ cups sifted all-purpose flour
½ tsp. baking powder
1 tsp. soda
¾ tsp. salt
½ tsp. cinnamon
½ tsp. cloves
⅓ cup chopped nuts
⅓ cup chopped dates

Cream shortening and sugar until light and fluffy. Add eggs, one at a time, beating well after each addition. Add squash. Sift together flour, baking powder, soda, salt and spices. Reserve ¼ cup flour mixture and work it into the dates and nuts. Add flour mixture to squash mixture. Stir dates and nuts into batter. Turn batter into greased 9 × 5 × 3½-inch pan. Bake at 350°F. for about 1 hour or until done. Makes 1 loaf.

Apple Spice Coffee Cake

This is a long-time favorite from Parkay® Margarine, so good it deserves company. A fall time, crisp apple time, coffee klatsch perhaps? Be sure to serve with plenty of coffee.

½ cup Parkay® Margarine
1 cup granulated sugar
¾ cup packed brown sugar
2 eggs
1 tsp. vanilla
3 cups flour
1 Tbs. baking powder
1 tsp. salt
1 tsp. ground allspice
1 tsp. ground cloves
1 cup milk
3 cups peeled apple slices
1 tsp. cinnamon

Cream margarine, ¾ cup granulated sugar and brown sugar until light and fluffy. Blend in eggs and vanilla. Add combined flour, baking powder, salt, allspice and cloves alternately with milk; mix well after each addition. Pour into greased 13 × 9-inch baking pan. Arrange apples on batter; sprinkle with combined ¼ cup granulated sugar and cinnamon. Bake at 375°F., 40–45 minutes or until wooden pick inserted in center comes out clean.

Quick Nut Bread

There's something very satisfying about this whole wheat sweet bread from Elam's. It's nothing sensational, but it's the kind of thing people ask if you've made lately when they drop in for a cup of coffee or tea.

- 3 cups Stone Ground 100% Whole Wheat Flour
- 4 tsps. baking powder
- 1 tsp. salt
- ½ cup soft shortening
- 1 cup sugar
- 3 eggs
- 2 tsps. vanilla
- 1¼ cups milk
- 1 cup finely chopped walnuts or pecans

Combine first 3 ingredients in bowl; mix well and reserve. Cream shortening; add sugar gradually beating well after each addition, Add eggs, one at a time, beating well after each addition. Stir in vanilla and milk; mix until smooth. Add dry ingredients, ¼ at a time, blending well after each addition. Fold in chopped nuts. Spoon into greased loaf pan (9 × 5 × 3-inch). Bake in moderate oven (350°F.) until done, 60–70 minutes. Cool in pan 10 minutes; loosen edges and remove bread from pan. Finish cooling on wire rack. Makes one loaf.

Old-Fashioned Date and Nut Bread

Here's the all time best American style recipe from the Dromedary Date people. I like it served with a bowl of cream cheese whipped up with a bit of sour cream and cups of fragrant freshly made coffee.

- ¾ cup water
- ¼ cup shortening
- 1 8-oz. package Dromedary Chopped Dates or Dromedary Pitted Dates, snipped.
- ¾ cup chopped walnuts
- 2 eggs, slightly beaten
- ½ tsp. vanilla extract
- 1½ cups all-purpose flour
- ¾ cup granulated sugar
- 1½ tsps. baking soda
- ½ tsp. salt

Preheat oven to 350°F. Grease and flour a 9 × 5 × 3-inch loaf pan. In small saucepan, bring water and shortening to a boil; pour over dates in a medium bowl. Allow mixture to stand 15 minutes. Stir to blend. Add nuts, eggs and vanilla. In small bowl, combine flour, sugar, baking soda and salt. Stir into date mixture until blended. Do not overmix. Pour into pan. Bake 65–70 minutes or until cake tester inserted in center comes out clean. Cool in pan on wire rack 10 minutes. Loosen edges with spatula; turn out on wire rack to cool completely. Makes 1 loaf.

Crescent Caramel Swirl

Birth of a new classic. This recipe won the $25,000 Grand Prize at the 27th Pillsbury Bake-Off® Contest in 1976.

- ½ cup margarine or butter
- ½ cup chopped nuts
- 1 cup firmly packed brown sugar
- 2 Tbs. water
- 2 8-oz. cans Pillsbury Refrigerated Quick Crescent Dinner Rolls

Heat oven to 375°F. (350°F. for colored fluted tube pan.) In small saucepan, melt margarine. Coat bottom and sides of 12-cup fluted tube pan (do not use pan with removable bottom) with 2 Tbs. of the melted margarine; sprinkle pan with 3 Tbs. of the nuts. Add remaining nuts, brown sugar and water to margarine; heat to boiling, stirring occasionally. Remove dough from cans in rolled sections; do not unroll. Cut each section into 4 slices. Arrange 8 slices in prepared pan, separating each pinwheel slightly to allow sauce to penetrate. Spoon half the caramel sauce over dough. Repeat with remaining dough, topping slices in pan; pour remaining caramel sauce over dough. Bake at 375°F. for 25–30 minutes (30–35 minutes for colored fluted tube pan) or until deep golden brown. Cool 3 minutes; turn onto serving platter or waxed paper. Makes 1 coffee cake ring.

Grandmother's Delicious Gingerbread

An old-fashioned favorite cake-like gingerbread, from the Crisco test kitchens. The recipe was developed almost 20 years ago but it's still in demand.

1 cup brown sugar
½ cup Crisco
2 eggs
¾ cup molasses
2¾ cups sifted regular flour
2 tsps. soda
2 tsps. ginger
1 tsp. cinnamon
½ tsp. salt
1 cup buttermilk or sour milk*
Ice cream, whipped cream or applesauce

* To sour milk, add 1 Tbs. vinegar to 1 cup milk.

Blend sugar, Crisco and eggs. Stir in molasses. Add combined dry ingredients alternately with buttermilk; beat well. Spread in a well-greased and floured 13 × 9 × 2-inch pan. Bake at 350°F. for 35–40 minutes. Serve warm with ice cream, whipped cream or applesauce.

Sugar-Coated Sour Milk Doughnuts

One of my friends in Maine has the distinction of frying the best doughnuts in the entire state. Her secret? Here's what she says, "It's not just the recipe, though that must be good, but it's the way you fry them too. I use Crisco and the recipe from the can but it's my 'knack' that really makes them so good." (See below).

4 cups sifted flour
1 tsp. baking soda
1 tsp. salt
1 tsp. ground nutmeg
½ tsp. cream of tartar
¾ cup sugar
¼ cup Crisco
3 eggs
1 cup sour milk (1 Tbs. vinegar plus enough milk to make 1 cup)
Crisco for deep frying

Combine the flour, baking soda, salt, nutmeg, and cream of tartar. In large mixing bowl, cream the ¾ cup sugar and the Crisco; beat in eggs. Add flour mixture alternately with sour milk, beating just till blended. Cover and chill at least 2 hours. On floured surface, roll dough ⅜ inch thick. Cut with floured 2½-inch doughnut cutter. Fry in deep Crisco heated to 365°F. till doughnuts are golden brown, about 2–3 minutes, turning once. Drain on paper toweling. Roll in granulated sugar. Makes 24 doughnuts and 24 holes.

My Friend's "knack" tips:

On lightly floured surface, roll chilled dough about ¼ inch thick. Dip doughnut cutter in flour between cuts; cut straight down.

Heat Crisco in saucepan to 365°F. using frying thermometer to check temperature. Fry a few doughnuts at a time, turning once.

Use a slotted spoon or fork to remove doughnuts from hot Crisco. Drain on paper toweling before frosting or sugar coating.

Delicious White Bread

Here's a classic "label" recipe from Pillsbury® that is very simple to make, yet is beautiful to look at and eat.

5 to 6 cups Pillsbury's® Best Bread Flour
3 Tbs. sugar
2 tsps. salt
2 packages active dry yeast
2 cups water
¼ cup oil or shortening

Grease two 8 × 4-inch or 9 × 5-inch loaf pans. Lightly spoon flour into measuring cup; level off. In large bowl, combine 2 cups flour, sugar, salt and yeast; blend well. In small saucepan, heat water and oil until very warm (120°F. to 130°F.). Add warm liquid to flour mixture. Blend at low speed until moistened; beat 3 minutes at medium speed. By hand, stir in 2½ to 3 cups flour until dough pulls cleanly away from sides of bowl. On floured surface, knead in ½ to 1 cup flour until dough is smooth and elastic with blisters under the surface, about 10 minutes. Place dough in greased bowl; cover loosely with plastic wrap and cloth towel. Let rise in warm place until light and doubled in size, about 1½ hours. Punch down dough several times to remove all air bubbles. Divide dough into 2 parts; mold into balls. Allow to rest on counter, covered with inverted bowl, for 15 minutes. Work dough with hands to remove large air bubbles. Shape into two loaves. Place in prepared pans. Cover; let rise in warm place until dough fills pans and tops of loaves are about 1 inch above pan edges, about 1 hour. Heat oven to 375°F. Bake for 45 to 55 minutes until loaves sound hollow when lightly tapped. Remove from pans immediately; cool on wire racks. If desired, for soft crusts brush tops of loaves with melted butter. Makes 2 loaves.

Buttermilk Bread

This back-of-the-label recipe, almost as old as the Fleischmann's® first test kitchen, has been updated and simplified, but the flavor remains as homey good as your grandmother's bread.

6 cups unsifted flour (about)
3 Tbs. sugar
2½ tsps. salt
¼ tsp. baking soda
1 package Fleischmann's® Active Dry Yeast
1 cup buttermilk
1 cup water
⅓ cup margarine

Combine 2 cups flour, sugar, salt, baking soda and undissolved yeast. Heat buttermilk, water and margarine over low heat until liquids are warm. (Mixture will appear curdled.) Add to dry ingredients; beat for 2 minutes at medium speed, scraping bowl occasionally. Add 1 cup flour. Beat at high speed for 2 minutes. Stir in enough flour to make a soft dough. Turn onto floured board; knead about 8 to 10 minutes. Place in greased bowl; grease top. Cover; let rise until doubled, about 1 hour. Punch down; turn onto floured board. Divide dough in half. Shape into loaves. Place each in a greased 8½ × 4½ × 2½-inch loaf pan. Cover; let rise until doubled, about 1 hour. Bake at 375°F. about 35 minutes, or until done. Remove from pans and cool on wire racks. Makes 2 loaves.

Quick Buttermilk Rolls

What could be easier than baking these prize-winning buttermilk yeast rolls? Alberta Beaty, who developed the recipe for a Red Star® Baking Contest, says they are both easy *and* delicious. Seems the judges agreed.

4 to 4½ cups all-purpose flour
2 packages Red Star® Instant Blend Dry Yeast
3 Tbs. sugar
1 tsp. salt
½ tsp. soda
1¼ cups buttermilk
½ cup water
½ cup shortening

Preheat oven to 400°F. In large mixer bowl, combine 1½ cups flour, yeast, sugar, salt and soda; mix well. In saucepan, heat buttermilk, water and shortening until warm (120°F. to 130°F., shortening does not need to melt). Add to flour mixture. Blend at low speed until moistened; beat 3 minutes at medium speed. By hand, gradually stir in enough remaining flour to make a firm dough. Knead on floured surface until smooth and elastic, about 5 minutes. Place in greased bowl, turning to grease top. Cover; let rise in warm place until light and doubled, about 20 minutes. Punch down dough. Divide dough into 24 pieces. Form into balls; place on greased cookie sheet or 15 × 10-inch pan. Cover; let rise in warm place until almost doubled, about 20 minutes. Bake at 400°F. for 15 to 20 minutes until golden brown. Remove from pan; brush with butter, if desired. Cool on racks. Makes 24 rolls.

Portuguese Sweet Bread

This is one of my favorite breads, and everyone who tries it is as pleased as I am with its just slightly sweet taste and light texture. It was featured on the back of Fleischmann's® Yeast package a few years ago and requests are so frequent it may be put back there again next season.

- 6¼ cups (about) unsifted flour
- ⅔ cup sugar
- 1 tsp. grated lemon peel
- ¼ tsp. ground mace
- 1 package Fleischmann's® Active Dry Yeast
- ⅔ cup potato water
- ½ cup milk
- ½ cup margarine
- 3 eggs (at room temperature)
- ½ cup unseasoned mashed potato
- Confectioners sugar

Combine 1½ cups flour, sugar, lemon peel, mace and undissolved yeast. Heat potato water, milk and margarine to 120°F. to 130°F. Add to dry ingredients; beat 2 minutes. Add eggs, mashed potato and ½ cup flour. Beat 2 minutes. Stir in more flour to make a soft dough. On floured board, knead 8 to 10 minutes. Place in greased bowl; turn to grease top. Cover; let rise until doubled, about 1¾ hours. Punch dough down, roll out to 16 × 10 inches. Roll up. Place, seam side down, in greased 10-inch tube pan. Pinch ends to form ring. Cover; let rise until doubled, about 1 hour. Bake at 350°F. 40 minutes or until done. Cool in pan 5 minutes. Remove. Cool. Dust with confectioners sugar.

Bran Yeast Loaf

If your mother or grandmother saved the Kellogg's® box the original version of this recipe appeared on, she would have a collectors' item. It was decorated with one of a

series of illustrations by Norman Rockwell; the recipe alone is a collectors' item.

- 2 packages active dry yeast
- 2¼ cups warm water (110°F. to 115°F.)
- ⅓ cup molasses
- 2 Tbs. vegetable oil
- 2 tsps. salt
- 5½ cups all-purpose flour
- 3 cups Kellogg's® 40% Bran Flakes® Cereal
- 2 Tbs. margarine or butter, melted

Dissolve yeast in warm water in large mixing bowl. Add molasses, oil, salt and 3 cups of the flour. Beat well. Stir in cereal. Add remaining flour to make a stiff dough. On lightly floured surface, knead dough about 10 minutes or until smooth and elastic. Place in greased bowl, turning once to grease top. Cover lightly. Let rise in warm place until double in volume (about 1 hour). Punch down dough. Let rest 15 minutes. Shape into 2 loaves and placed in greased 9 × 5 × 3-inch loaf pans. Brush with melted margarine. Cover and let rise in warm place until double in volume (about 30 minutes). Bake at 375°F. about 45 minutes or until golden brown. Remove from pans and cool on wire rack. Makes 2 loaves.

Whole Wheat Potato Bread

Another updated classic from Pillsbury®. My favorite friend says it's even good eaten plain, without butter; you may agree.

- 3½ cups Pillsbury's® Best Bread Flour
- 1½ cups Hungry Jack® Mashed Potato Flakes
- 1½ cups water
- 1¼ cups milk
- ¼ cups margarine or butter
- ¼ cup honey

2½ tsps. salt
2 packages active dry yeast
2 eggs
2½ to 3 cups Pillsbury's® Best Whole Wheat Flour

Grease two 8 × 4- or 9 × 5-inch loaf pans. Lightly spoon flour into measuring cup; level off. In large bowl, combine 2 cups bread flour, potato flakes, salt and yeast; blend well. In medium saucepan, heat water, milk, margarine and honey until very warm (120° to 130°F.). Add warm liquid and eggs to flour mixture. Blend at low speed until moistened; beat 4 minutes at medium speed. By hand, stir in 1½ cups bread flour and 1½ to 2 cups whole wheat flour until dough pulls cleanly away from sides of bowl. On floured surface, knead in remaining 1 to 1½ cups whole wheat flour until dough is smooth and elastic, about 10 minutes. Place dough in greased bowl, cover loosely with plastic wrap and cloth towel. Let rise in warm place until light and doubled in size, about 1½ hours. Punch down dough. Divide dough into two parts; mold into balls. Allow to rest on counter, covered with inverted bowl, for 15 minutes. Shape dough into 2 loaves; place in prepared pans. Cover; let rise in warm place until doubled in size, about 1 hour. Heat oven to 375°F. Bake loaves for 35 to 40 minutes or until deep golden brown and loaves sound hollow when lightly tapped. Immediately remove loaves from pans. If desired, brush with margarine or butter. Makes 2 loaves.

Ralston Whole Wheat Bread

This recipe for Ralston® Whole Wheat Bread has been revised, but it still has the same good flavor of the original one developed almost 30 years ago. Try toasting it for a real treat.

2¼	cups Instant or Regular Ralston® cereal	4	cups (1 quart) milk, scalded
¼	cup sugar	2	packages active dry yeast
1	Tbs. salt	½	cup warm water
⅓	cup vegetable shortening	7	to 8 cups all-purpose flour

Grease 3 8½ × 4½ × 2½-inch loaf pans. Combine Ralston®, sugar, salt and shortening in large bowl. Add hot, scalded milk. Stir until thoroughly moistened. Cool to warm (105°F. to 115°F.), stirring occasionally. Dissolve yeast in water. Stir into cereal mixture. Add 2 cups flour. Mix well. Gradually stir in enough additional flour to form a stiff dough. Place on floured surface. Knead until smooth and elastic (8 to 10 minutes). Work in additional flour as needed. Form into ball. Place in greased bowl. Turn to grease all sides. Cover. Let rise in warm place, free from draft, until double (about 1 hour). Punch dough down. Place on lightly floured surface. Knead about 2 minutes. Divide dough in thirds. Form into loaves. Place in pans. Cover. Let rise in warm place until almost double (about 30 minutes). Bake in preheated 400°F. oven about 30 minutes or until browned and bread sounds hollow when lightly tapped. Remove from pans at once. Cool on rack. Makes 3 loaves. Use 1 loaf fresh from the oven. Freeze two to enjoy later.

Note: For golden brown, shiny top, brush tops with beaten egg before baking.

Russian Black Bread

This hearty "old country" loaf has been a specialty of whole-grain bakers for almost 20 years. Fleischmann's® Yeast put it on their package label that long ago.

- 1 cup unsifted rye flour
- 2 to 2½ cups unsifted white flour
- ½ cup whole bran cereal
- 2 tsps. caraway seed, crushed
- 1 tsp. salt
- ½ tsp. sugar
- ½ tsp. instant coffee
- ½ tsp. onion powder
- ¼ tsp. fennel seed, crushed
- 1 package Fleischmann's® Active Dry Yeast
- 1 cup water
- 2 Tbs. white vinegar
- 2 Tbs. dark molasses
- 2 Tbs. Fleischmann's® Margarine
- ½ square (½ oz.) unsweetened chocolate
- ½ tsp. corn starch
- ¼ cup cold water

Combine rye and white flours. In a large bowl thoroughly mix 2 cups flour mixture with cereal, caraway seed, salt, sugar, instant coffee, onion powder, fennel seed and Fleischmann's® Active Dry Yeast. Combine 1 cup water, vinegar, molasses, Fleischmann's® Margarine and chocolate in a saucepan and heat over low heat until liquids are very warm (120°F. to 130°F.). Margarine and chocolate do not need to melt. Gradually add to dry ingredients and beat 2 minutes at medium speed of electric mixer, scraping bowl occasionally. Stir in enough additional flour mixture to make a soft dough. Turn out onto lightly floured board. Knead until smooth and elastic, 5 to 7 minutes. Cover; let rise in a warm place, free from draft, until doubled in bulk, about 1 hour. Bake at 350°F. for 45 to 50 minutes, or until done. Meanwhile, combine corn starch and cold water. Cook over medium heat, stirring constantly 1 minute. As soon as loaf is baked, brush corn starch mixture over top. Return bread to oven and bake 2 minutes longer, or until glaze is set. Remove from pan and cool on wire rack. Makes 1 loaf.

Coconut Breakfast Breads

This is bread for a special breakfast—Christmas morning maybe or New Year's Day. The Holland House® people recommend you make it any day to make the next morning a special one.

- ⅓ cup milk, scalded
- ¾ stick unsalted butter
- ½ cup Coco Casa® Cream of Coconut
- 1 tsp. vanilla extract
- ¾ tsp. salt
- 3 large eggs, lightly beaten
- 1 package dry active yeast, dissolved in 2 Tbs. warm water
- 4 cups unbleached flour
- 1 egg yolk mixed in 3 Tbs. water for glaze (page 360)

Filling

Stir together to form a paste

- ½ cup Coco Casa® Cream of Coconut
- 4 Tbs. coconut flakes
- 4 Tbs. chocolate bits or 4 Tbs. ground toasted almonds

Stir butter in scalded milk until dissolved. Add Cream of Coconut, vanilla and salt. Place eggs in bowl with milk mixture, yeast and flour. Knead until dough is pliable and satiny to the touch, adding more flour if necessary. Place in large buttered bowl. Cover with buttered foil. Let rise in warm place 2½ to 3 hours until it triples in volume. Punch down and shape into brioches or a loaf.

Brioches

Butter 12 small brioche molds. Flatten into a 4-inch circle enough dough to half fill mold. Place 1 Tbs. filling in center, fold into a cushion and place, seam down, in mold. Cut a cross on surface, and into this press a ball of dough the size of a walnut.

Loaf

Butter a 5 × 9-inch loaf pan. Roll dough in a 9-inch square. Spread filling evenly over surface, roll tightly and place seam down into pan.

Glaze for either loaf or brioche

Let dough rise again for 1 to 1½ hours or until doubled. Brush with egg glaze. Bake in preheated 400°F. oven. Brioches: 30 to 35 minutes. Loaf: 50 to 60 minutes.

Grandma's Cinnamon Rolls

A German grandmother from Minnesota passed on the recipe for these delicious rolls to Barbara Hawkins of Denton, Kansas, who entered them in a Red Star® Baking Contest. The "secret" that makes them special is the coffee and maple flavoring in the icing which is spread on the still warm rolls.

- 5½ to 6 cups all-purpose flour
- 2 packages Red Star® Instant Blend Dry Yeast
- ½ cup sugar
- 1½ tsps. salt
- 1 cup milk
- 1 cup water
- ¼ cup butter or margarine
- 2 eggs
- ⅓ cup butter or margarine, melted
- ¾ cup sugar
- 1½ tsps. cinnamon
- ½ cup chopped nuts

Glaze

- 3 Tbs. butter or margarine, melted
- 2 cups powdered sugar
- 3 to 4 Tbs. hot coffee
- ½ tsp. maple flavor

Preheat oven 375°F. In large mixer bowl, combine 2 cups flour, yeast, ½ cup sugar and salt; mix well. In saucepan, heat milk, water and butter until warm (120°F. to 130°F.; butter does not need to melt). Add to flour mixture. Add eggs. Blend at low speed until moistened; beat 3 minutes at medium speed. By hand, gradually stir in enough remaining flour to make a soft dough. Knead on floured surface until smooth and elastic, about 5 minutes. Place in greased bowl, turning to grease top. Cover; let rise in warm place until light and doubled, about 1 hour. Punch down dough. Divide into 2 parts. On lightly floured surface, roll or pat each half into a 12 × 9-inch rectangle. Brush each part with melted butter. Combine ¾ cup sugar, cinnamon and nuts. Sprinkle over butter. Starting with shorter side, roll up tightly, pressing dough into roll with each turn. Pinch edges to seal. Cut each roll into 12 pieces. Place cut-side down in greased 13 × 9-inch pans. Cover; let rise in warm place until almost doubled, about 30 minutes. Bake at 375°F. for 20 minutes until golden brown. Combine Glaze ingredients; blend until smooth. Drizzle over hot rolls. Cool on racks. Makes 24 rolls.

Viennese Crescent Ring

Talk about good cooks, this elegant coffee cake won a special 1980 contest held for three-time Bake Off® Finalists who were no longer eligible for Pillsbury's regular yearly contest.

- 1 cup finely ground almonds
- ⅓ cup powdered sugar
- 2 Tbs. margarine or butter, softened
- 1 tsp. almond extract
- 1 egg yolk (reserve egg white for topping)
- 2 8-oz. cans Pillsbury® Refrigerated Crescent Dinner Quick Rolls

Topping

- ⅓ cup apricot preserves
- ⅓ cup pineapple preserves
- Reserved egg white
- ¼ cup sliced unblanched almonds
- 1 Tbs. sugar

Heat oven to 350°F. In medium bowl, combine ground almonds, powdered sugar, margarine, almond extract and egg yolk; blend well. (Mixture will be stiff.) Set aside. Separate one can of dough into 4 rectangles. Place in ungreased 12-inch pizza pan; press over bottom, sealing perforations. Separate second can of dough into 8 triangles. Spread 1 rounded Tbs. of almond filling over each triangle. Roll up; start at shortest side of triangle and roll to opposite point. Arrange filled crescents, pointed-side-down, evenly around edge of dough-lined pan. In small bowl, combine preserves. Spoon evenly over center of dough spreading just to filled rolls. Beat egg white until frothy; brush over tops of filled crescents. Sprinkle with sliced almonds; sprinkle sugar evenly over almonds. Bake at 350°F. for 25 to 30 minutes or until golden brown. Cut into wedges to serve. Serve warm. Makes 8 servings.

Pita Bread

Another great recipe from Pillsbury® that deserves a gold star. These tender, crisp rolls are super easy to bring freshly baked to the table.

- ¾ cup boiling water
- 2 Tbs. margarine or butter, softened
- 1 package Pillsbury® Hot Roll Mix
- Cornmeal
- Milk, if desired
- Sesame seeds, if desired

Measure boiling water into large bowl; stir in margarine until completely melted. Sprinkle with yeast packet from Hot Roll mix; stir until dissolved. Add flour mixture; blend well. Knead dough on lightly floured surface for about 2 minutes until smooth. Cover; let rise in a warm place until doubled in size, 30 to 45 minutes. Lightly sprinkle cornmeal onto 2 ungreased cookie sheets. Divide dough into 6 equal pieces; shape into balls. On lightly floured surface, roll each piece into a 7-inch circle. Place 3 circles on each cookie sheet. Let rise again in warm place, 30 to 45 minutes, until light and slightly risen. For sesame seed pita bread, brush circles with small amount of milk and sprinkle lightly with sesame seeds. Bake in preheated 425°F. oven for 5 to 10 minutes or until light golden brown. Cut in half crosswise and slice to form pocket before storing. Makes 6 pita breads, 12 servings.

Sunland Vineyard Loaf

Super-good and super-quick, this raisin bread made from packaged hot roll mix made its debut in a Sun-Maid® booklet back in 1977. The recipe says to cool it, but I must admit I can't wait, so it's always served still slightly warm at our house.

- 1 cup Sun-Maid® Seedless Raisins
- ⅓ cup sherry
- 1 13¾-oz. package hot roll mix
- ¼ cup warm water
- ½ cup hot milk
- 2 Tbs. butter
- 1 Tbs. sugar
- 1 egg, beaten
- ½ cup chopped walnuts
- 4 bay leaves (optional)
- Melted butter

Chop raisins coarsely; add sherry. Let stand an hour or more. Dissolve yeast from mix in warm water. Combine milk, butter and sugar; when lukewarm, add yeast and egg. Beat in flour mixture from package. Mix in walnuts and drained raisins. Cover, and let rise in warm place until doubled, 1¼ to 1½ hours. Punch down. Divide into 8 portions. Shape each into a slender roll 8 inches long. Twist 2 together for each loaf; fit into greased pans, 5½ × 3 inches, with a bay leaf in bottom of pan. Brush with melted butter. Let rise until doubled, 30 to 40 minutes. Bake on low shelf at 375°F. 30 to 35 minutes. Turn out and cool.

Banana Nut Bread

This moist, well-textured bread was first used in a Wheat Chex® Cereal recipe book about 20 years ago. It's included in that company's all-time great recipe file.

- 1½ cups all-purpose flour
- ½ cup sugar
- 2½ tsps. baking powder
- ½ tsp. salt
- ½ tsp. baking soda
- 1 cup Wheat Chex® Cereal crushed to ½ cup
- ⅓ cup chopped nuts
- 1 egg, slightly beaten
- ¼ cup vegetable oil
- 2 Tbs. water
- 1½ cups mashed banana (3 large)
- 1 tsp. vanilla

Preheat oven to 350°F. Grease an 8½ × 4½ × 2½-inch loaf pan. Stir together flour, sugar, baking powder, salt, baking soda, Wheat Chex Cereal® and nuts. Combine egg, oil, water, mashed banana and vanilla. Add all at once to dry ingredients. Stir just until moistened. Spread evenly into pan. Bake 50 to 55 minutes or until tester inserted in center comes out clean. Let cool 15 minutes before removing from pan. Makes 1 loaf.

Note: May be baked in three 5¾ × 3¼ × 2-inch loaf pans (bake about 40 minutes) or six 4½ × 2½ × 1¼-inch loaf pans (bake about 30 minutes).

Fruit and Cereal Brunch Cake

From the General Mills® kitchens, an adaptation of a classic German recipe. Serve this rich coffee cake at breakfast, brunch or tea time.

- 2 cups Total® Cereal
- 1 cup orange juice
- ¼ cup vegetable oil
- 1 egg
- 2 medium bananas, mashed
- 1½ cups Gold Medal® All-Purpose Flour
- ¾ cup sugar
- ½ cup raisins, if desired
- 1 tsp. baking soda
- 1 tsp. ground cinnamon
- ½ tsp. salt
- Streusel Topping (below)

Heat oven to 350°F. Grease square pan, 9 × 9 × 2-inches. Mix cereal and orange juice in large bowl; let stand until softened, about 2 minutes. Mix in oil, egg and bananas. Stir in flour, sugar, raisins, baking soda, cinnamon and salt. Spread in pan. Bake until top springs back when touched, 40 to 45 minutes. Sprinkle Streusel Topping over warm coffee cake. Set oven control to broil and/or 550°F. Broil with top about 5 inches from heat until bubbly, about 1 minute. (Watch carefully to avoid burning.) Makes 9 to 12 servings.

Streusel Topping

- ½ cup packed brown sugar
- ½ cup chopped nuts
- ¼ cup Gold Medal All-Purpose Flour
- ¼ cup margarine or butter, softened
- ½ tsp. ground cinnamon

Mix all ingredients until crumbly.

Honeycomb Coffee Cake

Who doesn't like warm, fragrant buttery coffee cake sweetened with honey? A featured recipe on the inside label of Land O Lakes® Unsalted Butter. It's a treasure.

1¾ cups all-purpose flour
½ cup sugar
½ cup Land O Lakes® Unsalted Butter, softened
⅓ cup milk
2 eggs
2 tsp. baking powder
½ tsp. almond extract
½ tsp. orange extract
Topping (below)

Preheat oven to 350°F. Grease 9-inch square baking pan. In 3-quart mixer bowl combine all coffee cake ingredients. Beat at medium speed, scraping sides of bowl often, until well mixed (1 to 2 minutes). Spread into greased pan. Set aside. In heavy 2-quart saucepan combine all topping ingredients. Cook over medium heat, stirring occasionally, until mixture comes to a full boil (5 to 6 minutes). Continue cooking, stirring occasionally, until mixture boils (2 to 3 minutes). Pour topping evenly over coffee cake. Bake near center at 350°F. oven for 22 to 27 minutes or until wooden pick inserted in center comes out clean. Makes 1 9-inch square coffee cake.

Topping

½ cup Land O Lakes® Unsalted Butter
½ cup chopped pecans
¼ cup sugar
¼ cup honey
½ tsp. nutmeg
1 Tbs. milk
½ tsp. orange extract

Top-Stove Coffee Cake

In 1947 the Pet® Milk Company published an up-dated edition of their original 1932 *Gold Cookbook*. This recipe was included, and it's still on their most frequently requested list.

- 1 cup sifted all-purpose flour
- ⅓ cup sugar
- 2 tsp. baking powder
- ¾ tsp. cinnamon
- ½ tsp. salt
- 1 well-beaten egg
- ⅓ cup Pet® Milk
- ⅓ cup water
- 3 Tbs. melted shortening
- ¼ cup sugar
- ¾ tsp. cinnamon

Grease a heavy 9-inch skillet. Cover the bottom with 1 layer of heavy brown wrapping paper cut to fit. Grease top layer of paper. Sift together first 5 ingredients into bowl. Mix together the egg, Pet® Milk, water and shortening. Add, all at once, to flour mixture; mix quickly but thoroughly. Pour into prepared skillet. Sprinkle with a mixture of ¼ cup sugar and ¾ tsp. cinnamon. Cover and bake on top of range over very low heat 30 minutes, or until firm to the touch. Lift out carefully and remove paper while still hot. Decorate with shelled walnut halves, if desired. Serve warm or cold. Makes one 9-inch cake.

Note: To bake this cake in the oven, omit paper, place uncovered skillet on center shelf of a moderate oven (375°F.). Bake 25 minutes or until firm to the touch.

Mexican Corn Bread

This very different corn bread has been a favorite of Mrs. W. B. Stokely, III, for years; it is a much-requested recipe from the Stokely–Van Camp® test kitchens.

- 1⅓ cups yellow cornmeal
- 1⅓ cups all-purpose flour
- 3 Tbs. sugar
- ½ tsp. baking soda
- 1 tsp. salt
- 2 Tbs. bacon drippings
- 1 medium-size onion, finely chopped
- 6 strips bacon, cooked and crumbled

- 2 eggs
- 1 cup buttermilk
- 1 8½-oz. can Cream Style Golden Corn
- ¾ cup grated American cheese, divided
- 1 to 2 Tbs. chopped green chilies

Preheat oven to 400°F. Butter 9-inch square pan. Combine cornmeal, flour, sugar, baking soda and salt in large mixing bowl. Beat eggs and stir in buttermilk, Corn, bacon drippings, onion, bacon, ½ cup cheese and chilies. Add to cornmeal mixture; stir until well combined. Pour batter into prepared pan and sprinkle with remaining ¼ cup cheese. Bake 45 minutes. Makes 8 to 10 servings.

Cinnamon Apple Rolls

These rolls belong to the "sticky bun" family, of which I am an avid fan. You will be too when you try them. The recipe was developed by the Crisco® Oil people and it's one of their all-time most requested.

- 3 cups sifted all-purpose enriched flour
- 2 Tbs. sugar
- 4 tsps. double-acting baking powder
- 1 tsp. salt
- 1 cup milk
- ½ cup Crisco® Oil
- 2 cups chopped, pared apples
- ½ cup brown sugar
- 1 tsp. cinnamon
- 1 cup brown sugar
- ½ cup Crisco® Oil
- ½ cup chopped nuts

Combine flour, 2 Tbs. sugar, baking powder and salt. Add milk and ½ cup Crisco® Oil; stir just enough to hold dough together. Place on lightly floured surface and knead 10 to 12 strokes. Roll to ¼-inch thick rectangle. Cover dough with combined apples, ½ cup brown sugar and cinnamon. Roll up jelly-roll fashion. Cut into 1-inch thick pieces. Combine 1 cup brown sugar, ½ cup Crisco® Oil and nuts in bottom of 13 × 9 × 2-inch pan. Place rolls in pan. Bake at 425°F. for 15 to 20 minutes, until desired brownness. Immediately turn upside down onto large platter or cookie sheet. Serve warm. Makes about 8 rolls.

Bran Nut and Raisin Bread

The first in-flight meal to be served aboard a passenger plane took place on April 8, 1930. Fifteen presidents of Detroit women's organizations were served a luncheon prepared by Mary I. Barber, home economic director at the Kellogg® Company. It was a cooperative venture; Kellogg's® supplied the meal, and the Ford Motor Company provided the "Tin Goose" tri-motor club plane. A report on the outing stated that the Bran Nut and Raisin Bread was especially well received and, oh yes, the women enjoyed the flight.

- 1½ cups all-purpose flour
- 1 Tbs. baking powder
- 1 tsp. salt
- 1½ cups Kellogg's® All-Bran® Cereal
- ⅓ cup firmly packed brown sugar
- ¾ cup milk
- ¾ cup water
- ⅓ cup molasses
- ¾ cup English walnuts, broken
- ¾ cup seedless raisins

Stir together flour, baking powder and salt. Set aside. In large mixing bowl, mix together cereal, sugar, milk, water and molasses. Mix in flour mixture. Stir in walnuts and raisins. Spread in greased 9 × 5 × 3-inch loaf pan. Bake at 350°F. about 1 hour until wooden pick inserted near center comes out clean. Makes 1 loaf.

Saffron Loaves

Start the week off right with this bread. Monday won't look so bad and the rest of the week will look better when you treat yourself and friends to this delicious sunny-colored, sunny-tasting Dole® Banana Loaf.

- 1 cup butter
- 1 cup sugar
- 3 eggs, separated
- 2 medium ripe Dole® bananas
- 1 cup milk
- 3½ cups flour
- 4 tsps. baking powder
- 1 tsp. salt
- ⅛ tsp. saffron*
- 1 cup seedless raisins
- ½ cup coarsely chopped peanuts

Cream butter and sugar until light and fluffy. Beat in egg yolks until blended. Mash bananas to make 1 cup. Combine with milk. Combine remaining ingredients. Add to creamed mixture alternately with milk mixture until blended. Beat egg whites until stiff peaks form, but not dry. Fold into batter. Pour into two 8 × 4 × 2½-inch well-greased loaf pans. Bake in a 350°F. oven 50 to 60 minutes until cake tests done. Cool 10 minutes. Invert onto wire racks to complete cooling. Makes 2 loaves.

* Substitute 2 tsps. cinnamon

Biscuits

Remember Scarlett "stuffin'" biscuits before the big barbecue at Twelve Oaks? The recipe for these absolutely authentic Southern biscuits was one of the first to appear on the Pillsbury® self-rising flour bag. It's a classic for sure.

2 cups Pillsbury's® Best Self-Rising or Unbleached Self-Rising Flour
½ cup shortening
¾ cup milk

Heat oven to 450°F. Lightly spoon flour into measuring cup; level off. Cut shortening into flour with fork until consistency of coarse meal. Add milk all at once; stir with fork just until a soft dough forms. Turn dough onto lightly floured surface; sprinkle dough lightly with flour. Knead gently 10 times or until no longer sticky. Roll out dough to ½-inch thickness; cut with 2-inch floured biscuit cutter. Place biscuits on ungreased cookie sheet. Bake at 450°F. for 8 to 12 minutes or until golden brown. Makes 12 biscuits.

Variations:

Crispy Biscuits: Roll out dough to ⅛- to ¼-inch thickness. Cut with floured 2¾-inch biscuit cutter. Bake at 425°F. for 8 to 10 minutes.

Buttermilk Biscuits: Substitute buttermilk for milk. Add ¼ tsp. soda.

Sausage or Bacon Biscuits: Fry ½ lb. sausage or bacon. Drain well; crumble. Add to flour-shortening mixture. Refrigerate leftovers.

Cheese Biscuits: Add 8 oz. (2 cups) shredded Cheddar cheese to flour-shortening mixture.

Cornmeal Biscuits: Substitute ½ cup cornmeal for ½ cup flour.

Drop Biscuits: Increase milk to 1 cup. Drop dough by tablespoonfuls onto greased cookie sheet.

Irish Soda Bread

A favorite recipe featured on the Bisquick box in the 1970's and in Betty Crocker's® "Creative Recipes" booklet. Best served warm (not hot), cut into wedges, split and spread with soft butter.

- 4 cups Bisquick® Baking Mix
- 1 cup Gold Medal® Whole Wheat Flour
- 3 Tbs. sugar
- ¼ cup firm margarine or butter
- 2 eggs
- 1½ cups buttermilk

Heat oven to 350°F. Generously grease 1½-quart round casserole. Mix baking mix, flour and sugar in large bowl. Cut in margarine until crumbly. Beat eggs slightly; reserve 1 Tbs. Stir remaining eggs and the buttermilk into crumbly mixture until moistened. Turn dough onto well-floured cloth-covered board. Knead 20 times. Shape dough into ball; place in casserole. Cut 4-inch cross about ¼-inch deep in center of ball. Brush dough with reserved egg. Bake until wooden pick inserted in center comes out clean, 60 to 70 minutes. Cool 10 minutes; remove from casserole. Makes 1 loaf.

Peanut Butter Wheat Crackers

Quick, easy and absolutely delicious; a must-have, much-requested recipe from the Skippy® Peanut Butter kitchens.

- 1 cup unsifted flour
- 1 cup unsifted whole-wheat flour
- 1 cup Skippy® Super Chunk Peanut Butter
- ½ cup (about) water

¼ cup wheat germ
1½ tsps. caraway seeds
1 tsp. salt
½ tsp. baking soda
2 Tbs. cider vinegar
Milk
Coarse salt (optional)

In large bowl mix together flour, whole-wheat flour, wheat germ, caraway seeds, salt and baking soda. With pastry blender or two knives, cut in Peanut Butter until coarse crumbs form. Add water and vinegar; mix until dough holds together (if mixture is too dry additional water may be added 1 Tbs. at a time). Divide dough in half. On lightly floured surface roll half of dough out to ⅛-inch thickness. Cut with 3-inch round cookie cutter. Repeat with scraps and remaining half of dough. Place on ungreased cookie sheet. Brush surface with milk. If desired, sprinkle with coarse salt. Bake in 375°F. oven 13 to 15 minutes or until browned and crisp. Remove from pan and cool on wire racks. Store in airtight container. Makes about 40 crackers.

Whole Wheat Cheese Wafers

In 1907 the Kellogg Company ran a promotion campaign with newspaper advertisements that read, "Give the grocer a wink, and see what you get: KTC." KTC stood for Kellogg's® Toasted Corn Flakes® and every customer who winked at the grocer received a free cereal sample. In New York City alone sales increased from two railroad carloads monthly to a carload a day! A more recent but less-daring promotion featured this recipe for these delicious cheese wafers.

½ cup margarine or butter, softened
2 cups (8 ozs.) shredded sharp Cheddar cheese

3 cups Kellogg's® Rice Krispies® cereal, crushed to measure 1½ cups
¾ cup whole wheat flour

In large mixing bowl, beat margarine and cheese until very light and fluffy. Stir in crushed Cereal. Add flour, mixing until well combined. Portion dough using rounded measuring teaspoon. Shape in o balls. Place on ungreased baking sheets. Flatten with fork dipped in flour. Bake at 350°F. about 12 minutes or until lightly browned around edges. Remove immediately from baking sheets. Cool on wire racks. Makes about 7 dozen.

Surprise Muffins

These easy-to-make muffins made their debut back in the 1950's when the recipe appeared in a national Welsh® Concord Grape Jelly ad. Their homey, old-fashioned flavor is just right with freshly made coffee.

3 cups sifted all-purpose flour
4 tsps. double-acting baking powder
¼ cup sugar
1 tsp. salt
¼ cup butter or margarine
3 eggs, well beaten
1 cup milk
1 cup golden seedless raisins
½ cup Welch® Concord Grape Jelly

In a bowl, sift together flour, baking powder, sugar and salt. Cut in butter. Mix eggs, milk and raisins; blend into flour mixture. Stir lightly just to dampen flour. (If too dry, add few drops more milk.) Spoon into greased muffin-pan cups. Push 1 spoonful of grape jelly down into batter of each cup. Bake in a preheated hot oven (425°F.) approximately 20 minutes or until done. Serve hot. Makes 12.

Baking Powder Biscuits

This is the "remembered" Crisco recipe that's been used by over three generations of good cooks who "don't need a recipe to knock out a few biscuits for goodness' sake!"

2 cups sifted flour
3 tsps. baking powder
1 tsp. salt
⅓ cup Crisco
¾ cup milk

Preheat oven to 425°F. In bowl, combine the flour, baking powder and salt. Cut in Crisco until mixture resembles coarse meal. Add milk; stir with fork until blended. Transfer dough to a lightly floured surface. Knead gently, 8–10 times. Roll dough ½ inch thick. Cut with floured cutter. Bake on ungreased baking sheet at 425°F. for 12–15 minutes. Makes 12–16 biscuits.

9.
The Very Best Pies

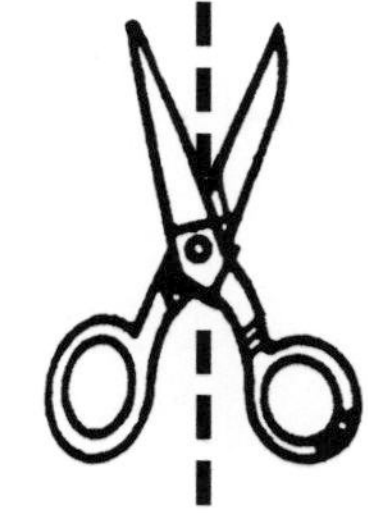

We Americans simply love pies. Our fondness for them dates back to the English settlers who founded Colonial America, for pies are as old as England itself. Our New England ancestors used native apples and the Indian gift of pumpkin for those early desserts, but pie-making was by no means limited to those first fruits. Moving westward, our pioneer families adopted local fruits to make mouth-watering fresh peach and plum pies. Sour cherries, blackberries and rhubarb, too, lent their tart-sweet taste to flaky pastry. Hoosier housewives created shoofly pie with dark sweet molasses, while Southern cooks concocted those made-in-heaven chocolate pies and that ultimate in glorious calorie-abandon, the pecan pie.

As for lemon pie, it knows no geographic limitations. Created at the turn of the century, lemon pie remains second only to chocolate cake as our all-time favorite dessert.

But many a cook has shied away from pie-making, afraid that special skills were needed to make a perfect pie. If you are one of them, hesitate no longer. This chapter has all of your favorites to make the results as certain as the rising sun, plus a handy fruit-pie chart.

Even pastry making, that sometimes forbidding art, has lost its terrors; flaky unbaked shells are available in every supermarket, and dependable pie-crust mixes are easily at hand. Also included here is a never-fail pie-crust recipe. So make your own pastry, use a mix or a ready-to-bake shell, whatever suits your time, your skill or your fancy, but do go ahead and delight your family and guests with a real, honest-to-goodness, homemade pie. No other dessert is as dear to the hearts of all of us than freshly made pie

Libby's Famous Pumpkin Pie

For seventy-five years this has been America's favorite pumpkin pie recipe and it is without doubt the best.

- 2 eggs, slightly beaten
- 1 16-ounce can Libby's Solid Pack Pumpkin
- ¾ cup sugar
- ½ tsp. salt
- 1 tsp. cinnamon
- ½ tsp. ginger
- ¼ tsp. cloves
- 1½ cups (12-ounce can) undiluted Carnation Evaporated Milk
- 1 9-inch unbaked pie shell with high fluted edge* **

Mix filling ingredients in order given. Pour into pie shell. Bake in preheated 425°F. oven for 15 minutes. Reduce temperature to 350°F. and continue baking for 45 minutes, until knife inserted in center of pie filling comes out clean. Cool. Garnish with whipped cream, if desired. Makes one 9-inch pie.

***Crunchy Pecan Topping:** In a small bowl, mix 1 cup coarsely chopped pecans with ⅔ cup firmly packed light brown sugar. Drizzle with 3 Tbs. melted butter or margarine; stir until uniformly moistened. Sprinkle over completely cooled pumpkin pie. Broil about 5 inches from heat for 1 to 2 minutes, until topping is bubbly. Serve while warm. Or, let cool, then garnish with whipped cream or dessert topping and extra pecan halves. Tops one 9-inch pie.

* If using regular frozen pie shells, recipe fills two. Bake on cookie sheet in preheated 425°F. oven for 15 minutes. Reduce heat to 350°F. and continue baking for about 30 minutes, until pies test done with knife, as noted above.

** If using deep-dish frozen pie shells, recipe fills one. Let shell thaw for ten minutes; then pinch edge so that it stands ½ inch above rim of pan. Bake filled pie on cookie sheet in preheated 425°F. oven for 15 minutes. Reduce heat to 350°F.; continue baking for about 50 minutes, until pie tests done with knife, as noted above.

Creamy Orange Pumpkin Pie

Here's another version of that famous Libby Pumpkin Pie. Gossamer light and delicately orange flavored, it made an instant hit when Libby added the recipe to its Solid Pack Pumpkin label several years ago.

- 1 9-inch unbaked pie shell
- 1 cup sugar, divided
- 1 envelope unflavored gelatine
- 1 tsp. pumpkin pie spice
- ½ tsp. salt
- 1½ cups (12-ounce can) undiluted Carnation Evaporated Milk
- 2 eggs, separated
- 1 16-ounce can Libby's Solid Pack Pumpkin
- ½ cup orange marmalade
- ½ cup chopped pecans or shredded coconut

Bake pie shell according to package directions. Stir together ½ cup sugar, gelatine, pumpkin pie spice and salt in 2-quart saucepan. Add evaporated milk. Heat, stirring constantly, to boil; remove from heat. Beat egg yolks. Pour a portion of hot mixture into beaten egg yolks. Pour egg mixture back into saucepan. Mix well. Heat, stirring constantly, until mixture thickens. Remove from heat. Stir in pumpkin and orange marmalade. Chill until mixture mounds from spoon. Beat egg whites until foamy; gradually beat in remaining ½ cup sugar until stiff peaks form; fold into pumpkin mixture. Pour into baked pie shell. Top with pecans or coconut. Chill until set. Makes one 9-inch pie.

Pecan Pie

This recipe for pecan pie was printed on the Karo label in 1945. Today, after more than thirty years, it is still one of the most popular.

- 3 eggs
- 1 cup Karo Light or Dark Corn Syrup
- 1 cup sugar
- 2 Tbs. corn oil margarine, melted
- 1 tsp. vanilla
- ⅛ tsp. salt
- 1 cup pecans
- 1 9-inch unbaked pastry shell

Beat eggs slightly in a small bowl with mixer at medium speed. Beat in corn syrup, sugar, margarine, vanilla and salt. Stir in pecans. Pour filling into pastry shell. Bake in 350°F. oven 55 to 65 minutes or until knife inserted halfway between center and edge comes out clean. Cool. If desired, serve with whipped cream. Makes one 9-inch pie.

Lemon Meringue Pie

The century was young, the horseless carriage was making a tentative appearance and ladies' skirts still swept the ground in the early 1900s when this classic recipe was printed on the Argo Corn Starch package.

- 1 cup sugar
- 3 Tbs. Argo Corn Starch
- 1½ cups cold water
- 3 egg yolks, slightly beaten
- 1 lemon's grated rind
- ¼ cup lemon juice
- 1 Tbs. margarine
- 1 9-inch baked pastry shell
- 3 egg whites
- ⅓ cup sugar

Stir together 1 cup sugar and cornstarch in a 2-quart saucepan. Gradually stir in water until smooth. Stir in egg yolks. Stirring constantly, bring to boil over medium heat and boil

1 minute. Remove from heat. Stir in lemon rind, lemon juice and margarine. Cool. Turn into pastry shell. Beat egg whites until foamy in small bowl with mixer at high speed. Add ⅓ cup sugar, 1 Tbs. at a time, beating well after each addition. Continue beating until stiff peaks form. Spread some meringue around edge of filling, first touching crust all around, then fill center. Bake in 350°F. oven 15 minutes, until lightly browned. Cool at room temperature away from draft. Makes 6 to 8 servings.

Key Lime Pie

If recipes were placed in leather-bound books to treasure forever this all-time favorite pie would be included. An inspired Florida genius created this recipe which first appeared on the Eagle Brand Condensed Milk can twenty years ago.

4 eggs, separated (reserve 3 whites for meringue)
1 can Eagle Brand Sweetened Condensed Milk
½ cup lime juice
2 to 3 teaspoons grated lime rind, optional
Few drops green food coloring
1 8- or 9-inch baked pastry shell, cooled
½ tsp. cream of tartar
⅓ cup sugar

Preheat oven to 350°F. In medium bowl, beat egg yolks; stir in sweetened condensed milk, lime juice, rind, and food coloring. In small bowl, stiffly beat 1 egg white; fold into sweetened condensed milk mixture. Turn into shell. Beat reserved egg whites with cream of tartar until foamy; gradually add sugar, beating until stiff but not dry. Spread meringue on top of pie, sealing carefully to edge of shell.

Bake 15 minutes or until meringue is golden brown. Cool. Chill before serving. Makes one 8- or 9-inch pie.

Chocolate Butterscotch Pie

America's two favorite flavors, chocolate and butterscotch, combine in this unusual pie recipe from Hershey's® famous 1934 cookbook.

- ¾ cup brown sugar, packed
- ⅓ cup all-purpose flour
- ½ tsp. salt
- 2½ cups milk
- 6 Tbs. Hershey's® Chocolate-Flavored Syrup
- 2 egg yolks, well beaten
- 2 Tbs. butter
- ½ tsp. vanilla
- 1 9-inch baked pie shell

Thoroughly combine sugar, flour and salt. Stir in milk, chocolate syrup and beaten egg yolks. Cook over medium heat until thick, stirring constantly. Remove from fire; blend in butter and vanilla. Pour into baked pie shell; cool. Chill in refrigerator. Serve with sweetened whipped cream if desired. Makes one 9-inch pie.

Chocolate Pie

Back in 1932 this easy chocolate pie became an instant success and the requests for the recipe are still coming in to the Pet Milk test kitchens.

¾ cup sugar
⅓ cup cornstarch
½ tsp. salt
1 13-ounce can Pet Evaporated Milk
1⅓ cups water
1 Tbs. vanilla
2 squares (1 ounce each) unsweetened chocolate, broken up
1 9-inch frozen Pet-Ritz "Deep Dish" Pie Shell, baked

Mix sugar, cornstarch and salt in large saucepan. Gradually stir in evaporated milk and water. Add chocolate. Cook and stir over medium heat until chocolate is completely melted and mixture boils. Boil 1 minute. Remove from heat. Stir in vanilla. Pour into baked crust. Chill pie at least 2 hours before serving. Serve topped with meringue or Whipped Topping, if desired. Makes one 9-inch pie.

Chocolate Pie With Pretzel Crust

I'll bet you never thought of a pretzel crust, did you? Well, here is one from Rold Gold Pretzels. It's a terrific taste combination and a great change from just plain pie crust.

Crust:

1 13-ounce package Rold Gold Pretzels
3 Tbs. sugar
½ cup butter or margarine, melted

Crush pretzels very fine in blender or between 2 sheets of waxed paper. Add sugar and butter or margarine. Mix thoroughly. Press half of mixture in 9-inch pie plate. Bake at 350°F. for 8 minutes. Cool. Pour in Chocolate Filling and top with remaining pretzel mixture. Chill. Makes one 9-inch pie.

Chocolate Filling:

⅔ cup sugar
3 egg yolks, slightly beaten

4 Tbs. cornstarch
2½ cups milk
3 1-ounce squares unsweetened chocolate, cut in small pieces
1 tsp. vanilla extract

Combine sugar, cornstarch, milk and chocolate in top of double boiler. Cook over boiling water until thickened, stirring constantly. Cover and cook for 15 minutes. Stir part of hot chocolate mixture into egg yolks. Add to chocolate mixture. Mix thoroughly. Cool. Add vanilla extract and mix thoroughly.

Grasshopper Pie

That Queen of Pies, the Grasshopper. Here's the recipe from the Hiram Walker people just as it appeared in all sorts of advertising a couple of years ago.

Crush 24 chocolate wafer cookies fine, then mix with 3 tablespoons of softened butter and press into a pie plate. Melt 24 marshmallows and ½ cup of milk in the top of a double boiler; after it has cooled, add ¼ cup Hiram Walker Crême de Menthe green and fold in 2 cups of Whipped Cream. Pour into pie shell and chill well. Then, immediately before the pie is served, decorate it with Whipped Cream. Makes one 9-inch pie.

Shoofly Pie

Have you ever baked a Shoofly pie? No? Well this classic from the Grandma's Molasses label is guaranteed to become a favorite at your house. I like it best served warm with a glob of sour cream on top.

- 1½ cups sifted all-purpose flour
- ½ cup sugar
- ⅛ tsp. salt
- ½ tsp. cinnamon
- ¼ tsp. ginger
- ¼ tsp. nutmeg
- ¼ cup butter or margarine
- ½ tsp. baking soda
- ½ cup Grandma's Unsulphured Molasses
- ¾ cup boiling water
- 1 unbaked 8-inch pastry shell

Mix together flour, sugar, salt and spices. Cut in butter or margarine until mixture resembles coarse meal. Mix together baking soda and molasses and immediately stir in boiling water. Stir in 1⅓ cups of the crumb mixture. Turn into pastry shell. Sprinkle remaining ⅔ cup of the crumb mixture over top. Bake in 375°F. oven for 30 to 40 minutes, until crust is lightly browned. Serves 6 to 8.

Della Robbia Holiday Pie

The recipe for this beautiful dessert appeared in the Amaretto di Saronno advertising some years ago, and customers still ask for it. The idea is to arrange the leaves and fruit into a "wreath" around the edge of the pie. Truly a spectacular highlight for a holiday buffet table.

- 1½ cups vanilla wafer crumbs
- ¼ cup chopped toasted almonds
- ⅓ cup Amaretto di Saronno liquer
- 1 cup heavy cream
- 2 Tbs. Amaretto di Saronno liquer
- ⅓ cup finely chopped mixed candied fruits
- ⅓ cup melted butter or margarine
- 1 quart vanilla ice cream
- Fresh mint leaves or crystallized mint leaves (optional)
- Candied mimosa and violets (optional)

1 lb. marzipan fruits or 2 cups assorted fruits—strawberry halves, green seedless grapes, maraschino cherries, peach slices, pineapple chunks, banana slices or plum slices

In a bowl, mix crumbs, almonds and butter or margarine. Press mixture firmly into an ungreased 9-inch pie pan. Chill. Soften ice cream and stir in ⅓ cup Amaretto di Saronno and fruits. Pour mixture into chilled pie shell. Freeze until hard. In a bowl, mix heavy cream, 2 Tbs. Amaretto di Saronno liqueur; beat until stiff. Pile whipped cream in mounds around the outer edge of pie. Freeze until ready to serve. Decorate pie with marzipan or fruits pressed into whipped cream. Add mint leaves, mimosa and violets if desired. Serve at once. Makes one 9-inch pie.

Never-Fail Pie Crust

Here's a pie crust recipe from Standard Milling Company. Once you have a great pie crust, there is a world of fillings to choose from, a world of pies and quiches you can make.

4 to 4¼ cups Hecker's unbleached flour, sifted
1 Tbs. sugar
3 tsps. salt
1 egg
1 Tbs. vinegar
½ cup water
1¾ cups shortening

Sift flour, sugar and salt into a large bowl. Beat the egg and combine with vinegar and water. Cut shortening into flour, sprinkle with egg mixture, and mix all together.

Gather the dough into a ball, wrap in wax paper and chill for about 30 minutes before using.

This dough can be kept in the refrigerator up to 1 week. Or you can divide it into 4 parts (1 pie shell each), wrap each securely and freeze. Makes 4 pie shells or two double crusts.

Jell-O® Strawberry Bavarian Pie

A beautiful dessert, gossamer light and smooth as silk. Garnish with whole fresh strawberries if you like.

- 1 3-ounce package Jell-O® Strawberry Gelatin
- 1 Tbs. sugar
- ⅛ tsp. salt
- 1 cup boiling water
- ½ cup cold water
- 1 10-ounce package Birds Eye® Quick Thaw Strawberries
- 1 cup Birds Eye® Cool Whip Non-Dairy Whipped Topping, thawed
- 1 baked 9-inch pie shell, cooled

Dissolve Jell-O®, sugar and salt in boiling water. Add cold water and frozen strawberries. Stir gently until fruit thaws and separates. Chill until slightly thickened. Add whipped topping; blend until smooth. (Mixture may appear slightly curdled but will smooth out on blending.) Pour into pie shell. Chill until firm, about 4 hours. Garnish with additional whipped topping, and mint leaves, if desired. Makes one 9-inch pie.

Fruit Pies—America's #1 Baked Dessert

From General Foods' kitchens, a handy chart for making the very best fresh fruit pies.

Fresh fruit pies thickened with tapioca are bright in taste as well as appearance. Prepare your own two-crust pastry, or make life simple by using a mix. (See directions on Page 119)

Fruit	*Prepared fruit*	*Minute tapioca (Tbs.)*	*Sugar (cups)*	*Salt (tsp.)*	*Flavorings (optional)*	*Butter or margarine (Tbs.)*
Apple*	5 cups (peeled and thinly sliced)	1½	¾	⅛	¾ tsp. cinnamon ¼ tsp. nutmeg	1
Blueberry	4 cups (stemmed)	4	1 to 1¼	¼	⅛ tsp. cinnamon 1½ Tbs. lemon juice	1
Red Sour Cherry	4 cups (pitted)	4	1½	¼	½ tsp. cinnamon ¼ tsp. nutmeg	1
Peach	4 cups (peeled and sliced)	3	¾ to 1	¼	1 Tbs. lemon juice	1
Plum	3 cups (sliced)	3	1	¼	⅛ tsp. cinnamon	1
Rhubarb	4 cups (diced)	3	1½	¼	1 tsp. grated orange rind	1
Strawberry	4 cups (hulled)	3	½	¼	1 tsp. lemon juice	None

* Use Greening, Cortland, Home Beauty, Wealthy or McIntosh.

Directions for using chart (page 389)

Combine all ingredients except butter. Let stand about 15 minutes. Pour into pastry-lined 9-inch pie pan. Dot with butter. Add top crust. Seal and flute edge. Cut and open slits in top crust to permit escape of steam. Bake at 425°F. until syrup boils with heavy bubbles that do not burst, 45 to 55 minutes. Cool before cutting.

Boston Cream Pie

This is a marvelous cake, one of America's best! Yes, this recipe did indeed originate in, or around, Boston and it's called a pie because "my dear, Boston pies are so elegant they are made with delicate cake layers instead of just plain pie crusts," or so I was told by a Boston lady. Hershey® cooks perfected this version.

- 2 cups unsifted all-purpose flour
- 1½ cups sugar
- 1 tsp. baking soda
- 1 tsp. baking powder
- ½ tsp. salt
- ¼ cup butter or margarine, softened
- ¼ cup shortening
- 1½ tsps. vanilla
- 1¼ cups buttermilk or sour milk*
- 4 egg whites (reserve 2 egg yolks for filling)
- Cream Filling and Chocolate Glaze (opposite)

Grease and dust with flour two 9-inch layer pans. Combine flour, sugar, baking soda, baking powder and salt in large mixer bowl. Add butter, shortening, vanilla and buttermilk. Blend on low speed 30 seconds; beat on medium speed 2 minutes. Add egg whites; beat 2 minutes. Pour into pans and bake at 350°F. for 30–35 minutes or until cake tester inserted

* *To Sour Milk:* Use 1 Tbs. plus 1 tsp. vinegar plus milk to equal 1¼ cups.

in center comes out clean. Cool 10 minutes; remove from pans. Cool completely.

Prepare Cream Filling. Spoon onto 1 cake layer. Carefully top with remaining layer. Prepare Chocolate Glaze. Immediately pour onto top of cake, allowing some to drizzle down side. Chill before serving. Makes 8–10 servings.

Cream Filling: Combine ⅓ cup sugar, 2 Tbs. cornstarch and ⅛ tsp. salt in saucepan. Gradually add 1½ cups milk and reserved 2 egg yolks; blend well. Cook and stir over medium heat until mixture boils; boil and stir 1 minute. Remove from heat; blend in 1 Tbs. butter and 1 tsp. vanilla. Cool 10 minutes.

Chocolate Glaze: Combine 3 Tbs. water and 2 Tbs. butter in small saucepan. Bring to full boil; remove from heat and add ¼ cup Hershey's® Cocoa. Stir until mixture leaves side of pan and forms ball. Beat in 1 cup confectioners' sugar and ½ tsp. vanilla until smooth.

Apple Pie with Cheese Topper

It's hard to imagine anything better to eat than a first-rate apple pie. And if ever one tasted a first-rate apple pie this is it; sweet but not too sweet, juicy but not too juicy, with a crust that is flaky and delicately brown. It's a perfect pie made even more perfect with a creamy Cheese Topping. The Crisco people tell me this recipe has received fan letters for years.

Crisco pastry for double-crust 9-inch pie
½ cup light raisins (optional)
6–8 tart apples, peeled, cored and sliced (6 cups)
½ tsp. grated lemon peel
1 tsp. lemon juice

- ¾ cup sugar
- 2 Tbs. flour
- ½ tsp. ground nutmeg
- Dash salt
- Cheese Topper (below)

Preheat oven to 400°F. Line a 9-inch pie plate with pastry. Pour boiling water over raisins and let stand 5 minutes; drain. Toss apples with lemon peel, juice and drained raisins. Combine sugar, flour, nutmeg and salt; mix with apples. Turn into pastry-lined pie plate. Place top crust over apples; seal and flute edges. Cut slits for escape of steam. Bake at 400°F. for 50–60 minutes or till done. Cover edges with foil after 15 minutes to prevent over-browning. Serve warm pie with Cheese Topper.

Cheese Topper: Have ½ cup (2 oz.) shredded Cheddar cheese and 1 package (3 oz.) cream cheese at room temperature. In small mixing bowl, combine cheeses and 2 Tbs. milk; beat till fluffy and nearly smooth.

Crunchy Pecan Pie

I'm not really sure about this recipe—is it a torte or is it a pie? One thing I am sure about, it's absolutely delicious and it's a snap to make. From the Nabisco Graham Cracker box, first printed in the 1940's.

- 3 egg whites
- 1 cup granulated sugar
- 12 squares Nabisco Graham Crackers, finely rolled (about 1 cup crumbs)
- 1 cup finely chopped pecans
- ¼ tsp. baking powder
- 1 cup heavy cream, whipped

Beat egg whites until soft peaks form; gradually add sugar, beating until stiff peaks form. Combine next three ingredients; fold into egg whites. Spread in a greased 9-inch pie plate. Bake in the center of preheated oven (350°F.) 30 minutes. Cool thoroughly. Spread with whipped cream. Chill 6 hours or overnight. Makes 8 3¾-inch wedges.

Southern Coconut Pie

A rich custard pie, lavish with coconut. The recipe was perfected by home economists at the Baker Coconut test kitchens. Southerners tell me it's the real thing.

- 2 Tbs. melted butter
- ⅓ cup sugar
- ¼ tsp. salt
- 3 eggs, slightly beaten
- 1 cup light corn syrup
- 1 tsp. vanilla
- ½ tsp. almond extract
- ⅔ cup Baker's Cookie Coconut
- 1 unbaked 9-inch pie shell

Blend butter, sugar and salt. Add eggs, syrup and extracts; stir well. Sprinkle coconut over bottom of pie shell. Pour filling over coconut. Bake in moderate oven (375°F.) 40–50 minutes. Cool. Serve with ice cream, prepared Dream Whip Whipped Topping or whipped cream, if desired. Makes 6–8 servings.

Chocolate Meringue Pie

Here, by insistent requests, is that "noble chocolate pie with the high and haughty meringue"—the chocolate pie that man in your life remembers. The recipe was first printed in *Baker's Chocolate and Coconut Favorites* cookbook in 1962. Today even after 18 years it's still a top favorite.

1¼ cups sugar
3 Tbs. cornstarch
½ tsp. salt
2 cups milk
1½ squares Baker's Unsweetened Chocolate, chopped
2 egg yolks, slightly beaten
1 Tbs. butter
1 tsp. vanilla
1 baked 8-inch pie shell, cooled
2 egg whites

Mix 1 cup sugar, the cornstarch and salt in a saucepan. Gradually stir in milk. Add chocolate; cook and stir over medium heat until mixture comes to a boil and is thickened. Then continue to cook and stir 1 minute longer. Remove from heat. Gradually stir at least half of the hot mixture into egg yolks. Then stir egg yolk mixture into mixture in saucepan. Cook and stir 1 minute longer. Remove from heat. Blend in butter and vanilla. Cool 20 minutes; then beat just until smooth—about 30 seconds. Pour into pie shell. Beat egg whites until foamy. Add ¼ cup sugar, a little at a time, beating well after each addition. Continue beating until stiff peaks will form. Spread over filling, carefully sealing to crust. Bake in hot oven (425°F.) 6–8 minutes, or until browned. Cool about 4 hours. Makes 6 servings.

Raisin Nut Pie

Raisin Nut Pie was among the winners in a Karo Corn Syrup contest held several years ago. You'll know why when you try it. Eunice Yeager of Lanesville, Indiana, sent in the recipe.

3 eggs
¾ cup Karo Dark Corn Syrup
½ cup firmly packed light brown sugar
¼ cup Mazola Margarine, melted
1 tsp. vanilla
¼ tsp. salt
1 cup raisins
½ cup chopped pecans or walnuts
1 unbaked (9-inch) pastry shell

In bowl beat eggs slightly. Stir in corn syrup, brown sugar, margarine, vanilla and salt. Stir in raisins and nuts. Turn into pastry shell. Bake in 350°F. oven 40–50 minutes or until knife inserted half-way between center and edge comes out clean. Cool on wire rack. If desired, serve with unsweetened whipped cream or vanilla ice cream. Makes 8 servings.

Vanilla Cream Pie

How long has it been since you've made a creamy, smooth egg custard pie? This is the original recipe and it's just as good now as it was in the 1940's when Argo and Kingsford first printed it on their cornstarch box.

⅔ cup sugar
¼ cup Argo or Kingsford's Corn Starch
½ tsp. salt
2½ cups milk
3 eggs, separated

1 tsp. vanilla
1 baked (9-inch) pastry shell
6 Tbs. sugar

In 2-quart saucepan mix together ⅔ cup sugar, cornstarch and salt. Gradually stir in milk until smooth. Stir in egg yolks, slightly beaten. Stirring constantly, bring to boil over medium-low heat and boil 1 minute. Remove from heat. Stir in vanilla. Cover surface with waxed paper or plastic wrap. Cool slightly (no longer than 1 hour). Turn filling into pastry shell. In small bowl with mixer at high speed beat egg whites until frothy peaks form. Gradually beat in 6 Tbs. sugar until stiff peaks form. Spread over filling sealing to edge of crust. Bake in 350°F. oven 15 to 20 minutes or until lightly browned. Cool at room temperature away from drafts. Makes 8 servings.

Banana Cream Pie: Follow recipe for Vanilla Cream Pie. Fill pastry shell with small amount of cooled filling. Arrange 2 bananas, sliced, over filling and cover with remaining filling.

Coconut Cream Pie: Follow recipe for Vanilla Cream Pie. Fold ¾ cup flaked coconut into cooled filling and sprinkle meringue with ¼ cup flaked coconut before baking. Bake in 425°F. oven 5 minutes or until meringue browns and coconut is toasted.

Chocolate Cream Pie: Follow recipe for Vanilla Cream Pie adding 2 squares (1 oz. each) unsweetened chocolate to milk mixture before cooking.

Impossible Coconut Pie

Here's a fantastic recipe from the Bisquick® Baking Mix box. It's so easy and so much fun to make. Try it once and it will become a favorite at your house.

2 cups milk
¾ cup sugar
½ cup Bisquick® Baking Mix
¼ cup margarine or butter
4 eggs
1½ tsps. vanilla
1 cup flaked or shredded coconut

Heat oven to 350°F. Lightly grease pie plate, 9 × 1¼ inches. Place all ingredients in blender container. Cover and blend on high speed 15 seconds. Pour into pie plate. Bake until golden brown and knife inserted in center comes out clean, 50–55 minutes. Refrigerate any remaining pie.

Impossible Chocolate Pie: Add 2 Tbs. cocoa.

Impossible Fruit Pie: Use 10-inch pie plate. Cool pie; spread 1 21-oz. can fruit pie filling over top. Refrigerate at least 2 hours.

Impossible Lemon Pie: Use 10-inch pie plate. Add ¼ cup lemon juice.

Impossible Macaroon Pie: Do not blend coconut; sprinkle over top of pie before baking.

Mystery Torte

"My mother used to make a pie with Saltine Crackers called a Mystery Torte. Do you have a recipe?" The Nabisco Company has been getting letters like this for years. They always write back. "Yes, we do!" And here it is:

10 Premium Saltine Crackers, coarsely rolled (about ⅔ cup crumbs)
½ cup chopped pecans
Chocolate-Cream Topping (optional—below)
½ tsp. baking powder
3 egg whites (at room temperature)
1 cup granulated sugar
½ tsp. vanilla extract

Combine cracker crumbs and pecans. Set aside. Add baking powder to egg whites. Beat until soft peaks form. Gradually add sugar and vanilla. Continue beating until egg whites are very stiff and glossy, but not dry. Fold in cracker mixture. Turn into 1 9-inch ungreased pie plate. Bake in a preheated oven (300°F.) 50 minutes. Chill several hours.

Chocolate-Cream Topping: For an excellent topping, combine ½ cup heavy cream with 3 Tbs. confectioners' sugar and 3 tsps. instant cocoa mix. Whip until stiff. Spoon over just before serving. Makes 4–6 servings.

Pumpkin Chiffon Pie

Here is the recipe for that "lighter" pumpkin pie that so many people told me is better than best. The secret of its lightness is the Knox Unflavored Gelatine. It is indeed such a lovely holiday pie.

1 envelope Knox Unflavored Gelatine
¾ cup brown sugar
½ tsp. salt
½ tsp. nutmeg
1 tsp. cinnamon
3 eggs, separated
¾ cup milk
1 16-oz. can pumpkin
¼ cup sugar
9-inch baked pastry shell

In medium saucepan, mix Unflavored Gelatine, brown sugar, salt and spices; blend in egg yolks beaten with milk. Let stand 1 minute. Stir over low heat until Gelatine is completely dissolved, about 8 minutes; blend in pumpkin. Pour into large bowl and chill, stirring occasionally, until mixture mounds slightly when dropped from spoon. In medium bowl, beat egg whites until soft peaks form; gradually add sugar and beat until stiff. Fold into Gelatine mixture. Turn into prepared crust and chill until firm. Garnish, if desired, with whipped cream. Makes about 8 servings.

Mr. & Mrs. Foster's Yogurt Pie

Pearl Byrd Foster developed this recipe for her famous American style New York restaurant. Although it's new on the scene, Dannon Yogurt has brought this pie hundreds of fans. It's sure to go down in history as an all-time favorite dessert.

- 1 Tbs. unflavored gelatin*
- ¼ cup cold water
- 2 egg yolks, slightly beaten
- ¼ cup milk
- 2 cups Dannon Plain Yogurt
- 1 tsp. Vanilla
- 8 oz. Neufchatel** cheese, room temperature
- 8 oz. cream cheese, room temperature
- 1 tsp. molasses
- 1 Tbs. clover honey
- ½ cup graham cracker crumbs
- 1 graham cracker crumb shell

Soften gelatin in cold water and dissolve over hot water. Add milk to the slightly beaten egg yolks and cook with the gelatin over gently boiling water until it coats a silver spoon. Set

* If a softer filling is desired—use less gelatin.

** If Neufchatel is not available, you may substitute an additional 8 oz. cream cheese.

aside to cool. Cream the cheese, vanilla, molasses and honey together (if mixing machine used—cream on low speed only), add one cup of Dannon Yogurt and continue to cream until smooth. Pour the cold gelatin mixture slowly over the cheese, stirring constantly. Add the second cup of Dannon Yogurt. Mix well. Pour into baked graham cracker crumb shell and chill until firm. When ready to serve, sprinkle top with graham cracker crumbs. Makes 1 10-inch pie.

Alaska Pie

Baked Alaska was a featured dessert at Delmonicos Restaurant in old New York. Kraft® perfected this easy adaptation.

- 1½ cups graham cracker crumbs
- 3 Tbs. sugar
- 6 Tbs. margarine, melted
- 1 qt. ice cream, softened*
- 3 egg whites
- Dash of salt
- 1 cup Kraft® Marshmallow Creme

Combine crumbs, sugar and margarine; press onto bottom and sides of 9-inch pie plate. Bake at 375°F., 8 minutes. Cool. Fill crust with softened ice cream. Freeze. Beat egg whites and salt until soft peaks form. Gradually add marshmallow creme, beating until stiff peaks form. Spread over frozen ice cream pie, sealing to edge of crust. Bake at 500°F., 3 minutes or until lightly browned. Serve immediately.

To Make Ahead: Prepare recipe as directed, except for final baking. Freeze several hours or overnight. When ready to serve, bake as directed.

* Almost any ice cream is delicious in this meringue-topped pie. Try fresh peach, strawberry, chocolate, fudge-nut or New York cherry.

Easy Fruit Tarts

You know those beautiful little glistening fruit tarts that look so beguiling but sound so difficult to make? Well, Jell-O® has made them easy. If you would like to make your reputation as a great hostess, serve these at your next party.

- 1 3¼-oz. package Jell-O® Vanilla Pudding and Pie Filling
- 8 baked 3-inch tart shells (frozen, packaged, or home-baked)
- 1–2 cups assorted fruit (see suggested fruits below)
- 1 3-oz. package Jell-O® Strawberry, Raspberry or Orange Gelatin

Prepare pudding as directed on package; chill. Divide evenly among tart shells. Top with any of the fruit combinations below, arranging in neat design. Chill. Meanwhile, prepare gelatin as directed on package. Chill until thickened. Spoon gelatin over tarts, using just enough to cover fruit with a smooth glaze. Chill until ready to serve. Pour remaining gelatin into serving dish and chill to use at another time. Garnish with prepared Dream Whip Whipped Topping or whipped cream, if desired. Makes 8 tarts.

Note: Recipe may be doubled for party serving.

Suggested fruits:

Blueberries and grapes
Blueberries and peaches
Strawberries and green grapes
Strawberries and bananas
Blueberries and green grapes
Green grapes and mandarin orange sections
Blueberries with whole strawberry in center
Apricot halves garnished with mint sprigs
Layered peach slices
Whole strawberries

Canned pineapple slice with
stemmed Bing Cherry in center

Rosy Apple Pie

Apple pie is America's own. Years of intensive baking by ardent cooks have given it its present shape, infinite variety, goodness and overwhelming popularity. This one, with a pinky amber, sweet tart filling was created by the cooks at the Crisco® test kitchens. You'll love it, as have almost a million other lovers of great apple pie.

Crisco® Oil Pie Crust
(For 9-inch double crust)

2⅔ cups sifted all purpose enriched flour
1 teaspoon salt
¾ cup Crisco® Oil
¼ cup water

Mix flour and salt in a bowl. Add Crisco® Oil and water. Stir with a fork until blended and dough holds together. Divide in half and form to flat circles.

Roll out half the dough between two squares of waxed paper until circle of dough touches edges of paper. Dampen working surface to prevent waxed paper from slipping as dough is rolled.

Peel off top paper. Pick up rolled dough with bottom paper and turn onto pie plate, paper side up. Carefully peel off paper and press dough into pie plate. Trim dough even with edge of plate.

Roll remaining dough in the same way for the top crust. Add filling to pastry-lined pie plate. Peel waxed paper from top crust and place over filling. Trim about ½ inch beyond edge of pie plate. Fold edge of top crust under edge of bottom crust. Seal by fluting with fingers or fork. Prick or slit top crust to allow for escape of steam. Bake as directed under filling recipe.

Rosy Apple Filling

¾ cup sugar
½ cup water
¼ cup red cinnamon candies (red hots)
5 medium cooking apples (about 5 cups apple slices)
1 Tbs. flour
1 tsp. lemon juice
1 Tbs. butter or margarine

In a medium saucepan combine sugar, water and cinnamon candies; cook until candies dissolve. Pare, core, and slice apples; add to sugar mixture; simmer until apples are red. Drain; save syrup. Blend flour into cooled syrup and add lemon juice. Spread apples in a pastry-lined 9-inch pie plate; pour syrup over apples. Dot with butter. Cover with top crust; seal and flute edges. Cut slits for escape of steam. Bake at 400°F. about 30 minutes, until desired brownness. Makes 1 pie.

Deep-Dish Apple Pie

A simply beautiful and extra-festive pie. A sensation ever since it first appeared in 1970 on the Pepperidge Farm® Frozen Patty Shell package.

- 2 1-lb. 4-oz. cans apple pie filling
- 2 Tbs. grated orange rind
- 1 tsp. grated lemon rind
- 1 10-oz. package frozen patty shells, thawed
- 1 egg yolk
- 1 Tbs. water

Combine apple pie filling, orange rind and grated lemon rind. Pour into 1½-quart deep pie plate. Press the patty shells together. Roll out to make a circle ½ inch larger than top of pie plate. Trim off a ½-inch margin and fit this onto edge of pie crust on top of pastry rim on dish. Press lightly to seal. Trim off any surplus pastry. Crimp edges. Brush top with egg yolk mixed with water. Fashion shapes from pastry trimmings and use to decorate the crust. Brush the trimmings with the egg yolk and water mixture. Bake at 450°F. for 20 to 25 minutes.

Love Apple Pie

Love this Love Apple Pie. It's a Heinz® Tomato Ketchup classic recipe chosen from their 100 all-time top favorites. You don't really taste the ketchup but it gives this pie an intriguing sweet/tart taste.

- ⅓ cup Heinz® Tomato Ketchup
- 2 tsps. lemon juice
- 5 cups thinly sliced, pared cooking apples
- ¾ cup granulated sugar
- ¾ cup all-purpose flour
- ½ tsp. ground cinnamon
- ⅓ cup butter or margarine, softened
- 1 unbaked 9-inch pie shell

Blend Ketchup and lemon juice;* combine with apples. Combine sugar, flour and cinnamon; cut in butter until thoroughly mixed. Fill pie shell with apples; top with sugar mixture. Bake in 375°F. oven, 40 to 45 minutes or until apples are cooked. Serve warm with vanilla ice cream, if desired. Makes one 9-inch pie.

Cherry Cheese Pie

Cherry Cheese Pie is probably today's most popular recipe using Eagle® Brand Sweetened Condensed Milk and the one requested most by people. It appeared almost 20 years ago as Cherry-O Cream Cheese Pie in a recipe booklet and since has been on the can label and in advertisements. A similar recipe, however, was part of the first Eagle® Brand cookbook done in 1919.

- 1 9-inch graham cracker crumb crust
- 1 8-oz. package cream cheese, softened
- 1 14-oz. can Eagle® Brand Sweetened Condensed Milk (*not* evaporated milk)
- ⅓ cup ReaLemon® Reconstituted Lemon Juice
- Canned cherry pie filling, chilled
- Ambrosia Topping *or* Cranberry Nut Topping (page 406)

In large mixer bowl, beat cheese until fluffy. Beat in Eagle® Brand until smooth. Stir in ReaLemon® and vanilla. Pour into crust. Chill 3 hours or until set. Top with desired amount of pie filling before serving. Refrigerate leftovers. Makes one 9-inch pie.

* If apples are very tart, add 1 to 2 Tbs. sugar to Ketchup mixture.

Ambrosia Topping

- ½ cup peach or apricot preserves
- ¼ cup flaked coconut
- 2 Tbs. orange-flavored liqueur
- 2 tsps. corn starch
- fresh orange sections (1 or 2 oranges)

In small saucepan, combine first four ingredients. Cook and stir until thickened. Remove from heat. Chill thoroughly. Spread over pie; arrange orange sections over top.

Cranberry Nut Topping

- 1 cup chilled cranberry-orange relish
- ½ cup chopped walnuts
- 1 tsp. grated orange rind

In small bowl, combine relish, walnuts and orange rind. Spread over pie. Garnish with orange twists, if desired.

No-Bake Pumpkin Pie

In 1931, the Borden® Company offered cooks $25 for new recipes made with Eagle® Brand Sweetened Condensed Milk. All of 80,000 recipes were read and graded and of those, 1,000 new recipes were tested in the kitchens. No-Bake Pumpkin Pie was among those selected and included in a booklet called "The Most Amazing Short-Cuts in Cooking You Ever Heard Of." It's still one of the most popular in their all-time favorites file.

- 1 envelope Knox® Unflavored Gelatine
- 1 tsp. ground cinnamon
- 2 eggs, well beaten
- 1 16-oz. can pumpkin (about 2 cups)

½ tsp. ground ginger
½ tsp. ground nutmeg
½ tsp. salt
1 14-oz. can Eagle® Brand Sweetened Condensed Milk (*not* evaporated milk)
1 graham cracker or butter flavored Ready® Crust pie crust

In heavy medium saucepan, combine unflavored gelatine, cinnamon, ginger, nutmeg and salt; stir in Sweetened Condensed Milk and eggs. Mix well. Let stand 1 minute. Over *low* heat, cook and stir constantly until gelatine dissolves and mixture thickens slightly, about 10 minutes. Remove from heat. Stir in pumpkin; mix well. Pour into prepared crust. Chill 3 hours or until set. Garnish as desired. Refrigerate leftovers.

Walnut Meringue Pie

This wonderful confection was first made for me by my Aunt Sally in Shreveport, Louisiana. It's a perfect dessert for special occasions; a luscious creation from Pet Ritz® that truly looks like a celebration. Tastes like one too!

3 egg whites, room temperature
¼ tsp. salt
½ tsp. baking powder
1 cup granulated sugar
1 tsp. vanilla extract
⅔ cup broken walnuts
20 Ritz Crackers, broken in fourths
4 cups cut-up fresh fruits in season, or canned, very well-drained
½ cup heavy cream, whipped, unsweetened

Beat egg whites until soft peaks form. Add salt and baking powder. Gradually beat in sugar; continue beating until stiff and glossy. Add vanilla extract. Lightly fold in next two ingredients. Spread mixture over bottom and sides of well-greased pie plate. Build up sides. Bake in a preheated slow oven

(325°F.) 25 to 30 minutes. Cool completely on wire rack. Just before serving, fill center with fruit. Serve cream separately. Makes 8 (3½-inch) wedges.

Southern Sweet Chocolate Pie

Most men adore chocolate pie—but I know one New York food editor whose favorite is not just chocolate but Southern chocolate pie. As he spent his childhood in the deep South, it's no wonder and I must admit this recipe that he sent me has a unique flavor unbuyable at any bakery. Baker's® German Sweet Chocolate gets the credit.

- 1 4-oz. package Baker's® German Sweet Chocolate
- ¼ cup butter or margarine
- 1 13-oz. can evaporated milk
- 1 cup sugar
- 3 eggs
- 1 tsp. vanilla
- 1 unbaked 9-inch pie shell, with high-fluted rim*
- 1⅓ cups (about) Baker's® Angel Flake Coconut
- ½ cup chopped pecans

Heat Chocolate with butter in saucepan over low heat, stirring until melted and smooth. Remove from heat; gradually blend in evaporated milk and sugar. Beat in eggs and vanilla. Gradually blend in chocolate mixture. Pour into pie shell; sprinkle with coconut and nuts. (Shell will be quite full, but filling will not rise over sides.) Bake at 375°F. for 45 to 50 minutes, or until top is puffed and browned. (Filling will be soft, but will set while cooling.) Cool at least 4 hours.

Note: If topping browns too quickly, cover loosely with aluminum foil during the last 15 minutes of baking. Pie may be wrapped and stored in freezer; thaw before serving.

* Or Use 2 unbaked 8-inch pie shells, baked about 45 minutes.

Coconut Pear Pie Supreme

Part of the popularity of this luxurious dessert is its ease of preparation, but it is the rich and elegant taste that has made it one of the top ten best recipes in the Holland House® test kitchen as well as with its consumers.

- 1 fully baked 8- or 9-inch pie shell
- 1 15-oz. container whole milk Ricotta cheese
- ¾ cup Coco Casa® Cream of Coconut
- 1 Tbs. candied fruit
- 1 Tbs. mini chocolate bits
- 6 to 8 pear halves, stewed or canned
- Apricot glaze, warmed
- Bitter chocolate curls or rounds for garnish

Whip Ricotta cheese until smooth and glossy. Add Cream of Coconut and mix well. Fold in candied fruit and chocolate bits. Refrigerate for 3 hours or overnight. Spread Ricotta filling evenly into pie shell. Place drained pears in an attractive pattern over filling and brush with apricot glaze. Decorate with curls or rounds of chocolate.

Orange Ambrosia Pie

There's always a reason when a recipe becomes a "top favorite" and "an all-time great." I think it's the contrast of the fresh orange filling to this crunchy crust that makes this one such a heavenly hit.

- 3 to 4 oranges, peeled and cut into small pieces (2½ cups)
- ½ cup and ⅓ cup sugar
- 1 cup orange juice (approximately)
- 3 tablespoons corn starch
- 1 3 oz. package cream cheese, softened
- ¼ teaspoon ground ginger
- 1 tablespoon milk
- ¼ to ½ cup flaked coconut
- Chex® Crust (page 410)

To prepare Filling, mix orange pieces and ½ cup sugar. Set aside while preparing Chex Crust (below). Then continue with Filling: Drain syrup from oranges. Add enough orange juice to make 1½ cups. In medium-size saucepan combine corn starch and remaining ⅓ cup sugar. Add orange juice. Cook and stir over medium heat until very thick and clear. Cool to lukewarm. Combine cream cheese, ginger and milk. Spread on bottom and sides of crust. Stir orange pieces into sauce. Turn into crust. Sprinkle with coconut. Chill at least two hours or until sauce is set. For easy serving, set pie plate in warm water for 1 minute before cutting.

Chex® Crust

- 4 cups Rice Chex® Cereal crushed to 1 cup
- ¼ cup packed brown sugar
- ¼ tsp. ground ginger
- ⅓ cup butter or margarine, melted

Preheat oven to 300°F. Butter 9-inch pie plate. Combine Rice Chex® crumbs, sugar and ginger. Add butter. Mix thoroughly. Press evenly onto bottom and sides of pie plate. Bake 10 minutes. Cool completely.

Creamy Cheese Pie

Oh my, this is good! It's a snap, crackle and pop kind of recipe from the Kellogg's® people. You'll be smiled upon for preparing it, I assure you.

- 3 cups Kellogg's® Rice Krispies® cereal, crushed to measure 1½ cups
- ¼ cup sugar
- ½ tsp. ground cinnamon
- 1 tsp. vanilla flavoring
- ⅓ cup sugar
- 1 tsp. lemon juice
- 1 8-oz. carton (1 cup) dairy sour cream

- ½ cup margarine or butter, melted
- 4 3-oz. packages cream cheese, softened
- 2 eggs
- 2 Tbs. sugar
- 1 1-lb., 5-oz. can cherry pie filling
- 1 tsp. lemon juice

Combine crushed Rice Krispies® Cereal, ¼ cup sugar and cinnamon with the margarine. Press firmly in 9-inch pie pan to form crust. Set aside. In large mixing bowl, beat cream cheese until smooth. Add eggs, vanilla, ⅓ cup sugar and 1 teaspoon lemon juice, mixing until well combined. Pour mixture into crust. Bake in oven at 375°F. about 20 minutes, or until set. While pie is baking, stir together sour cream and 2 Tbs. sugar. Remove pie from oven. Spread sour cream mixture over top. Return to oven. Bake 5 minutes longer. Remove from oven. Cool. Stir together pie filling and the remaining 1 tsp. lemon juice. Spread over top of cooled pie. Chill. Makes 1 9-inch pie.

Fudge Sundae Pie

When this easy-to-prepare ice cream pie was featured in a series of national advertisements by Kellogg's®, it was an instant success. It's just plain delicious.

- ¼ cup corn syrup
- 2 Tbs. firmly packed brown sugar
- 3 Tbs. margarine or butter
- 2½ cups Kellogg's® Rice Krispies® Cereal
- ¼ cup peanut butter
- ¼ cup fudge sauce for ice cream
- 3 Tbs. corn syrup
- 1 quart vanilla ice cream

Combine ¼ cup corn syrup, brown sugar and margarine in medium-size saucepan. Cook over low heat, stirring occasionally, until mixture begins to boil. Remove from heat. Add Rice Krispies® Cereal, stirring until well coated. Press evenly in 9-inch pie pan to form crust. Stir together peanut butter, fudge sauce and the corn syrup. Spread half the peanut butter mixture over crust. Freeze until firm. Allow ice cream to soften slightly. Spoon into frozen pie crust, spreading evenly. Freeze until firm. Let pie stand at room temperature about 10 minutes before cutting. Warm remaining peanut butter mixture and drizzle over top. Makes 8 servings.

Frosty Mint Ice Cream Pies

These deliciously different pies are from a special *Pillsbury® Plus Cookbook*. The crust puffs during baking and then collapses to form the pie shell shape. A beautiful dessert.

Pie Shells

1 package Pillsbury® Plus Chocolate Mint, Devil's Food or Dark Chocolate Cake Mix
¾ cup Pillsbury® Ready To Spread Chocolate Fudge Frosting Supreme
¾ cup water
¼ cup oil

Filling

6 cups (1¼ quarts) mint chocolate chip or your favorite ice cream, softened

Heat oven to 350°F. Generously grease bottom, sides and rim of two 9-inch pie pans or round cake pans.* In large bowl, blend all shell ingredients at low speed until moistened; beat 2 minutes at highest speed. Spread half of batter (2¼ cups) in bottom of each pan. Do not spread up sides of pan. Bake at 350°F. for 25 to 30 minutes; *Do not overbake.* Cakes will collapse to form shells. Cool completely. In large bowl, blend ice cream until smooth; spread evenly in center of each shell leaving a ½-inch rim. If desired, heat remaining frosting just until softened. Drop by spoonfuls on top of ice cream and swirl with knife. Freeze at least 2 hours. Store in freezer. Wrap frozen pies airtight to avoid freezer burn. Makes 2 pies, 12 servings.

Fresh Coconut Cream Pie

Now here's a pie for you; a real "coconutty" coconut pie. It's from the inside label of the Holland House® Cream of Coconut can. They tell me at Holland House® that this is the recipe that makes over a half-million people buy their second and third can of this lovely liquid.

- 1 10-inch baked pie shell
- 6 ozs. Coco Casa® Cream of Coconut
- ¼ cup milk
- 10 ozs. mini-marshmallows
- 3 cups heavy cream, whipped stiff
- 2 cups coconut flakes (fresh or canned)

Mix Cream of Coconut with milk. Add marshmallows. Cook over low heat until marshmallows melt. Cool in bowl and refrigerate 1 hour or until mixture starts to jell. Beat jelled mixture with electric mixer until frothy. Carefully, fold in

* Do not use 8-inch pie or cake pans.

whipped cream. Blend in 1 cup flaked coconut, by hand. Pour into baked pie shell. Sprinkle remaining cup of flaked coconut (toast if desired) over pie and refrigerate at least 6 hours before serving. Makes 1 10-inch pie.

Vanilla Nut Crumb Crust

Here's the accurate and predictable, as well as delectable, nut crumb pie crust that you and just about every good cook has asked for.

- 1 cup finely crushed vanilla wafers (about 29)
- ½ cup Planters® Pecan Pieces, Planters® Walnut Pieces, Planters® Blanched Almonds or Planters® Salted Peanuts, ground
- ⅓ cup Blue Bonnet® Margarine, melted*

In a small bowl, combine vanilla wafer crumbs, ground Planters® nuts and Blue Bonnet® Margarine. Press mixture against sides and bottom of a 9-inch pie plate. Bake at 375°F. for 7 to 8 minutes, or until lightly browned. Cool. Fill as desired.

Chocolate Variation: Use 1 cup finely crushed chocolate wafers (about 17) in place of vanilla wafers.

Peach Gem Pie

This lovely pie from the Jell-O® kitchens has inspired more than a few people to try their hand at pie making, and with good reason; it's a snap to make and just about any fresh or canned fruit may be substituted for the peaches. Try strawberry Jello® and chopped fresh strawberries or lime Jello® with blueberries—or, try your own ideas.

* If Planters® Salted Peanuts are used increase margarine to 6 Tbs.

1 3-oz. package Jell-O® Orange Gelatin
1 cup boiling water
2 cups ice cubes
½ tsp. almond extract
2 cups sliced peeled fresh peaches*
1 baked 9-inch pie shell, cooled

Dissolve gelatin in boiling water. Add ice cubes and stir constantly until gelatin starts to thicken—3 to 5 minutes. Remove any unmelted ice. Add almond extract and peaches. Pour into pie shell. Chill until firm—about 3 hours. Garnish with whipped topping and toasted almonds, if desired. Makes 1 9-inch pie.

Coffee Yogurt Chiffon Pie

At your insistence, here's "a" famous Dannon® Yogurt Pie. I must admit it's really delicious.

Crumb crust
1⅓ cups chocolate wafer crumbs
3 Tbs. butter or margarine, melted

Combine cookie crumbs and butter. Reserve 3 Tbs. of crumbs for top of pie and press remaining crumbs on bottom and sides of 9-inch pie plate.

Filling
1 envelope Knox® Unflavored Gelatine
⅔ cup sugar, divided
3 eggs, separated
¾ cup milk
1 8-oz. container Dannon® Coffee Yogurt

* Or use 1 16-oz. can sliced peaches, drained

Mix Gelatine and ⅓ cup sugar in saucepan. Beat egg yolks and milk together and stir into Gelatine mixture. Cook, stirring constantly over low heat for 4 or 5 minutes, until gelatine dissolves and mixture thickens slightly. Cool slightly and blend in yogurt. Chill, stirring occasionally, until mixture mounds slightly when dropped from a spoon. Beat egg whites until soft peaks form. Gradually beat in remaining ⅓ cup sugar, beat until stiff. Fold into Gelatine mixture. Turn into prepared pie shell and chill until firm. Garnish with reserved cookie crumbs. Makes 1 9-inch pie.

Planters® Nut Crust

A perfected all-nut crust that is constantly requested.

- 2 cups Planters® Salted Peanuts, Planters® Walnuts, Planters® Pecan Pieces, or Planters® Blanched Almonds, ground
- 3 Tbs. Blue Bonnet® Margarine, melted*
- 1 Tbs. sugar

Combine ground Nuts, Blue Bonnet® Margarine and sugar. Press evenly into bottom and on sides of 9-inch pie plate. Bake at 350°F. for 10 to 12 minutes. Cool and fill as desired.

Nutty Meringue Pie Shell

The other most requested pie shell from Planters®. It's angels' food, no less.

- 3 egg whites (at room temperature)
- ¼ tsp. cream of tartar
- ¼ cup Planters® Pecan Pieces, Planters® Walnuts, Planters®

* Increase to 4 Tbs. margarine for walnut or pecan crust.

⅛ tsp. salt
¾ cup sugar
½ tsp. vanilla extract
Blanched Almonds, or Planters® Salted Peanuts, coarsely chopped

Combine egg whites, cream of tartar and salt in small bowl of electric mixer. Beat on high speed until soft peaks form. Gradually add sugar, beating until stiff peaks form. Mix in vanilla. Spread meringue evenly over bottom and sides of a greased and floured 9-inch pie plate. Sprinkle Planters® Nuts over meringue in bottom of shell. Bake at 300°F. for 40 to 45 minutes, or until lightly browned. Cool. Fill as desired.

Foolproof Meringue

Terrific, just terrific. The enthusiasm for this recipe has been going strong since Kraft® developed it some 15 years ago.

3 egg whites
Dash of salt
1 cup (½ of 7-oz. jar) Kraft® Marshmallow Creme

Beat egg whites and salt until soft peaks form. Gradually add marshmallow creme, beating until stiff peaks form. Spread over pie filling, sealing to edge of crust. Bake at 350°F. 12 to 15 minutes or until lightly browned. Cool.

Brandy Alexander Pie

Brandy Alexanders were a favorite drink concocted in the 1920's during prohibition. The pie came later—about 1950—thanks to the Knox Gelatine good cooks and it proved to be almost as much of a sensation.

- 2 envelopes Knox Unflavored Gelatine
- ¾ cup cold whipping or heavy cream
- ¾ cup milk, heated to boiling
- ¼ cup sugar
- 3 Tbs. brandy
- 3 Tbs. creme de cacao
- 1 cup ice cubes (about 6–8)
- Chocolate-Coconut Crust (below) or 9-inch graham cracker crust

In 5-cup blender, sprinkle Unflavored Gelatine over chilled cream; let stand 3–4 minutes. Add hot milk and process at low speed until gelatine is completely dissolved, about 2 minutes. Add sugar, brandy and creme de cacao; process at high speed until blended. Add ice cubes, one at a time; process at high speed until ice is melted. Pour into prepared crust and chill until firm. Garnish, if desired, with maraschino cherries. Makes about 8 servings.

Chocolate-Coconut Crust: In medium bowl, combine one square (1 oz.) unsweetened chocolate, melted, and 2 Tbs. milk; stir in 2 cups flaked coconut and ½ cup confectioners' sugar. Press into 9-inch pie pan.

10.

Prize-Winning Cakes

If it's a festive occasion, it's time for a cake! The very word sounds special: wedding cake, birthday cake, Christmas cake—all great and wonderful days call for nothing less than a beautiful, big, homemade cake.

Way back in the Forties there was an immensely popular, if silly, song, "If I'd Known You Were Coming, I'd Have Baked a Cake." It was fun, and it did put into words that special something about a homemade cake. Despite all this, a lot of people put off cake making. Why? I suspect because they think of cake making as troublesome and not a few are haunted by late-lamented failures. Well, put all that behind you. Cake making is fun when the experts have worked out recipes that are super-easy and super-sure of success. You can rest assured that *every* recipe in this chapter has been perfected to the point where it simply can't fail.

And what recipes! Deep, dark, rich devil's food; airy angel cake; a butterscotch chiffon cake, creamy textured with an all-time favorite butterscotch flavor; and there are $25,000 prize-winning cakes from the Pillsbury Bake Off, and cakes that made Bacardi® Rum household words; plus frostings, fillings and glazes to crown each success with new laurels—from dependable old-fashioned seven-minute frosting to a rich rum filling. Last but not least, an authentic Linzer Torte.

Wouldn't it be fun to surprise your family with a luscious, big cake tonight? As for parties, there's no more beautiful sight on a buffet table than a perfect cake, and, may I let you in on a very special party secret? A famous hostess, known for her fabulous parties down in Dallas, Texas, where the sky's the limit when it comes to parties, never fails to have a luscious devil's food cake and a pot of always hot coffee on a side table when she gives one of her justly celebrated cocktail buffets. It seems her guests love this combination as the best "one for the road" ever.

Now if I had known you were coming I would have baked you a cake—in fact I will anyway. Maybe you will drop in this afternoon and it pays to be ready.

Devil's Food Cake

For the thousands of people who thought they had lost it forever, here's that great Devil's Food cake recipe from the Swans Down Cake Flour box. It's the *best* devil's food cake that ever was. I've made it for thirty years.

- 2½ cups sifted Swans Down Cake Flour
- 1¾ cups sugar
- 1¾ tsps. baking soda
- 1 tsp. salt
- ⅔ cup shortening (at room temperature)
- 1⅓ cups milk
- 1 tsp. vanilla
- 2 eggs
- 3 squares Baker's Unsweetened Chocolate, melted and cooled

Sift flour with sugar, soda, and salt. Stir shortening to soften. Add flour mixture, 1 cup milk, and vanilla; mix until flour is dampened. Then beat 2 minutes at medium speed of electric mixer or 300 vigorous strokes by hand. Add eggs, melted chocolate and remaining ⅓ cup milk; beat 1 minute longer with mixer or 150 strokes by hand. Pour into two greased and floured 9-inch layer pans. Bake at 350°F. about 35 minutes, until cake tester inserted in center comes out clean. Cool 10 minutes in pans; remove from pans and cool thoroughly on racks.

Alternate baking pans: This cake may also be baked at 350°F. in three 8-inch layer pans about 30 minutes or in a 13 × 9-inch pan about 40 minutes. Recipe may be doubled, if desired. If necessary, refrigerate part of the batter while first layers bake.

Seven-Minute Frosting

And here's the perfect icing for devil's food or almost any cake. Peaks of this snowy white frosting crown a cake in regal fashion.

2 egg whites
1½ cups sugar
Dash of salt
⅓ cup water
2 tsps. light corn syrup
1 tsp. vanilla

Combine egg whites, sugar, salt, water, and corn syrup in top of double boiler. Beat 1 minute or until thoroughly mixed. Then place over boiling water and beat constantly at high speed of electric mixer or with rotary beater for 7 minutes, until frosting will stand in stiff peaks; stir frosting up from bottom and sides of pan occasionally. Remove from boiling water and pour at once into a large bowl. Add vanilla and beat 1 minute, until thick enough to spread. Makes about 4½ cups, enough to cover tops and sides of two 8- or 9-inch layers or a 10-inch tube cake.

Variation: For your Devil's Food Cake, you might like to try . . .

Vanilla "Philly" Frosting

We couldn't go to press without this all-time classic recipe for frosting. Kraft® tells us over two million good cooks have asked for the recipe since it was offered on an early Kraft® television show. Thousands of plaintive cries to replace "the one I saved from the Philadelphia Cream Cheese package" come in to the Kraft® kitchens each year.

1 8-ounce package Philadelphia Brand Cream Cheese
1 Tbs. milk
1 tsp. vanilla
Dash of salt
5½ cups sifted confectioners' sugar

Blend together softened cream cheese, milk, vanilla and salt. Add sugar, 1 cup at a time, mixing well after each addition. Fills and frosts two 8- or 9-inch cake layers.

Variations:

Substitute 1 tsp. almond extract for vanilla.
Stir in ¼ cup crushed peppermint candy.
Stir in ¼ cup crushed lemon drops and 1 tsp. lemon juice.

German Sweet Chocolate Cake

In 1958 this all-time favorite cake appeared on Baker's Sweet Chocolate package. As the years passed, its popularity grew. Today it's one of the most requested recipes of the General Foods' kitchens.

- 1 4-ounce package Baker's German Sweet Chocolate
- ½ cup boiling water
- 2½ cups sifted Swans Down Cake Flour*
- 1 tsp. baking soda
- ½ tsp. salt
- 1 cup butter or margarine
- 2 cups sugar
- 4 egg yolks
- 1 tsp. vanilla
- 1 cup buttermilk
- 4 egg whites
- Coconut-Pecan Filling and Frosting

Melt chocolate in boiling water; cool. Sift flour with soda and salt. Cream butter and sugar until light and fluffy. Add egg yolks, one at a time, beating after each addition. Blend in vanilla and melted chocolate. Add flour mixture, alternately with the buttermilk, beating after each addition until smooth. Beat egg whites until they form stiff peaks; fold into batter. Pour batter into three 9-inch layer pans which have been lined on bottoms with paper. Bake at 350°F. for 30 to 35 minutes, until cake springs back when lightly pressed in center. Cool cake in pans 15 minutes; then remove and cool on rack. Spread Coconut-Pecan Filling and Frosting between layers and over top of cake.

* Or use 2¼ cups sifted all-purpose flour.

Note: This delicate cake will have a flat slightly sugary top crust which tends to crack.

Coconut-Pecan Filling and Frosting

- 1 cup evaporated milk or heavy cream
- 1 cup sugar
- 3 egg yolks, slightly beaten
- ½ cup butter or margarine
- 1 tsp. vanilla
- 1⅓ cups (about) Baker's Angel Flake or Premium Shred Coconut
- 1 cup chopped pecans

Combine milk, sugar, egg yolks, butter and vanilla in a saucepan. Cook over medium heat, stirring constantly until mixture thickens, about 12 minutes. Remove from heat. Add coconut and pecans. Cool until of spreading consistency, beating occasionally.

Makes 2½ cups or enough to cover tops of three 9-inch layers.

Note: For thinner frosting, use only 2 egg yolks.

Hershey's® Red Velvet Cocoa Cake

In the Thirties money was scarce and luxuries were few. No wonder this economy-minded cake recipe from Hershey's® Cocoa was a favorite then. It still is! Moist and rich tasting, it calls for only ½ cup of shortening and two eggs, but it tastes as extravagant as any cake you've ever made.

- ½ cup shortening
- 1½ cups sugar
- 2 eggs
- 1 tsp. vanilla
- 3 Tbs. Hershey's® Cocoa
- 2 ounces red food coloring
- 2½ cups sifted cake flour
- 1 cup buttermilk
- 1 tsp. salt
- 1 tsp. soda
- 1 Tbs. vinegar

Cream shortening and sugar. Add eggs and vanilla. Beat well. In a separate dish, blend cocoa and food coloring; add to sugar mixture. Add flour, buttermilk, and salt alternately. Mix soda and vinegar in cup and add.

Bake in two 9-inch cake pans, greased and floured, at 350°F. for 30 to 35 minutes. If desired, divide batter between three 8-inch pans. Let cool before frosting.

Note: A red paste coloring usually does a prettier job than some liquid types. They are available in specialty shops or in cake decorating supply sections of department stores.

Lovelight Chiffon Yellow Cake

Here's that famous all-time favorite cake from Wesson Oil.

- 2 eggs, separated
- 1½ cups of sugar
- 2¼ cups sifted cake flour
- 3 tsps. baking powder
- 1 tsp. salt
- ⅓ cup Wesson Oil
- 1 cup milk
- 1½ tsps. vanilla

Heat oven to 350°F. Lightly oil and dust with flour two round 8- or 9-inch layer pans. Beat egg whites until frothy. Gradually beat in ½ cup of sugar. Continue beating until very stiff and glossy. Sift remaining sugar, flour, baking powder and salt into another bowl. Add Wesson Oil, half the milk, and vanilla. Beat 1 minute, medium speed on the mixer, or 150 strokes by hand. Scrape sides and bottom of bowl constantly.

Add remaining milk, and egg yolks, then beat 1 minute more, scraping the sides of the bowl constantly. Fold in meringue. Pour into prepared pans. Bake layers for 30 to 35 minutes. Cool then frost with Seven-Minute Frosting

Chocolate Mayonnaise Cake

Mayonnaise in a cake? Yes, and what's more, thousands of cooks have written in for copies of this old favorite printed on the Hellmann's jar.

- 2 cups unsifted flour
- ⅔ cup unsweetened cocoa
- 1¼ tsps. baking soda
- ¼ tsp. baking powder
- 1⅔ cups sugar
- 3 eggs
- 1 tsp. vanilla
- 1 cup Hellmann's or Best Foods Real Mayonnaise
- 1⅓ cups water

Grease and flour bottoms of two 9 × 1½-inch round baking pans. In medium bowl stir together flour, cocoa, baking soda and baking powder; set aside. In large bowl with mixer at high speed beat sugar, eggs and vanilla, occasionally scraping bowl, 3 minutes or until light and fluffy. Reduce speed to low; beat in mayonnaise. Add flour mixture in 4 additions alternately with water, beginning and ending with flour. Pour into prepared pans. Bake in 350°F. oven for 30 to 35 minutes or until cake tester inserted in center comes out clean. Cool in pans for 10 minutes. Remove; cool on wire racks. Frost as desired. Garnish with sliced almonds. Makes two 9-inch layers.

Angel Food Cake

Did you think I would leave this one out? It's a classic from Swans Down.

- 1¼ cups sifted Swans Down Cake Flour
- ½ cup sugar
- 1½ cups (about 12) egg whites (at room temperature)
- ¼ tsp. salt
- 1¼ tsps. cream of tartar
- 1 tsp. vanilla
- ¼ tsp. almond extract
- 1⅓ cups sugar
- Butter Cream Frosting or Sweet Chocolate Glaze

Sift flour with ½ cup sugar four times. Combine egg whites, salt, cream of tartar and flavorings in large bowl. Beat with a flat wire whip, rotary beater or high speed of electric mixer until moist, glossy; soft peaks will form. Add 1⅓ cups sugar, sprinkling in ⅓ cup at a time and beating until blended after each addition, about 25 strokes by hand. Sift in flour mixture in four additions, folding in with 15 complete fold-over strokes after each addition and turning bowl often. After last addition, use 10 to 20 extra strokes. Pour into an ungreased 10-inch tube pan. Bake at 375°F. for 35 to 40 minutes, or until the top springs back when pressed lightly. Invert on rack and cool thoroughly. Then remove from pan and frost.

Butter Cream Frosting

Fluffier than most, this butter frosting adds to your cake's elegance.

- ½ cup butter or margarine
- ⅛ tsp. salt
- 1 lb. unsifted confectioners' sugar
- 1 egg or 2 egg yolks
- 1 tsp. vanilla
- 2 Tbs. (about) milk

Cream butter and salt; gradually add part of the sugar, blending well after each addition. Stir in egg and vanilla. Add remaining sugar alternately with milk, until of spreading consistency, beating after each addition until smooth. Makes 2½ cups, or enough to cover tops and sides of two 9-inch layers, three 8-inch layers, a 9-inch square, a 13 × 9-inch cake, or a 10-inch tube cake.

Coffee Butter Cream Frosting. Prepare as for Butter Cream Frosting, adding 1 Tbs. Instant Maxwell House, Sanka, or Yuban Coffee and decreasing the vanilla to ½ tsp.

Sweet Chocolate Glaze

Just enough dark, glossy glaze to crown a cake beautifully, deliciously.

- 1 4-ounce package Baker's German Sweet Chocolate
- 1 Tbs. butter
- 3 Tbs. water
- 1 cup sifted confectioners' sugar
- Dash of salt
- ½ tsp. vanilla

Combine chocolate, butter and water in a small saucepan; stir over low heat until blended and smooth. Combine sugar and salt in mixing bowl. Gradually add chocolate mixture, blending well. Add vanilla. (For thinner glaze, stir in a little hot water; for thicker glaze, cool mixture until of desired consistency). Makes ¾ cup, or enough to glaze top of a 9- or 10-inch tube cake, 8- or 9-inch layer, or 13 × 9-inch cake.

Fantasy Sponge Cake

Swans Down's traditional six-egg cake—a good basis for hundreds of desserts.

- 6 egg whites (¾ cup), room temperature
- 1 tsp. cream of tartar
- 1½ cups sifted sugar
- 1⅓ cups sifted Swans Down Cake Flour
- ½ tsp. Calumet Baking Powder
- ½ tsp. salt
- 6 egg yolks (½ cup)
- ¼ cup water
- 1 tsp. lemon extract

Beat egg whites with cream of tartar in a large bowl until soft mounds begin to form, using high speed of electric mixer or rotary beater or flat wire whip. Beat in ½ cup of sugar, 2 Tbs. at a time; then beat until very stiff peaks form; do not underbeat. Sift flour with remaining 1 cup sugar, baking powder and salt into a small bowl. Add egg yolks, water and lemon extract; beat with a spoon just until blended (about 75 strokes). Carefully fold into egg white mixture, using about 30 fold-over strokes; do not stir or beat. Pour into an ungreased 10-inch tube pan; gently cut through batter to remove large air bubbles. Bake at 375°F. for about 35 minutes, until cake springs back when pressed lightly. Invert and cool thoroughly in pan. Remove from pan; sprinkle with sifted confectioners' sugar or top with a glaze, if desired. Makes one 10-inch tube cake.

Spicy Butterscotch Chiffon Cake

Here is a recipe for an unusual Butterscotch Chiffon Cake that appeared on the Domino Sugar carton a few years ago. It's a delightfully different cake, light and spicy. I like it best with Seven-Minute Frosting (page 123).

- 2¼ cups sifted cake flour
- 3 tsps. double-acting baking powder
- 1 tsp. salt
- ½ tsp. *each* allspice, cinnamon, cloves and nutmeg
- 2 cups Domino Light Brown Sugar
- ½ cup salad oil
- 5 egg yolks
- ¾ cup water
- 2 tsps. vanilla
- 1 cup egg whites, room temperature
- ½ tsp. cream of tartar

Sift together flour, baking powder, salt and spices in large mixing bowl. Stir sugar into mixture. Make a well in dry ingredients; add oil, yolks, water and extract. Beat thoroughly until sugar is dissolved and batter is smooth.

Place egg whites in large mixing bowl. Sprinkle cream of tartar on whites. Beat at highest speed until whites stand in peaks but are not dry. Gradually fold batter into beaten egg whites, turning mixture over lightly from bottom with rubber spatula until well blended. Do not stir or overmix.

Turn into ungreased 10-inch tube pan. Bake in slow 325°F oven, for 80 to 85 minutes until cake springs back when touched lightly. Invert pan on funnel or suspend over cooling rack. Allow cake to hang until cool. Remove by running a sharp thin-bladed knife around sides of pan with one long steady stroke. Tap pan sharply until cake comes free. Makes one 10-inch cake.

Happy Day Cake

This is an all-time favorite from the Swans Down Cake Flour package.

- 2½ cups sifted Swans Down Cake Flour
- 1½ cups sugar
- 3 tsps. Calumet Baking Powder
- 1 tsp. salt
- ½ cup shortening (at room temperature)
- 1 cup milk
- 1 tsp. vanilla
- 2 eggs

Sift flour with sugar, baking powder, and salt. Stir shortening to soften. Add flour mixture, ¾ cup of the milk, and vanilla. Mix until all flour is dampened; then beat 2 minutes at medium speed of electric mixer or 300 vigorous strokes by hand. Add eggs and remaining ¼ cup milk; beat 1 minute longer with mixer or 150 strokes by hand. Pour into two 9-inch layer pans that have been lined on bottoms with paper. Bake at 350°F. for 25 to 30 minutes, or until cake tester inserted in center comes out clean. Cool 10 minutes in pans; remove from pans and cool thoroughly on racks. Frost with any favorite frosting.

Alternate baking pans: This cake may also be baked at 350°F. in three 8-inch layer pans for 25 to 35 minutes, or in a 13 × 9-inch pan for 30 to 35 minutes. Or spoon the batter into 36 medium paper baking cups in muffin pans, filling each half full; then bake at 375°F. for 20 to 25 minutes.

Coconut Praline Cake: Prepare as for Happy Day Cake, adding ⅔ cup Baker's Angel Flake Coconut with the eggs; bake in 13 × 9-inch pan as directed. Meanwhile, prepare Coconut Praline Topping. Spread topping over hot cake in pan; broil until bubbly and golden brown.

Coconut Praline Topping

A broiled-on topping that's delicious hot or cool.

Melt ½ cup butter; then add 1 cup firmly packed brown sugar, 1⅓ cups (about) Baker's Angel Flake Coconut, and ⅓ cup light cream, mixing well. Let stand about 5 minutes. Then spread mixture over top of either warm or cold cake. Broil until topping is bubbly and golden brown, about 3 minutes. Serve warm or cold. Makes about 1⅔ cups, or enough to cover top of a 13 × 9-inch cake or a 10-inch tube cake.

Plum Good Cake

Ever think of using baby food to make a cake? The Gerber people did and printed this recipe on their strained plum jars years ago. It's a lovely, moist, rich cake and a snap to make.

2 cups unsifted flour
2 cups granulated sugar
½ tsp. baking powder
½ tsp. baking soda

- ½ tsp. salt
- ½ tsp. cloves
- 1 cup salad oil
- 3 eggs
- 2 jars (4¾ ounces each) Gerber Strained Plums with Tapioca
- 1 tsp. cinnamon
- 1 Tbs. red food coloring
- 1 cup chopped black walnuts or other nuts (optional)

Mix all ingredients at one time with electric beater until eggs are well mixed. Pour into greased Bundt or tube cake pan. Bake in preheated 300°F. oven for 1 hour and 10 minutes or until sides of cake pull away from pan. Remove cake from pan while still hot. Frost while hot.

Frosting: 1 cup confectioners sugar combined with 1 Tbs. lemon juice (will be quite thick). Let cool before serving.

Nutty Graham Picnic Cake

A Pillsbury Bake-Off winner! A brown sugar glaze topped with nuts adds just the right finish to this moist, hearty cake.

- 2 cups Pillsbury's Best All Purpose or Unbleached Flour*
- 1 cup (14 squares) graham craker crumbs
- 1 cup firmly packed brown sugar
- ½ cup sugar
- 1 tsp. salt
- 1 tsp. baking powder
- 1 tsp. baking soda
- ½ tsp. cinnamon
- 1 cup margarine or butter, softened
- 1 cup orange juice
- 1 Tbs. grated orange peel
- 3 eggs
- 1 cup chopped nuts

* If you use Pillsbury's Best Self-Rising Flour, omit salt and baking powder and reduce soda to ¼ tsp.

Glaze:

2 Tbs. brown sugar
5 tsps. milk
1 Tbs. margarine or butter
¾ cup powdered sugar
¼ cup chopped nuts

Heat oven to 350°F. Using 1 Tbs. solid shortening, generously grease and flour 12-cup fluted tube pan or 10-inch tube pan (non-stick finish). Lightly spoon flour into measuring cup; level off. In large bowl, combine all cake ingredients except nuts; beat 3 minutes at medium speed. Stir in nuts. Pour into prepared pan. Bake at 350°F. for 45 to 50 minutes or until toothpick inserted in center comes out clean. Cool upright in pan for 15 minutes; invert onto serving plate, cool completely.

Glaze: In small saucepan, heat 2 Tbs. brown sugar, milk and butter just until melted. Remove from heat; add powdered sugar and blend until smooth. Drizzle over cake; sprinkle with nuts. Makes 12 to 16 servings.

High Altitude: Above 3500 feet, bake at 350°F. for 50 to 55 minutes.

Bacardi® Rum Cake

Here's the very first cake to incorporate a pudding mix. It's simply fabulous.

Cake:

1 cup chopped pecans or walnuts
1 18½-ounce package yellow cake mix
1 3¾-ounce package Jell-O® Instant Vanilla Pudding mix
4 eggs
¼ cup cold water
½ cup Wesson oil
½ cup Bacardi® Dark Rum (80 proof)

Glaze:

¼ lb. butter
¼ cup water
1 cup granulated sugar
½ cup Bacardi® Dark Rum (80 proof)

Preheat oven to 325°F. Grease and flour 10-inch tube or 12-cup Bundt pan. Sprinkle nuts over bottom of pan. Mix all cake ingredients together. Pour batter over nuts. Bake 1 hour. Cool. Invert on serving plate. Prick top. Drizzle and smooth glaze evenly over top and sides. Allow cake to absorb glaze. Repeat till all glaze is used up.

Glaze: Melt butter in saucepan. Stir in water and sugar. Boil 5 minutes, stirring constantly. Remove from heat. Stir in rum.

Optional: Decorate with whole maraschino cherries and border of sugar frosting or whipped cream. Serve with seedless green grapes dusted with powdered sugar.

Orange Kiss-Me Cake

This cake is still as good as it was in 1950 when it was named the $25,000 Pillsbury Bake-Off winner. The delicious flavor comes from a fresh orange, raisins and walnuts ground together. Modern methods make it so easy to prepare that you can enjoy this cake often. A blender or food processor makes short work of grinding the fruit and nuts.

- 2 cups Pillsbury's Best All Purpose or Unbleached Flour
- 1 orange
- 1 cup raisins
- ⅓ cup walnuts
- 1 cup sugar
- 1 tsp. baking soda
- 1 tsp. salt
- 1 cup milk
- ½ cup shortening
- 2 eggs

Topping:

- Reserved ⅓ cup orange juice
- ⅓ cup sugar
- 1 tsp. cinnamon
- ¼ cup finely chopped walnuts
- Orange slices, to garnish

Heat oven to 350°F. (325°F. for glass pan). Grease (not oil) and flour 13 × 9-inch pan. Lightly spoon flour into measuring cup; level off. Squeeze orange; reserve ⅓ cup juice. Grind orange peel and pulp, raisins and ⅓ cup walnuts together. Set aside. In large bowl, blend flour, sugar, soda, salt, milk, shortening and eggs. Beat for 3 minutes at medium speed. Stir in orange-raisin mixture. Pour into prepared pan.

Bake at 350°F. for 35 to 40 minutes or until toothpick inserted in center comes out clean.

Topping: Drizzle reserved orange juice over warm cake. Combine sugar, cinnamon and walnuts; sprinkle over cake. If desired, garnish with orange slices. Makes a 13 × 9-inch cake.

Notes: Self-rising flour not recommended. A blender may be used to grind orange-raisin mixture if grinder is unavailable. This has not been tested in a food processor, but it should work.

High Altitude: Above 3500 feet, add 2 Tbs. flour; bake at 375°F. for 35 to 40 minutes.

Bacardi® Rum Piña Colada Cake

Can you believe it? It's even better than the original rum cake—if that's possible!

Cake:

- 1 package (2-layer size) white cake mix
- 1 package (4-serving size) Jell-O® Coconut Cream Flavor or Vanilla Instant Pudding and Pie Filling*
- 4 eggs
- ¼ cup water*
- ⅓ cup Bacardi® Dark Rum (80 proof)
- ¼ cup Wesson oil
- 1 cup flaked coconut

* With vanilla flavor filling, increase water to ¾ cup; add 1 cup flaked coconut to batter.

Frosting:

- 1 8-ounce can crushed pineapple (in juice)
- 1 package (4-serving size) Jell-O® Coconut Cream Flavor or Vanilla Instant Pudding and Pie Filling
- ⅓ cup Bacardi® Dark Rum (80 proof)
- 1 9-ounce container frozen whipped topping, thawed

Blend all ingredients except coconut in large mixer bowl. Beat 4 minutes at medium speed of electric mixer. Pour into two greased and floured 9-inch layer pans. Bake at 350°F. for 25 to 30 minutes or until cake springs back when lightly pressed. Do not underbake. Cool in pan for 15 minutes; remove and cool on racks. Fill and frost; sprinkle with coconut. Chill. Refrigerate leftover cake.

Frosting: Combine all ingredients except whipped topping in a bowl; beat until well blended. Fold in thawed whipped topping.

Dream Cake

The idea of adding to a cake mix isn't so new after all. In 1969 General Foods developed this recipe for a luscious, creamy cake that uses a packet of Dream Whip for its velvety taste and texture.

- 1 package (2-layer size) yellow, white or devil's food cake mix
- 1 envelope Dream Whip Whipped Topping Mix*
- 4 eggs
- 1 cup cold water

* Do not whip; use right from envelope.

Combine cake mix, whipped topping mix right from envelope, eggs and water in large bowl of electric mixer. Blend until moistened. Beat at medium speed for 4 minutes. Pour into greased and floured 10-inch tube pan. Bake at 350°F. for 45 to 50 minutes or until cake tester inserted into center of cake comes out clean. Cool in pan 15 minutes. Then loosen from sides and center tube with knife and gently remove cake. Finish cooling on rack.

Note: Reduce temperature to 325°F. when using glass baking dishes.

Alternate baking pans: This cake may also be baked in the following greased and floured pans, cooling in pans 10 minutes:

Two 9-inch layer pans for 30 minutes.
Two 8-inch square pans for about 30 minutes.
Three 8-inch layer pans for about 35 minutes.
Three 8 × 3½-inch aluminum loaf pans for 30 to 40 minutes.
Two 9 × 5-inch loaf pans for 45 minutes.
One 13 × 9-inch pan for 40 to 45 minutes.
Two 15 × 10-inch jelly roll pans for 12 to 14 minutes.
40 medium cupcake pans (one-half to two-thirds full) for 20 minutes.
One 10-inch Bundt pan for 40 minutes; cool in pan for 15 minutes.
Three 8 × 4-inch loaf pans for 30 to 40 minutes.

Tomato Spice Cake

A half century of good cooks have baked this Campbell's Tomato Soup cake. It's as moist, delicate and delicious today as it was fifty years ago.

2¼ cups cake flour or 2 cups all-purpose flour
1⅓ cups sugar
4 tsps. baking powder

1 tsp. baking soda
1½ tsps. allspice
1 tsp. cinnamon
½ tsp. ground cloves
1 10¾-ounce can Campbell's Condensed Tomato Soup
½ cup shortening
2 eggs
¼ cup water

Preheat oven to 350°F. Generously grease and flour two round 8- or 9-inch layer pans, or a 13 × 9 × 2-inch oblong pan. Measure dry ingredients into large bowl. Add soup and shortening. Beat at low to medium speed for 2 minutes or 300 strokes with a spoon, scraping sides and bottom of bowl constantly. Add eggs and water. Beat 2 minutes more, scraping bowl frequently. Pour into pans. Bake for 35 to 40 minutes. Let stand 10 minutes; remove. Cool. Use Vanilla Philly Frosting (page 123).

Bundt pan: Proceed as above. Bake in well-greased and lightly floured 2½-quart Bundt pan at 350°F. for 50 to 60 minutes or until done. Cool right-side-up in pan for 15 minutes; remove from pan. Cool. If desired, sprinkle with confectioners' sugar.

It's-A-Snap Cheesecake

The Knox Gelatine people printed this sure-fire recipe for cheesecake on their package years ago. It's become a classic, so don't hesitate. Make it for dessert the next time you want to serve something impressive.

1 envelope Knox Unflavored Gelatine
½ cup sugar
1 cup boiling water
2 8-ounce packages cream cheese, softened
1 tsp. vanilla (optional)
1 9-inch graham cracker crust

In a large bowl, mix Knox Unflavored Gelatine and sugar; add boiling water and stir until gelatine is completely dissolved. With electric mixer, beat in cream cheese and vanilla until smooth. Pour into prepared crust; chill until firm, about 2 hours. Top, if desired, with fresh or canned fruit. Makes about 8 servings.

For delicious variations try:

Marbled Cheesecake: Before chilling, marble in ⅓ cup chocolate fudge, butterscotch or your favorite flavor ice cream topping.

Lemon or Almond Cheesecake: Substitute ½ to ¾ teaspoon lemon or almond extract for vanilla extract.

Fruit 'n Creamy Cheesecake: Chill cheesecake for 10 minutes, then swirl in ⅓ cup strawberry or raspberry preserves.

Sunshine Cheesecake: Substitute ½ teaspoon orange extract for vanilla extract and add 1 teaspoon grated orange rind.

Bacardi® Rum Chocolate Cake

And now there's a chocolate version to split and fill with a heady chocolate filling.

- 1 18½-ounce package chocolate cake mix
- 1 package (4-serving size) Jell-O® Chocolate Instant Pudding and Pie Filling
- 4 eggs
- ½ cup Bacardi® Dark Rum (80 proof)
- ¼ cup cold water
- ½ cup Wesson oil
- ½ cup slivered almonds, optional

Filling:

- 1½ cups cold milk

Instant Pudding and Pie Filling

¼ cup Bacardi® Dark Rum (80 proof)
1 package (4-serving size) Jell-O® Chocolate
1 envelope Dream Whip Topping Mix

Preheat oven to 350°F. Grease and flour two 9-inch layer cake pans. Combine all cake ingredients together in large bowl. Blend well, then beat at medium mixer speed for 2 minutes. Turn into prepared pans. Bake for 30 minutes or until cake tests done. Do not underbake. Cool in pans for 10 minutes. Remove from pans, finish cooling on racks. Split layers in half horizontally. Spread 1 cup filling between each layer and over top of cake. Stack. Keep cake chilled. Serve cold.

Optional: Garnish with chocolate curls.

Filling: Combine milk, rum, pudding mix and topping mix in deep narrow-bottom bowl. Blend well at high speed for 4 minutes, until light and fluffy. Makes 4 cups.

Goodie Apple Sauce Cake

The Stokely Company printed this recipe on its apple sauce label. It's cake that stays fresh for days!

2½ cups all-purpose flour
1 cup sugar
¼ tsp. baking powder
1½ tsps. baking soda
1½ tsps. salt
¾ tsp. cinnamon
½ tsp. cloves, ground
½ tsp. allspice
½ cup shortening, softened
½ cup water
½ cup nut meats, broken
1 cup raisins, cut up
1 1-lb. can Stokely's Finest Gravenstein Apple Sauce
1 large egg

Sift together first eight ingredients. Add next four ingredients and beat for 2 minutes. Add last two ingredients and beat 2 more minutes. Pour into greased and floured 12 × 7½-inch pan and bake at 350°F. for 45 to 50 minutes. Top with your favorite lemon frosting. Makes 18 servings.

Note: For best flavor, bake the day before serving.

Linzer Torte

A dozen years ago Blue Diamond Almonds introduced this scrumptious and authentic Linzer Torte. Serve it with clouds of real whipped cream in true Viennese fashion and don't forget the coffee.

- 1½ cups Blue Diamond Whole Natural Almonds
- 1 cup butter or margarine
- 1 cup sugar
- 2 egg yolks, beaten
- 1½ tsps. grated lemon rind
- 2 cups sifted all-purpose flour
- 1 Tbs. cinnamon
- ½ tsp. ground cloves
- 1 cup raspberry jam

Grind almonds in blender or food processor; set aside. Cream butter and sugar. Add egg yolks, ground almonds and lemon rind. Sift together flour and spices and add to creamed mixture. Knead until dough is firm and holds together. Pat two-thirds of dough into a 9-inch round cake pan, covering bottom and sides. The layer should be about ½ inch thick. Spread with jam. Form eight ½-inch thick strips with remaining dough. Make lattice top by placing four strips one way and 4 the opposite. Bake in 350°F. oven for 30 to 40 minutes. Cool. Cut into pie-shaped wedges 1 inch wide at the rim. Makes about 30 pieces.

Old-Fashioned Jelly Roll

How long since you've had a slice of homemade jelly roll cake? Too long I'll bet. If your mother didn't save her recipe, here it is, just as printed on the Welch® Concord Grape Jelly jar over 15 years ago.

4 eggs
¾ cup sifted all-purpose or cake flour
1 tsp. baking powder
¼ tsp. salt
¾ cup sugar
1 tsp. vanilla extract or 1 Tbs. grated orange peel
Confectioners sugar
1 10-oz. jar Welch's® Concord Grape Jelly

In electric mixer bowl, let eggs warm to room temperature (about 1 hour). Sift together flour, baking powder and salt; set aside. At high speed, beat eggs until thick and lemon colored. Gradually beat in sugar, 2 Tbs. at a time, continuing to beat until very thick and light (about 5 minutes). At low speed, blend in sifted dry ingredients and vanilla just until combined. Spread evenly in a jelly-roll pan, 15 × 10½ × 1 inches, lined with greased wax paper. Bake in a preheated hot oven (400°F.) until surface springs back when gently pressed with fingertip (about 10 to 13 minutes). Sift confectioners sugar on a clean towel in a 15 × 10-inch oblong. With sharp knife, loosen sides of cake from pan. Turn onto the sugared towel; gently peel off wax paper and trim off crisp edges. Starting with 10-inch side, roll cake in towel; place seam side down on wire rack until cool. Gently unroll cake, remove towel and spread with jelly (beaten with fork to spreading consistency). Reroll and place seam side down, on serving plate; cover loosely with foil. Chill at least 1 hour. Serve topped with sifted confectioners sugar. Serves 10.

Golden Beauty Prune Cake

A half-century of good cooks have baked this Sunsweet® Prune Cake. It's as moist, rich and delicious today as it was 50 years ago.

- 1 cup snipped cooked Sunsweet® Prunes
- ½ cup butter or margarine
- 1 cup granulated sugar
- ½ cup brown sugar, packed
- 1 tsp. vanilla
- 2 large eggs, beaten
- 2½ cups sifted all-purpose flour
- ¾ tsp. baking powder
- ¾ tsp. baking soda
- ¾ tsp. salt
- ½ tsp. cinnamon
- ¼ tsp. nutmeg
- ¼ tsp. cloves
- 1 cup buttermilk
- Mocha Frosting (below)

Cook prunes by package directions; drain and snip. Cream butter with sugars and vanilla until light and fluffy. Beat in eggs. (Mixture may appear slightly curdled.) Resift flour with baking powder, soda, salt and spices. Blend into creamed mixture alternately with buttermilk, beginning and ending with flour mixture. Fold in prunes. Turn into 2 well greased, 8-inch layer cake pans. Bake in oven center at 375°F. for about 30 minutes, until cakes test done. Remove from oven; let stand 10 minutes, then turn out onto wire racks to cool. When cold, spread Mocha Frosting between layers and on top and sides of cake. Makes 1 8-inch cake.

Mocha Frosting

- 1 tsp. instant coffee powder
- ¼ cup milk
- ⅓ cup soft butter or margarine
- 1 lb. powdered sugar, sifted.

Dissolve coffee powder in milk. Combine with butter or margarine and powdered sugar. Beat until smooth, adding a few drops more milk if needed for good spreading consistency.

Famous Chocolate Wafer Roll

Here is another of those "too good to take off the package" recipes. Ridiculously easy to make, fabulously rich-tasting and positively exotic when sliced and served. It's the Famous Chocolate Wafers® that have made this a famous American classic dessert.

1 cup heavy cream
¼ cup confectioners sugar
½ tsp. vanilla extract
20 Famous Chocolate Wafers®

Whip cream with sugar and vanilla, until stiff. Reserve 1 cup. Spread Famous Chocolate Wafers® with remaining cream and arrange in stacks of 4 or 5. Chill 15 minutes. Lay stacks on edge to make one long roll. Spread remaining cream on outside of roll. Chill 3 to 4 hours, or overnight, covered. To serve, cut diagonally.

Makes 8 ¾-inch slices.

Variation: Substitute 1 Tbs. instant coffee for vanilla extract, and garnish with chocolate curls.

Deluxe Shortcake

No true American cookbook would be complete without a real shortcake made with your own, not-too-sweet, biscuit-like layers, not with "store-bought" sponge cake.

- 2 cups Pillsbury's® Best Self-Rising or Unbleached Self-Rising Flour
- 2 Tbs. sugar
- ½ cup shortening
- ¾ cup half-and-half or whipping cream
- 2 Tbs. margarine or butter, melted
- 1 Tbs. sugar
- 1 cup whipping cream, whipped
- 6 cups sliced strawberries or other favorite fruit

Heat oven to 425°F. Lightly spoon flour into measuring cup; level off. In large bowl, combine flour and sugar. Cut shortening into flour mixture with fork until consistency of coarse meal. Add half-and-half to flour mixture; stir just until moistened. Spread batter in 2 ungreased 8-inch round pans. Brush melted margarine over batter; sprinkle with sugar. Bake at 425°F. for 12 to 18 minutes or until light golden brown. Immediately remove from pans; cool completely. Fill and top layers with whipped cream and strawberries. Refrigerate leftovers. Makes 12 servings.

Old-Fashioned Cocoa Mint Cake

Memories were soon made when this "pepperminty-chocolatey" recipe was first printed in Hershey's® 1930 cookbook.

- 2/3 cup butter
- 1 2/3 cups granulated sugar
- 3 eggs
- 2 cups all-purpose flour
- 2/3 cup Hershey's® Cocoa
- 1 1/4 tsps. baking soda
- 1/4 tsp. baking powder
- 1 tsp. salt
- 1 1/3 cups milk
- 1/2 cup crushed peppermint candy
- Cocoa Peppermint Icing (below)

Cream butter, sugar and eggs until fluffy, and beat vigorously 3 minutes (high speed of mixer). Combine flour, cocoa, baking soda, baking powder and salt; add alternately with milk to creamed mixture. Blend in crushed candy. Pour batter into 2 greased and floured 9-inch cake pans. Bake in a moderate oven (350°) for 35 minutes. Cool 10 minutes before removing from pans. Ice cake with Cocoa Peppermint Icing.

Cocoa Peppermint Icing

- 1/2 cup butter
- 1/2 cup Hershey's® Cocoa
- 3 2/3 cups (1-lb. box) confectioners sugar
- 7 Tbs. milk
- 1 tsp. vanilla
- 1 Tbs. crushed peppermint candy

Melt the butter in a saucepan; add the Cocoa and heat 1 minute or until smooth, stirring constantly. Alternately add sugar and milk, beating to spreading consistency. Blend in vanilla and peppermint candy. Makes about 2 1/4 cups icing or enough for an 8- or 9-inch layer cake.

Holiday Gift Cake

On the label of Philadelphia® Brand Cream Cheese a long time ago, but still a much-requested recipe.

- 1 8-oz. package Philadelphia® Brand Cream Cheese
- 1 cup Parkay® Margarine
- 1½ cups sugar
- 1½ tsps. vanilla
- 4 eggs
- 2¼ cups sifted cake flour
- 1½ tsps. baking powder
- ¾ cup well-drained chopped Maraschino cherries
- ½ cup chopped pecans
- ½ cup finely chopped pecans
- 1½ cups sifted confectioners sugar
- 2 Tbs. milk

Combine softened cream cheese, margarine, sugar and vanilla, mixing until well blended. Add eggs, one at a time, mixing well after each addition. Gradually add 2 cups flour sifted with baking powder, mixing well after each addition. Toss remaining flour with cherries and chopped nuts; fold into batter. Grease a 10-inch Bundt or tube pan; sprinkle with finely chopped nuts. Pour batter into pan; bake at 325°F. 1 hour and 20 minutes. Cool 5 minutes; remove from pan. Cool thoroughly. Glaze with mixture of confectioners sugar and milk. Garnish with cherries and nuts, if desired. Makes 1 cake.

Chocolate Upside-Down Cake

In the 1940's when upside-down cakes were at their height of popularity, this one rated four stars. They tell me at the Hershey® test kitchens it has been rediscovered, and requests for the recipe have doubled in the last few years. No wonder; it is *good!*

- 3 Tbs. butter, melted
- ½ cup light brown sugar, packed
- 2 Tbs. light corn syrup
- ½ cup butter or margarine
- 1¼ cups sugar
- 2 eggs
- 1 tsp. vanilla

- 1 29-oz. can sliced peaches or pear halves, well drained
- Maraschino cherries, halved
- ½ cup chopped nuts (optional)
- 1¼ cups unsifted all-purpose flour
- ⅓ cup Hershey's® Cocoa
- ¾ tsp. baking soda
- ½ tsp. salt
- ⅔ cup buttermilk or sour milk*

Combine 3 Tbs. butter, brown sugar and corn syrup in bottom of a 12-cup Bundt pan or 10-inch tube pan. (Do not use a removable-bottom tube pan.) Arrange sliced peaches or pear halves and cherries in a decorative design. Sprinkle with nuts. Cream ½ cup butter and sugar until light and fluffy. Add eggs, one at a time, beating well after each addition; add vanilla. Combine flour, cocoa, baking soda and salt; add to creamed mixture alternately with buttermilk. Pour batter evenly over fruit and nuts in pan. Bake at 350°F. for 40 to 45 minutes for Bundt pan, 50 to 55 minutes for tube pan or until cake tester inserted in center comes out clean. Immediately invert onto serving plate; leave pan over cake a few minutes. Serve warm with sweetened whipped cream if desired.

Amazin' Raisin Cake

The name fits; a rather terrific cake. When it appeared in a national ad the response from consumers was, in a word, amazing.

- 3 cups unsifted flour
- 2 cups sugar
- ½ tsp. salt
- ¼ tsp. ground cloves

* To Sour Milk: Use 2 tsps. vinegar plus milk to equal ⅔ cup.

- 1 cup Hellmann's® Best Foods Real Mayonnaise
- ⅓ cup milk
- 2 eggs
- 2 tsps. baking soda
- 1½ tsps. ground cinnamon
- ½ tsp. ground nutmeg
- 3 cups chopped peeled apples
- 1 cup seedless raisins
- 1 cup coarsely chopped walnuts
- 2 cups whipped cream

Grease and flour 2 9-inch round baking pans. In large bowl with mixer at low speed, scraping bowl frequently, beat together flour, sugar, Real Mayonnaise, milk, eggs, baking soda, cinnamon, nutmeg, salt and cloves 2 minutes or beat vigorously 300 strokes by hand. (Batter will be thick.) With spoon stir in apples, raisins and nuts. Spoon into prepared pans. Bake in 350°F. oven 45 minutes or until cake tester inserted in center comes out clean. Cool in pans on wire racks 10 minutes. Remove and cool on wire racks. Fill and frost with whipped cream. Makes 8 servings.

Amaretto Raisin Bundt Cake

This cake is a positive triumph. It is a party cake for sure. Thousands have written in for copies of this recipe since it appeared only a few short years ago in a national magazine advertisement for Hiram Walker® Amaretto.

- 1 package Pillsbury® Pound Cake Supreme Bundt Cake Mix
- ½ cup dairy sour cream
- ¼ cup margarine or butter, softened
- ½ cup water
- ⅓ cup Hiram Walker® Amaretto
- 3 eggs
- 2 cups (1 lb.) candied fruit mixture
- 1 cup Sun-Maid® Raisins
- 1 cup chopped nuts
- Sauce (opposite)

Heat oven to 325°F. Grease 12-cup Bundt pan. In large bowl, combine two clear packets of Cake Mix and remaining cake ingredients, except fruit, raisins and nuts. Blend until moistened; beat 2 minutes at medium speed. Fold in fruit, raisins and nuts. Pour into pan. Bake at 325°F. for 70 to 80 minutes until toothpick inserted in center comes out clean. *Cool upright* in pan on rack 25 minutes; invert onto plate. Cool completely. Sprinkle or sift topping packet over top of cake. Makes 16 servings.

Sauce

- 1½ cups sugar
- 4 Tbs. corn starch
- 1½ cups water
- 4 Tbs. margarine or butter
- ¼ cup Hiram Walker® Amaretto
- 2 Tbs. lemon juice
- ½ cup Sun-Maid® Raisins

To prepare sauce, mix sugar and corn starch in saucepan. Gradually stir in water. Over medium heat stirring constantly, heat to boiling; boil 1 minute. Remove from heat; stir in margarine, Amaretto, juice and raisins. Serve warm over cooled cake.

Carrot Cake

A "top-request" recipe and a particular favorite at the Betty Crocker® test kitchens. Made to order for mid-morning coffee, afternoon tea or after-school milk.

- 2 cups Bisquick® Baking Mix
- ½ cup packed brown sugar
- ½ cup chopped nuts
- 2 tsps. ground cinnamon
- 1 tsp. ground nutmeg
- 1½ cups shredded carrots
- ⅓ cup vegetable oil
- 3 eggs
- ¼ cup chopped nuts
- Cream Cheese Frosting (page 452)

Heat oven to 350°F. Grease and flour square pan, 9 × 9 × 2 inches. Beat all ingredients except frosting and ¼ c. nuts on low speed, scraping bowl constantly, 30 seconds. Beat on medium speed, scraping bowl occasionally, 2 minutes. Pour into pan. Bake until wooden pick inserted in center comes out clean, about 30 minutes. Cool; frost with Cream Cheese Frosting. Sprinkle with nuts. Refrigerate any remaining cake.

Cream Cheese Frosting

1 3-oz. package cream cheese, softened
2 cups powdered sugar
1 Tbs. margarine or butter, softened
2 to 3 tsps. milk

Mix all ingredients until texture is smooth.

Cheese Cake Almondine

One of the simplest of all cheese cakes to make, it won a popularity contest back in the 1950's because of its sensational richness and flavor, from Planters®.

1½ cups finely crushed vanilla wafer crumbs
1¼ cups sugar
½ cup chopped Planters® Pecans
½ tsp. grated lemon rind
¼ cup Blue Bonnet® Margarine, melted
3 8-oz. packages cream cheese, softened
3 eggs
⅔ cup chopped Planters® Blanched Almonds
¾ tsp. almond extract
1 cup dairy sour cream
⅓ cup Planters® Sliced Almonds

Combine vanilla wafer crumbs, 2 Tbs. sugar, Planters® Pecans and lemon rind. Add melted Blue Bonnet® Margarine. Combine well and press mixture into the bottom of a lightly greased 8-inch spring-form pan. Refrigerate. Cream the cheese and 1 cup of the remaining sugar in large bowl until light and fluffy. Add eggs, one at a time, beating well after each addition. Blend in Planters® Blanched Almonds and ½ teaspoon almond extract. Pour into chilled crust. Bake at 375°F. for 45 minutes. Cool at room temperature for 30 minutes. Meanwhile, blend sour cream, remaining 2 Tbs. sugar and ¼ tsp. almond extract. Spread mixture over cooled cheese filling. Bake for an additional 10 minutes. Sprinkle with Planters® Sliced Almonds and cool. Refrigerate overnight before serving. Makes 1 cake.

Devil's Delight Cake

An old-fashioned honest-to-goodness Devil's Food Cake from Hershey's® 1934 Cookbook. This was always my choice for my own birthday, filled and lavishly covered with Creole Icing made with strong and clear black coffee.

- 4 squares Hershey's® Baking Chocolate, melted
- ⅔ cup brown sugar, packed
- 1 cup milk
- 1 egg yolk
- ⅓ cup butter
- ½ cup brown sugar, packed
- 2 egg yolks
- 2 cups sifted cake flour
- ¼ tsp. salt
- 1 tsp. baking soda
- ½ cup milk
- 1 tsp. vanilla
- 3 egg whites
- ½ cup brown sugar, packed
- Orange slices sprinkled with minced nutmeats and minced citron or candied ginger for garnishes

Combine melted baking chocolate with ⅔ cup brown sugar, 1 cup milk and 1 beaten egg yolk, and stir over simmering water until well blended. Cool slightly. Cream butter, then add ½ cup brown sugar gradually, while beating constantly. Add 2 egg yolks well-beaten. Sift flour, salt and baking soda 3 times, and add to creamed mixture alternately with ½ cup milk, beating thoroughly. Add chocolate mixture and vanilla, and beat. Beat egg whites until foamy; gradually add ½ cup brown sugar and beat until stiff. Fold into batter. Pour into 2 buttered and floured 9-inch round cake pans. Bake in a moderate oven (350°F.) for 35 minutes. Spread layers and top with any favorite frosting, and garnish with orange slices, sprinkled with minced nutmeats and minced citron or candied ginger.

Creole Icing

- 1 Tbs. softened butter
- ¼ cup clear black coffee
- 3 Tbs. Hershey's® Cocoa
- Pinch of cinnamon
- 3¼ cups confectioners sugar

Combine butter, coffee, Cocoa and cinnamon. Gradually add sugar, beating to spreading consistency. Makes 1½ cups icing or enough for an 8- or 9-inch layer cake.

Sun-Maid® Victory Cake

Sun-Maid® developed this easy-make cake back in the days of World War II. It's still one of their best.

- 1 cup Sun-Maid® Raisins
- 1 cup brown sugar (packed)
- 1 cup water
- ½ cup shortening
- 1 tsp. cinnamon
- 1 tsp. nutmeg
- 1 tsp. cloves
- 2 cups sifted all-purpose flour
- 1 tsp. soda
- ½ tsp. salt
- ½ cup chopped walnuts

Combine Raisins, sugar, water, shortening and spices; heat to boiling and simmer 2 minutes. Cool 1 hour. Resift flour with soda and salt. Stir into raisin mixture, along with walnuts. Turn into greased 9-inch tube or square pan. Bake in slow oven (300°F.) 50 to 60 minutes, just until cake tests done. Cool in pan. Makes 1 9-inch cake.

Almond Candy Cake

One of the most popular cakes ever to appear in a national ad by the California Almond Growers Exchange.

- 1 large sponge or chiffon cake
- Filling (page 456)
- Maple Crisp topping (page 456)
- 1 cup toasted blanched almond halves

Split cake into 4 equal layers. Spread about half of Filling between cake layers. Spread remainder over top and sides of cake. Cover cake very thickly with Maple Crisp Topping, and stick almond halves porcupine fashion over top and sides of cake. Makes 16 to 20 servings.

Filling

2 cups whipping cream
2 Tbs. sugar
⅛ tsp. maple flavoring

Whip cream with sugar and flavoring.

Maple Crisp Topping

1½ cups sugar
⅓ cup water
¼ cup light corn syrup
1 Tbs. sifted baking soda
2 tsps. maple flavoring

Combine sugar, water and corn syrup in a saucepan, stirring until well blended. Boil over moderate heat to hard-crack stage (310°F.), until a small amount of syrup dropped into cold water will break with a brittle snap. Remove from heat, and stir in soda and maple flavoring. Stir vigorously until well blended, but not enough to destroy foam made by soda. Turn at once into ungreased shallow pan, about 9 inches square. Let stand without moving until completely cold. Knock out of pan and crush between sheets of waxed paper to make coarse crumbs.

Apple Spice Cake with Brandy Hard Sauce

Land O Lakes® Butter printed this scrumptious buttery spice cake recipe in an in-store recipe brochure. Serve it at your next dessert party and don't forget the coffee.

Cake

- 2 cups finely chopped apples
- ¼ cup water
- 1½ cups Land O Lakes® Unsalted (Sweet) Butter, softened
- 2 cups sugar
- 2 eggs
- 4 cups all-purpose flour
- 4 tsp. baking soda
- 2 tsp. *each* cinnamon and nutmeg
- 1 tsp. *each* salt and cloves
- 1 cup currants
- 1 cup chopped pecans
- ½ cup all-purpose flour

Hard Sauce

- ½ cup Land O Lakes® Unsalted (Sweet) Butter, softened
- 1 cup confectioners sugar
- 1 Tbs. brandy

Heat oven to 325°F. In 3-quart saucepan combine apples and water. Cook, uncovered, over medium heat, stirring occasionally, until apples are crisply tender (7 to 9 minutes). Remove from heat. Stir in butter until melted. Stir in sugar and eggs until well blended. In bowl combine 4 cups flour, baking soda, cinnamon, nutmeg, salt and cloves. Stir into apple mixture. In same bowl toss currants and pecans with ½ cup flour until coated. Stir into batter until well mixed. Spoon into 10-inch greased Bundt pan or tube pan. Bake in Bundt pan for 65 to 75 minutes (or tube pan for 70 to 80 minutes) until wooden pick inserted in center comes out clean. Cool in pan 15 minutes. Meanwhile, in 1½-quart mixer bowl combine all hard-sauce ingredients. Beat at medium speed until light and fluffy (3 to 5 minutes). Invert cake onto serving plate. Serve slices of warm cake with a dollop of 1 Tbs. hard sauce on each slice. Makes 1 10-inch cake with 1¼ cups hard sauce (20 servings).

Bavarian Apple Torte

Kraft® tells me this *is* a Bavarian torte, but I do believe it is a first cousin to the Pennsylvania Dutch apple torte. Well no matter, I'm not one to quarrel with ancestry when the results are this good.

½ cup Parkay® Margarine
⅓ cup sugar
¼ tsp. vanilla
1 cup flour
1 8-oz. package Philadelphia Brand Cream Cheese
¼ cup sugar
1 egg
½ tsp. vanilla
4 cups thin peeled apple slices
⅓ cup sugar
½ tsp. cinnamon
¼ cup sliced almonds

Cream margarine and sugar until light and fluffy. Blend in vanilla. Add flour; mix well. Spread on bottom and sides of 9-inch springform pan. Combine softened cream cheese and sugar, mixing until well blended. Blend in egg and vanilla. Pour into pastry-lined pan. Toss apples with combined sugar and cinnamon; spoon over cream cheese layer. Sprinkle with nuts. Bake at 450°F., 10 minutes. Reduce oven temperature to 400°F.; continue baking 25 minutes. Loosen crust from rim of pan; cool before removing rim of pan. Makes 8–10 servings.

Hunt's® Very Special Spice Cake

An all-time favorite from Hunt's® Tomato Sauce label. This cake stays marvelously moist for days.

- 3 cups sifted flour
- 1½ cups sugar
- 1½ tsp. baking powder
- 1½ tsp. cinnamon
- ¾ tsp. nutmeg
- ¾ tsp. cloves
- ¾ tsp. allspice
- ¾ tsp. salt
- 1 8-oz. can Hunt's® Tomato Sauce
- 1½ tsp. baking soda
- 2 eggs, beaten
- ¾ cup pure vegetable oil
- 1 cup chopped nuts
- 1½ cup golden raisins
- ½ cup orange or pineapple juice

In large mixing bowl, combine flour, sugar, baking powder, spices and salt. Thoroughly mix Hunt's® Tomato Sauce and soda in small bowl; add to flour mixture. Stir in eggs, oil, nuts, raisins and fruit juice; mix well. Pour into greased 10-inch Bundt or tube pan. Bake at 350°F. 45–55 minutes. Cool in pan 15 minutes before turning out on serving plate. Dust top with powdered sugar. Makes one 10-inch cake.

Grandma's Upside-Down Cake

I'm told that Fannie Farmer made this cake famous. In her day it was a sensation. It still is, thanks to this excellent recipe from the Dole® test kitchens.

- 1 1 lb., 4 oz. can Dole® Sliced Pineapple
- ¼ cup butter
- ⅔ cup brown sugar, firmly packed
- Maraschino cherries
- 1 cup flour
- ¾ cup sugar
- 1½ tsp. baking powder
- ½ tsp. salt
- ½ cup milk
- ¼ cup shortening

1 egg
1 tsp. lemon juice
1 tsp. vanilla
¼ tsp. grated lemon peel

Drain pineapple, reserving 2 Tbs. syrup. Melt butter in a 10-inch cast iron skillet.* Stir in brown sugar until blended. Remove from heat. Arrange pineapple slices in sugar mixture. Place a Maraschino cherry in center of each slice. Combine flour, sugar, baking powder and salt. Add milk and shortening; beat 2 minutes. Add egg, reserved syrup, lemon juice, vanilla and lemon peel; beat 2 minutes. Pour over pineapple in skillet, spreading evenly. Bake in a 350°F. oven 40 minutes. Cool on wire rack 5 minutes. Invert onto serving plate. Serve warm. Makes 8 servings.

Hollywood Cheesecake

This is the famous Philadelphia Brand Cream Cheese cheesecake recipe that made cheesecake popular in the 1940's, not just in California and New York, but across the country. As most good cooks know, you can top it with anything from fresh strawberries to canned (drained) cherries, pineapple or raspberry jam—and so on and so on.

1 cup graham cracker crumbs
3 Tbs. sugar
3 Tbs. margarine, melted
½ cup sugar
1 Tbs. lemon juice
1 tsp. grated lemon rind
½ tsp. vanilla

* If using a skillet with wooden handle, wrap well with foil.

2 8-oz. packages Philadelphia Brand Cream Cheese

2 eggs, separated
1 cup dairy sour cream
2 Tbs. sugar
1 tsp. vanilla

Combine crumbs, sugar and margarine, press onto bottom of 9-inch springform pan. Bake at 325°F., 10 minutes. Combine softened cream cheese, sugar, lemon juice, rind and vanilla, mixing at medium speed on electric mixer until well blended. Add egg yolks, one at a time, mixing well after each addition. Fold in stiffly beaten egg whites; pour over crust. Bake at 300°F., 45 minutes. Combine sour cream, sugar and vanilla. Carefully spread over cheesecake; continue baking 10 minutes. Loosen cake rim of pan; cool before removing rim of pan. Chill.

Black Forest Cake

There are days when I just long to get out to the kitchen and create something really special and this is certainly the recipe for those times. High, wide and handsome, it's a spectacular from Parkay® Margarine.

1¼ cups sugar
⅔ cup Squeeze Parkay® Margarine
3 eggs
3 1-oz. squares unsweetened chocolate, melted
1
1 tsp. vanilla

1¾ cups flour
1 tsp. baking powder
1 tsp. baking soda
1 tsp. salt
⅔ cup buttermilk
Chocolate Filling (page 462)
Brandied Cherry Filling (page 462)
Whipped Cream Frosting (page 463)

Combine sugar and margarine. Add eggs, one at a time, mixing well after each addition. Blend in chocolate and vanilla. Add combined dry ingredients alternately with buttermilk, mixing well after each addition. Pour into two greased and floured 8-inch layer pans. Bake at 350°F., 30–35 minutes or until wooden pick inserted in center comes out clean. Cool 10 minutes; remove from pans. Cool; split each layer in half horizontally. Spread one layer with Chocolate Filling; top with second layer spread with Brandied Cherry Filling. Repeat with remaining layers. Frost sides with Whipped Cream Frosting.

Chocolate Filling

- 1 cup heavy cream
- ¼ cup confectioners' sugar
- 1 Tbs. cocoa
- ½ tsp. vanilla

Beat cream until slightly thickened; gradually add sugar, cocoa and vanilla, beating until stiff peaks form.

Brandied Cherry Filling

- 1 16-oz. can pitted sour cherries or
- 1 16-oz. package frozen sour cherries, thawed
- 2 Tbs. cornstarch
- ¼ cup sugar
- 2 Tbs. brandy

Drain cherries, reserving ¾ cup syrup. Combine cornstarch and sugar in saucepan; gradually add reserved syrup. Cook over medium heat until mixture is clear and thickened. Stir in cherries and brandy. Cool.

Whipped Cream Frosting

1 cup heavy cream
¼ cup confectioners' sugar
½ tsp. vanilla

Beat cream until slightly thickened; gradually add sugar and vanilla, beating until stiff peaks form.

Sour Cream Chocolate Cake

A half-century of good cooks have baked this Chocolate Sour Cream Cake. It's as moist, rich and delicious as it was when it was first printed on the back of Hershey's® Baking Chocolate package some 20 years ago.

3 blocks (3 oz.) Hershey's® Baking Chocolate
½ cup butter or margarine
1 cup boiling water
2 cups light brown sugar, packed
2 cups all-purpose flour
1½ tsps. baking soda
1 tsp. salt
2 eggs
½ cup dairy sour cream
1 tsp. vanilla
Sour Cream Filling and Icing (see recipe below)

Combine baking chocolate, butter or margarine and boiling water in a small bowl; stir until chocolate and butter or margarine are melted. Thoroughly combine brown sugar, flour, baking soda and salt in a large mixer bowl. Gradually add chocolate mixture, beating until thoroughly combined. Blend in eggs, sour cream and vanilla; beat one minute at medium speed. Pour into a greased and floured 13 × 9 × 2-inch pan. Bake at 350°F. for 35–40 minutes. Cool and frost.

Chocolate Sour Cream Filling and Icing

- 2 cups granulated sugar
- 6 Tbs. Hershey's® Chocolate Flavored Syrup
- ⅔ cup sour cream (dairy)
- 1 tsp. vanilla

In a saucepan, combine the sugar and chocolate syrup. When well mixed, add the sour cream, and cook over medium heat to the soft-ball stage (234°F.). Remove from the fire; add vanilla and beat until thick enough to spread. Add nuts of any kind for variety. Yields 1½ cups icing.

Sweet Chocolate Cake

A truly memorable classic from Baker's Chocolate.

- 1 4-oz. package Baker's German's Sweet Chocolate
- ½ cup boiling water
- 1 cup butter or margarine
- 2 cups sugar
- 4 egg yolks
- 1 tsp. vanilla
- 2½ cups sifted cake flour
- 1 tsp. soda

½ tsp. salt
1 cup buttermilk
4 egg whites, stiffly beaten
Coconut-Pecan Frosting (below)

Melt chocolate in boiling water. Cool. Cream butter and sugar until light and fluffy. Add egg yolks, one at a time, beating after each addition. Add vanilla and melted chocolate; mix until blended. Measure sifted flour, soda, and salt and sift together. Then add flour mixture and buttermilk alternately to chocolate mixture, beating after each addition until batter is smooth. Fold in egg whites. Pour batter into three 8- or 9-inch layer pans, lined on bottoms with paper. Bake in moderate oven (350°F.) for 35–40 minutes for 8-inch layers or 30–35 minutes for 9-inch layers. Cool. (This delicate cake will have a flat contour and a slightly sugary top crust which tends to crack.) Frost top and between layers with Coconut-Pecan Frosting.

Coconut-Pecan Frosting

A heavenly icing just made for Sweet Chocolate Cake.

1 cup evaporated milk
1 cup sugar
3 egg yolks, slightly beaten
¼ lb. (½ cup) butter or margarine
1 tsp. vanilla
1⅓ cups (about) Baker's Angel Flake Coconut
1 cup chopped pecans

Combine milk, sugar, egg yolks, butter, and vanilla in a saucepan. Cook and stir over medium heat until thickened—about 12 minutes. Remove from heat. Add coconut and pecans. Beat until cool and thick enough to spread. Makes 2½ cups, or enough for tops of three 8- or 9-inch layers.

Fudge Cake

Perhaps this isn't the very first fudge cake recipe ever written but certainly it's one of the best, as two generations of good cooks will attest. Hershey® Chocolate Company first printed it on their cocoa box label way back in the 1930's.

½ cup shortening
1½ cups sugar
2 eggs
1 tsp. vanilla
½ cup plus 1 Tbs. hot water
⅔ cup Hershey's® Cocoa
1¾ cup unsifted all-purpose flour
1 tsp. baking soda
1 tsp. baking powder
½ tsp. salt
1 cup sour milk*

Grease bottoms and sides of two 9-inch layer pans. Cream shortening and sugar until fluffy. Add eggs, one at a time, beating well after each addition; blend in vanilla. Stir hot water into cocoa to form a smooth paste; gradually add to creamed mixture. Combine flour, baking soda, baking powder and salt; add alternately with sour milk to creamed mixture. Pour batter into pans. Bake at 350°F. for 30–35 minutes or until cake tester inserted in center comes out clean. Cool 10 minutes. Remove from pans; cool completely. Frost with your favorite frosting.

* *To Sour Milk:* Use 1 Tbs. vinegar plus milk to equal 1 cup.

Chocolate Town Special Cake

One of the best ever Chocolate Cake recipes to come from Chocolate Town, Hershey®, Pennsylvania. A long-time favorite from the Hershey® Cocoa box label.

- ½ cup Hershey's® Cocoa
- ½ cup boiling water
- ⅔ cup shortening
- 1¾ cups sugar
- 1 tsp. vanilla
- 2 eggs
- 2¼ cups unsifted all-purpose flour
- 1½ tsps. baking soda
- ½ tsp. salt
- 1⅓ cups buttermilk or sour milk*

Grease and dust with flour two 9-inch cake pans. Make smooth paste of cocoa and boiling water; cool slightly. Cream shortening, sugar and vanilla in large mixer bowl; blend in eggs. Combine flour, baking soda and salt; add alternately with buttermilk to creamed mixture. Add cocoa paste to batter, blending well. Pour batter into pans. Bake at 350°F. for 35–40 minutes or until cake tester inserted in center comes out clean. Frost as desired.

Golden Coconut Frosting

- ½ cup butter or margarine
- 1⅓ cups (about) Baker's Angel Flake Coconut**
- 1 cup firmly packed brown sugar
- ¼ cup milk
- 2 cups (about) sifted confectioners' sugar

* *To Sour Milk:* Use 1 Tbs. plus 1 tsp. vinegar plus milk to equal 1⅓ cups.
** Or use 1 cup Baker's Cookie Coconut

Melt 2 Tbs. butter in a skillet. Add coconut and stir until golden brown. Remove about half the coconut; set aside. Melt remaining butter in skillet with coconut. Add brown sugar. Cook and stir over low heat 2 minutes, or until blended. Then add milk; bring to a boil. Remove from heat. Cool. Gradually add confectioners' sugar until it's the right consistency to spread, beating well after each addition. Spread on cake. Sprinkle with remaining coconut. Makes 2 cups frosting, or enough to cover tops and sides of two 8-inch layers, one 9-inch square, or 24 cupcakes.

Glazed Chocolate Torte

Now there comes a time when only a real pretty "dress up" dinner party will suit the occasion and this is certainly the dessert to crown the meal. Beautiful—just beautiful. It's from the Hershey® Baking Chocolate box.

- ¼ cup shortening
- ¾ cup sugar
- 3 egg yolks
- 1 tsp. vanilla
- ⅓ cup blanched ground almonds
- 3 blocks (3 ounces) Hershey's® Baking Chocolate, melted
- 1 cup sifted all-purpose flour
- ½ tsp. baking powder
- ½ tsp. baking soda
- ½ tsp. salt
- ¾ cup milk, room temperature
- 3 egg whites
- ¼ cup sugar
- Filling (opposite)
- Glaze (opposite)

Cream shortening with sugar. Add egg yolks and vanilla; beat well. Stir in ground almonds, then baking chocolate. Sift together flour, baking powder, baking soda and salt. Add to creamed mixture alternately with milk, blending well after each addition. Beat egg whites until frothy, gradually add sugar and beat until stiff peaks form. Carefully fold into chocolate mixture and turn into two greased and cocoa-dusted 8-inch round layer pans. Bake at 350°F. for 20 minutes or until done. Cool 10 minutes; remove from pans. When completely cool, split layers and fill with whipped cream.

Filling: 1½ cups whipping cream, sweetened and whipped or 3 cups non-dairy whipped topping.

Glaze

1 block (1 oz.) Hershey's® Baking Chocolate
2 Tbs. butter
1 Tbs. light corn syrup
1 cup confectioners' sugar
2 Tbs. hot water

Combine chocolate, butter and corn syrup in top of double boiler over simmering water. Stir in confectioners' sugar and hot water. While still warm, pour glaze over torte. Spread quickly, allowing glaze to run down the sides. Refrigerate until serving time.

Prize Coconut Cake

This is the recipe for coconut cake that so many people requested; "the one with coconut in the batter not just in the frosting." It first appeared in *Baker's Chocolate and Coconut Favorites* cookbook in 1962. It's also in the latest edition and yes, it's just as good as you remembered.

1¾ cups sifted cake flour
2¼ tsps. Calumet Baking Powder
¾ tsp. salt
½ cup butter or margarine
1 cup plus 2 Tbs. sugar
2 eggs
⅔ cup milk

1 tsp. vanilla
⅔ cup Baker's Cookie or Angel Flake Coconut

Measure sifted flour, baking powder and salt; sift together. Cream butter. Gradually add sugar; cream until light and fluffy. Add eggs, one at a time, beating well after each addition. Alternately add flour mixture and milk, beating after each addition until smooth. Stir in vanilla and coconut. Pour batter into two 8-inch layer pans, lined on bottoms with paper. Bake in moderate oven (350°F.) 30–35 minutes. Cool in pans 10 minutes; then remove from pans and finish cooling on racks. Frost with Golden Coconut Frosting.

Delicate Graham Cracker Cake

Do you remember this one? It's been one of Nabisco's most requested recipes for 40 years. Actually more of a torte than a cake. Fill and frost with sweetened whipped cream for a taste of old Vienna.

⅔ cup all-purpose flour
¾ cup granulated sugar
2½ tsps. baking powder
½ tsp. salt
1⅓ cups Nabisco Graham Cracker Crumbs
½ cup shortening
¾ cup milk
1 tsp. vanilla extract
2 eggs

Combine flour, sugar, baking powder, salt and Nabisco Graham Cracker Crumbs. Place shortening in a bowl. Add dry ingredients, milk and vanilla; mix until dry ingredients are moistened. Beat 2 minutes in electric mixer or 300 strokes by hand. Add eggs and beat 1 minute or 150 strokes by hand. Pour into 2 heavily greased 8-inch layer cake pans; bake in a preheated moderate oven (350°F.) about 25 minutes, or until done. Cool. Fill and frost as desired.

Peanut Butter Picnic Cake

An old favorite from Parkay® Margarine. Children especially like it, I'm told, but so do the men in my life—every one of them from six to sixty years.

- ½ cup Parkay® Margarine
- 1⅓ cups sugar
- ¼ cup peanut butter
- 2 eggs
- 1 tsp. vanilla
- 2 cups flour
- 1 Tbs. baking powder
- 1 tsp. salt
- 1 cup milk
- 1 10-oz. jar Kraft® Strawberry Preserves or Grape Jelly
- Peanut Butter Frosting (below)

Cream margarine and sugar until light and fluffy. Blend in peanut butter, eggs and vanilla. Add combined dry ingredients alternately with milk, mixing well after each addition. Pour into two greased and floured 8- or 9-inch layer pans. Bake at 350°F., 35–40 minutes or until wooden pick inserted in center comes out clean. Cool 10 minutes; remove from pans. Spread ⅔ cup preserves between layers. Frost with Peanut Butter Frosting. Decorate with additional preserves.

Peanut Butter Frosting

- ¼ cup Parkay® margarine
- ¼ cup peanut butter
- 1 tsp. vanilla
- Dash of salt
- 2½ cups sifted confectioners' sugar
- 3 Tbs. milk

Cream margarine; blend in peanut butter, vanilla and salt. Add sugar alternately with milk, beating until light and fluffy.

Tennessee Jam Cake

My Aunt Della made a version of this cake back in Memphis. It's a Southern tradition for Sunday dinner dessert. This one is from Kraft®, who seem to have a "hand" with old-fashioned "receipts."

- 1 cup margarine
- 1½ cups granulated sugar
- 1 10-oz. jar Kraft® Strawberry, Raspberry or Blackberry Preserves
- 4 eggs
- 2½ cups flour
- Brown Sugar Frosting (below)
- Confectioners' sugar
- 1 tsp. soda
- 1 tsp. nutmeg
- 1 tsp. cinnamon
- 1 tsp. cloves
- ¼ tsp. salt
- 1 cup buttermilk
- 1½ cups chopped pecans

Cream margarine and granulated sugar until light and fluffy. Blend in preserves and eggs. Add combined dry ingredients to creamed mixture, alternately with buttermilk, mixing well after each addition. Stir in nuts. Pour into three greased and floured 9-inch layer pans. Bake at 350°F., 30–35 minutes. Cool 10 minutes; remove from pans. Fill and frost sides with Brown Sugar Frosting. Sift confectioners' sugar over top of cake.

Brown Sugar Frosting: Combine 1 cup packed brown sugar, ½ cup margarine and ¼ cup milk; bring to boil, stirring constantly. Remove from heat; cool 10 minutes. Gradually add 3 cups sifted confectioners' sugar, beating until well blended.

Peach Upside-Down Cake

Upside-down cake was popular when Shirley Temple was a star, remember? I'm sure your mother does. This

version, made with fresh peaches, is from the test kitchen of Parkay® Margarine.

- Parkay® Margarine
- ½ cup packed brown sugar
- 1½ cups fresh peach slices
- ⅔ cup granulated sugar
- 1 egg
- ½ tsp. vanilla
- 1½ cups flour
- 1½ tsps. baking powder
- ½ tsp. salt
- ½ cup milk

Melt 3 Tbs. margarine in 8- or 9-inch oven-proof skillet or layer pan; sprinkle with brown sugar. Arrange fruit in skillet. Cream ⅓ cup margarine and granulated sugar until light and fluffy. Blend in egg and vanilla. Add combined dry ingredients alternately with milk, mixing well after each addition. Carefully pour batter over fruit. Bake at 350°F., 40–45 minutes or until wooden pick inserted in center comes out clean. Immediately invert onto serving platter.

Variation: Substitute 16-oz. can peach slices, drained, for fresh peaches.

Fresh Apple Cake

A new cake from the Kellogg's kitchens destined to become an old favorite. The perfect afternoon snack cake. Great with icy cold milk, superb with freshly made steaming hot coffee.

- 1½ cups all-purpose flour
- 2 tsps. baking soda
- ½ tsp. salt
- ½ cup margarine or butter, softened
- 1 cup granulated sugar
- 1 tsp. ground cinnamon
- 1 tsp. ground nutmeg
- 1 3-oz. package cream cheese, softened
- 1 Tbs. margarine or butter, softened

- 2 eggs
- 4 cups finely chopped, pared apples
- 1 cup Kellogg's All-Bran® cereal or Kellogg's Bran Buds® cereal
- 1 tsp. vanilla flavoring
- 1½ cups sifted confectioners' sugar

Stir together flour, soda, salt, cinnamon and nutmeg. Beat the ½ cup margarine and the granulated sugar. Beat in eggs. Stir in apples, cereal and flour mixture. Spread in greased 9 × 9 × 2-inch baking pan. Bake at 350°F. about 45 minutes or until done.

To make frosting, beat cream cheese, the 1 Tbs. margarine and vanilla. Gradually add confectioners' sugar, beating until smooth. If frosting is too thick, add 1–2 tsps. milk. Spread on cooled cake. Yield 12 servings.

Variations: In place of Kellogg's All-Bran® cereal, use 2 cups Kellogg's 40% Bran Flakes® cereal. Or crush 1⅓ cups Kellogg's Cracklin' Bran® cereal to coarse crumbs.

Sun Maid® Raisin Nut Cake

A top request recipe since it first appeared on the Sun Maid® Raisin box over fifty years ago. Made to order for tea time and the coffee hour.

- ½ lb. self-raising flour
- ½ tsp. salt
- 1 tsp. mixed spices
- 2 oz. chopped nuts
- 4½ oz. Sun Maid® Seedless Raisins
- 4 oz. margarine
- 6 oz. granulated sugar
- 2 eggs

Grease and flour a loaf tin, 9½ × 5½ × 2½ inches. Sieve together first three ingredients and add the nuts and raisins.

Cream the margarine and sugar thoroughly and add the eggs, one at a time, beating thoroughly after each addition. Add the flour mixture alternately with the milk, beating well after each addition, and bake in the prepared tin in a moderate oven (350°F.) for about 1–1¼ hours.

Orange-Raisin Whole Wheat Cake

Several years ago a Pillsbury Bake-Off® winner and a real star. People love it, it's one of the new "mix-it-all-in-one-bowl" cakes, made with whole wheat flour and just delicious.

1¼ cups Pillsbury's Best® All-Purpose Flour
1 cup Pillsbury's Best® Whole Wheat Flour
1 cup brown sugar
1 tsp. baking soda
½ tsp. salt
1 cup orange juice
½ cup oil
1 tsp. grated orange rind
1 egg
½ cup raisins

Heat oven to 350°F. Grease and flour 8- or 9-inch square pan. Combine all ingredients except raisins; beat 2 minutes at medium speed. Stir in raisins. Pour into prepared pan. Bake at 350°F. for 40–50 minutes or until toothpick inserted in center comes out clean. Serve with Honey-Nut Topping, if desired. Makes 9 servings.

Honey-Nut Topping

1 Tbs. cornstarch
½ cup chopped walnuts
½ cup water
½ cup honey
½ cup butter

In small saucepan, combine cornstarch and honey; add remaining ingredients. Cook over medium heat, stirring constantly, until mixture starts to boil. Continue cooking and stirring about 1 minute or until slightly thickened. Serve warm. Makes 1¾ cups.

Fruit Gâteau

Pretty and so simple. A light-as-air sponge cake layer topped with fresh seasonal fruit, an especially pretty idea for a summer party dessert. (I like fresh peaches best.) An old favorite from the Argo Cornstarch box.

2 eggs
⅓ cup sugar
¼ tsp. salt
⅓ cup sifted flour
¼ cup Argo or Kingsford's Corn Starch
2 cups assorted fresh fruit (mandarin oranges, sliced strawberries, peaches, apricot halves, grapes, etc.)
Glaze (opposite)
Whipped cream

Grease 9 × 1½-inch round layer pan. Line with waxed paper and grease again. In small bowl with mixer at high speed beat eggs until fluffy. Gradually add sugar and salt; beat until mixture is doubled in bulk and mounds slightly when dropped from a spoon, about 5 minutes. Sift flour and corn starch over egg mixture; thoroughly fold in. Pour into prepared pan. Bake in 350°F. oven 25 minutes or until cake springs back when lightly touched. Cool 10 minutes. Remove from pan; cool completely on wire rack. Place on serving plate. Arrange fruit as desired on top of sponge layer. Spoon glaze evenly over fruit. Let set 30 minutes. Garnish with whipped cream. Makes 8 servings.

Glaze: In small saucepan mix together 1 Tbs. corn starch, 1 cup apple juice and 1 Tbs. lemon juice. Stirring constantly, bring to boil over medium heat and boil 1 minute. Cool. Makes 1 cup.

11.
Fabulous Desserts

Desserts are "soul food," the crown of the meal, the sweet ending which, "like in the movies," everybody wants. In fact, there is something unfinished about a meal without dessert.

So here we give you a collection to satisfy your soul, to end on a sweet note that leaves everyone happy. Some of them have been pleasing people for half a century, some are new; all are as easy as smiling and every one tastes scrumptious. These are professional recipes, created by true professionals. You can be sure of perfect results each and every time you decide to make each and every recipe.

Cointreau Crêpes

One day the Prince of Wales requested a thin French® pancake with a blend of orange and lemon peel and Cointreau Liqueur. By accident the liqueur caught fire, and with no time to re-do the dish, the pancakes were served flaming. They were a triumph, and the rest is history. The Cointreau people claim this is the true story of the origin of "Crêpes Suzette." No matter, the sauce is lovely and will turn these easy-to-make crêpes into a truly festive dessert.

Crêpes:

2 eggs
2 egg yolks
1 cup milk
1 Tbs. Cointreau Liqueur
2 Tbs. melted butter
¾ cup flour
1 Tbs. sugar
½ tsp. salt

Beat to combine eggs, egg yolks, milk, Cointreau and melted butter. Stir in dry ingredients until smooth. Heat 6- or 7-inch skillet; brush with butter. Pour in 2 Tbs. batter, tilting pan to spread. Brown both sides. Repeat with rest of batter. Makes about 16 crêpes.

Cointreau Crêpe Sauce: Prepare one dozen dessert crêpes and fold into triangles. In a chafing dish, heat 1 stick butter, 8 sugar cubes, ½ teaspoon grated orange rind (or more to taste) and the juice of 1 orange. Cook, stirring until smooth. Turn crêpes in this mixture and arrange neatly in pan. Pour over ½ cup Cointreau Liqueur, basting crêpes until flames subside. Serves 4.

Crêpes L'Ananas Deluxe

Straight from a deluxe restaurant, voilà! Very special crêpes dreamed up by Dole® Pineapple for your next party.

- 1 can (1 lb., 4 ounces) Dole® Crushed Pineapple in Juice
- 2 egg yolks, slightly beaten
- ½ cup sugar
- 1 tsp. grated lemon peel
- ⅛ tsp. salt
- 2 Tbs. unflavored gelatine
- 1½ cups cottage cheese
- 1½ tsps. vanilla
- 1 cup whipped cream
- 5 to 6 Dessert Crêpes

Drain pineapple, reserving all juice. Set aside 2 Tbs. pineapple for garnish. Combine egg yolks, sugar, lemon peel, salt and 1 Tbs. pineapple juice in a double boiler. Cook over medium heat, stirring continuously until mixture is smooth and thickened, about 5 minutes. Remove from heat. Soften gelatine in remaining pineapple juice; add to cooked mixture, stirring until thoroughly dissolved. Blend in crushed pineapple, cottage cheese and vanilla. Cool slightly. Reserve ¼ cup whipped cream for garnish. Fold balance of whipped cream into pineapple mixture. Chill. Place one crêpe on a pedestal cake plate or other serving dish. Spread 1 cup pineapple mixture evenly over crêpe. Top with second crêpe. Repeat until crêpe stack is 4 to 5 layers high. Top with reserved ¼ cup whipped cream and 2 Tbs. crushed pineapple in center. Chill before serving. Makes 4 to 6 servings.

Note: For extra ease in cutting, freeze dessert for 40 minutes before serving. Use a long, sharp knife to cut.

Dessert Crêpes

- 3 eggs
- ½ cup milk
- 2 Tbs. butter, melted
- ½ cup flour
- 1 tsp. sugar
- Dash salt

Combine all ingredients and blend well. Refrigerate for at least 1 hour. Lightly oil a 6-inch crêpe pan. Set pan over medium heat. Pour ⅛ cup crêpe batter into pan. Tilt and swirl batter to coat pan evenly. Cook until edges darken slightly. Lift with spatula and cook on other side. Lift onto a sheet of wax paper. Continue with remaining batter. Stack crêpes with a sheet of wax paper separating each. Store in refrigerator or freezer.

Note: If you use an electric crêpe machine, prepare crêpes according to manufacturer's instructions.

Chocolate-Marshmallow Cream Roll

A simply beautiful and extra-festive dessert. A sensation ever since it appeared in a 1930s Hershey® advertisement.

- 6 egg yolks
- 6 Tbs. Hershey's® Cocoa
- 1 heaping cup 4X sugar (confectioners')
- Dash of salt
- ½ cup cake flour
- 1 tsp. vanilla
- 6 egg whites, stiffly beaten

Beat egg yolks until thick and lemon-colored; add cocoa, sugar, salt, flour and vanilla (mixture will be stiff). Fold in one-fourth of the stiffly beaten egg whites; blend well. Fold in remaining egg whites; turn into a greased 15 × 9 × 2-inch pan lined with waxed paper. Bake in a 350°F. oven 20 minutes. Turn out onto a damp towel, roll up and let rest 1 minute. Unroll and reroll without towel. Cool on rack covered with waxed paper. Fill with Marshmallow Peppermint Icing and cover with half recipe Bitter Chocolate Butter Icing. If desired, garnish with flowers made by cutting marshmallows into very thin strips, using candied cherries as centers. Makes 12 servings.

Marshmallow Peppermint Icing

2 Tbs. water
½ cup granulated sugar
1 egg white, beaten stiff
¾ cup marshmallow whip
¼ tsp. peppermint extract
Few drops red food coloring
Few grains salt

Boil water and sugar together until the soft ball stage is reached (234°F.). Slowly pour hot syrup over beaten egg white, beating constantly. Add marshmallow whip, salt, extract and food coloring; beat until cool. Makes 2¼ cups icing or enough for a 13 × 9 × 2-inch loaf cake.

Bitter Chocolate Butter Icing

½ cup butter
2 cups 4X sugar (confectioners')
2 Tbs. light cream
4 squares Hershey's® Baking Chocolate, melted

Cream butter and sugar together; add cream and beat well. Gradually add melted baking chocolate, and beat thoroughly to reach spreading consistency. (Additional cream may be needed.) Makes 2 cups icing, or enough for an 8- or 9-inch layer cake.

All-American Apple Soufflé

Can't-fail soufflé, as delicious as it is different, from the label of the Dole® Pineapple Slices can.

- 4 large apples
- 1 20-ounce can Dole® Pineapple Slices, in syrup
- 1 envelope unflavored gelatine
- ¾ tsp. cinammon
- ¼ tsp. cardamom
- 1 tsp. lime juice
- 2 Tbs. finely chopped almonds
- ½ cup whipping cream

Pare, core and slice apples. Drain pineapple, reserving syrup. Cook apples and ½ cup pineapple syrup until soft. Sprinkle gelatine over remaining syrup and let stand 5 minutes. Stir into hot apple sauce until dissolved. Put apple mixture through food mill or purée in blender. Stir in spices, lime juice and almonds. Chill until mixture mounds on spoon. Whip cream and fold in. Stand pineapple slices around sides of 1½-quart soufflé dish. Pour in apple sauce mixture and chill until firm. Garnish with remaining pineapple slices and additional apple slices, if desired. Makes 4 to 6 servings.

Easy Apple Crisp

A great "quickie" from the Maypo Oatmeal box.

- ⅔ cup brown sugar, firmly packed
- ½ cup sifted flour
- 1 cup Maypo 30-Second Oatmeal
- ½ cup melted butter or margarine
- 1 can (1 lb., 4 ounces) apple pie filling

Mix dry ingredients together; blend in melted butter. Press two-thirds of mixture into a lightly buttered 8-inch square cake pan. Cover with pie filling. Sprinkle with remaining Maypo mixture. Bake in preheated 350°F. oven for 30 to 35 minutes, until lightly browned. Cool; cut into squares; serve topped with ice cream or whipped cream. Makes one 8-inch square.

Easy Cherry Pudding

Here's an old-fashioned favorite that appeared on cans of Stokely's Finest Red Sour Cherries thirty years back. Good enough for a party dinner, yet easy even for children to make. Serve warm with whipped cream if you like.

- ½ cup butter or margarine
- 1 cup sugar
- 1 cup flour
- 2 tsps. baking powder
- ¾ cup milk
- 1 1-lb. can Red Sour Pitted Cherries
- ½ cup sugar

In 9-inch square pan, melt butter or margarine. In bowl, combine next 4 ingredients. Mix until well blended. Pour over melted butter; do not stir. Pour undrained cherries over batter; do not stir. Sprinkle ½ cup sugar over cherries; do not stir. Bake at 325°F. for 1 hour. Makes 9 servings.

Mince Meat Tarts

Mince meat pie is an American tradition, a holiday must. These tarts, from the people who bottle Angostura® Bitters, are lovely served just pleasantly warm from the oven, topped with chilled, lightly sweetened and brandied whipped cream.

1 14-oz. can pineapple chunks
1 9-oz. package mince meat
1 Tbs. Angostura®
2 packages pastry mix

Drain pineapple. Measure juice and add enough water to make 1½ cups. Slice chunks. Break up mince meat, add to liquid and simmer 2 minutes. Add pineapple. Cool and add Angostura®. Mix pastry according to directions on package. Roll one half of mixture at a time. Cut into 4-inch rounds. With small cutter, remove centers from half of the rounds. Arrange whole rounds on baking sheet and moisten edges. Place rounded Tbs. mince meat mixture in center of rounds, cover with pastry rings and press edges together. Bake in hot oven (450°F.) about 20 minutes until pastry is lightly browned. Makes 12 tarts.

Kahlua® Mousse

A dozen years ago Kahlua® introduced this fabulous version of a French® classic. Prepare it for a special-occasion dinner party. It's a sensational dessert.

1 cup Kahlua®
¾ cup strong, brewed coffee
Instant decaffeinated-coffee granules
1 cup confectioners sugar
¼ tsp. almond extract
1 envelope unflavored gelatin
7 egg yolks, beaten
7 egg whites, beaten until stiff
1½ cups heavy cream, whipped stiff
½ cup heavy cream
2 Tbs. confectioners sugar
Finely chopped pecans (optional)

Fold waxed paper, 26 inches long, in thirds. With string, tie around 1-quart soufflé dish, to form collar 2 inches high. In top of double boiler, combine Kahlua, brewed coffee, ¾ tsp. coffee granules, confectioners sugar, almond extract, gelatin and egg yolks: mix well. Cook over boiling water (water should not touch bottom of double boiler), stirring occasionally, until mixture thickens and mounds when dropped from spoon. With wire whisk, using an under-and-over motion, fold egg whites and whipped cream into gelatin mixture. Turn mixture into prepared soufflé dish, wineglasses or dessert dishes. Refrigerate until firm—several hours or overnight. Before serving: In Chilled bowl, combine ½ cup heavy cream and 2 Tbs. confectioners sugar; beat together until stiff. Spoon into pastry bag with a number-6 star tip. Sprinkle lightly with coffee granules. If desired, press finely chopped pecans around edge. Makes 8 to 10 servings.

Crunchy Lemon Squares

Remember this one? I'll bet your mother does. It appeared on the Eagle Brand Condensed Milk can in 1947. It's still a popular and easy "company special" dessert.

- 1 cup quick oats, uncooked
- 1 cup flour
- ½ cup flaked coconut
- ½ cup coarsely chopped pecans
- ½ cup butter or margarine, melted
- 1 can Eagle Brand Sweetened Condensed Milk

- ½ cup firmly packed light brown sugar
- 1 tsp. baking powder
- ½ cup ReaLemon Reconstituted Juice
- 1 Tbs. grated lemon rind

Preheat oven to 350°F. (325°F. if using glass dish). In medium bowl, combine oats, flour, coconut, nuts, sugar, baking powder and butter; stir to form a crumbly mixture. Set aside. In medium bowl, combine sweetened condensed milk, lemon juice and rind. Pat half of crumb mixture evenly on bottom of 9 × 9-inch baking pan. Spread sweetened condensed milk mixture on top and sprinkle with remaining crumbs. Bake for 25 to 30 minutes or until lightly browned. Cool thoroughly before cutting. Makes 9 servings.

All-Time Favorite Puff Pudding

Although this interesting pudding did not appear on the Post Grape-Nuts package until 1952, it was originally developed for a book about Post Cereal's founder, C. W. Post, way back in 1926. It's a lovely dessert with a cake-like top layer and a creamy, lemony custard below.

- ¼ cup butter or margarine
- ½ cup sugar or honey
- 1 tsp. grated lemon rind
- ¼ cup Post Grape-Nuts Brand Cereal
- 1 cup milk
- 2 egg yolks
- 3 Tbs. lemon juice
- 2 Tbs. all-purpose flour
- 2 egg whites, stiffly beaten

Thoroughly cream butter with sugar and lemon rind. Add egg yolks; beat until light and fluffy. Blend in lemon juice, flour, cereal and milk. (Mixture will look curdled, but this will not affect finished product.) Fold in beaten egg whites. Pour into greased 1-quart baking dish; place the dish in pan of hot water. Bake at 325°F. for 1 hour and 15 minutes or until top springs back when lightly touched. When done, pudding has a cakelike layer on top with custard below. Serve warm or cold with cream or prepared whipped topping, if desired. Makes 4 to 6 servings.

Note: For individual puddings, pour mixture into five 5-ounce or four 6-ounce custard or soufflé cups. Bake for about 40 minutes.

Rice Pudding

Old-fashioned rice pudding. This recipe was a favorite even before Carolina Rice printed it on their box in the early 1940s. It's still the homey, familiar dessert everyone loves.

2 cups milk
½ cup uncooked Carolina Rice
¼ tsp. salt
3 egg yolks
3 Tbs. sugar
¾ cup heavy cream

Bring milk to boil; stir in rice and salt. Cook over hot water until milk is absorbed, about 30 minutes. Beat egg yolks with sugar and cream. Combine with rice mixture. Add raisins, if desired. Pour into baking dish. Bake in preheated 350°F. oven for 15 minutes, until top browns. Makes 8 servings.

Sierra Snow Cap

Remember Grandma's prune whip? This light, but lavish, dessert from Sun-Sweet® Apricots is a sophisticated version.

1¼ cups Sun-Sweet® Apricots
1¼ cups water
½ cup sugar
5 egg whites, unbeaten
¼ tsp. salt
3 to 4 Tbs. brandy (or ¼ tsp. almond extract)

Cook apricots in water 10 minutes, until soft. Cool. Drain and measure 1 cup. Chop and combine with sugar, egg whites and salt in top of double boiler. Beat over boiling water with rotary beater until thick enough to hold its shape, about 5 minutes. Remove from heat; gently fold in brandy. Serve warm or cold, garnished with reserved apricots. Makes 4 to 6 servings.

Frosty Orange Stars

Here's the recipe that gives the "how to" for preparing star-shaped orange shells. It's one of Sunkist® growers "most requested."

Grated peel of 1 Sunkist® Orange
1 peach, nectarine, banana or kiwi, peeled, mashed
1 pint vanilla ice cream, softened
2 Sunkist® oranges, cut into 4 star-shaped shells*

In bowl, combine orange peel, peach and ice cream; return to freezer. Scoop frozen ice cream into orange shells. Makes 4 servings.

Variation: Substitute orange sherbet for orange peel, mashed peach and vanilla ice cream.

* To make 2-star shaped orange shells, cut each orange as follows: Insert tip of paring knife, diagonally, half way between stem and blossom ends. Cut around orange (inserting knife in and pulling out) in a zigzag pattern. Make sure to cut through to center of orange. Give a slight twist to pull apart halves. Carefully ream out juice; drink or reserve for cooking. Scrape shells "clean" with spoon.

Plum Cobbler

Do people really make cobblers these days? Of course they do. Requests come into the Karo® test kitchens in a steady stream for this recipe. It was on the label quite some time ago, but word of mouth keeps its reputation going.

- ¾ cup Karo® Light Corn Syrup
- 1 Tbs. corn starch
- ½ tsp. ground cinnamon
- 2 lb. ripe fresh plums, pitted, quartered
- 1¼ cups buttermilk baking mix
- ½ cup finely chopped nuts (optional)
- ⅓ cup milk
- ¼ cup sugar

Stir together first 3 ingredients; toss with plums. Spoon into 8 × 8 × 2-inch baking dish. Bake in 400°F. oven 15 minutes. Meanwhile, mix remaining ingredients. Beat vigorously 20 strokes. Drop by spoonfuls onto hot plums. Bake 15 to 20 minutes longer. Serves 6.

Butter-Cream Baked Apples

Most people remember these classic Land O Lakes® baked apples as "comforting" food of their childhood. Baked with butter and sugar that turns into a rich sauce when cream is added, they are just as comforting and delicious today.

- 4 medium baking apples, cored and not peeled
- 1 cup sugar
- ½ cup Land O Lakes® Sweet Cream Butter
- 1 Tbs. corn starch
- 1 Tbs. cold water
- ½ cup whipping cream

Preheat oven to 450°F. Place apples in 1½- or 2-quart round glass baking dish. Sprinkle with sugar; dot with butter. Bake near center of 450°F. oven for 20 to 30 minutes, stirring, basting and turning two times, until apples are fork tender. Meanwhile, combine corn starch and water; add to cream; set aside. Remove apples; stir in cream and corn starch mixture. Return apples to pan. Return to oven for 8 to 10 minutes or until sauce thickens and bubbles all over. Serve apples with sauce spooned over. Makes 4 servings.

Blueberry Chocolate Puffs

Here's a superb, very French®, pastry dessert that's as easy to make as it is delectable to eat. From the test kitchens of Pepperidge Farm®.

- 1 package 17¼-oz Pepperidge Farm® Frozen Puff Pastry Sheets
- 1 egg mixed with 1 tsp. water
- ⅔ cup blueberry jam
- 3 squares(3ozs.)semi-sweet chocolate
- 2 Tbs. vegetable shortening

Thaw pastry 20 minutes, then unfold. Roll each square lightly until exactly 10 inches square. Cut each sheet into 25 2-inch rounds. Place rounds on ungreased baking sheets and brush with egg mixture; chill 10 minutes. Bake pastry rounds in preheated 425°F. oven for 12 to 15 minutes or until puffed and golden brown. Transfer to wire racks and cool completely. With a sharp knife, split each puff and spread bottom half with ½ tsp. blueberry jam; replace top half to make a sandwich. Repeat until all puffs are filled. Melt chocolate; add shortening and stir until smooth. Using a spoon drizzle chocolate back and forth over each puff. Let puffs stand until chocolate hardens. Makes 25 puffs.

Homemade Blueberry Jam

2½ cups fresh or dry-pack frozen blueberries
3 cups sugar
⅓ cup orange juice
1 Tbs. lemon juice
½ bottle (3 ozs.) fruit pectin

Wash blueberries. Measure 2½ cups into an enamel or stainless steel pan. Crush blueberries in pan. Add sugar and fruit juices. Mix well. Bring to a full rolling boil and boil hard for one minute, stirring constantly. Remove from heat. Stir in pectin. Seal in hot sterilized jars. Refrigerate. Can be kept for two months. Makes 3 cups 4 6-oz. jars.

Swiss Chocolate Squares

The good cooks at the Parkay® Margarine test kitchens developed this "new" way to mix up a cake back in the 1960's. It's terrific—and quick.

1 cup water
½ cup Parkay® Margarine
1½ 1-oz. squares unsweetened chocolate
2 cups flour
2 cups sugar
2 eggs
½ cup dairy sour cream
1 tsp. baking soda
½ tsp. salt
½ cup Parkay® Margarine
6 Tbs. milk
1½ 1-oz. squares unsweetened chocolate
4½ cups sifted confectioners sugar
1 tsp. vanilla
½ cup chopped nuts

Combine water, margarine and chocolate in saucepan; bring to boil. Remove from heat. Stir in combined flour and sugar. Add eggs, sour cream, baking soda and salt; mix well. Pour into greased and floured 15½ × 10½-inch jelly roll pan. Bake at 375°F. 20 to 25 minutes. Combine margarine, milk and chocolate in saucepan; bring to boil. Remove from heat. Add sugar; beat until smooth. Stir in vanilla. Frost cake while warm; sprinkle with nuts. Cool; cut into squares. Makes about 24 squares.

Cantaloupe Sherbet

A 1970's "summertime, and the living is easy" time dessert from Karo®. It's one of the simplest of recipes to put together, and it's light, airy and refreshing.

- 1 envelope unflavored gelatin
- ½ cup milk
- 3 cups cubed cantaloupe
- 1 cup Karo® Light Corn Syrup

In small saucepan sprinkle gelatin over milk. Stir over low heat until dissolved. Place in blender container with cantaloupe and corn syrup; cover. Blend on high speed 30 seconds. Pour into 9 × 9 × 2-inch baking pan. Cover; freeze overnight. Soften slightly at room temperature, about 10 to 15 minutes. Spoon into large bowl; with mixer at low speed, beat until smooth, but not melted. Pour into 4-cup mold or freezer container. Cover; freeze about 4 hours or until firm. Unmold or soften at room temperature for easier scooping. Makes about 4 cups.

Blueberry Sherbet: Follow basic recipe. Use 3 cups whole blueberries; omit cantaloupe. Makes about 3½ cups.

Honeydew Sherbet: Follow basic recipe. Use 3 cups cubed honeydew melon; omit cantaloupe. Makes about 4 cups.

Nectarine or Peach Sherbet: Follow basic recipe. Use 3 cups cubed nectarines or peaches and 1 Tbs. lemon juice; omit cantaloupe. Makes about 4 cups.

Papaya Sherbet: Follow basic recipe. Use 3 cups cubed papaya and 1 Tbs. lemon juice; omit cantaloupe. Makes about 4 cups.

Pineapple Sherbet: Follow basic recipe. Use 3 cups cubed pineapple; omit cantaloupe. Makes about 4 cups.

Strawberry Sherbet: Follow basic recipe. Use 3 cups whole strawberries; omit cantaloupe. Makes about 3½ cups.

Watermelon Sherbet: Follow basic recipe. Use 3 cups cubed watermelon; omit cantaloupe. Makes about 4 cups.

Brandied Raspberry Bavarian

For many years this was a favorite recipe on the Dole® Crushed Pineapple label. It was so popular it was reprinted in a booklet and used in national advertisements, too.

- 1 1-lb., 4-oz. can Dole® Crushed Pineapple in Juice
- 2 6-oz. packages raspberry gelatin
- 3 cups boiling water
- 2 cups cold water
- 1 tsp. grated lemon peel
- ½ cup brandy
- ½ pint whipping cream
- 2 Tbs. sugar

Drain pineapple reserving all juice. Dissolve gelatin in boiling water. Stir in reserved pineapple juice, cold water, lemon peel and brandy. Chill to consistency of unbeaten egg white. Whip cream with sugar. Fold into thickened gelatin along with drained pineapple. Pour into Bundt pan. Chill overnight. Makes 10 servings.

Broken Window Glass Cake

The way food looks is second only to the way it tastes. In the "sweet ending" class, one seldom comes by a dessert that has such style and appeal as this elegant gelatin-cake combination. It comes from *The New Joys of Jello-O®* book, first printed in 1973.

- 1 3-oz. package Jell-O® Brand Orange Flavor Gelatin
- 1 3-oz. package Jell-O® Brand Cherry Flavor Gelatin
- 1 3 oz. package Jell-O® Brand Lime Flavor Gelatin
- 3 cups boiling water
- 1½ cups cold water
- 1½ cups graham cracker crumbs
- ⅓ cup butter or margarine, melted
- 1 3-oz. package Jell-O® Brand Lemon Flavor Gelatin
- ¼ cup sugar
- 1 cup boiling water
- ½ cup canned pineapple juice
- 1 8-oz. container Birds Eye® Cool Whip Non-Dairy Whipped Topping, thawed

Prepare the orange, cherry and lime gelatins separately, dissolving each in 1 cup boiling water and adding ½ cup of the cold water. Pour each flavor into separate 8-inch square pan. Chill until firm, at least 3 hours or overnight. Cut into ½-inch cubes. Mix crumbs with butter. Set aside about ¼ cup for garnish, if desired, and press remaining crumb mixture evenly over bottom and up sides to within 1 inch from top of 9-inch springform or tube pan. Chill. Dissolve lemon gelatin and sugar in 1 cup boiling water; add pineapple juice. Chill until slightly thickened. Blend in whipped topping. Fold in gelatin cubes. Spoon into crumb-lined pan. Chill overnight or until firm. Just before serving, run a spatula around sides of pan; then gently remove sides. Garnish with reserved crumbs or with additional whipped topping and flaked coconut, tinted, if desired. Makes 12 to 16 servings.

Mai-Tai Mold

The recipe for this beautiful dessert appeared in Dole® Pineapple advertising some years ago and customers still ask for it. I depart from the last line directions; I unmold it, but serve the whipped cream on the side. It's just too pretty to cover when it first comes to the table.

- 1 1-lb., 4-oz. can Dole® Pineapple Chunks in Juice
- 2 6-oz. packages orange gelatin
- 3 cups boiling water
- 2 cups cold water
- ½ cup dark rum or orange juice
- 3 large mint sprigs
- 12 Maraschino cherries
- 1 orange, peeled and sectioned
- Sweetened whipped cream

Drain pineapple, reserving all juice. Dissolve gelatin in boiling water. Stir in cold water and rum. Arrange mint sprigs, 3 or 4 cherries and several pineapple chunks in bottom of Bundt pan. Pour in ½ cup gelatin mixture. Chill firm. Chill remaining gelatin to consistency of unbeaten egg white. Fold in pineapple, cherries and orange sections. Pour over mint sprigs. Chill firm overnight. Unmold and top with whipped cream to serve. Makes 8 to 10 servings.

Crème de Menthe Crown

Here's a superb extra-easy dessert to end dinner in style. It is from the Dole® Pineapple people—a recipe worth keeping for special occasions and special people.

- 1 1-lb., 4-oz. can Dole® Sliced Pineapple
- 2 6-oz. packages lime gelatin
- 3 cups boiling water
- 1½ cups cold water
- 6 Tbs. Crème de Menthe
- ½ pint whipping cream
- ¼ cup sugar
- 1 tsp. vanilla

Drain pineapple, reserving all syrup. Dissolve gelatin in boiling water. Stir in pineapple syrup, cold water and Crème de Menthe. Pour 1 cup mixture into bottom of Bundt pan. Arrange 3 slices of pineapple, cut in halves, in gelatin mixture in bottom of Bundt pan. Chill firm. Cut through gelatin with spatula at pan ridges. Stand remaining slices in ridges. Chill remainder to consistency of unbeaten egg white. Whip cream with sugar and vanilla until stiff. Fold into thickened gelatin mixture. Spoon into Bundt pan between pineapple slices and over top. Chill until firm overnight. Makes 10 servings.

Pineapple Crème Brûlée

Sensationally rich and flavorful but one of the simplest of all desserts to make. An elegant friend served it not too long ago at one of her elegant dinner parties. She was nice enough to tell me where to find the recipe: on the inside label of Coco Casa® Piña Colada mix.

- 3 cups heavy cream
- 1 2-inch piece vanilla bean (split lengthwise) or 2 tsps. vanilla extract
- 2 tsps. corn starch
- 6 egg yolks
- 1 cup Coco Casa® Piña Colada Mix
- 2 Tbs. cognac or brandy
- 2 Tbs. dark brown sugar

In a saucepan, combine heavy cream and vanilla; heat until scalded. In a bowl, beat egg yolks and corn starch until smooth. Slowly stir in scalded cream, Piña Colada mix and liquor. Strain mixture into a baking dish. Place dish in a pan containing 1 inch hot water. Bake at 325°F. for 35 to 40 minutes or until set. Chill several hours or overnight. Before serving, sprinkle surface with brown sugar. Place dish over ice in a baking pan. Place under a preheated broiler until sugar is melted, about 5 minutes. Serve immediately. Serves 6 to 8.

Basic Dannon Yogurt Dessert

This has become a classic and part of our true American cuisine.

- 2 cups Dannon® Plain Yogurt
- ½ cup sugar
- 2 Tbs. lemon juice
- 3 Tbs. orange liqueur
- 1 pint softened vanilla ice cream

Mix sugar, lemon juice, orange liqueur and Dannon® Plain Yogurt. Stir softened vanilla ice cream and fold into other ingredients. Serves about 4 people.

Variations:

Mold in salad mold and freeze. Unmold on serving plate and surround with fresh strawberries, peaches, blueberries, raspberries, grapes, etc.

Alternate layers in a glass bowl: grapes, raspberries, blueberries, melon balls and Basic Dannon® Yogurt Dessert.

Mix any type of fruit and Basic Dannon® Yogurt Dessert and use as a filling for crêpes.

Mix any type of fruit and Basic Dannon® Yogurt Dessert and spoon into pie crust and freeze until set.

SOUFFLÉS

Some like it hot—some like it cold—but everyone loves a dessert soufflé and believe it or not the experts at Kraft® have made dessert soufflés fail proof. Honest, you can't miss. Cooks everywhere have been whipping them up successfully for at least ten years.

Chocolate "Philly" Soufflé

- 2 Tbs. margarine
- 2 Tbs. flour
- ½ cup milk
- ½ tsp. salt
- 1 8-oz. package Philadelphia Brand Cream Cheese, cubed
- ⅔ cup sugar
- 2 1-oz. squares unsweetened chocolate, melted
- 1½ tsps. vanilla
- 4 eggs, separated

Make a white sauce with margarine, flour, milk and salt. Add cream cheese, ⅓ cup sugar, chocolate and vanilla; stir over low heat until smooth. Remove from heat. Gradually add slightly beaten egg yolks; cool slightly. Beat egg whites until soft peaks form. Gradually add remaining sugar, beating until stiff peaks form. Fold cream cheese mixture into egg whites. Pour into 1¼-quart soufflé dish or casserole. Bake at 350°F. for 1 hour. Serve immediately. Makes 6 servings.

Strawberry Romanoff Soufflé

- 1 envelope unflavored gelatin
- ¼ cup cold water
- ¼ cup Cointreau liqueur
- 2 egg whites
- 1 8-oz. package cream cheese
- 1 10-oz. package frozen strawberries, thawed

- 1 7-oz. jar Kraft® Marshmallow Creme
- 1 cup heavy cream, whipped

Combine gelatin and water in saucepan; let stand 1 minute. Stir over medium heat until dissolved. Gradually add to softened cream cheese, mixing until well blended. Stir in strawberries and liqueur; chill until slightly thickened. Beat egg whites until soft peaks form. Gradually add marshmallow creme, beating until stiff peaks form. Fold in egg white mixture and whipped cream into gelatin mixture. Wrap a 3-inch collar of aluminum foil around top of 1-quart soufflé dish; secure with tape. Pour mixture into dish; chill until firm. Remove foil collar before serving. Makes 8–10 servings.

Variation: Frozen raspberries can be substituted for strawberries.

Caramel Praline Soufflé

- 1 envelope unflavored gelatin
- 1½ cups cold water
- 28 Kraft® Caramels
- 2 Tbs. sugar
- 5 eggs, separated
- 1 cup heavy cream, whipped
- 2 Tbs. sugar
- ¼ cup chopped pecans, toasted

Combine gelatin and ½ cup cold water. Melt caramels and sugar with remaining water in saucepan over low heat. Stir frequently until sauce is smooth. Stir small amount of hot mixture into egg yolks; return to hot mixture. Cook 3–5 minutes over low heat, stirring constantly, until thickened. Stir in gelatin. Cool to room temperature. Fold stiffly beaten egg whites and whipped cream into caramel mixture. Wrap a 3-inch collar of aluminum foil around top of 1-quart soufflé dish; secure with tape. Pour mixture into dish; chill until firm. Remove foil collar before serving.

Melt sugar in skillet over medium heat until clear and caramel colored. Stir in nuts; spoon onto greased cookie sheet. Immediately separate nuts with two forks. Cool; break into small pieces. Sprinkle over soufflé before serving. Makes 6 servings.

Coconut Sponge Roll

A simply beautiful and very festive dessert. Sensational for a party. Baker's Coconut test kitchens made it easy!

¾ tsp. Calumet Baking Powder
½ tsp. salt
4 eggs (at room temperature)
¾ cup sugar
¾ cup sifted cake flour
1 tsp. vanilla
Coconut Whipped Cream (page 504)
½ cup Baker's Coconut

Combine baking powder, salt and eggs in bowl. Beat, gradually adding sugar, until mixture becomes thick and light colored. Gradually fold in sifted flour; add vanilla. Line a 15 × 10 × 1-inch jelly roll pan on bottom with paper; then grease sides and paper. Pour batter into pan. Bake in a hot oven (400°F.) for 13 minutes.

Turn cake out onto cloth, which has been sprinkled with confectioners' sugar. Quickly remove paper and cut off crisp edges of cake. Then roll cake, rolling cloth up in cake. Let stand on cake rack about 30 minutes. Unroll cake, spread about 2 cups of Coconut Whipped Cream on roll and roll again. Spread with remaining filling and sprinkle with coconut. Chill.

Coconut Whipped Cream

- 1½ cups whipping cream
- 1 Tbs. confectioners' sugar
- ¾ tsp. vanilla
- ½ cup Baker's Coconut

Combine all ingredients in a chilled bowl. Whip cream until thick but still glossy. (Do not overbeat.) Makes about 3 cups, or enough to top a 13 × 9 × 2-inch cake, two 9-inch layers, or to fill and frost a cake roll.

Shortcake Supreme

I've always said that no one could improve an old-fashioned shortcake; well, now I take it all back. This super shortcake is just fabulous. Kraft® featured it on their television series and it has gotten raves ever since.

- 2 cups flour
- 2 Tbs. sugar
- 1 Tbs. baking powder
- ½ tsp. salt
- 1 egg, slightly beaten
- ⅔ cup milk
- ½ cup Parkay® Margarine, melted
- 1 cup Kraft® Marshmallow Creme
- 1 cup heavy cream, whipped
- 1 tsp. vanilla
- 1½ cups peach slices
- 1½ cups strawberry slices
- ½ cup blueberries

Combine dry ingredients. Add combined egg, milk and margarine, mixing just until moistened. Spread into greased and floured 8-inch layer pan. Bake at 450°F., 12–15 minutes or until golden brown. Cool 10 minutes; remove from pan. Cool.

Combine marshmallow creme, 2 Tbs. heavy cream and vanilla; mix until well blended. Whip remaining heavy cream until stiff. Fold in marshmallow creme mixture. Split shortcake in half horizontally; fill with half of fruit and marshmallow creme mixture. Top with remaining fruit and marshmallow creme mixture. Makes 8–10 servings.

Fudgy Casserole à la Mode

Do you have children? Or a husband? Make them all happy with this chocolatey chocolate dessert. It's been an easy-to-make favorite since Hershey® printed it on their Baking Chocolate box a dozen years ago.

3 blocks (3 oz.) Hershey's® Baking Chocolate
½ cup + 1 Tbs. butter or margarine, softened
1½ cups sugar
3 eggs
1½ tsps. vanilla
¾ cup sifted all-purpose flour
¾ cup chopped pecans
Vanilla ice cream

Melt baking chocolate in top of a double boiler over simmering water. Remove from heat. Beat in butter or margarine, sugar, eggs and vanilla. Blend in flour; add chopped pecans. Pour into buttered 1- or 1½-quart casserole. Bake at 350°F. for 55 minutes. Spoon into individual dishes and serve warm with ice cream. Makes 6–8 servings.

Brandied Cherry Chocolate Mousse

One of the most popular recipes to ever appear on the Hershey® Chocolate package in the last 20 years.

1 cup pitted, dark sweet cherries, drained (reserve juice)
¼ cup brandy or cherry juice
3 blocks (3 oz.) Hershey's® Baking Chocolate
⅓ cup cherry juice
1 cup sugar
3 egg yolks, well beaten
2 cups whipping cream, sweetened and whipped

Cut cherries into quarters. Pour brandy over cherries and marinate several hours. (If using cherry juice, no need to marinate.) Melt baking chocolate with ⅓ cup cherry juice in saucepan, stirring constantly over medium-low heat. Add sugar; cook until dissolved. Gradually stir hot mixture into egg yolks. Return to saucepan and cook until mixture boils. Cool. Drain cherries and stir brandy or ¼ cup juice into chocolate mixture. Carefully fold chocolate mixture into whipped cream. Fold in cherries and pour into oiled 1½-quart bowl. Cover; freeze overnight. At serving time, remove from freezer; let stand 10 minutes. Loosen with spatula and unmold. Cut 10–12 wedges and serve.

Chocolate Pudding

This is what I call a "comforting recipe"—real, honest, made with milk and eggs, chocolate pudding to enjoy and remember because it's been around since the 1920's when Hershey® printed it on their Baking Chocolate box.

1 cup sugar
¼ cup cornstarch
½ tsp. salt
2½ cups milk
3 egg yolks, well-beaten
2 blocks (2 oz.) Hershey's® Baking Chocolate
1 Tbs. butter
1 tsp. vanilla

Combine sugar, cornstarch and salt in medium saucepan; gradually stir in milk and egg yolks. Add baking chocolate, broken into pieces; cook and stir over medium heat until mixture boils. Boil and stir one minute; remove from heat. Add butter and vanilla; pour into individual serving dishes. Chill. Serve with sweetened whipped cream topping. Makes 6 servings.

Mt. Gretna Chocolate Fondue

When this recipe appeared on the Hershey® Chocolate package its reputation spread fast—here was a Chocolate Fondue that was rich as sin but didn't become too thick while waiting to be dipped into.

3½ blocks (3½ oz.) Hershey's® Baking Chocolate
1¼ cups (14-oz. can) sweetened condensed milk
½ cup marshmallow creme
1 Tbs. milk
1½ tsps. vanilla
1 Tbs. creamy peanut butter (optional)

Combine baking chocolate and condensed milk in saucepan; stir constantly over medium-low heat until chocolate is melted and mixture is smooth. Blend in marshmallow creme and milk. Just before serving, stir in vanilla and peanut butter. Transfer to fondue pot. Makes 2 cups.

Serve by dipping any of the following into warm fondue: Apple, pear, peach or banana slices; strawberries, pineapple chunks, mandarin orange segments, cherries, nut halves, marshmallows, ladyfingers, pieces of angel food or pound cake.

Sun-Maid® Raisin Brown Betty

Developed in the 1930's before World War II, this old-fashioned favorite appeared on the Sun-Maid® box almost 50 years ago.

- 3 cups finely chopped tart apples
- 1 cup Sun-Maid® Seedless Raisins
- ½ cup brown sugar (packed)
- ¼ tsp. nutmeg
- ¼ tsp. cinnamon
- 1 cup soft bread crumbs
- 1 Tbs. butter
- ⅓ cup water

Arrange alternating layers of apples and raisins in greased baking dish. Sprinkle each layer with sugar blended with nutmeg and cinnamon. Add water. Top with crumbs mixed with melted butter. Cover. Bake in hot oven (400°F.) 30–40 minutes until apples are tender. Remove cover and continue baking to brown top. Serve with cream or hard sauce. Makes 6 servings.

Saucy Lemon Pudding

An old-fashioned favorite, this pudding separates as it bakes into a delicate sponge layer and a creamy lemon sauce. A Parkay® "1965 classic."

⅓ cup Parkay® Margarine
1 cup sugar
2 eggs, separated
2 Tbs. lemon juice
1 Tbs. grated lemon rind
⅓ cup flour
1 cup milk

Cream margarine and ¾ cup sugar until light and fluffy. Blend in egg yolks, lemon juice and rind. Add flour; mix well. Stir in milk. Beat egg whites until soft peaks form. Gradually add remaining sugar, beating until stiff peaks form. Fold into batter; pour into 8 6-oz. custard cups. Set custard cups in baking pan; pour in boiling water to ½-inch depth. Bake at 350°F., 35–40 minutes. Remove from water; cool 10 minutes. Invert on dessert dishes. Makes 8 servings.

Variation: Prepare recipe as directed. Pour batter into 1-quart casserole. Bake at 350°F., 40–45 minutes. Cool 20 minutes; invert on serving plate.

Banana Pudding

Remember home-made Banana Pudding? Most Southerners do. This is the real thing, made from scratch. The recipe, a consistent favorite, was on the Nabisco Nilla Wafers package way back when I was a child.

¾ cup sugar, granulated
3 Tbs. all-purpose flour
Dash of salt
4 eggs
2 cups milk
½ tsp. vanilla extract
Nabisco Nilla Wafers
5–6 medium size fully ripe bananas, sliced

Combine ½ cup sugar, flour and salt in top of double boiler. Mix in 1 whole egg and 3 egg yolks. Stir in milk. Cook, uncovered, over boiling water, stirring constantly, until thickened. Remove from heat; add vanilla. Spread small amount on bottom of 1½-quart casserole; cover with layer of Nilla Wafers. Top with layer of sliced bananas. Pour about ⅓ of custard over bananas. Continue to layer wafers, bananas and custard to make 3 layers of each ending with custard. Beat remaining 3 egg whites until stiff, but not dry; gradually add remaining ¼ cup sugar and beat until mixture forms stiff peaks. Pile on top of pudding covering entire surface. Bake in preheated hot oven (425°F.) 5 minutes or until delicately browned. Serve warm or chilled. Makes 8 (about ¾-cup) servings.

Basic Vanilla Chiffon

The Knox Company has been inserting this extra-easy recipe in their Gelatine package for dozens of years. It's such a favorite with "creative" cooks who want to do their "own thing" with special flavoring and such that it simply can't be left out.

1 envelope Knox Unflavored Gelatine
¼ cup sugar
2 eggs, separated
1¾ cups milk
1 tsp. vanilla extract

In medium saucepan, mix Unflavored Gelatine with 2 Tbs. sugar; blend in egg yolks beaten with milk. Let stand 1 minute. Stir over low heat until Gelatine is completely dissolved, about 5 minutes; add vanilla. Pour into large bowl and chill, stirring occasionally, until mixture mounds slightly when dropped from spoon. In medium bowl, beat egg whites until soft peaks form; gradually add remaining sugar and beat until stiff. Fold into Gelatine mixture. Turn into 4-cup bowl or dessert dishes and chill until set. Makes about 8 servings.

Variations:

Chocolate Chiffon: After Gelatine is completely dissolved, stir in ½ cup semi-sweet chocolate chips. Continue cooking, stirring constantly, until chocolate is melted. With wire whip or rotary beater, beat mixture until chocolate is blended.

Coffee Chiffon: Mix 1 Tbs. instant coffee powder with Gelatine and sugar.

Lemon Chiffon: Omit vanilla. After Gelatine is completely dissolved, cool mixture completely. Add 2 Tbs. lemon juice and 2 tsps. grated lemon peel.

Peppermint Chiffon: Substitute ¼ tsp. peppermint extract for vanilla; if desired, add a few drops red food coloring.

Soufflé: Turn the chiffon mixture into a soufflé dish, using a collar for the characteristic high-rise effect. To make collar, fold foil into four thicknesses 3 inches wide and long enough to go around the soufflé dish with generous overlap. Attach to dish with tape, leaving collar 2 inches higher than rim of dish. The volume of the Gelatine mixture should be about 4 cups *more* than the volume of the dish without the collar.

Charlotte: Turn chiffon mixture into a bowl, loaf pan or springform pan lined with lady fingers. For an 8-inch bowl you need about 12 ladyfingers. Split ladyfingers, and place upright, rounded side out, around side of bowl.

Basic Fruit Juice Whip

You asked for it—and Knox test kitchens did it—way back in the 1960's. A low-calorie but really great-tasting dessert.

1 envelope Knox Unflavored Gelatine
2 Tbs. sugar
1 cup water or fruit juice, heated to boiling*
1 cup cold fruit juice

In large bowl, mix Unflavored Gelatine with sugar; add boiling water or fruit juice and stir until Gelatine is completely dissolved. Stir in cold juice. Chill, stirring occasionally, until mixture is consistency of unbeaten egg whites. With electric mixer, beat at high speed until mixture triples in volume; about 10 minutes. Turn into dessert dishes or large bowl and chill until set. Makes about 8 servings.

Variations: Try any of the following fruit juices—orange, pineapple (do not use fresh or frozen), grape juice, apricot or peach nectar or cranberry juice cocktail.

Grasshopper Dessert

A variation of a favorite, lighter than grasshopper pie, it's been a "collectible recipe" since Jell-O® printed it on their Lime Jell-O® box a decade ago.

2 3-oz. packages or 1 6-oz. package Jell-O® Lime Gelatin
1½ cups cold water
¼ cup sugar

* NOTE: Use all juices for fruitier flavor. If *less* sweetness is desired, reduce sugar.

- 2 cups boiling water
- 2 Tbs. green creme de menthe liqueur
- 1 envelope Dream Whip Whipped Topping mix

Dissolve gelatin and sugar in boiling water. Add cold water and liqueur. Pour 1 cup into a bowl and chill slightly, until slightly thickened. Pour remaining gelatin mixture into a 9-inch square pan. Chill until firm—at least 3 hours. Cut into ½-inch squares.

Meanwhile, prepare whipped topping mix as directed on package. Blend into slightly thickened gelatin. Pour into a 3-cup bowl. Chill until firm—about 3 hours. Unmold the creamy gelatin in the center of a shallow serving bowl. Arrange gelatin cubes around the mold. Garnish with chocolate curls, if desired. Makes about 5 cups or 8–10 servings.

Topaz Parfait

Beautiful to look at and absolutely divine to eat. A perfect "make ahead" dessert for your next dinner party. The recipe is from the Lemon Jell-O® box. If you meant to save it but didn't, fret not, here it is.

- 1 cup strong coffee
- 1 3-oz. package Jell-O® Lemon Gelatin
- ⅓ cup sugar
- ½ cup cold water*
- ¼ cup brandy or dark rum*
- 1 envelope Dream Whip Whipped Topping mix
- 2 Tbs. brown sugar
- 1 Tbs. brandy or dark rum**

* Or increase cold water to ¾ cup and add 1 tsp. brandy extract.

** Or use ½ tsp. brandy extract.

Bring coffee to a boil. Add gelatin and sugar and stir until dissolved. Add cold water and ¼ cup brandy. Pour into an 8-inch square pan. Chill until firm—about 4 hours. Cut into cubes. Prepare whipped topping as directed adding brown sugar and 1 Tbs. brandy. Layer coffee cubes and topping in parfait glasses or top cubes in sherbet glasses with topping. Makes 4 servings.
Note: Recipe may be doubled.

Patriotic Mold

It's the Fourth of July! Plan a porch supper of cold fried chicken, corn on the cob, sliced tomatoes and onions; wind up with this red, white and blue spectacular! As much fun as fireworks, and a dream to taste.

Red Layer:

1 3-oz. package Jell-O® Strawberry Gelatin
1⅓ cups boiling water
1 10-oz. package Birds-Eye® Quick-Thaw Strawberries

White Layer:

1 3-oz. package Jell-O® Lemon Gelatin
1 cup boiling water
1 pint vanilla ice cream, slightly softened

Blue Layer:

1 package 3-oz. Jell-O®—Lemon, Black Cherry, Concord Grape or Black Raspberry—Gelatin
¼ cup sugar
1 cup boiling water
½ cup cold water
1½ cups fresh, frozen or drained canned blueberries, mashed.

Dissolve strawberry gelatin in 1⅓ cups boiling water. Add frozen strawberries. Stir gently until fruit thaws and separates. Chill until thickened. Pour into an 8-cup mold (star-shaped, if desired), a 9-cup Bundt pan, or straight-sided saucepan. Chill until set, but not firm.

Dissolve 1 package lemon gelatin in 1 cup boiling water. Blend in ice cream, beating until smooth. Chill until thickened. Spoon over strawberry mixture in mold. Chill until set, but not firm.

Dissolve remaining package of gelatin and the sugar in 1 cup boiling water. Add ½ cup cold water; chill until thickened. Stir in blueberries and spoon over lemon ice cream mixture in mold. Chill until firm, or overnight. Unmold. Makes about 8 cups or 12–14 servings.

Frozen Pumpkin Dessert Squares

This "new" way to serve pumpkin made its appearance back in 1960 when the recipe was first printed on Libby's solid pack pumpkin can. It's as American as pumpkin pie and just as delicious.

1½ cups graham cracker crumbs
¼ cup sugar
¼ cup butter or margarine, melted
1 16-oz. can Libby's Solid Pack Pumpkin
½ cup brown sugar
½ tsp. salt
1 tsp. ground cinnamon
¼ tsp. ground ginger
⅛ tsp. ground cloves
1 quart vanilla ice cream, softened
Whipped cream and toasted coconut (optional)

Mix crumbs with sugar and butter. Press into bottom of 9-inch square pan. Combine pumpkin with brown sugar, salt and spices. Fold in ice cream. Pour into crumb-lined pan. Cover; freeze until firm. Take out of freezer about 20 minutes before serving. Cut into squares; top each square with whipped cream and toasted coconut. Yields 9 3-inch squares.

Ice Cream Sandwiches

A Sunday best dessert, easy to do and prepared ahead of time. Kellogg's® Rice Krispies cereal featured the ice cream treat in national advertising two summers ago, and put it on their cereal box too.

½ cup corn syrup
½ cup peanut butter
4 cups Kellogg's® Rice Krispies cereal
1 pint ice cream, cut into 6 slices

In medium size mixing bowl, stir together corn syrup and peanut butter. Add Kellogg's® Rice Krispies cereal. Stir until well coated. Press mixture evenly in buttered 13 × 9 × 2-inch pan. Place in freezer or coldest part of refrigerator until firm. Cut cereal mixture into twelve 3-inch squares. Sandwich each slice of ice cream between 2 squares. Freeze until firm. Cut each large sandwich in half and wrap individually in foil. Store in freezer until needed. Makes 12 sandwiches.

PET® EVAPORATED MILK ICE CREAMS

I just went wild when I sampled these luxurious Ice Creams. So instead of stingily giving you just one I have included them all.

Fudge Marlow

- 1 13-oz. can Pet® Evaporated Milk, divided usage
- ⅔ cup sugar
- ⅓ cup cocoa
- Few grains salt
- ½ cup water
- 16 large marshmallows
- 2 tsps. vanilla

Freeze 1 cup evaporated milk in small mixing bowl until ice crystals form along edges. Stir together sugar, cocoa and salt in small saucepan. Add ⅔ cup evaporated milk and water. Cook and stir over low heat until smooth. Add marshmallows and cook until half melted. Remove from heat. Stir until completely melted. Stir in vanilla. Pour into medium bowl. Refrigerate until well chilled. Beat icy evaporated milk until stiff. Fold into chilled cocoa mixture. Pour into 2½ quart bowl. Freeze until firm. Makes about 2 quarts.

Coffee Pecan Ice Cream

- 2 eggs
- 1⅓ cups sugar
- 2 13-oz. cans Pet® Evaporated Milk
- 1 cup whole milk
- 1 Tbs. vanilla
- 2 Tbs. instant coffee
- ¼ cup boiling water
- 1 cup chopped pecans

Beat eggs and sugar in large mixing bowl until well blended. Stir in evaporated milk, milk and vanilla. Dissolve coffee in boiling water. Add to milk mixture. Refrigerate until well chilled. Pour into ice cream freezer container. Churn and freeze according to manufacturer's directions. When ice cream is finished, stir in pecans.

Mint Chip Ice Cream

- 3 eggs
- 1½ cups sugar
- 2 13-oz. cans Pet® Evaporated Milk
- ¾ tsp. peppermint extract
- ⅛ tsp. green food coloring
- 1½ cups (6 oz.) grated milk chocolate

Beat eggs and sugar in large mixing bowl until well blended. Stir in evaporated milk, peppermint extract and food coloring. Gently stir in grated chocolate. Refrigerate until well chilled. Pour into ice cream freezer container. Churn and freeze according to manufacturer's directions. Makes about 2 quarts.

Cinnamon Chocolate Ice Cream

- 3 13-oz. cans Pet® Evaporated Milk, divided usage
- 2½ 1-oz. squares unsweetened chocolate
- 2 eggs
- 1 cup sugar
- ½ tsp. cinnamon
- ¼ tsp. nutmeg

Combine 1 can (1⅔ cups) evaporated milk and chocolate in small saucepan. Cook over medium heat, stirring frequently, until chocolate melts and mixture is smooth. Meanwhile beat eggs, sugar, cinnamon and nutmeg in large mixing bowl until well blended. Stir in hot chocolate mixture. Stir in remaining 2 cans (3⅓ cups) evaporated milk.

Refrigerate until well chilled. Pour into ice cream freezer container. Churn and freeze according to manufacturer's directions. Makes 2 quarts.

Peanut Butter Chocolate Ice Cream

- 2 13-oz. cans Pet® Evaporated Milk, divided usage
- 2 squares (2 oz.) unsweetened chocolate
- 2 eggs
- ¾ cup sugar
- 4–6 Tbs. chunky peanut butter

Combine 1 cup evaporated milk and chocolate in small saucepan. Cook over medium heat, stirring frequently, until chocolate melts and mixture is smooth. Meanwhile beat eggs and sugar in large mixing bowl until well blended. Beat in peanut butter until smooth. Stir in hot chocolate mixture. Stir in remaining 2⅓ cups evaporated milk. Refrigerate until well chilled. Pour into ice cream freezer container. Churn and freeze according to manufacturer's directions. Makes about 2 quarts.

A PAIR OF OLD-FASHIONED, WELL-LOVED PUDDINGS FROM GENERAL FOODS KITCHENS

Chocolate Tapioca Pudding

Here's a nourishing milk-and-egg dessert that's fast to fix and a favorite with chocolate lovers. Add instant coffee when you'd like a mocha flavor.

- 1 cup sugar
- 3 Tbs. Minute Tapioca
- ⅛ tsp. salt
- 3⅔ cups milk
- 1 egg, slightly beaten
- 1 tsp. vanilla
- 2 1-ounce squares Baker's Unsweetened Chocolate
- 2 to 3 tsps. Maxwell House Instant Coffee (optional)

Combine sugar, tapioca and salt in saucepan; stir in milk and egg. Let stand 5 minutes. Add chocolate and instant coffee. Cook and stir over medium heat until mixture comes to a full boil and chocolate is well blended, about 15 minutes. Remove from heat. Stir in vanilla. Cool for 20 minutes; stir. Chill. Serve with prepared Dream Whip Whipped Topping, if desired. Makes about 8 servings.

Heavenly Hash

Your little angels will sing for more of this heavenly treat with marshmallows and fruits floating amid clouds of pudding.

- 1 egg
- ⅓ cup sugar
- 2⅓ cups milk
- 3 Tbs. Minute Tapioca
- ¼ tsp. salt
- 1 8¼-ounce can crushed pineapple, drained
- 8 marshmallows, quartered
- 1 cup prepared Dream Whip Whipped Topping
- 2 Tbs. chopped maraschino cherries

Beat egg until thick and light in color. Gradually add sugar, beating thoroughly after each addition. Blend in milk, tapioca and salt. Let stand for 5 minutes. Pour into saucepan. Cook and stir over medium heat until mixture comes to a full boil. (Pudding thickens as it cools.) Cool for 20 minutes; fold in pineapple and marshmallows. Chill for at least 1 hour. Just before serving, fold in whipped topping and cherries. Makes 3½ cups or 6 or 7 servings.

Hot Curried Fruit

Here's a superb extra-easy dessert to end dinner with a flourish. It's from the Hiram Walker Cordials Entertaining Book.

Drain canned peaches, pears, pineapple, apricots and cherries. Layer in a Pyrex dish—first fruit, then dot with butter, sprinkle with brown sugar and curry powder, drizzle with Hiram Walker Blackberry Brandy. Make at least 3 layers. Bake one hour at 325°F.

P.S. I like it swathed in sour cream.

Ribbon Icebox Dessert

An old-fashioned favorite, from Pet Milk's 1932 Cookbook.

- 1 30-ounce can fruit cocktail, drained, reserving liquid
- 2 3-ounce packages strawberry-flavored gelatine
- 30 graham crackers, each 2½ inches square
- ½ cup butter or margarine, softened
- 2 cups powdered sugar
- 1 13-ounce can Pet Evaporated Milk
- ½ cup water

Heat 1½ cups fruit cocktail liquid to boiling (if not enough liquid, add water to make 1½ cups liquid). Add gelatine; stir until dissolved. Cool to room temperature. Place half of graham crackers in one layer on bottom of 13 × 9 × 2-inch pan. Beat butter until creamy; gradually beat in powdered sugar; add ⅓ cup evaporated milk, stirring in about 1 Tbs. at a time; beat well after each addition; spread over graham crackers in pan. Top with remaining graham crackers in a single layer. Refrigerate. Divide cooled gelatine into two equal portions. Stir 1⅓ cups evaporated milk into one portion. Chill until slightly thicker than unbeaten egg whites. Beat until fluffy. Spread over graham crackers. Refrigerate until firm. Stir ½ cup water and drained fruit cocktail into remaining dissolved gelatine. Pour over chilled gelatine–evaporated milk mixture. Chill until firm. Cut into squares and serve. Makes 12 servings.

HERSHEY'S® CHOCOLATE SAUCES

Here are two great chocolate sauces from the Hershey® Company's 1934 Cookbook. Either one will transform just plain ice cream into a fabulous dessert. If you want to create something "extra special," try either one over poached pear or peach halves.

Chocolate Marshmallow Sauce

- 2 cups granulated sugar
- 1 cup boiling water
- ¼ cup Hershey's® Cocoa
- 1 tsp. vanilla
- ½ cup shredded fresh marshallows
  or
- ½ cup miniature marshmallows

Cook sugar and water in saucepan to 220°F. Remove from heat; stir in cocoa, vanilla and marshmallows until melted. Cool, without stirring, until bottom of pan just feels warm to hand. Beat to thicken and serve warm over ice cream. Makes 2 cups of sauce.

Chocolate Caramel Sauce

- 1 cup brown sugar, packed
  Dash of salt
- 3 Tbs. water
- ¼ cup Hershey's® Chocolate Flavored Syrup
- 1 Tbs. butter
- 1 Tbs. cornstarch
- 1 cup hot water
- ½ tsp. vanilla

Cook sugar and salt with 3 Tbs. water to a light caramel brown. Remove from heat; add chocolate syrup, butter and cornstarch mixed to a paste and 1 cup hot water. Cook over direct heat until thick (220°F.), for about 15 minutes; add vanilla. Serve with cottage pudding or other hot desserts. This sauce is very nice with ice cream. Makes 1 cup of sauce.

Sunkist Fresh Lemon Ice Cream

Leave it to a Californian to dream up this delicate, refreshingly different ice cream.

2 cups whipping cream or half-and-half
1 cup sugar
1 to 2 Tbs. fresh grated Sunkist Lemon Peel
⅓ cup fresh-squeezed Sunkist Lemon Juice

In large bowl, stir together cream and sugar until sugar is thoroughly dissolved. Mix in lemon peel and juice. Pour into 8-inch square pan, or directly into sherbet dishes or scooped-out lemon boats. Freeze several hours until firm. Garnish with lemon cartwheel twists, if desired. Makes about 1½ pints.

12.

Cookies and Special Sweets

For a while there I began to think nobody made cookies anymore—or homemade candy, for that matter. Everyone seemed to be so "into gourmet" that the humble cookie and the plate of homemade fudge became somewhat out of fashion. Well, the cookie is back; and who can wonder why after they taste cookies like our California Gold Bars or deep, dark, chewy Chocolate Brownies? As for candy, a lot of people are discovering that a plate of homemade candies offered with small cups of hot strong coffee makes the perfect finale to the most elegant dinner party.

Nothing could be easier or more satisfying than to whip up a few dozen cookies or a platter of candy. Even busier-than-ever cooks can find the few moments it takes with any of the recipes included here. As for saving money as well as time, homemade beats "store bought" by a country mile.

Once again I assure you that each recipe here is a proven success, easy, quick and dependable time after time—tested over and over again in the kitchens of our most famous food companies. All you need to worry about is making enough; the cookies and candies included here have a way of vanishing—fast!

Peanut Butter Kisses

A classic from the Skippy® Peanut Butter label; easy to make, inexpensive and they love 'em.

2 egg whites
⅛ tsp. cream of tartar
⅔ cup sugar
½ cup Skippy® Creamy or Super Chunk Peanut Butter

In small bowl with mixer at high speed beat egg whites and cream of tartar until mixture holds stiff peaks when beater is raised. Add sugar, 1 Tbs. at a time, beating well after each addition. Continue beating until mixture holds very stiff peaks when beater is raised. Lightly fold in peanut butter just until mixed. Drop by teaspoonfuls onto greased cookie sheet. Bake in 300°F. oven 25 minutes or until lightly browned. Remove from cookie sheet immediately. Makes about 3 dozen cookies.

Brown-Eyed Susans

A rich, chocolate-topped cookie with almond "eyes"—the popularity of this Parkay® "classic" dates from the 1940's and has not diminished with passing time.

1 cup Parkay® Margarine
¼ cup sugar
½ tsp. almond extract
2 cups flour
½ tsp. salt
Chocolate Frosting (page 528)
Whole almonds

Cream margarine and sugar until light and fluffy. Blend in extract. Add flour and salt; mix well. Shape rounded teaspoonfuls of dough into balls. Place on ungreased cookie sheet; flatten slightly. Bake at 375°F., 10 to 12 minutes. Cool. Frost with Chocolate Frosting; top with almonds. Makes approximately 5 dozen.

Chocolate Frosting

1 cup confectioners sugar, sifted
2 Tbs. cocoa
1 Tbs. hot water
½ tsp. vanilla

Combine sugar and cocoa. Add water and vanilla and mix well.

Butter Pecan Turtle Cookies

An irresistibly good cookie made easy by the talented cooks at the Land O Lakes® test kitchens.

Crust

2 cups all-purpose flour
1 cup firmly packed brown sugar
½ cup Land O Lakes® Sweet Cream Butter, softened
1 cup whole pecan halves (not chopped)

Preheat oven to 350°F. In 3-quart mixer bowl combine crust ingredients. Mix at medium speed, scraping sides of bowl often, until well mixed and particles are fine (2 to 3 minutes). Pat firmly into ungreased 13 × 9 × 2-inch pan. Sprinkle pecans evenly over unbaked crust. Prepare caramel layer; pour evenly over pecans and crust. Bake near center of 350°F. oven for 18 to 22 minutes or until entire caramel layer is bubbly and crust is light golden brown. Remove from oven. Immediately sprinkle with chips. Allow chips to melt slightly (2 to 3 minutes). Slightly swirl chips as they melt; leave some whole for a marbled effect. Do *not* spread chips. Cool completely; cut into bars. Makes 3 to 4 dozen bars.

Caramel Layer
⅔ cup Land O Lakes® Sweet Cream Butter
½ cup firmly packed brown sugar
1 cup milk-chocolate chips

Caramel Layer: In heavy 1-quart saucepan combine butter and brown sugar. Cook over medium heat, stirring constantly, until entire surface of mixture begins to boil. Boil ½ to 1 minute, stirring constantly.

Chewy Walnut Squares

We've been making these cookies from the Diamond® Walnut Growers every Christmas as far back as I can remember. "They are so good they deserve to be put in your book" wrote several different fans.

1 egg, unbeaten
1 cup brown sugar, packed
1 tsp. vanilla
½ cup sifted all-purpose flour
¼ tsp. baking soda
¼ tsp. salt
1 cup coarsely chopped Diamond® Walnuts

Grease an 8-inch square pan. Stir together the egg, brown sugar and vanilla. Quickly stir in flour, baking soda and salt. Add Walnuts. Spread in pan and bake at 350°F. for 18 to 20 minutes. (Cookies should be soft in center when taken from oven.) Leave in pan; cut into 2-inch squares. Makes 16 squares.

Butterscotch Brownies

These old-fashioned cookies from Nestlé® have been making butterscotch fanciers happy for a very long time.

2 cups unsifted flour
2 tsps. baking powder
1½ tsps. salt
One 12-oz. package (2 cups) Nestlé® Butterscotch Morsels
½ cup butter
2 cups firmly packed brown sugar
4 eggs
1 tsp. vanilla extract
1 cup chopped nuts

Preheat oven to 350°F. In small bowl, combine flour, baking powder and salt; set aside. Melt over hot (not boiling) water, Nestlé® Butterscotch Morsels and butter; remove from heat and transfer to large bowl. Stir in brown sugar. Cool 5 minutes. Beat in eggs and vanilla extract. Blend in flour mixture. Stir in nuts. Spread evenly into greased 15 × 10 × 1-inch baking pan. Bake at 350°F. for 30 minutes. Cool. Cut into 2-inch squares. Makes 35 2-inch squares.

Note: For one 6-oz. package, recipe may be divided in half. Spread into greased 13 × 9 × 2-inch baking pan. Bake for 25 to 30 minutes. Makes 24 2-inch squares.

"Philly" Sprites

A cream cheese version of spritz and a Kraft® classic.

1 cup margarine
1 8-oz. package Philadelphia® Brand Cream Cheese
⅔ cup sugar
1 tsp. vanilla
2 cups flour
Dash of salt

Combine margarine, softened Cream Cheese and sugar, mixing until well blended. Blend in vanilla. Add flour and salt; mix well. Chill. Force dough through cookie press onto ungreased cookie sheet. Bake at 400°F., 8 to 10 minutes. Makes approximately 8 dozen.

Spritz Cookies

These buttery rich "no chill" cookies from the Land O Lakes® Sweet Cream Butter carton have been a favorite for a generation.

- 1 cup Land O Lakes® Sweet Cream Butter, softened
- ⅔ cup sugar
- 1 egg
- 2 tsp. vanilla *or* almond *or* lemon flavoring
- 2¼ cups all-purpose flour
- ½ tsp. salt

Preheat oven to 400°F. In 3-quart mixer bowl combine butter, sugar, egg and flavoring. Beat at medium speed, scraping sides of bowl often, until light and fluffy. Reduce to low speed (or by hand); stir in flour and salt until well combined. Dough can be divided and tinted if desired. If dough is too soft, chill for easier handling. Force dough through a cookie press onto ungreased baking sheet. Decorate with colored sugar or cinnamon candies, etc. Bake near center of 400°F. oven for 8 to 14 minutes or until cookies are light golden around edges. Makes 6 dozen cookies.

Tip: For green or pink cookies, add 3 to 4 drops green or red food coloring.

Cross-Country Oatmeal Cookies

Americans have been munching these old-fashioned oatmeal cookies since they were first introduced by Mazola® in the mid 1930's, but the updated version is as modern as tomorrow. They are low in fat and have only a moderate amount of cholesterol, sugar and salt.

- ¾ cup Mazola® Corn Oil
- 1 cup quick-cooking oats

1 cup firmly packed brown sugar
2 eggs
1 tsp. vanilla
1½ cups unsifted flour
1½ tsps. baking powder
½ tsp. salt
½ tsp. ground cinnamon
½ cup coarsely chopped nuts

In large bowl with mixer at medium speed beat corn oil, sugar, eggs and vanilla until thick. Add flour, oats, baking powder, salt and cinnamon. Beat at low speed until blended. Stir in nuts. Drop by level tablespoonfuls 2 inches apart on greased cookie sheet. Bake in 350°F. oven 12 to 15 minutes or until browned. Makes about 3½ dozen.

Oatmeal Scotchies

Oatmeal, brown sugar and Nestlé® Butterscotch Morsels have made these moist and rich cookies a favorite since the 1950's.

2 cups *unsifted* flour
2 tsps. baking powder
1 tsp. baking soda
1 tsp. salt
1 cup butter, softened
1½ cups firmly packed brown sugar
2 eggs
1 Tbs. water
1½ cups quick oats, uncooked
One 12-oz. package (2 cups) Nestlé® Butterscotch Morsels
½ tsp. orange extract

Preheat oven to 375°F. In small bowl, combine flour, baking powder, baking soda and salt; set aside. In large bowl, combine butter, brown sugar, eggs and water; beat until creamy. Gradually add flour mixture. Stir in oats, Nestlé® Butterscotch Morsels and orange extract. Drop by slightly rounded tablespoonfuls onto greased cookie sheets. Bake at 375°F. for 10 to 12 minutes. Makes 4 dozen 3-inch cookies.

Double Chocolate Oatmeal Cookies

A top-request recipe and a particular favorite with the Betty Crocker® staff. Made to order for after-school treats.

- 1½ cups sugar
- 1 cup margarine or butter, softened
- 1 egg
- ¼ cup water
- 1 tsp. vanilla
- 1¼ cups Gold Medal® All-Purpose Flour*
- ⅓ cup cocoa
- ½ tsp. baking soda
- ½ tsp. salt
- 3 cups quick-cooking oats
- 1 6-oz. package semi-sweet chocolate chips

Heat oven to 350°F. Mix sugar, margarine, egg, water and vanilla. Stir in remaining ingredients. Drop dough by rounded teaspoonfuls about 2 inches apart onto ungreased cookie sheet. Bake until almost no indentation remains when touched, 10 to 12 minutes. Immediately remove from cookie sheet. About 5½ dozen cookies.

Note: Unbleached flour can be used in this recipe.

* If using self-rising flour, omit baking soda and salt.

Snowy Apricot Bars

An old-fashioned favorite from Bisquick®; these rich fruit and nut bars often appear at showers, weddings and holiday buffets.

- 1 6-oz. package dried apricots (1⅓ cups)
- ½ cup firm margarine or butter
- ½ cup granulated sugar
- 2½ cups Bisquick® Baking Mix
- 2 cups packed brown sugar
- 4 eggs, beaten
- ⅔ cup Bisquick® Baking Mix
- 1 tsp. vanilla
- 1 cup chopped nuts
- Powdered sugar

Place apricots in 2-quart saucepan; add enough water to cover. Heat to boiling; reduce heat. Simmer uncovered 10 minutes; drain. Cool; chop and reserve. Heat oven to 350°F. Cut margarine into granulated sugar and 2½ cups Baking Mix until crumbly. Pat in ungreased jelly roll pan, 15½ × 1-inch. Bake 10 minutes. Beat brown sugar and eggs. Stir in apricots, ⅔ cup Baking Mix, the vanilla and nuts. Spread over baked layer. Bake 30 minutes longer. Cool completely; cut into bars, about 2 × 1 inches each. Roll in powdered sugar. Makes 75 cookies.

Speedy Little Devils

A very "early on" creamy-center bar cookie from the label of a Duncan Hines® Cake Mix box; printed way back when most people thought cake mixes only made cakes. Love these cookies; my only complaint is how in heaven's name can anyone follow the last line of the directions in the recipe. "Serve one piece at a time?" You just can't do that at my house.

- 1 package Duncan Hines® II Devil's Food Cake Mix
- 1 stick butter or margarine, melted
- ¾ cup creamy peanut butter
- 1 7 to 7½-oz. jar marshmallow creme

Combine melted butter and dry Cake Mix (let butter cool down a couple of minutes before adding to dry mix. Mixture should be crumbly. If butter is too hot, the result will be a sticky mass rather than a crumbly mixture.) Reserve 1½ cups of this mixture for topping. Pat remaining crumb mixture into an ungreased 13 × 9 × 2-inch pan. Combine peanut butter and marshmallow creme and spread evenly over the crumb mixture in the pan. Crumble the reserved 1½ cups of cake mixture over the peanut butter/marshmallow creme layer. Bake 20 minutes at 350°F. Let cool, cut into bars, and serve one piece at a time. Makes 3 dozen 1¼-inch bars.

Baby Ruth Cookies

Remember how you loved them? The recipe, from a booklet printed in the early 1950's, has been one of the "most requested" at the Standard Brands' kitchens for over 25 years. Due to its popularity it was reprinted on the package in the late 1970's. People who remember making them for their children now want a reprint of the recipe for their grandchildren.

- 1¼ cups unsifted flour
- ½ tsp. baking soda
- ½ tsp. salt
- ½ cup (1 stick) Blue Bonnet Margarine
- ¾ cup sugar
- 1 egg
- ½ tsp. vanilla
- 1 cup chopped Curtiss® Baby Ruth Candy Bars

Sift together flour, baking soda and salt; set aside. Cream together Blue Bonnet® Margarine and sugar until light and fluffy. Beat in egg and vanilla. Stir in Curtiss® Baby Ruths and dry ingredients until well blended. Chill for 30 minutes. Drop dough by ½-teaspoonfuls onto greased baking sheets. Bake at 350°F. for 10 to 12 minutes, or until done. Remove from sheets and cool on wire racks.

Choco-Almond Confections

This positively elegant "very adult" confection is from Blue Diamond.®

- 1¼ cups Blue Diamond® Chopped Natural Almonds, toasted
- 3 1-oz. squares milk chocolate
- ½ cup orange juice
- ½ cup granulated sugar
- 3 cups crushed lemon, orange or vanilla wafers
- 2 Tbs. Curacao or orange juice

In blender or food processor, finely grind ¼ cup of the almonds; set aside. Combine chocolate with orange juice and sugar in saucepan. Cook over medium heat, stirring constantly until sugar is dissolved and chocolate is melted. Remove from heat and mix in crushed wafers, Curacao and the chopped almonds. Chill mixture at least one hour. Form into small balls; roll in the ground almonds. Refrigerate in airtight container for several days for best flavor to develop. Makes about 3 dozen.

Applesauce Bars

Rich, moist and spicy good. The entire family will love these cookies from Stokely–Van Camp.®

2½ cups all-purpose flour
1 cup sugar
¼ tsp. baking powder
1½ tsps. baking soda
1½ tsps. salt
¾ tsp. cinnamon
½ tsp. cloves
½ tsp. allspice
½ cup vegetable shortening, at room temperature
½ cup water
1 16½-oz. can Applesauce
1 egg
½ cup chopped nuts
1 cup chopped raisins
Caramel Frosting (below)

Preheat oven to 350°F. Grease and flour 15 × 10 × 1-inch jelly-roll pan. Sift all dry ingredients into a large mixing bowl. Add shortening, water, applesauce and egg. Beat 4 minutes with electric mixer on medium speed. Gently fold in nuts and raisins. Pour into prepared pan and bake 30 minutes. Cool in pan. Frost cake in pan and cut into bars. Makes 48 bars.

Caramel Frosting

¼ cup butter or margarine
½ cup firmly packed brown sugar
3 Tbs. milk
About 1½ cups sifted confectioners sugar

Melt butter, add brown sugar; boil for 1 minute, stirring constantly. Cool slightly. Stir in milk. Gradually add confectioners sugar and beat until of spreading consistency.

Yugoslav Kifle (Filled Butterhorn Cookie)

A sweet walnut-meringue cookie made with a yeast dough. Your mother may have called them Butterhorns

and found the recipe on a Fleischmann's® Yeast label. If she made them you'll remember; once tried they are never forgotten.

- ½ cup dairy sour cream
- 1 Tbs. boiling water
- 1 package Fleischmann's® Active Dry Yeast
- ½ cup (1 stick) Fleischmann's® Margarine, softened
- 1¾ to 2¼ cups unsifted flour
- 2 egg yolks (at room temperature)
- 1 cup finely chopped Planters® Walnuts
- ½ cup sugar
- 1 tsp. vanilla extract
- 2 egg whites, stiffly beaten
- Confectioners sugar
- Melted Fleischmann's® Margarine

Combine sour cream and boiling water; mix well. Stir in undissolved Fleischmann's® Active Dry Yeast; let stand 3 minutes. Stir until yeast is completely dissolved; set aside. Place softened Fleischmann's® Margarine and ½ cup flour in small bowl. Add sour cream mixture and beat 1 minute at low speed of electric mixer, scraping bowl occasionally. Add egg yolks and ¼ cup flour; beat at medium speed 1 minute, scraping bowl occasionally. Stir in enough additional flour to make a soft dough. Turn out onto lightly floured board; knead 8 to 10 minutes. (Dough will not be smooth.) Divide dough into 3 equal pieces. Wrap in wax paper. Chill at least 2 hours or up to 5 days. When ready to shape, combine Planters® Walnuts, sugar and vanilla extract. Fold in stiffly beaten egg whites. On a board dusted with confectioners sugar, roll each piece of dough into a 10-inch circle; cut each into 8 pie-shaped wedges. Top wide edge of each wedge with about 1 Tbs. nut filling mixture. Roll up from wide end to point. Place on greased baking sheets, with points underneath. Brush with melted Fleischmann's® Margarine. Bake at 375°F. for 20 minutes, or until golden brown.

Remove from baking sheets and place on wire racks to cool. Immediately sprinkle with confectioners sugar if desired. Makes 2 dozen cookies.

Crunchy Fudge Sandwiches

No one knows how many millions of cupfuls of Kellogg's® Rice Krispies® have been used for this sensational recipe.

- One 6-oz. package (1 cup) butterscotch-flavored morsels
- ½ cup peanut butter
- 4 cups Kellogg's® Rice Krispies® Cereal
- One 6-oz. package (1 cup) semi-sweet chocolate morsels
- ½ cup sifted confectioners sugar
- 2 Tbs. margarine or butter, softened
- 1 Tbs. water

In large saucepan, melt butterscotch-flavored morsels and peanut butter over very low heat, stirring constantly until smooth. Stir in Cereal. Press half the mixture in a buttered 8 × 8 × 2-inch pan. Chill. Set remaining mixture aside. Melt over hot (not boiling) water semi-sweet morsels, sugar, margarine and water, stirring constantly until smooth. Spread over chilled Cereal mixture. Spread remaining Cereal mixture evenly over top. Press in gently. Chill until firm (1 hour). Makes 25 squares, 1½ × 1½ inches each.

Pecan Turtles

Here's a very special and extremely popular recipe for Turtles, made with Planters® Pecans. Great for special occasions, for gift giving or just for you.

½ cup (1 stick) Blue Bonnet® Margarine
1 cup firmly packed light brown sugar
Dash salt
½ cup light corn syrup
⅔ cup sweetened condensed milk
1½ cups Planters® Pecan Pieces
½ tsp. vanilla extract
1 6-oz. package semi-sweet chocolate morsels, melted

Melt Blue Bonnet® Margarine over medium heat in a medium saucepan. Stir in brown sugar and salt. Mix in corn syrup and sweetened condensed milk. Cook, stirring occasionally, to 245°F. (firm-ball stage), about 15 to 20 minutes. Remove from heat; stir in Planters® Pecan Pieces and vanilla. Drop by tablespoonfuls onto greased baking sheets. When cooled and firm, dip into melted chocolate to coat top. Return to greased baking sheet and cool until chocolate is set. Store candies in a closed container in a cool place.

Crunchy Mounds

It's impossible to fail with this crunchy crisp and delicious candy from Skippy® Peanut Butter. You don't even need a candy thermometer. A teenage favorite to make and to eat.

1 6-oz. package semi-sweet chocolate pieces
¼ cup Skippy® Creamy or Super Chunk Peanut Butter
2⅓ cups corn flakes
⅓ cup dry-roated peanuts

In 1-quart saucepan stir together chocolate pieces and peanut butter. Cook over low heat until melted. Stir in corn flakes and nuts. Drop by teaspoonfuls onto waxed paper. Cool 15 to 20 minutes or until set. Makes about 32 1½-inch cookies.

Creamy-Sure Fudge

A number of different people sent me this "can't fail" fudge recipe from Diamond® Walnuts. They voted it "best of the best."

- 1⅓ cups granulated sugar
- ⅔ cup (1 small can) undiluted evaporated milk
- ¼ cup butter
- 1 jar regular size (approximately 7 ozs.) marshmallow creme, *or* 16 large marshmallows, quartered
- ¼ tsp. salt
- 1 12-oz. package (2 cups) semi-sweet chocolate pieces
- 1 tsp. vanilla
- 1 cup coarsely chopped Diamond® Walnuts

Combine sugar, undiluted milk, butter, marshmallow creme *or* marshmallows and salt in 2-quart saucepan. Cook, stirring constantly, until mixture has boiled for exactly 5 minutes. Remove from heat; add chocolate pieces and vanilla and stir until chocolate is melted. Stir in walnuts. Turn into buttered 8-inch square pan. Let stand until firm, then cut into squares. Makes about 2½ lbs. candy.

Country Club Two-Story Fudge

Some inspired candy aficionado at the Hershey® test kitchens came up with this very festive fudge variation in the early 1940's.

First Story:

- 2½ cups granulated sugar
- 1 cup milk
- 3 squares Hershey's® Baking Chocolate
- 1 Tbs. light corn syrup
- 2 Tbs. butter
- 1 tsp. vanilla
- ½ cup chopped nutmeats

Combine sugar, milk, Baking Chocolate broken into small pieces, and the corn syrup in a heavy saucepan (3-quart).

Place over medium heat and stir gently till Baking Chocolate is melted, then cook with very little stirring to soft-ball stage (234°F.). Remove from the fire; add butter and vanilla. Cool, undisturbed, to lukewarm (110°F.). Beat vigorously until fudge thickens and starts to lose its gloss; add nuts and quickly pour into a buttered 9 × 9 × 1¾-inch pan. Set aside to cool.

Second Story:

- 2½ cups granulated sugar
- ½ cup light cream
- ½ cup milk
- ¼ tsp. salt
- 1 Tbs. light corn syrup
- 2 Tbs. butter
- 1 tsp. vanilla
- ⅓ cupful chopped glâcé cherries

Butter sides of a heavy saucepan (2-quart). In it combine sugar, cream, milk, salt and corn syrup. Place over medium heat, and stir until sugar is dissolved, then cook to soft-ball stage (236°F.). Remove from fire; add butter and vanilla. Cool, undisturbed, to lukewarm (110°F.). Beat vigorously until mixture becomes very thick and starts to lose its gloss. Quickly stir in glâcé cherries, and pour over the dark fudge, smoothing the surface with a knife. Cut into squares while still warm. Makes 4 dozen pieces.

Chocolate Seafoam

Light and airy, but rich as only good chocolate candy can be; a Hershey® Town classic.

- 2 cups light brown sugar, packed
- ¾ cup cold water
- ½ cup (5½-oz. can) Hershey's® Chocolate Flavored Syrup
- 2 egg whites
- 1 tsp. vanilla
- 1 square Hershey's® Baking Chocolate, melted
- ½ cup nutmeats

Mix together sugar, water and Chocolate Syrup in a heavy saucepan (3-quart). Cook over medium heat, stirring constantly, till sugar dissolves and mixture boils. Then cook to hard-ball stage (250°F.) without stirring. Remove pan from heat. Immediately beat egg whites till stiff. Pour hot syrup in a thin stream over beaten egg whites, beating constantly at high speed on mixer. Continue beating till mixture forms peaks when dropped from spoon, about 10 minutes. Quickly stir in vanilla and melted baking chocolate by hand. Blend in nutmeats. Drop by teaspoonfuls onto waxed paper. Cool. Makes 3 to 4 dozen pieces.

Crispy Confections

Quick and delicious—an all-time Kraft® favorite.

49 Kraft® caramels (14-oz. bag)
3 Tbs. water
2 cups crisp rice cereal
2 cups corn flakes
1 4-oz. package shredded coconut

Melt caramels with water in saucepan over low heat. Stir frequently until sauce is smooth. Pour over combined cereals and coconut; toss until well coated. Drop rounded tablespoonfuls onto greased cookie sheet; let stand until firm. Makes 4 dozen.

HOMEMADE ALMOND CANDIES

A perfect ending to a little supper party might be this assortment of fine homemade candy from Blue Diamond® Almonds and the California Almond Growers Exchange. All three come from their permanent files of all-time favorite classics.

Almond Brittle

- 2 cups sugar
- ⅓ cup light corn syrup
- ⅔ cup cold water
- ¼ cup butter or margarine
- 1 tsp. vanilla
- ½ tsp. baking soda
- 1½ cups diced roasted almonds

Combine sugar, syrup, water and butter, and cook and stir until sugar is dissolved. Continue cooking without stirring to 300°F. or when syrup separates into hard brittle threads when dropped into cold water. Remove from heat and stir in vanilla, soda and almonds. Pour onto greased cookie sheet. When slightly cooled, pull edges to make a thin sheet. When thoroughly cold, break into pieces. Makes about 1½ lbs. candy.

Almond Penuche

- 3 cups brown sugar, packed
- ⅛ tsp. salt
- 1 cup milk
- 2 Tbs. light corn syrup
- 2 Tbs. butter or margarine
- 1 tsp. vanilla
- 1 cup toasted blanched slivered almonds

In saucepan combine sugar, salt, milk and syrup. Cook over low heat, stirring constantly until sugar is dissolved. Boil gently, stirring often to 235°F., or until a little mixture forms a soft ball in cold water. Remove from heat. Add butter and cool without stirring. Add vanilla. Beat until creamy and no longer shiny. Stir in almonds and pour into buttered 8-inch square pan. Cool and cut into squares. Makes 36 squares.

Fruit-Nut Balls

- 1 cup golden seedless raisins
- ½ cup shredded coconut, toasted

1 cup dried apricots
Water
1 cup whole natural almonds
1 to 2 Tbs. honey
Powdered sugar

Combine raisins and apricots in saucepan with water to partially cover. Simmer, covered, 5 minutes. Drain. Put fruits and almonds through food chopper, using medium blade. Add coconut and honey and mix thoroughly. Shape into small balls. Roll in powdered sugar. Makes about 18 balls.

California Gold Bars

Oh my, these are good! A top-request recipe. If you bought a 2-pound box of Domino® Granulated Sugar about 5 years ago, you may already have it on file.

1½ cups (11-oz. package) dried apricots
4 eggs
2 cups Domino® Granulated Sugar
½ tsp. salt
2 tsps. grated orange rind
2 cups sifted all-purpose flour
2 tsps. double-acting baking powder
½ tsp. nutmeg
1 cup chopped pecans or walnuts
Domino® Confectioners' 10-X Powdered Sugar

Soak apricots in water until soft. Drain well; cut into small pieces. Beat eggs well in large bowl. Gradually beat sugar and salt into eggs until light and foamy. Add orange rind. Sift together flour, baking powder and nutmeg; gradually blend into egg mixture. Add apricots and nuts; mix briefly. Spread batter into 2 greased 9-inch square pans. Bake in moderate oven, 350°F., 30–35 minutes or until done. When partially cool, cut 1½ × 3-inch bars and roll in confectioners' sugar. Remove to cooling rack. If necessary to store bars, place in air-tight container with waxed paper between layers; roll again in confectioners' sugar before serving. Yields 54 bars.

Lemony Bars

I just love this recipe; it's super easy, inexpensive and so delicious. Makes super bars to serve as cookies, but I also like to cut it into squares and serve with a scoop of vanilla ice cream or a fluff of whipped cream as a heavenly dessert. The cooks at the Checkerboard Kitchens dreamed it up for their Rice Chex® Cereal box about six years ago.

Base

1 cup sifted all-purpose flour
¾ cup sugar
½ tsp. baking powder
¼ tsp. salt
2 cups Rice Chex® cereal crushed to ½ cup
½ cup butter or margarine

Topping

2 eggs, beaten
¾ cup sugar
2 Tbs. all-purpose flour
¼ tsp. baking powder
4 tsps. lemon juice
1 tsp. grated lemon peel

Preheat oven to 350°F. Grease 9-inch square baking pan. To prepare *base*, sift together flour, sugar, baking powder and salt. Stir in Rice Chex crumbs. Cut in butter until very fine crumbs. Press mixture firmly into pan. Bake 12 minutes.

Meanwhile, prepare *topping*. Combine all ingredients. Mix until well blended. Pour over hot base. Return to oven for additional 15–20 minutes or until top is set but not browned. Cool. Sprinkle with confectioners' sugar. Cut into bars. Makes 24 (2¼ × 1½-inch) bars.

Almond Blondies

Here's another recipe for cookie bars that can be cut into squares and can double as a very special dessert. It's from the Blue-Diamond® Almond can and I think you will love it.

- ⅓ cup shortening
- 1 cup granulated sugar
- 2 eggs
- 2 tsps. vanilla extract
- 1⅓ cups all-purpose flour (do not sift)
- 1 cup flaked coconut
- 2 tsps. baking powder
- ½ tsp. salt
- Topping (below)

Cream shortening with granulated sugar; beat in eggs and vanilla. Sprinkle flour, coconut, baking powder and salt over creamed mixture; beat well. Spread over bottom of 9-inch square baking pan. Spoon Topping over evenly. Bake in 350°F. oven 40 to 50 minutes or until a light touch in center leaves no impression. Cut into 1½-inch rectangles. Makes about 3 dozen.

Topping

- ½ cup Blue-Diamond® Whole Blanched Almonds, toasted
- ½ cup packed brown sugar
- 1 Tbs. all-purpose flour
- 1 egg
- ¼ cup heavy cream

Coarsely chop almonds. Combine with brown sugar and flour. Stir in egg and cream.

Crunchy Chews

Rich, moist, chewy and delicious; quick and easy to prepare. You'll love these bar cookies from the Skippy® Peanut Butter kitchens.

- ¾ cup sugar
- ¾ cup Karo Dark Corn Syrup
- ¾ cup Skippy® Super Chunk Peanut Butter
- 4½ cups corn flakes, crisp rice cereal or round oat cereal
- ¾ cup peanuts or broken mixed nuts (optional)

Grease 13 × 9 × 2-inch baking pan. In saucepan mix together sugar and corn syrup. Bring to boil, stirring constantly, over medium heat. Boil 1 minute. Mix in peanut butter. Turn into prepared pan. Stir in corn flakes and nuts. Press together firmly. Cool. Cut into squares. Makes 4½ dozen (1½-inch) squares.

Fudgy Brownies

Here it is, just what you asked for, that *other* brownie recipe, the chewy, fudgy dark chocolate kind. From Baker's Chocolate.

- 4 squares Baker's Unsweetened Chocolate
- ½ cup butter or margarine
- 2 cups sugar
- 4 eggs, beaten
- 1 cup sifted flour
- 1 tsp. vanilla
- 1 cup coarsely chopped walnuts

Melt chocolate and butter together over hot water. Cool slightly. Gradually add sugar to eggs, beating thoroughly after each addition. Blend in chocolate mixture. Stir in flour.

Then add vanilla and nuts. Spread in greased 9-inch square pan. Bake in slow oven (325°F.) about 40 minutes. Cool in pan. Cut into squares. Makes about 2 dozen brownies.

Chocolate Peppermint Brownies: Prepare Fudgy Brownies, arranging 15–20 chocolate peppermint patties over top of hot brownies; return to oven about 3 minutes to soften patties. Then spread to cover entire top of the brownies. Cool and cut.

Nut-Topped Brownies: Prepare Fudgy Brownies, omitting walnuts from batter. Pour batter into pan and sprinkle with ½ cup coarsely chopped walnuts, pecans or peanuts. Bake. If desired, melt 1 square Baker's Unsweetened or Semi-Sweet Chocolate with 1 tsp. butter; blend, and dribble over top of baked brownies.

Honey Brownies (formerly Honeybear Brownies)

Was the first baking you ever did a pan of Honeybear Brownies? Mine was. The recipe was from the label of a can of Hershey's® Cocoa and everyone said they were the

"best ever." I still make them and you know what? They still say just that.

- ⅓ cup butter or margarine
- ¾ cup sugar
- ⅓ cup honey
- 2 tsps. vanilla
- 2 eggs
- ½ cup unsifted all-purpose flour
- ⅓ cup Hershey's® Cocoa
- ½ tsp. salt
- 1 cup chopped nuts

Grease one 9-inch pan. Cream butter and sugar in small mixer bowl; blend in honey and vanilla. Add eggs, one at a time, beating well after each addition. Combine flour, cocoa and salt; gradually add to creamed mixture. Stir in nuts. Pour into pan. Bake at 350°F. for 25–30 minutes or until brownies begin to pull away from edge of pan. Cool in pan. Makes 16 brownies.

Peanut Butter Brownies

Two American favorites; chocolate and peanut butter combine in these moist, rich and delicious brownies. The recipe was perfected by the good cooks at Reese's.

- ½ cup butter or margarine, softened
- Peanut Butter Brownie Frosting (opposite)
- 1 cup sugar
- 1 tsp. vanilla
- 2 eggs
- 1¼ cups unsifted all-purpose flour
- ⅛ tsp. baking soda
- ¾ cup Hershey's® Chocolate Syrup
- 1 cup Reese's Peanut Butter Chips

Cream butter or margarine, sugar and vanilla. Add eggs; beat well. Combine flour and baking soda; add alternately with chocolate syrup to creamed mixture. Stir in peanut butter chips. Pour batter into greased 13 × 9 × 2-inch pan; bake at 350°F. for 30–35 minutes. Cool; frost with Peanut Butter Brownie Frosting. Makes 24 brownies.

Peanut Butter Brownie Frosting: Combine ⅓ cup sugar, ¼ cup evaporated milk and 2 Tbs. butter in a small saucepan. Stir over medium heat until mixture comes to full boil; remove from heat. Quickly stir in 1 cup Reese's Peanut Butter Chips until melted; add 1 tsp. vanilla. Beat to spreading consistency; frost brownies. Cut into 24 brownies.

Queen's Lace Cookies

The nuns at the convent near our house in Louisiana used to make cookies like these; I always thought they were impossibly difficult until I discovered the recipe in the Parkay® Margarine cookbook. If you want to make an impression at your next party, these are for you.

- ¼ cup Squeeze Parkay® Margarine
- ¼ cup granulated sugar
- 2 Tbs. dark corn syrup
- 1 tsp. brandy
- ½ cup flour
- ½ tsp. grated lemon rind
- ¼ tsp. ginger
- Brandied Whipped Cream (page 552)

Heat margarine, granulated sugar and corn syrup over low heat in heavy skillet or saucepan, stirring until sugar is dissolved. Remove from heat; beat in brandy and combined flour, lemon rind and ginger. Drop level teaspoonfuls of batter, 3 inches apart, onto greased cookie sheet. Bake at 350°F., 8–10 minutes or until deep golden brown. Remove from oven; wait 10–15 seconds for cookies to set. Remove cookies one at a time; turn smooth-side up and wrap around handle of a wooden spoon spread with margarine. Slip cookie off; repeat with remaining cookies, working quickly. If cookies become too firm to roll, return to oven for 1–2 minutes to soften. When ready to serve, fill cookies with Brandied Whipped Cream.

Brandied Whipped Cream

1 cup heavy cream
2 Tbs. confectioners' sugar
1 Tbs. brandy

Whip cream until slightly thickened; gradually add sugar and brandy, beating until stiff peaks form. Makes enough to fill approximately 1½ dozen cookies.

Melting Moments

The Argo Company tells me there have been dozens of variations on this recipe since it first appeared on their packaging some thirty years ago, but this was the original and the texture and flavor can't be improved. You can add chopped nuts, coconut or candied fruit or top each cookie with a whole pecan, almond, or candied cherry—but then I don't have to tell you, do I?

1 cup unsifted flour
½ cup Argo or Kingsford's Corn Starch
½ cup confectioners' sugar
¾ cup Nucoa or Mazola Margarine

In medium bowl stir flour, cornstarch and confectioners' sugar. In large bowl with mixer at medium speed beat margarine until smooth. Add flour mixture and beat until combined. Refrigerate 1 hour. Shape into 1-inch balls. Place about 1½ inches apart on ungreased cookie sheet; flatten with lightly floured fork. Bake in 300°F. oven 20 minutes or until edges are lightly browned. Makes about 3 dozen cookies.

Chinese Almond Cookies

This recipe was developed because of popular demand. When Oriental cooking started to become popular in this country about ten years ago, requests came in to the Almond Growers Exchange so hot and heavy that a recipe had to be perfected. This one is perfection indeed.

½ cup Blue-Diamond® Whole Natural Almonds
1 cup sifted all-purpose flour
½ tsp. baking powder
¼ tsp. salt
½ cup butter or margarine
⅓ cup granulated sugar
½ tsp. almond extract
1 Tbs. gin, vodka or water

Reserve 36 whole almonds; finely chop or grind remainder. Sift flour with baking powder and salt. Thoroughly cream butter and sugar. Stir in all remaining ingredients except whole almonds. Form dough into 36 balls. Place on greased cookie sheets. Press a whole almond in center of each ball. Bake in 350°F. oven for 20 minutes or until lightly browned. Makes about 3 dozen.

Old-Fashioned Molasses Cookies

If there are children in your house, these cookies belong in a cookie jar on a low shelf in your kitchen. Made with Elam's extra-nutritional flours.

- 1 cup Stone Ground 100% Whole Wheat Flour
- ¾ cup Unbleached White Flour with Wheat Germ
- ½ tsp. salt
- ½ tsp. baking soda
- ½ tsp. cinnamon
- ½ cup soft shortening or butter
- ¾ cup (packed) brown sugar
- 1 egg
- ¼ cup molasses

Combine and mix first 5 ingredients in bowl; reserve. Beat shortening or butter until creamy. Add brown sugar gradually; beat well after each addition. Add egg and molasses; beat until smooth. Blend in dry ingredients; mix well. Chill dough 1–2 hours. Shape dough into balls using a level Tbs. of dough for each. Place balls 2 inches apart on ungreased baking sheets. Bake in slow oven (325°F.) until done, 15–18 minutes. Transfer to wire racks to cool. Yields about 3½ dozen cookies, 2½ inches in diameter.

Oatmeal Drop Cookies

Old friends are best, and what better and older friends does a child of any age have than an oatmeal cookie and a glass of cold milk. These are the real thing from Elam's. Great tasting and nutritional, too.

- 2 cups Stone Ground 100% Whole Wheat Flour
- 1 tsp. salt
- 1 tsp. baking soda
- 1 egg
- 2 tsps. vanilla
- ½ cup light corn syrup
- ⅓ cup milk

- 1 tsp. cinnamon
- 2 cups Steel Cut Oatmeal
- 1 cup soft shortening
- ½ cup (packed) brown sugar
- 1 cup seedless raisins
- 1 cup chopped pecans or walnuts

Combine and mix whole wheat flour, salt, soda and cinnamon. Stir in oatmeal; reserve. Beat shortening and sugar together until creamy. Beat in egg and vanilla. Add dry ingredients alternately with corn syrup and milk, blending well after each addition. Stir in raisins and nuts. Drop rounded tablespoonfuls of dough onto ungreased baking sheets. Bake in moderate oven (350°F.) until done and brown, 12–14 minutes. Yields 5½ about dozen cookies, about 2½ inches in diameter.

Hiram Walker Amaretto Cookies

These are the most melt-in-the-mouth Italian-style cookies—more like macaroons actually. Brew up some espresso coffee and enjoy!

- ½ cup egg whites (3 eggs)
- 1¼ cup sugar
- ¼ tsp. salt
- ⅓ cup Hiram Walker Amaretto liqueur
- 3¼ ounces flaked coconut
- 4 ounces almonds, finely chopped

Beat egg whites until stiff. Then gradually beat in sugar, 1 Tbs. at a time, until stiff and glossy. Add salt. Gradually beat in Amaretto. Fold in coconut and almonds.

Foil-line cookie sheets. Drop mixture by heaping teaspoons onto foil. Bake at 325°F. for 20 minutes. Cool cookies on foil. Store in air-tight container. Makes 4 dozen.

Chocolate Date and Nut Bars

Rich, moist, chewy and delicious. You'll love these cookies from Hershey®.

- 2 eggs
- ½ cup granulated sugar
- ½ cup sifted all-purpose flour
- 1 tsp. baking powder
- 6 Tbs. Hershey's® Chocolate Flavored Syrup
- 1 tsp. vanilla
- ½ cup walnut meats, chopped
- ½ cup dates, chopped in small pieces

Beat eggs thoroughly; gradually beat in sugar. Sift flour and baking powder; add to egg–sugar mixture; then add chocolate syrup, vanilla, nuts and dates. Beat mixture together; spread in a greased shallow 9 × 9-inch pan. Bake in a 350°F. oven for 25 minutes. Cool. Cut into 1 × 3-inch strips. Sprinkle with confectioners' sugar. Makes about 2 dozen bars.

Coconut Macaroons

These delicate-tasting, easy-to-make macaroons made their debut back in 1962 when the recipe appeared on Baker's Angel Flake Coconut packages. Despite their chewy goodness they are extra-low in calories, a sweet even the dieter can enjoy.

- 1⅓ cups (about) Baker's Angel Flake Coconut
- ⅓ cup sugar
- 2 Tbs. all-purpose flour
- ⅛ tsp. salt
- 2 egg whites
- ½ tsp. almond extract

Combine coconut, sugar, flour and salt in mixing bowl. Stir in egg whites and almond extract; mix well. Drop by teaspoonfuls onto lightly greased baking sheets. Garnish with candied cherry halves, if desired. Bake at 325°F. for 20 to 25 minutes, until edges of cookies are golden brown. Remove from baking sheets immediately. Makes about 1½ dozen.

Choco-Scotch Clusters

Some inspired genius in the Kellogg kitchen came up with this luscious combination of chocolate, butterscotch and peanut butter in the early 1940s.

- 1 6-ounce package semi-sweet chocolate morsels
- 1 6-ounce package butterscotch morsels
- 2 Tbs. peanut butter
- 4 cups Kellogg's Rice Krispies cereal

Melt chocolate, butterscotch morsels and peanut butter together in top section of double boiler over hot but not boiling water, or in heavy saucepan over very low heat, stirring constantly until well blended. Remove from heat. Add Rice Krispies; stir until well coated.

Drop by level measuring-tablespoon onto waxed paper or buttered baking sheets. Let stand in cool place until firm. Makes about 4 dozen Choco-Scotch Clusters, 1½ inches in diameter.

Note: Mixture may be pressed into buttered 9 × 9 × 2-inch square pan. Cut into squares when firm. Yields 3 dozen 1½ × 1½-inch Choco-Scotch Clusters.

Tiger Cookies

Kellogg's Tiger on the box inspired this great cookie recipe. It's been making chocolate fanciers happy for years.

- 1¾ cups all-purpose flour
- ½ tsp. baking soda
- ½ tsp. salt
- 3 cups Kellogg's Sugar Frosted Flakes of Corn cereal, crushed to measure 1½ cups

- 1 cup margarine or butter, softened
- 1 cup sugar
- 2 eggs
- 1 tsp. vanilla
- 1 6-ounce package semi-sweet chocolate morsels, melted

Stir together flour, soda and salt. Set aside. In large mixing bowl, beat margarine and sugar until light and fluffy. Add eggs and vanilla. Beat well. Add flour mixture, mixing until well combined. Stir in crushed Sugar Frosted Flakes of Corn cereal. Drizzle melted chocolate over dough. With knife, swirl melted chocolate gently through dough to achieve marbled appearance. Drop by rounded measuring-tablespoon onto ungreased baking sheets. Bake in 350°F. oven for about 12 minutes, until lightly browned. Remove immediately from baking sheets. Cool on wire racks. Makes about 5 dozen cookies.

Cherry Winks

These great Christmas cookies are from Kellogg. Moist, rich and festive, they have been a favorite for a generation.

- 2¼ cups all-purpose flour
- 2 tsps. baking powder
- ½ tsp. salt
- ¾ cup margarine or butter, softened
- 1 cup sugar
- 2 eggs
- 2 Tbs. milk
- 1 tsp. vanilla
- 1 cup chopped nuts
- 1 cup finely cut pitted dates
- ⅓ cup finely chopped candied red cherries
- 2⅔ cups Kellogg's Corn Flakes cereal, crushed to measure 1⅓ cups
- 15 candied red cherries, cut into quarters

Stir together flour, baking powder and salt. Set aside. In large mixing bowl, beat margarine and sugar until light and fluffy.

Add eggs. Beat well. Stir in milk and vanilla. Add flour mixture. Mix until well combined. Stir in nuts, dates and chopped cherries. Using level measuring-tablespoon, shape dough into balls. Roll in crushed Corn Flakes cereal. Place about 2 inches apart on greased baking sheets. Top each with cherry quarter. Bake in 375°F. oven for about 10 minutes, until lightly browned. Remove immediately from baking sheets. Cool on wire racks. Makes about 5 dozen.

Brownies

Two generations of American cooks have followed this recipe for brownies from the back of Baker's Unsweetened Chocolate package.

- 2 1-ounce squares Baker's Unsweetened Chocolate
- ⅓ cup soft butter or other shortening
- ⅔ cup all-purpose flour
- ½ tsp. Calumet Baking Powder
- ¼ tsp. salt
- 2 eggs
- 1 cup sugar
- 1 tsp. vanilla
- ½ cup chopped nuts

Melt chocolate with butter over low heat. Mix flour with baking powder and salt. Beat eggs well; then gradually beat in sugar. Blend in chocolate mixture and vanilla. Add flour mixture and mix well. Stir in nuts. Spread in greased 8-inch square pan. Bake at 350°F. for 25 minutes (for moist, chewy brownies); or about 30 minutes, or until cake tester inserted in center comes out clean (for cakelike brownies). Cool in pan; then cut into squares. Makes about 20 brownies.

Note: Recipe may be doubled; bake in greased 13 × 9 × 2-inch pan at 350°F. for 25 or 30 minutes, as directed. Makes about 40 brownies.

Famous Oatmeal Cookies

Quaker Oats first printed this cookie recipe on their oats package in 1955 but I suspect it was a favorite even before that.

- ¾ cup shortening, soft
- 1 cup firmly packed brown sugar
- 1 tsp. vanilla
- 1 cup sifted all-purpose flour
- 1 tsp. salt
- ½ cup granulated sugar
- 1 egg
- ¼ cup water
- ½ tsp. baking soda
- 3 cups uncooked Quaker Oats

Beat together shortening, sugars, egg, water and vanilla until creamy. Sift together flour, salt and soda; add to creamed mixture; blend. Stir in oats. Drop by teaspoonfuls onto greased cookie sheets. Bake in preheated 350°F. oven for 12 to 15 minutes. Makes 5 dozen cookies.

Toll House Cookies With Variations

Remember Empress Eugenie hats? If you do, you were around in 1939 when the Nestlé Company first printed this now famous cookie recipe on their Semi-Sweet Chocolate Morsels package.

- 2¼ cups unsifted all-purpose flour*
- 1 tsp. baking soda
- 1 tsp. salt
- 1 cup butter, softened
- 1 tsp. vanilla
- 2 eggs
- 1 package (12 ounces) Nestlé Semi-Sweet Real Chocolate Morsels

* For Whole-Wheat Toll House Cookies, substitute whole-wheat flour for all or half of all-purpose flour.

¾ cup sugar
¾ cup firmly packed brown sugar
1 cup chopped nuts

Preheat oven to 375°F. Combine flour, baking soda and salt in a small bowl; set aside. Combine butter, sugars, and vanilla extract in large bowl; beat until creamy. Beat in eggs. Gradually add flour mixture; blend well. Stir in Nestlé Semi-Sweet Real Chocolate Morsels and nuts. Drop by rounded teaspoonfuls onto ungreased cookie sheets. Bake at 375°F. for 8 to 10 minutes. Makes 100 2-inch cookies.

Variations: Omit nuts and substitute one of the following: 4 cups crisp ready-to-eat cereal; 2 cups chopped dates; 1 Tbs. grated orange rind; or 2 cups raisins.

Corn Flakes Macaroons

Kellogg developed these chewy cookies over twenty years ago, but cooks all over the country still write in for "that marvelous macaroon recipe."

4 egg whites
¼ tsp. cream of tartar
1 tsp. vanilla
1⅓ cups sugar
1 cup chopped pecans
1 cup shredded coconut
3 cups Kellogg's Corn Flakes cereal

In large mixing bowl, beat egg whites until foamy. Stir in cream of tartar and vanilla. Gradually add sugar, beating until stiff and glossy. Fold in pecans, coconut and Corn Flakes cereal. Drop by rounded measuring-tablespoon onto well-greased baking sheets. Bake in 325°F. oven for about 20 minutes or until lightly browned. Remove immediately from baking sheets. Cool on wire racks. Makes about 3 dozen macaroons.

Variation: Merry Macaroons: Fold in ½ cup crushed peppermint candy with pecans, coconut and cereal.

Magic Cookie Bars

Children have delighted in this recipe ever since it appeared on the Eagle Brand Condensed Milk can light-years ago. As easy for kids to make as it is for them to eat.

- ½ cup butter or margarine
- 1 can Eagle Brand Sweetened Condensed Milk
- 1 6-ounce package semi-sweet chocolate morsels
- 1½ cups graham cracker crumbs
- 1 3-ounce can flaked coconut
- 1 cup chopped nuts

Preheat oven to 350°F. (or 325°F. if you use a glass dish). In 13 × 9-inch baking pan, melt butter. Sprinkle crumbs over butter. Pour sweetened condensed milk evenly over crumbs. Top evenly with chocolate morsels, coconut, and nuts; press down gently. Bake for 25 to 30 minutes or until lightly browned. Cool thoroughly before cutting. Makes 24 bars.

Crisp Peanut Butter Cookies

One of the best peanut butter cookie recipies, a long-time favorite from the Skippy® Peanut Butter label.

- 2½ cups unsifted flour
- 1 tsp. baking powder
- 1 tsp. baking soda
- 1 tsp. salt
- 1 cup corn oil margarine
- 1 cup Skippy® Creamy or Super Chunk Peanut Butter
- 1 cup sugar
- 1 cup firmly packed brown sugar
- 2 eggs, beaten
- 1 tsp. vanilla

Stir together flour, baking powder, baking soda and salt. In large bowl with mixer at medium speed beat margarine and peanut butter until smooth. Beat in sugars until blended. Beat in eggs and vanilla. Add flour mixture and beat well. If necessary, chill dough. Shape into 1-inch balls. Place on ungreased cookie sheet 2 inches apart. Flatten with floured fork, making criss-cross pattern. Bake in 350°F. oven for 12 minutes or until lightly browned. Cool on wire rack. Makes 6 dozen 2-inch cookies.

Peanut Butter Sandwich Cookies: Follow basic recipe. Spread bottoms of half of baked cookies with peanut butter; top with remaining cookies. Makes about 3 dozen cookies.

Jelly Thumbprint Cookies: Follow basic recipe. Instead of flattening with fork, press small indentation in each with thumb. While still warm press again with thumb. Cool. Fill indentation with jelly or jam.

Peanut Butter Refrigerator Cookies: Follow basic recipe. Shape into 2 rolls 1½-inches in diameter. Wrap in plastic wrap and refrigerate. Slice into ¼-inch thick slices. Bake as directed. Makes about 8 dozen cookies.

Peanut Butter Crackles: Follow basic recipe. Roll in sugar before placing on cookie sheet; do not flatten. Bake as directed for 15 to 18 minutes. Immediately press chocolate candy kiss firmly into top of each cookie (cookie will crack around edges).

Marshmallow Treats

As long as there are children, these easy marshmallow "cookies-candies" will be favorites.

- ¼ cup margarine or butter
- 1 10-ounce package marshmallows or 4 cups miniature marshmallows
- 5 cups Kellogg's Rice Krispies cereal

Melt margarine in large saucepan over low heat. Add marshmallows and stir until completely melted. Cook over low heat for 3 minutes longer, stirring constantly. Remove from heat. Add Rice Krispies cereal. Stir until well coated. Using buttered spatula or waxed paper, press mixture evenly into buttered 13 × 9 × 2-inch pan. Cut into 2-inch squares when cool. Makes 24 squares.

Note: Best results are obtained when using fresh marshmallows.

Variations: To make thicker squares, press warm mixture into buttered 9 × 9 × 2-inch pan.

Marshmallow Crême Treats: About 2 cups marshmallow crême may be substituted for marshmallows. Add to melted margarine and stir until well blended. Cook over low heat for about 5 minutes longer, stirring constantly. Remove from heat. Proceed as directed in step 2 above.

Peanut Treats: Add 1 cup salted cocktail peanuts with the cereal.

Peanut Butter Treats: Stir ¼ cup peanut butter into marshmallow mixture just before adding cereal.

Raisin Treats: Add 1 cup seedless raisins with cereal.

Cocoa Krispies Cereal Treats: 6 cups Cocoa Krispies cereal may be substituted for 5 cups Rice Krispies cereal.

Magic Marshmallow Crescent Puffs

These sweet puffs have become a favorite of many. They were the best of the twentieth Pillsbury Bake-Off contest in 1968. The recipe for them has been requested over and over again.

- ¼ cup sugar
- 1 tsp. cinnamon
- 2 8-ounce cans Pillsbury Refrigerated Quick Crescent Dinner Rolls
- 16 large marshmallows
- ¼ cup margarine or butter, melted
- ¼ cup chopped nuts, if desired

Glaze:

- ½ cup powdered sugar
- 2 to 3 tsps. milk
- ½ tsp. vanilla

Heat oven to 375°F. Combine sugar and cinnamon. Separate crescent dough into 16 triangles. Dip a marshmallow in melted margarine; roll in sugar-cinnamon mixture. Place marshmallow on shortest side of triangle. Fold corners over marshmallow and roll to opposite point, completely covering marshmallow and pinching edges of dough to seal. Dip in melted margarine and place margarine side down in deep muffin cup. Repeat with remaining marshmallows. Place pan on foil or cookie sheet during baking to guard against spillage. Bake at 375°F. for 10 to 15 minutes or until golden brown. Immediately remove from pans.

Glaze: Combine Glaze ingredients; drizzle over warm rolls. Sprinkle with nuts. Makes 16 rolls.

Note: To reheat, wrap in foil; heat at 375°F. for 5 to 10 minutes.

High Altitude: No change.

Index